Family Planning in the Legacy of Islam

FAMILY PLANNING IN THE LEGACY OF ISLAM

Professor Abdel Rahim Omran

Published with the support of the
United Nations Population Fund

London and New York

First published 1992
by Routledge
11 New Fetter Lane, London EC4P 4EE

Simultaneously published in the USA and Canada
by Routledge
a division of Routledge, Chapman and Hall, Inc.
29 West 35th Street, New York, NY 10001

© 1992 United Nations Population Fund

Typeset by Leaper & Gard Ltd, Bristol
Printed and Bound in Great Britain by
Mackays of Chatham PLC, Chatham, Kent

All rights reserved. No part of this book may be reprinted or reproduced or utilized in any form or by any electronic, mechanical or other means, now known or hereafter invented, including photocopying and recording, or in any information storage or retrieval system, without permission in writing from the publishers.

British Library Cataloguing in Publication Data
A catalogue record for this book is available from the British Library

ISBN 0-415-05541-5

Library of Congress Cataloging in Publication Data
Omran, Abdel R.
    Family planning in Islam / Abdel Rahim Omran.
      p. cm.
    Includes bibliographical references and index.
    1. Birth control—Religious aspects—Islam. 2. Birth control
(Islamic law) 3. Family—Koranic teaching. I. Title.
HQ766.37.O47   1992
297′.197836666—dc20
                                                                           92-11914
                                                                             CIP

ISBN 0-415-05541-5

"وَمَا كَانَ لِمُؤْمِنٍ وَلَا مُؤْمِنَةٍ إِذَا قَضَى اللَّهُ وَرَسُولُهُ أَمْرًا أَن يَكُونَ لَهُمُ الْخِيَرَةُ مِنْ أَمْرِهِمْ وَمَن يَعْصِ اللَّهَ وَرَسُولَهُ فَقَدْ ضَلَّ ضَلَالًا مُّبِينًا ۞"

سورة الأحزاب (٣٣)

It is not fitting for a believer, man or woman, when a matter has been decided by Allah and His messenger, to have any option about their decision. If anyone disobeys Allah and His messenger, he is indeed on a clearly wrong path.

al-Ahzab (Sura 33: 36)

Contents

List of figures   xiii
List of tables   xiv
Foreword: *Nafis Sadik, UNFPA*   xv
Foreword: *H. Munawir Sjadzali, Republic of Indonesia*   xvi
Foreword: *Professor Gamal Serour, Al-Azhar University*   xvii
Preface   xviii
Acknowledgments   xxi
Introduction   1
    A working definition of family planning   4

Prologue:

Views of Sheikh Jadel Haq, the Grand Imam of Al-Azhar, on family planning   6

Part I   The Islamic Context

Chapter 1   Family and marriage in Islam   13
    The family in Islam   13
        Role of the family   13
        The relationship between husband and wife   13
    Marriage in Islam   15
        General summary   15
        Marriage as a basic institution   16
        Marriage as a solemn covenant   17
        Marriage as a grave responsibility   17
        Age at marriage   18

CONTENTS

Polygyny	19
Definition	19
Permissibility of polygyny	19
The wife can disallow polygyny	21
The elements of planning in family and marriage	22
Genetic considerations	22
Cultural considerations	23
Social considerations	26
Marital competence	26
Pregnancy planning	26

Chapter 2   *Parent and child: rights of one, obligations of the other*   27

Rights of parents in Islam	27
Rights of children in Islam	30
Introduction	30
Value of children in Muslim societies	30
Children's rights and parents' obligations	32
The enormity of the responsibility	38
The need for planning	39

Chapter 3   *The status of women in Islam*   40

Introduction	40
Women personalities in the Qur'an	41
The question of equality	43
The human partnership	43
Equality in religious duties	44
Women's share in the Islamic revolution	44
Equality in education	46
Equality in the principle of *jihad* (religious war)	46
Equity in treatment as daughters	48
Equality in choosing marital partners	49
Right to share in public life	50
Women's privileges over men	50
Men's privileges over women	51
Controversies resolved	52
Inheritance differentials and the status of women	52
Woman as witness	55
Women speak up for their rights	56

Chapter 4   *Family planning and the basic precepts of Islam*   59

Introduction	59
A religion of ease (*yusr*) not hardship (*'usr*)	59

A religion of moderation	61
A religion for quality	62
A religion for planning	62
A religion for all times	65
Changing population	65
Islam and population change	67

Part II Family Planning in the Qur'an and the Sunnah

Chapter 5 **Sources of Islamic jurisprudence** — 73
  Introduction and definitions — 73
  Sources and venues of Islamic jurisprudence — 74
    1 The primary and prerequisite sources: — 74
    2 Complementary sources of law:
      consensus and analogy — 77
    3 Supplementary venues — 78
    4 Broad principles — 79
  Application to family planning — 79
    Adaptability of Islamic law — 81
  Requirements of a new legal ruling or *fatwa* — 83

Chapter 6 **The Qur'an and family planning including the question of multitude** — 85
  General statement — 85
    Use of the Qur'an — 86
  The issue of equating family planning with
  Infanticide (*wa'd*) — 86
    Opponents — 86
    Proponents — 87
  Predestination (*qadar*), provision (*rizq*) and reliance on
  Allah (*tawakkul*) — 89
    Predestination (*qadar*) — 89
    Provision (*rizq*) — 90
    Reliance on Allah (*tawakkul*) — 90
  Procreation — 92
    Procreation and the value of children — 92
    Procreation and marriage — 94
  Additional arguments — 96
    Opponents refer to children as Allah's gifts — 96
    Proponents find evidence for spacing — 96
  The question of multitude (*kathrah*) — 97

CONTENTS

	Advocates of multitude	98
	Response by proponents of family planning	102
	Multitude versus harm to the mother: a juristic evaluation	111
	A demographic and cultural note	111
	Requirements of Islamic multitude	112

Chapter 7 ***The Sunnah and family planning*** 113
    Collections of *Hadith* (tradition) 113
        A survey and classification of traditions concerning *al-azl* into nine categories: 115
          1 The experience of the Companions with *al-azl*, (Jabir's traditions) (three traditions) 115
          2 Traditions denoting tacit approval by the Prophet of *al-azl* (three traditions) 120
          3 Traditions in which sanction was verbalized by the Prophet (three traditions) 121
          4 *Al-azl* and 'your wives are as tilth unto you' (five traditions) 123
          5 *Al-azl* is allowed with a wife's consent (two traditions) 125
          6 Traditions with seemingly equivocal support for *al-azl* (six traditions) 126
          7 *Al-azl* and *al-ghayla* (two traditions) 129
          8 Traditions referring to *al-azl* as hidden infanticide (one tradition) 130
          9 Traditions denying that *al-azl* is minor infanticide (seven traditions) 131
    Appraisal of the evidence from the *Sunnah* 134
        The permissibility of *al-azl* 134
        Arguments against *al-azl* based on Judama's tradition 136
        Refutation of the prohibition 137
        In summary 141

Part III *Family Planning in Islamic Jurisprudence*

Chapter 8 ***Family planning in Islamic jurisprudence (legal schools) from the seventh to the nineteenth century*** 145
    A chronology of scholarship 145
        Issues discussed by jurists 146
    Schools of Islamic jurisprudence (*al-madhahib al-fiqhiyya*) 146

	The Sunni schools	147
	The Kharijite movement and the Ibaddi school	147
	The Shi'ites	148
	A final note	152
	Views of legal schools on family planning	152
	Common or *jumhour* position in Islam	152
	The Hanafi school (Sunni)	153
	The Maliki school (Sunni)	155
	The Shafe'i school (Sunni)	159
	The Hanbali school (Sunni)	162
	The Zaydi school (Shi'ite)	165
	The Imami (Twelvers) school (Shi'ite)	165
	The Isma'ili school (Shi'ite)	167
	The Zahiri school	167
	The Ibaddi school (Kharijite)	167
Chapter 9	***Justifications for contraception in Islamic jurisprudence***	**168**
	General consideration	168
	Specified justifications by leading jurists	168
	Comment on the economic justifications	171
	Comment on the health justifications	173
	Comparison with Islamic medicine (from the earlier Islamic period)	173
	Back to jurisprudence	174
	Modern medicine	178
	Comment on the cultural justifications	182
Chapter 10	***Family planning in Islamic jurisprudence: the more problematical issues***	**184**
	Infertility and sterilization	184
	Infertility and artificial insemination	184
	The question of sterilization	187
	The question of abortion	190
	Opinion of legal schools	191
	Summary: four classes before 120 days	192
	After ensoulment: 120 days	192
	Views of other theologians	193
	The question of repudiating a child conceived despite contraception	193
	How the question arose	193
	How the jurists prepared themselves	194

CONTENTS

The jurists' knowledge of reproduction	194
Explaining predestination in the traditions	195
The question of repudiation	196

Part IV Islam and Family Planning in the Twentieth Century

Chapter 11 Conferences and publications by jurists on Islam and family planning — 201
- New challenges to juristic research — 201
- New challenges to the juristic process — 202
- Theologians who oppose family planning — 203
- Books by theologians on Islam and family planning — 209
- Conferences on Islam and family planning — 214
  - Introduction — 214
  - *Fatwa* Committees and Councils — 215
  - The Rabat Conference — 216
  - The Banjul (sub-Saharan) Conference — 217
  - The Dakar Seminar — 218
  - The Aceh Congress — 219
  - The Mogadishu Conference — 223

Chapter 12 Fatwas and opinions of other twentieth-century jurists on Islam and family planning — 225
- A commentary on *fatwas* on family planning — 225
- *Fatwas* from the Indian subcontinent — 229
- Opinions of other twentieth-century scholars ('*ulama*') — 230
- A grand finale: The Grand Imam of Al-Azhar reconfirms in 1991 his views of 1979-80 — 238

Epilogue:

A poem on family planning by Sheikh Abdul-Fattah M. Khattab — 241

Appendix 1: A chronology of theologians cited in this book — 243
Appendix 2: Text of the fatwas — 250

Notes — 260
Bibliography — 267
Index — 276

Figures

1.1	Consanguineous marriages	24
2.1	The ten cardinal rights of children in Islam	32
2.2	The human life cycle	38
4.1	World population growth, past and projected	66
4.2	Models of growth in Muslim countries	68
5.1	Sources and venues of Islamic jurisprudence	75
6.1	Requirements of Islamic multitude	112
7.1	The common compilations of *hadith*	116
8.1	Genealogy of founders of the Shi'ite schools and the Abbasid dynasty	148
8.2	Founders of schools of jurisprudence	150
8.3	Schools of Islamic jurisprudence (*al-madhahib al-fiqhiyya*)	150
9.1	Justifications acceptable to jurists (and the key theologians who promoted them)	169
9.2	Selected texts of Islamic medicine	174
9.3	Excerpt from Avicinna	175
9.4	Excerpt from Ali Abbas	176
9.5	Excerpt from al-Jurjani	176
9.6	Excerpt from Ibn al-Jami'	177
9.7	Health risks associated with family formation	179
9.8	The health theme in family planning	182
11.1	How to calculate population growth	212

Tables

9.1 Maternal mortality per 100,000 live births in Matab, Bangladesh — 182
9.2 Maternal mortality per 100,000 live births in Menufia, Egypt — 182
9.3 Maternal deaths that could be prevented — 183

Foreword

The United Nations Population Fund (UNFPA), is pleased to present this in-depth study of *Family Planning in the Legacy of Islam*. It was prepared as a result of growing interest in the topic throughout the Islamic countries, and at their request. The work surveys Islamic views on family life and family planning through fourteen centuries up to the present day, clarifying and updating teachings and opinions while dispelling misunderstandings. The text was prepared by Professor Abdel Rahim Omran, an expert in population and a long-standing student of the Islamic tradition.

Many leading scholars and theologians were consulted during the preparation of the text. The draft manuscript underwent the scrutiny of a committee of scholars from Muslim countries, which strongly endorsed the basic work, made several constructive suggestions and recommended unanimously that the final manuscript be translated into the key languages spoken by Muslim peoples. UNFPA is most grateful to the members of the committee for their contribution. In addition, quotations from the Qur'an and the traditions of the Prophet were reviewed and authenticated by a committee of theologians from Al-Azhar University in Cairo. We thank them for their work, and hope the result will be a valuable contribution to personal and family life.

The UNFPA is most pleased to have been able to facilitate this work and respond positively to the requests of Muslim countries. I do hope that this book will contribute to better understanding of family values in Islam and will lead to improvement of life of families throughout the Muslim World.

Nafis Sadik
Executive Director, UNFPA
October 1991

Foreword

It is a great honor for me to write a foreword to this most valuable work by Professor Omran on *Family Planning in the Legacy of Islam*. I have known Professor Omran for quite sometime and have been following his distinguished career with interest and admiration. He is a world authority on population, health and Islamic studies and is founding father of the World Association of Muslim Scholars for Population, Health and Development of which I became the chairman.

In this study, Dr Omran surveys the source books of Islamic jurisprudence from the eighth to the twentieth century in search for views on family formation and family planning. He has reviewed, in each century, the writing of leading theologians in each of the schools of jurisprudence (*al-madhahib al-fiqhiyya*), classifying their work, comparing their views and referring everything back to the foundation of Islamic jurisprudence namely the Qur'an and the *Sunnah* (the Prophet's tradition). The result of this in-depth study is neatly organized in logical sequence in the book.

The book covers so many areas of inquiry about Islam and family planning, and covers them well. This is a most comprehensive documentation of the subject by one author carrying the survey from family formation, to family planning in the Qur'an and *Sunnah*, to the views of the various schools of jurisprudence ending with the views, *fatwas*, books and conferences on the subject by scholars of the twentieth century. All in all I find it a most informative and engaging volume.

I would like to take this opportunity to thank Professor Omran for this study and the UNFPA for supporting it. I am looking forward to seeing this book translated into the native languages of the Muslim peoples, including my own.

H. Munawir Sjadzali
Minister of Religious Affairs
Republic of Indonesia
October 1991

Foreword

It is most rewarding for me to introduce this well-researched, thoroughly documented and elegantly presented study on *Family Planning in the Legacy of Islam* by Professor Abdel Rahim Omran, the consultant to our International Islamic Center for Population Studies and Research of Al-Azhar University.

The work addresses the various issues of family formation, child spacing, and fertility regulation in a commendable scholarly way. In so doing, the study puts the record straight and dispels misconceptions and misunderstandings of the subject not only among non-Muslims, but also among some Muslims as well. Because the work draws heavily on quotations from the *Qur'an* and *Sunnah* (Prophet's tradition), it was necessary to have such quotations reviewed and authenticated by a specialized committee. The Center has willingly convened, for this purpose, a committee drawn from Al-Azhar theologians. The membership included Dr Sheikh Ahmad Omar Hashim, Vice-President of Al-Azhar University (chairman of the Committee), Dr Sheikh El-Sayed Rizq Al-Taweel, Dean of Al-Azhar College of Islamic Studies in Cairo and Dr Sheikh Mohamed Ra'fat Osman, Dean of the Al-Azhar College of Shari'ah in Tanta (of the Gharbiya Province). The Committee reviewed the quotations and assured their authenticity.

It is therefore with pleasure and pride that I recommend this book to all concerned with population sciences, particularly in the Islamic world. I am sure they will find it as informative and enjoyable as I did.

Prof. Dr Gamal Serour
Director, International
Islamic Center for
Population Studies and Research
Al-Azhar University
December 1991

Preface

IN THE NAME OF ALLAH, THE BENEFICENT, THE MERCIFUL

A theological committee was convened under the Chairmanship of Dr Ahmad Omar Hashim, Vice President of Al-Azhar University and the specialist in Prophetic traditions (*Hadith*), and membership of Dr El-Sayed Rizq Al-Taweel, Dean of the Faculty of Islamic and Arab Studies and a specialist in the Arabic language, Dr Mohamed Ra'fat Osman, Dean of the Faculty of Shari'ah (religious law) at Tanta, and a specialist in jurisprudence (*fiqh*) and with the presence of Dr Gamal Serour, Director of the International Islamic Center for Population Studies and Research of Al-Azhar University and a specialist in human reproduction. The purpose of the meetings on 14–16 October 1991 was to review and authenticate the quotations from the Qu'ran and Prophetic traditions (*Hadith*) used in the text prepared by Professor Dr Abdel Rahim Omran under the title of *Family Planning in the Legacy of Islam*. The committee found that all the Qu'ranic quotations were correct and conformed with the [preferred] Othmanic script. Likewise, the Prophetic traditions were properly reported along with their respective source books. The committee completed the sources for a few traditions used and provided some Arabic explanations for some words to be used in the Arabic edition of the book.

The committee completed its work on 16 October at 10 a.m. and the members signed this statement which was hence stamped by the Official Seal of the Al-Azhar University.

Chairman	Members of the committee	
Dr Ahmed Omar Hashim	Dr El-Sayed Rizq Al-Taweel	Dr Mohamed Ra'fat Osman

PREFACE

جامعة الازهر
مكتب نائب رئيس الجامعــة
لشئون الطلاب

بسم الله الرحمـــن الرحيــم

اجتمعت اللجنه المكونة برئاسة الاستاذ الدكتور / أحمد عمر هاشم نائب رئيس جامعة الازهر وعالم الحديث ، والاستاذ الدكتور / السيد رزق الطويل عميد كلية الدراسات الاسلامية والعربيــــة بنين القاهرة وعالم اللغة ، والاستاذ الدكتور / محمد رأفت عثمان عميد كلية الشريعة بطنطا وعالــم الفقــه ، وبحضور أ.د/ جمال أبو السـرور مدير المركز الدولى الاسلامى للدراسات والبحوث السكانية بجامعة الازهـــر وعالم التكاثر البشــرى وذلك فى أيام من ١٤ - ١٦ أكتوبر سنة ١٩٩١ للنظر فى النصوص القرآنيـــه والاحاديث بكتاب تنظيم الأسرة فى التراث الاسلامى بقلم الاستاذ الدكـــــتور/ عبد الرحيم عمـــران واطلعت اللجنة على النصوص القرآنيـــة والأحاديث التى جاءت بالكتاب المذكـــور فوجدت كل النصوص القرآنيـــة مطابقة للرسم العثمانى بالمصحف الشريف . ووجدت أن الاحاديث مخرجـه تخريجا صحيحا ، وأضافت اللجنة التخريج لبعض الاحاديث التى لم يكتب تخريجها كما أضافت بعــــض التفسيرات اللغويـــة للاستفادة بها فى النسخلا العربيــــة .

هـــــذا وقد أنتهت اللجنة من أعمالهـــــا يوم ١٩٩١/١٠/١٦ فى تمام الساعـــــــة الثانية عشره صــباحا .

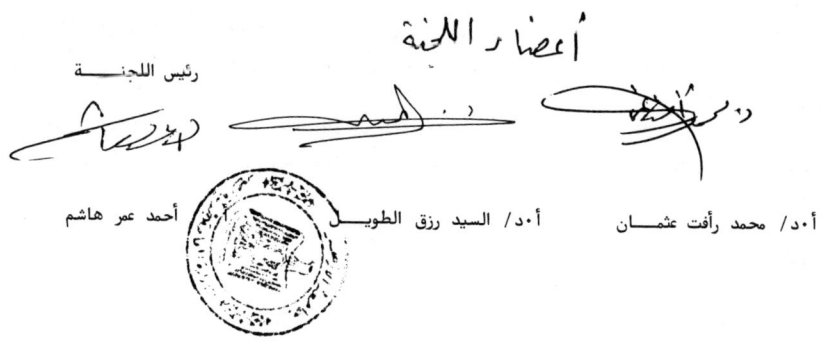

أعضاء اللجنة

رئيس اللجنـــة

أ.د/ محمد رأفت عثمـــان   أ.د/ السيد رزق الطويــل   أحمد عمر هاشم

Acknowledgements

This work would not have been possible without the help and encouragement of many institutions and individuals. Particular appreciation is due to the members of the international review committee:

H.E. Mr Munawir Sjadzali, Minister of Religious Affairs, Republic of Indonesia.

H.E. Dr Mohammad Afazal, Rector of International Islamic University, Islamabad, Pakistan.

Sheikh Said Toihir Ben Said Ahmad, Qadi (justice), Comoros.

Dr Huseyin Atay, Professor, College of Religion, Turkey.

Dr Fu'ad Hefnawi, Professor and Director of the Al-Azhar International Islamic Centre for Population Studies and Research, Al-Azhar, Egypt.

Dr Sulaiman Huzayyin, Professor and Former Director of Cairo Demographic Center (UN), Cairo, Egypt.

Dr Badr Gamal Mursy, Legal Advisor, Permanent Mission of the State of Qatar to United Nations.

Mr Rawani Mbaye, Director of Islamic Institute, Dakar, Senegal.

Dr Abdel Rahim Omran, Chief Advisor, Al-Azhar International Islamic Center for Population Studies and Research, Cairo, Egypt, Director of Population and Health Programs, University of Maryland and Professor of Health Care Sciences, George Washington University, USA.

The views expressed in this book are presented as a contribution to knowledge, thinking and discussion of the subjects covered. They do not necessarily imply the expression or endorsement of any opinion whatsoever on the part of UNFPA.

IN THE NAME OF ALLAH, THE COMPASSIONATE, THE MERCIFUL

Introduction

It is no wonder that Islam has considered the family as the basic social unit of Islamic society and has emphasized that family formation is a grave responsibility of couples. Family relations are specified in Islamic jurisprudence to achieve the welfare and useful life of its members. The rights of children in particular have been stressed as the future builders of society and upholders (and defenders) of the faith.

It is a wonder, however, to the thinkers of today that Islam should give so much concern to child spacing and family planning so early in human history and in the absence of compelling population pressures. The Companions (*sahaba*) of the Prophet (PBUH)* were allowed to practice coitus interruptus (*al-azl*) to ward off health, social or economic hardships. Certainly, there was no doubting the ability of Allah to provide for all creatures; neither was there antagonism to predestination (*qadar*) or reliance on Allah (*tawakkul*).

This pioneering achievement by Islam should not be a total surprise to Muslims. They know that Islam is not merely a religion of worship, but is also a social system, a culture and a civilization. Islamic legislation is most comprehensive and deals with human needs, activities and concerns. It has considered the question of family planning with objectivity and compassion for the believers, being a religion of ease (*yusr*) not hardship (*'usr*), and, having sponsored planning in all individual, communal and societal affairs, birth planning is no exception.

The subject matter, however, could not break the traditional inclinations not to interfere with the process of procreation. This and one tradition that was interpreted by some theologians as prohibiting or discouraging contraception have made the discussions and research on birth planning most lively throughout. Since the time of the Prophet (PBUH), almost all source books of Islamic jurisprudence spanning fourteen centuries have encompassed vivid discussions on *al-azl* or coitus interruptus, either in a few lines, a few paragraphs or as a detailed section or chapter. Birth planning was discussed openly in

---
*Peace Be Upon Him

INTRODUCTION

mosques, religious gatherings and institutes of learning.

It was timely, therefore, to undertake a serious effort to screen the sources of jurisprudence (*fiqh*), the writings of theologians (*'ulama*) and jurists (*fuqaha'*) from different schools (*madhahib*) and periods in the history of Islam. The enormity of the task cannot be over-emphasized in view of the huge treasury of Islamic jurisprudence, contained in regular and special libraries, both in Muslim and non-Muslim countries. I also found volumes at Al-Azhar University that are still in manuscript form. My job was made easier by copying the relevant pages of manuscripts rather than carrying hundreds of volumes wherever I went.

In addition to examining these texts most thoroughly and comparing their contents, I have consulted repeatedly with theologians at Al-Azhar, and other institutes of Islamic learning in both Egypt and elsewhere.

I also had the advantage of the advice of the international committee convened in New York by UNFPA to review the draft manuscripts. Member scholars came from various countries and provided constructive suggestions and support. In addition, I had the continued advice of the prominent scholar, Sheikh Sayyid Sabiq, author of *Fiqh al-Sunnah* and Professor of *fiqh* at Umm al-Qura University in Makkah, Saudi Arabia. Sheikh Abdel Fattah Barakah, Secretary General of the Academy of Islamic Research read the manuscript carefully and made constructive suggestions. I also received suggestions and guidance from Sheikh Abdel-Aziz 'Iesa (former minister of Al-Azhar and member of the Academy of Islamic Research) and Sheikh Sayyid Tantawi, the current Mufti of Egypt.

The manuscript is essentially a synthesis of theological writings rather than fixed ideas of my own. That is why the book avoids conclusions that favor one argument above another. It is a *reference volume*, and if the weight of one argument seems to overwhelm the other, this is the nature of things rather than my own doing. Of course, I am totally responsible for the contents of this volume and their arrangement. If I have succeeded, it is due to the nature of the material and the advice of so many. If I have failed, it is my own responsibility.

The work has been divided into four parts and twelve chapters. A prologue opens the subject area by presenting the views of Sheikh Jadel Haq Ali Jadel Haq, the Grand Imam of Al-Azhar. This provides a stimulating background not only because of the special position of Sheikh Jadel Haq but also because the views are comprehensive and well researched.

Part I provides the Islamic context on the family and family planning. It begins by considering the value of the family and the centrality of marriage as an institution. This is followed by a statement of the rights and obligations of parents and children and a special review of women in Islam. The part closes by showing the inherent support of Islamic precepts for the principles of family planning.

INTRODUCTION

Part II considers how the Qur'an and the *Sunnah* (the Prophet's tradition) deal with the concept of family planning. It introduces the subject through a brief orientation of the sources of Islamic jurisprudence. This is followed by a chapter on the Qur'an and family planning, with special reference to the question of multitude (*kathrah*). Multitude figures high among the topics considered and a survey of views which favor absolute multitude and those which favor quality multitude is made. The next chapter on the *Sunnah* and family planning classifies a considerable number of Prophetic traditions (*ahadith*, singular *hadith*) into nine homogeneous groups according to the subject matter or style. This is followed by commentaries on the *Sunnah* by theologians from different schools and different periods.

This arrangement of chapters is for good reason. The Qur'an supercedes the *Sunnah* and should be considered first. The inclusion of the account on multitude, given in Chapter 6, is also for good reason. First, there is repeated reference to the Qur'an in relation to multitude. Second, it includes a vivid discussion on the issue by opponents and proponents of family planning. This, I suspect, is provocative enough to draw attention to the intricacies of the subject. Had the details of the *Sunnah* been given first, many of the traditions would have been glossed over. In other words, this arrangement increases the appreciation of the *Sunnah* which is strikingly rich in information on contraception.

Part III is devoted to family planning in Islamic jurisprudence from the seventh to the nineteenth century. It provides first a résumé of the origin and distinction of each of nine schools. This is followed by a survey of views on family planning in each school with reference to some leading theologians therein. Another chapter is devoted to reasons for practicing family planning considered acceptable by theologians and is followed by a chapter on more problematical issues, including sterilization, genetic engineering, abortion and repudiation of a child conceived despite the use of coitus interruptus.

Part IV is devoted to family planning in Islamic jurisprudence in the twentieth century. This reflects the many new challenges that were ushered in by the twentieth century, ranging from unprecedented population pressures and the health aspects of family planning, to new methods of contraception and the concept of a family planning movement. Another factor is that the format of giving juristic views has been expanded to official Muftis (appointed jurists), theological councils, *fatwa* committees and even open conferences. Chapter 11 deals with these developments and presents the results of conferences and comments on books on family planning specially written by theologians. Chapter 12 presents a commentary on the *fatwas* from different parts of the Islamic world and the views of prominent scholars of the twentieth century on family planning.

This is followed by the epilogue: a poem on family planning written by a theologian, Sheikh Abdul-Fattah Khattab.

INTRODUCTION

Great care was taken in compiling a chronology of scholars, century by century, from the seventh to the nineteenth century and this is given in Appendix 1, while Appendix 2 provides the translated texts of the *fatwas* from 1937 to 1991.

It is also to be noted that the Qur'anic verses have been presented in the classical Othman script approved by Al-Azhar and other Islamic institutions. The traditions of the Prophet (PBUH) have been identified by the *hadith* compilations where they were authenticated. They have been written in the regular Arabic script.

Before closing this introduction, a working definition of family planning may be helpful and may prevent some misunderstanding.

A WORKING DEFINITION OF FAMILY PLANNING

Family planning as used in this text refers to the use of contraceptive methods by a husband and wife with mutual agreement between them, to regulate their fertility with a view to ward off health, social and economic hardships and to enable them to shoulder their responsibilities towards their children and society.

It encompasses the following:

(a) Spacing of children to allow breast-feeding and safeguard the health of the mother and child.
(b) Timing of pregnancies to occur at a safe age.
(c) Adjusting the number of children, not only to the family's need, but also to its physical, financial, educational and child raising capabilities.

The rule is that such a choice should be voluntary with no coercion or law fixing the number of children per family.

Prevention and control of infertility in both the male and the female is an integral part of family planning. The terms family planning, contraception and birth planning are interchangeably used.

The method used in earlier time was coitus interruptus (*al-azl*) and because all the books of jurisprudence until recently use the term *al-azl*, I have kept that word most of the time. All the rulings on *al-azl* apply, by analogous reasoning, to other methods of contraception. This was emphasized by many jurists.

With great compassion for the Muslim family and for the love of Muslim children, this research has been undertaken. I do hope it will serve a noble purpose.

Abdel Rahim Omran, Cairo/Washington　　　　　　　　　　AH 1412, AD 1992

PROLOGUE

Views of Sheikh Jadel Haq Ali Jadel Haq, the Grand Imam of Al-Azhar, on family planning

Given in 1979 and 1980 and published as *fatwas* in 1983 (subtitles added)

THE LEGALITY OF CONTRACEPTION

The Qur'an and the *Sunnah*

The reference sources of *Shari'ah* law as to permissibility (*halal*) or prohibition (*haram*) are the glorious Qur'an and the tradition (*Sunnah*) of His messenger (PBUH).

A thorough review of the Qur'an reveals no text (*nuss*) prohibiting the prevention of pregnancy or diminution of the number of children, but there are several traditions of the Prophet that indicate its permissibility. This was accepted by jurists of Islamic *Shari'ah*. While there is also in the *Sunnah* what can appear to be prohibiting, the majority (*jumhour*) of jurists (*fuqaha'*) in the legal schools (*madhahib*) agree with the permissibility of *al-azl* (coitus interruptus) where the husband ejaculates outside his wife's vagina.

Position of legal schools (*madhahib*)

In his book *Ihya' Ulum al-Din*, Imam al-Ghazali, who is a Shafe'i, classified earlier and contemporary opinions of his time into four groups: unconditional permission; permission if wife consents and prohibition if she does not; permission with slave but not with free wives (now obsolete); and unconditional prohibition. Al-Ghazali then said '*The correct* way to us (in the Shafe'i school), is that it is permitted.' He then specified five acceptable reasons for preventing pregnancy which include preservation of *the wife's beauty and fitness* and protecting her life from the dangers of labor (*talq*), and the need to avoid *economic embarrassment* and physical hardship entailed in having to work to support too many children. Al-Ghazali said 'to reduce economic embarrassment sustains piety'.

Al-Ghazali made a clear distinction between prevention of conception and abortion, permitting the former and rejecting the latter.

The Hanafi school permits coitus interruptus (*al-azl*) with the wife's consent, while later scholars allowed her consent to be bypassed in 'bad times' (times of religious decline) and to avoid 'bad' offspring (lacking piety). The opinion in the Maliki and Hanbali schools is permission with wife's consent, as it is in the Zaydi Shi'ite school. The Imami Shi'ites prefer to obtain the wife's permission at the time of the marriage contract.

Imam Shawkani adds that 'among the reasons for *al-azl* is to *protect a suckling child* from the dangers of changed milk from a pregnant mother; another is to *avoid getting too many children*, or avoiding getting them at all [*al-firar min husulihim min al-azl*].'

From this brief review of jurisprudence, it is evident that *al-azl* for temporary prevention of pregnancy is permissible (*ja'iz*). The *sahaba* themselves practised *al-azl* at the time of the Prophet (PBUH). He came to know about it and did not prohibit them according to Jabir's tradition reported in Muslim, and while the Qur'an was being revealed as reported in al-Bukhari.* Thus, prevention of pregnancy is lawful as stated above.

MODERN METHODS

It is true that early scholars of Islamic law did not mention other methods because *al-azl* was the method known to them at the time and before their time. By analogous reasoning (*qiyas*) alternative methods of contraception can be allowed as long as the purpose is to prevent pregnancy. Some of these methods may be barriers used by the man or the woman, or medicines prescribed by physicians for temporary contraception. There is no harm in allowing, by analogy, the modern methods as long as they will not destroy fecundity or the ability to procreate.

That is why the Hanafi jurists extended permission to blocking the mouth of the uterus, with the husband's consent. For the same reason the Shafe'i scholars allowed temporary delay of pregnancy for a period of time.

Hence temporary methods like contraceptive pills or the coil (IUDs) or other methods are permitted as long as there is no permanent impairment of fertility. Actually the modern methods are better than *al-azl* because they allow normal and complete marital relations.

---

*Muslim's and al-Bukhari's are the two leading compilations of prophetic traditions; each is called *sahih* or 'the accurate'.

PROLOGUE

Al-tawakkul and *rizq*

Such temporary contraception is no contradiction to reliance on Allah (*tawakkul*) because the use of these methods is to take expedients while putting trust in Allah, as Muslims always do. The Prophet advised his Companion, saying

«اعقِلْها وتوكّل»

رواه الترمذي والبيهقي والطبراني

Hobble her and put your trust in Allah.
　　　　　　　　Reported by al-Tirmidhi, al-Baihaqi and al-Tabarani

That is how the Prophet (PBUH) interpreted *tawakkul*. Imam al-Ghazali who is an authority on *tawakkul*, said that *al-azl* to escape economic embarrassment is not unlawful. As to the verse in the Qur'an which says

وَمَا مِن دَآبَّةٍ فِى ٱلْأَرْضِ إِلَّا عَلَى ٱللَّهِ رِزْقُهَا ...

هود(١١)

There is no moving creature on Earth, but its sustenance is on Allah.
　　　　　　　　　　　　　　　　　　　Hud (Sura 11:6)

This does not mean that a person should be lazy and neglect to earn a living while asking Allah to provide for them without work. The real meaning of *tawakkul* is that given by Sayyidna Omar Ibn al-Khattab, who equated it with a farmer who puts the seeds in the earth and puts his trust in Allah (for a good crop). Hence, *tawakkul* should be associated with taking expedients (*al-akhth bil-asbab*).

Sterilization

Other than for pressing health reasons, sterilization through surgery or through drugs is not permissible if it causes permanent loss of fertility. Sterilization may be used when it is established that a hereditary disease may pass to children or causes pain. In that case sterilization becomes mandatory, based on the juristic principle of permitting an injury to avoid a greater injury. This is conditional on the diseases being incurable and must take into consideration advances in medical technology.

Abortion

The Hanafi opinion supports abortion provided it is performed within 120 days of conception. During this period the fetus is not believed to be a complete human soul. Early abortion is held to be *makrouh*, (disliked but not forbidden) when it lacks valid reasons or justifications. Reported valid reasons included a woman's inability to breast-feed her baby and the family's inability to afford a wet nurse. Some Shafe'i scholars share these Hanafi views. Others like al-Ghazali do not. The Zaydi Shi'ite school allows abortion unconditionally with or without valid reason, provided it precedes 'ensoulment', calling it *ja'iz* or permitted. The Zahiri and Maliki jurists forbid it under all circumstances, calling it *haram*, but some Hanbali jurists allow it before 40 days.

Juristic consensus exists only on the point that abortion after a period of *four months* from the date of conception amounts to taking a life. Yet this limit may also be *set aside* if, according to medical opinion, there is a definite risk of death to the mother. The mother's life takes precedence over the child's life on the juristic principle: 'the root is more valuable than the branch.'

PREDESTINATION

Ways of Allah are unknown to man. Man lives in the small world of cause and effect, of action and reaction. It does not lie in the power of man to defy Allah's will whatever means man may use to carry out his intention. This is the reasoning used by the Prophet himself when he was asked about contraception. On the authority of Abu Sa'id al-Khudri, the Prophet (PBUH) said 'If Allah wills to create a soul, no one can stop Him.'

TWO ADDITIONS FROM AN INTERVIEW WITH THE GRAND IMAM, ALSO PUBLISHED WITH THE *FATWA*
Contraception is no murder

Question
Is birth control a form of killing i.e. does it come under the meaning of the verse 'Do not kill your children in fear of want'?

Answer
Prevention of pregnancy is neither a killing nor an abortion of a fetus, because the semen (*nutfa*) from which a fetus is created, is not in itself a human being. After the semen mingles with the woman's ovum in the process of fertilization, a fetus is formed which, as we already indicated, would not become an ensouled creature (*khalqan a'akhar*) until after 120 days.

Prevention of pregnancy is the act of preventing the semen of a man from mingling with the ovum of the woman and this is not killing. What the verse is referring to is the pre-Islamic custom of burying children in fear of poverty.

PROLOGUE

The state can help but no coercive laws

Question
Is it lawful for the state to make laws which compel parents to limit family size, particularly if such laws are in the national interest?

Answer
Islam goes to the extent of ensuring that, on the question of family size, one parent does not impose his or her will on the other. How can it sanction *coercive laws* which may ignore the needs and circumstances of individual families?

The state can, of course, help people take correct decisions by providing them with opportunities to act on these decisions and also creating conditions which abolish the need for a large family. This means wider, but sensible use of mass media and other educational channels for showing the advantage of a small family, with easier availability of contraceptives and of relevant information about the technological changes available to help reduce the family's dependence on its manpower as an economic unit. The last is very important. Posters, slogans and TV programmes cannot alter human behaviour *if* social and economic conditions obstruct the change.

Source
Al-Fatawa al-Islamiyyah, vol. 9, pp. 3087–92, pp. 3110–13, and pp. 3093–3193, High Council of Islamic Affairs, Cairo (1983) (includes the interview quoted above). Issued by *Darel-Ifta' al-Masriyyah* under the supervision of the Grand Imam, the Minister of Religious Affairs, the Mufti of the Republic and the Secretary General of the High Council of Islamic Affairs.

PART I

The Islamic Context

1

Family and marriage in Islam

The family is the basic social unit in Islamic society, and marriage is the fundamental Islamic institution. Marriage and family formation are grave responsibilities and are subject to specific regulations. Their planning is, therefore, in order.

THE FAMILY IN ISLAM
Role of the family
Islam has a pervasive social character and the family is the core of its society. Islam tends to consider the family as something absolutely good and almost sacred. Besides providing tranquility and mutual support and understanding between husband and wife, the obvious function of a family is to provide a culturally and legally acceptable way of satisfying the sexual instinct as well as to raise children as the new generation. Islam has more essential roles for the family, however. It is within the family system that Muslims acquire their religious training, develop their moral character, establish close social relationships and sustain loyalty both to the family and to society at large. The support system in the family (both financial, social and emotional) is paramount in establishing the peace of mind and security needed for the journey of life. This is particularly important for the socially dependent members, namely the children, the elderly, the single adults (especially females), as well as the sick or handicapped.

The family in Islam includes both the nuclear (husband, wife and their children) and extended varieties by caring for all the relatives (*ahl*). There are special laws governing family relations, details of which are beyond this account.

The relationship between husband and wife
The husband and wife are the principals of family formation. Their relationship in marriage is described in the Qur'an as of two major qualities: *love* (pas-

THE ISLAMIC CONTEXT

sion, friendship, companionship) on the one hand, and *mercy* (understanding, reconciliation, tolerance, forgiveness) on the other within the overall objective of tranquility. The Qur'an says

$$\text{وَمِنْ ءَايَٰتِهِۦٓ أَنْ خَلَقَ لَكُم مِّنْ أَنفُسِكُمْ أَزْوَٰجًا لِّتَسْكُنُوٓا۟ إِلَيْهَا وَجَعَلَ بَيْنَكُم مَّوَدَّةً وَرَحْمَةً ... ﴿٢١﴾ الروم (٣٠)}$$

And one of [Allah's] signs is, that He has created for you mates
from yourselves, that you may dwell in tranquility with them, and
has ordained between you Love and Mercy.
al-Roum (Sura 30: 21)

This is a verse frequently quoted to describe one of the purposes of family life. It starts by referring to the unity of origin of husband and wife, which is a confirmation of equality and a basis for harmony between them. It must follow then that both husband and wife will find tranquility (*sakan*) in one another. This key verse concludes by referring to the social relationships within the family, which range from love and tenderness, to understanding, empathy and mercy.

There can be no better expression of the relationship between two human beings living together in blessed marital bondage. Such a relationship is so highly valued that Allah made it among His signs, and it is.

This is confirmed further by another verse in which Muslims are reminded in the same manner of the first human family.

$$\text{هُوَ ٱلَّذِى خَلَقَكُم مِّن نَّفْسٍ وَٰحِدَةٍ وَجَعَلَ مِنْهَا زَوْجَهَا لِيَسْكُنَ إِلَيْهَا ... ﴿١٨٩﴾ الأعراف (٧)}$$

It is He who created you from a single soul (*nafs*) and therefrom
did make his mate, that he might dwell in tranquility with her.
al-A'raf (Sura 7: 189)

It is ironic that neither verse mentioned children or procreation. This suggests that tranquility is an overall purpose of marriage, which is more equitable since all couples can achieve tranquility, but not all couples are fertile. Procreation is also important to maintain the human race. Other verses in the Qur'an do mention procreation. For example,

وَاللَّهُ جَعَلَ لَكُم مِّنْ أَنفُسِكُمْ أَزْوَاجًا وَجَعَلَ لَكُم مِّنْ أَزْوَاجِكُم بَنِينَ وَحَفَدَةً ... ﴿٧٢﴾ النحل(١٦)

And Allah has made for you mates from yourselves and made for you out of them, children and grandchildren.

al-Nahl (Sura 16: 72)

Taking the three verses together, it is possible to infer that, while procreation is an expectation in marriage, it is not its exclusive purpose. When procreation takes place, however, it should support and endorse tranquility rather than disrupt it. It also means that sexual relations in marriage need not always be for the purpose of having children. This is a point of departure from other religions where procreation is the exclusive purpose of marital relations.

MARRIAGE IN ISLAM

General summary

Marriage is basic to family formation in Islam. When Islam came to Arabia, there were several forms of marriage. All were banned save one – a marriage with the free consent of the wife, as practiced today. Polygyny is allowed but monogamy is preferred. An equity condition (to treat all wives equally) is an important restriction and suggests that pologyny is conditionally allowed. Marriage is to be made public; the dowry and financial and household needs are the responsibility of the husband.

Parents are held responsible for the social, cultural and moral training of children as well as for their physical and health care. Those unable to undertake these responsibilities should postpone marriage. In return, parents (especially mothers) are held in great esteem and should receive respect and tender loving care from their children. As they grow old and fail to support themselves, the children (or adults) should provide shelter and adequate financial support for their parents in addition to continuing social support. Ageing, sick or handicapped parents should never be abandoned. This is the built-in social security system in Islamic society.

Marriage is a solemn covenant; divorce is possible but is strongly discouraged unless there is no alternative.

Contemporary Muslim families are undergoing change, becoming less extended, with more wives educated and gainfully employed. Arranged marriages are declining and the age of marriage is rising; modern contraceptives are slowly becoming more prevalent in certain communities.

Marriage as a basic institution

Marriage is basic to family formation in Islam. It has been hailed by the Prophet (PBUH) as a part of his way (*Sunnah*). Self-imposed permanent celibacy is not the Islamic way. It was solemnly prohibited by the Prophet. Some of the Companions of the Prophet, in their zeal for devoted, uninterrupted worship, wanted to wear rough wool clothes (wool in Arabic is *suf*, hence Sufism), abandon sex (actually be castrated), fast continuously, etc. When this was related to the Prophet he became angry and reprimanded those concerned in no kind words, as shown below.

«جاء ثلاثة رهط إلى بيوت أزواج النبي صلى الله عليه وسلم يسألون عن عبادته ، فلما أخبروا كأنهم تقالوها ، فقالوا : أين نحن من رسول الله ، قد غفر الله له ما تقدم من ذنبه وما تأخر،فقال أحدهم : أمّا أنا فإني أصلي الليل أبدا ، وقال آخر وأنا أصوم الدهر ولا أفطر ، وقال آخر وأنا أعتزل النساء فلا أتزوج ، فجاء رسول الله وقال : أنتم قلتم كذا وكذا ؟ أما والله إني لأخشاكم لله . وأتقاكم لله ، ولكني أصوم وأفطر ، وأصلي وأرقد ، وأتزوج النساء ، فمن رغب عن سنتي فليس مني »

متفق عليه

Three groups of people came to the residence of the Prophet to ask about his mode of worship. When they were told of it, they seemed to have belittled it [they expected more]. Then they said 'Where are we compared to the Prophet (PBUH)? He has already been forgiven by Allah for anything that he did or would do.'

Then one of them said 'As far as I am concerned, I will pray all night forever'; another said 'And I will fast continuously'; still another one said 'I will desert women and will never marry'.

When the Prophet (PBUH) returned, he asked them 'Are you the ones who said so and so?' And solemnly stated: 'By Allah, I am more God-fearing and devout than you. Nevertheless, I fast and I break my fast, I pray and I go to sleep, and I marry. He who deviates from my way is none of me'.

Agreed upon by al-Bukhari and Muslim the most trustworthy compilers of traditions

Despite this endorsement, Islam stopped short of making marriage mandatory for every Muslim (*fard ayn*). Some Muslims may, for financial, personal or other reasons, choose to postpone marriage until their circumstances improve. Marriage can also be bypassed altogether by a few for good reasons.

Marriage as a solemn covenant
Marriage, which is basic to family formation, is a solemn covenant and not a casual arrangement. The Qur'an calls marriage 'a solemn covenant' (*mithaq ghalith*).

$$\text{وَأَخَذْنَ مِنكُم مِّيثَاقًا غَلِيظًا ۝}$$
$$\text{النساء(٤)}$$

And they [the wives] have taken from you a solemn covenant.

al-Nisa' (Sura 4: 21)

This is contrary to the 'western' concept of marriage in Islam. Western writers tend to describe it as a status that one can get in and out of with ease. They refer, of course, to the legality of divorce in Islam. The notoriety of 'Islamic divorce' in western literature relates more to its permissibility than to its prevalence. Despite its permissibility, divorce is gravely discouraged in Islam, but, if inevitable, it can be practiced. The Prophet (PBUH) says

$$\text{«أبغض الحلال عند الله الطلاق»}$$
$$\text{رواه أبو داود وابن ماجة}$$

Verily, the most hateful to Allah of the lawful things is divorce.
Authenticated by Abu Dawoud and Ibn Maja

$$\text{«تزوجوا ولا تُطلِّقوا ، فإن الله لا يحب الذوَّاقين والذوَّاقات»}$$
$$\text{أخرجه الطبراني}$$

Marry but do not divorce. For, Allah does not like men and women who desire only a taste of marriage.
Authenticated by al-Tabarani

Marriage as a grave responsibility
Marriage is thus a grave responsibility and as such it should be planned for, with a view especially to ensuring the ability of a man to care for a wife and a household and for the couple to raise their children as pious, healthy, educated, useful and well-behaved citizens. Otherwise, marriage should be postponed. The Qur'an says

$$\text{وَلْيَسْتَعْفِفِ ٱلَّذِينَ لَا يَجِدُونَ نِكَاحًا حَتَّىٰ يُغْنِيَهُمُ ٱللَّهُ مِن فَضْلِهِۦ ... ۝}$$
$$\text{النور(٢٤)}$$

Let those who find not the wherewithal for marriage, keep themselves chaste, until Allah gives them means out of His grace.

al-Nour (Sura 24: 33)

The Prophet says

«يا معشرَ الشباب ، من استطاع منكم الباءة فليتزوج ، فإنه أغضُّ للبصر وأحصن للفرج ، فمن لم يستطع فعليه بالصوم ، فإنه له وجاء»

متفق عليه من حديث عبد الله بن مسعود

O young men! Those of you who can support a wife and household should marry. For, marriage keeps you from looking with lust at women and preserves you from promiscuity. But those who cannot, should take to fasting which is a means of tampering sexual desires.

Agreed upon

Imam al-Ghazali (d.AD1111) uses the interesting argument that as marriage can be postponed or bypassed altogether by some Muslims (which is legal) so can begetting children. He used this argument in his discussion of the legality of *al-azl* (withdrawal or coitus interruptus) as a method to avoid pregnancy.[1]

Age at marriage

Age at marriage has biological, socio-cultural and demographic significance. *Biologically*, intercourse with very young wives (who are not physically mature) may lead to genital pain, lacerations and tears. Furthermore, should pregnancy occur it carries great risks both to the mother and child. *Socio-culturally* the couple (particularly the wife) should be able to cope with the social requirements of marriage, running a household and raising children. Too young an age means that an element mentioned in the Qur'an will sometimes be missing, namely, the element of dwelling in tranquility (*sakan*). This also means that the element of 'free consent' is missing at a young age and the marriage may end in failure and divorce. *Demographically* higher ages of marriage are ways to reduce fertility without the use of contraception.

In Islam there is *no* fixed age of marriage, although some Muslim countries may have enacted legislation fixing a minimum age. In some texts of *fiqh* (e.g. al-Ajali's *al-Sara'ir Fil-Fiqh*[2] and Hilli's *Shar'i'ah al-Islam*[3]) there is a mention of age nine, without explaining why and on what grounds this age was based. These same texts mention, however, that if marriage occurs at such a young age, and if intercourse results in tears in the vagina and urethral wall leading to permanent incontinence, the husband is held responsible (*damin*, as in malpractice). They term this condition *ifda'*. In modern medicine, this is what is called 'vesico-vaginal fistula', a condition prevalent unfortunately in some Muslim countries such as Sudan, Nigeria, Somalia, Yemen and Bangladesh.

It is due more to early pregnancy than simple intercourse.

There are also general references in the Qur'an regarding the age of marriage and the age of sound judgement, without specifying a fixed age.

وَٱبْتَلُواْ ٱلْيَتَٰمَىٰ حَتَّىٰٓ إِذَا بَلَغُواْ ٱلنِّكَاحَ فَإِنْ ءَانَسْتُم مِّنْهُمْ رُشْدًا فَٱدْفَعُوٓاْ إِلَيْهِمْ أَمْوَٰلَهُمْ وَلَا تَأْكُلُوهَآ إِسْرَافًا وَبِدَارًا أَن يَكْبَرُواْ ...﴿٦﴾

النساء(٤)

And make trial of orphans until they reach the *age of marriage*; and if then you perceive in them a *sound judgement*, then hand over their property to them, but consume it not wastefully nor in haste against their growing up.

al-Nisa' (Sura 4: 6)

Imam Abu Hanifa is reported to have mentioned an age of 18 for boys and 17 for girls (See al-Sa'ih 1974)[4]. These were the figures used in the Ottoman Family Law before the First World War (1914). Modifications have been introduced since then in the region formerly controlled by the Ottoman Empire.

Currently many countries have legislation fixing ages of marriage that are not too different from the above. This is, however, a matter for further research by Muslim jurists and physicians.

POLYGYNY

Definition
Polygyny denotes multiple wives, polyandry denotes multiple husbands; polygamy includes both polygyny and polyandry.

Permissibility of polygyny
Polygyny in Islam is notorious not because of its prevalence but because of its possibility. Certainly the licence to marry more than one wife has been grossly abused by some Muslims who did not appreciate it as a conditional permission. Even with that abuse its occurrence is no more than 3 per cent and with the increasing education of women and reformed understanding of the real Islam, polygyny is on the decline.

The licence to practice polygyny, which was a restricting order to limit the number of wives, came from the following verses in the Qur'an:

THE ISLAMIC CONTEXT

$$\text{وَإِنْ خِفْتُمْ أَلَّا تُقْسِطُوا فِي الْيَتَامَىٰ فَانْكِحُوا مَا طَابَ لَكُمْ مِنَ النِّسَاءِ مَثْنَىٰ وَثُلَاثَ وَرُبَاعَ ۖ فَإِنْ خِفْتُمْ أَلَّا تَعْدِلُوا فَوَاحِدَةً ...}$$ (٣)

النساء(٤)

And if you are apprehensive that you shall not deal justly with orphans, then, marry women of your choice, two, three or four. But if you fear that you shall not be able to deal justly [with them], then only one.

al-Nisa' (Sura 4: 3)

Later in the same Sura, the Qur'an says

$$\text{وَلَنْ تَسْتَطِيعُوا أَنْ تَعْدِلُوا بَيْنَ النِّسَاءِ وَلَوْ حَرَصْتُمْ ...}$$ (١٢٩)

النساء(٤)

And you will not have it in your power to treat your wives equitably, even if it is your ardent desire.

al-Nisa' (Sura 4:129)

In considering the verses, most jurists believe that the permission is clear and that the condition of just treatment refers to 'controllable' aspects such as housing, clothing, feeding, recreation, care of the wife and equity in treatment of the children. To them the verses cannot mean being equal also in affection, because this is uncontrollable. They reiterate that limiting the number to a maximum of four was a hardship at the time of the Prophet when many husbands had more than four wives. They also sincerely believe that polygyny, for acceptable reasons and without abuse, is preferred to divorce. A dependent wife might prefer to share her husband with another wife, allowing her children to continue to be raised in their own home with both parents, notwithstanding a part-time father.[5]

Some theologians and thinkers believe that verse 3 in Sura 4 is a promotion of monogamy. Let us quote from an English commentary on the Qur'an by Abdullah Yusuf Ali which was included in his widely used translation of the meaning of the holy Qur'an (p. 179).

About the orphans' linkage:

> Notice the conditional clause about orphans, introducing the rules about marriage. This reminds us of the immediate occasion of the promulgation of this verse. It was after [the battle of] Uhud, when the Muslim community was left with many orphans and widows, and some captives of war. Their treatment was to be governed by principles of the greatest humanity and equity. The occasion is past, but the principles remain.

> Marry the orphans if you are quite sure that you will in that way protect their interest and their property, with perfect justice to them and to your own dependants if you have any; if not, make other arrangements.

About equitable dealings:

> The unrestricted number of wives of '*Jahiliyya*' [the age of ignorance] was now strictly limited to a maximum of four, provided you could treat them with perfect equity, in material things as well as in affection and immaterial things. As this condition is most difficult to fulfil, *I understand the recommendation to be towards monogamy.*[6]

The wife can disallow polygyny

From the early period of Islam, jurists have allowed the inclusion in the marriage contract of a solemn promise that the husband would not take another wife. If he does, the wife has the right to ask for divorce.

Sheikh Sayyid Sabiq, in his encyclopedia *Fiqh al-Sunnah* states

> As Islam has restricted polygyny to the ability of equitable dealing and restricted the number to four, it gave the woman or her guardian the right to include in the marriage contract the condition that the husband will not marry a second woman. If she makes that condition it becomes a part of the contract. She then has the right of divorce if the husband does not fulfil this condition. Her right for divorce is established unless she voluntarily removes this condition and *allows* her husband to take another wife.
>
> This is the opinion of Imam Ahmad, founder of the Hanbali school (*madhab*) and is further preferred by Ibn Taymiyah and Ibn-al-Qayyim.
>
> They also allowed the *condition* to be verbal [not necessarily written] or if it is the norm (*'urf*) for the girl's family, i.e. if the girl's family is known to oppose having another wife next to their daughter.[7]

Because of the significance of this quotation, I will give the statement in Arabic.

حق المرأة في اشتراط عدم التزوج عليها

«كما أنَّ الاسلام قيَّد التعدد بالقدرة على العدل ، وقصره على أربع ، فقد جعل من حق المرأة أو وليّها أن تشترط ألاَّ يتزوج الرجل عليها . فلو شرطت الزوجة

في عقد الزواج على زوجها ألاَّ يتزوج عليها صح الشرط ولزم . وكان لها
حق فسخ الزواج إذا لم يفِ بالشرط . ولا يسقط حقها في الفسخ إلا إذا
أسقطته هي ، ورضيت بمخالفته .

وإلى هذا ذهب الإمام أحمد ورجحه ابن تيمية وابن القيم وذهبوا كذلك إلى
أن الشرط يمكن أن يكون لفظيا،وفي بعض الأحوال يمكن أن يكون عرفياً ،
إذا جاءت الفتاة من أسرة يُعرف عنها أنها لا تقبل أن يتزوَّجَ عليها زوجُها»
انتهى كلام الشيخ سابق

THE ELEMENTS OF PLANNING IN FAMILY AND MARRIAGE

It is quite clear that marriage and family formation in Islam require a good deal of planning, including the following considerations.

Genetic considerations
In order to avoid genetic problems, the Prophet (PBUH) instructed that these genetic traits be considered.

Genetic counseling:
He said

«تخيَّروا لنطفكم فإن العرق دسّاس أو نزَّاع»

رواه ابن ماجة

Choose where you deposit your sperm for the line of descent is conducive.

Authenticated by Ibn Maja

Inbreeding is discouraged:
It is also a common advice (not *hadith*):

«اغتربوا لا تُضْنُوا»

Marry from outside your kin and kith, lest you beget puny children.

Caliph Omar told the clan of al-Sa'ib, who concentrated marriages within their clan:

«يا آل السائب ، قد أضْوَيتم ، فانكحوا في النزائع»

رواه ابراهيم الحربي في غريب الحديث

You have had puny children, you should marry outside the clan.

Authenticated by Ibrahim al-Harbi

Imam al-Ghazali emphasized that the wife should not be from among the close relatives (first cousins) lest the children would be puny (weak).[8]

Modern medicine has found that certain genetic disease conditions prevail with repeated consanguinity and inbreeding. These include sickle cell anaemia, cystic fibrosis (of the lung and pancreas), thalassemia (a blood disease), and phenylketonuria (PKU) (a deficiency of an essential liver enzyme).

All these diseases result from the marriage of two carriers of the abornmal genes. The genes are called recessive, because if only one spouse carries them and the other is normal, no disease results among the offspring, though some may become carriers of the harmful genes. With inbreeding or with repetitive consanguinity from grandparents, to parents, to the couple concerned, and in families known to have these diseases or to carry the harmful genes, the probability increases of a marriage between two carriers leading to affected children. Figure 1.1. may simplify this technical issue.

Despite this, I should emphasize that marriage between cousins is not prohibited in Islam. After all, the Prophet (PBUH) allowed his daughter Fatima to marry his cousin Ali; but this was in a healthy family. However, if genetic diseases occur in the family or if puny children are found, then the family is well advised to disallow intermarriages within the family. This medical advice can come under the general rule of 'no harm and no harassment'.

Note: Since we are in the area of genetics, I must refer to the fact that the husband is the one responsible for the sex of the child. I mention this because many husbands who have only daughters, marry another woman to give them sons. This may not succeed because sperms are of different character: some female sperms have the XX chromosomes which will produce a female child. Other sperms are male and carry the XY chromosomes and produce a male child. The wife provides X chromosome. Thus, producing only female children is not grounds for divorce or another marriage.

Cultural considerations

Islam emphasizes the religious and moral character of the marriage partner as evident in the following self-explanatory quotations. The Prophet (PBUH) says

THE ISLAMIC CONTEXT

Figure 1.1 **Consanguineous marriages**

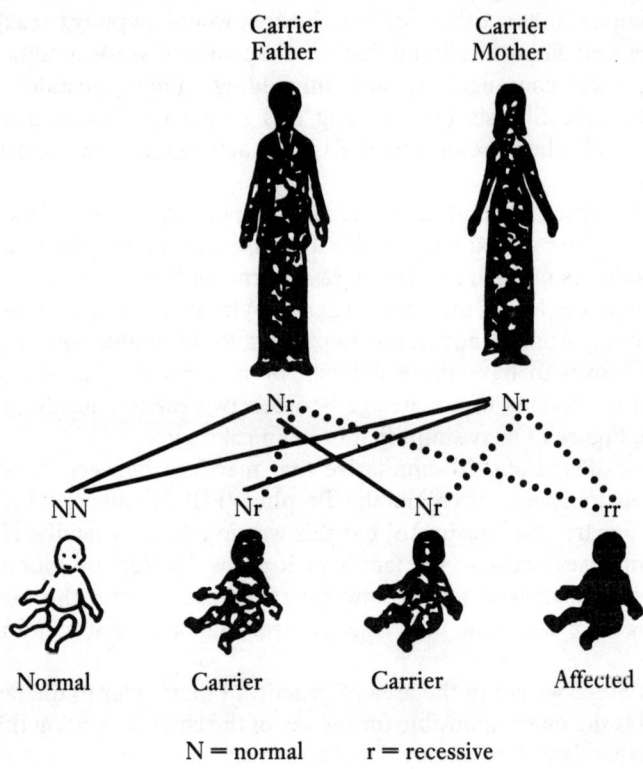

N = normal   r = recessive

From the pedigree it is apparent that each offspring has:
(a) a 25 per cent chance of being normal (NN);
(b) a 25 per cent chance of being affected (rr);
(c) a 50 per cent chance of being a carrier (Nr) like the parents.

Should the carrier son or daughter marry a carrier spouse the same risk (shown in pedigree 2) of transmitting the disease to the next generation occurs.

Close to 1,000 conditions are inherited recessively and are usually more severe than the conditions transmitted dominantly. Examples include the following:

- Cystic fibrosis
- Phenylketonuria (PKU) a deficiency of an essential liver enzyme
- Sickle cell anaemia
- Thalassemia, a blood disease

Genetic defects occurring within consanguineous marriages are of this recessive variety.

About the wife:

قال صلى الله عليه وسلم:

«ألا أخبركم بخير ما يكنز المرء ؟ المرأة الصالحة التي إذا نظر إليها سرَّته ، وإذا غاب عنها حفظته ، وإذا أمرها أطاعته»

رواه أصحاب السنن

وفي رواية

«التي تسره إذا نظر ، وتطيعه إذا أمر ، ولا تخالفه في نفسها ولا ماله بما يكره»

رواه أبو داود والنسائي

Shall I tell you what the best fortune is for a man to treasure up? A good woman who would be pleasing to look at, would stand up for him in his absence, and would obey him if he commands [her].

Authenticated by Ibn Maja and other Sunans

وقال:

«تُنكح المرأة لأربع : لمالها ولحسبها ولجمالها ولدينها ، فاظفر بذات الدين تربت يداك»

متفق عليه من حديث أبي هريرة

A woman is taken in marriage for four qualities: her wealth, her family, her beauty and her religiosity. So get hold of the religious one, and you will be blessed.

Agreed upon

وقال:

«إيّاكم وخضراءَ الدَّمن ، قالوا وما خضراءُ الدَّمن يارسولَ الله ، قال : المرأة الحسناء في المنبت السوء»

رواه الدارقطني وتفرد به الواقدى

Beware of the verdant midden: someone asked 'O Messenger of Allah. What is a verdant midden?', He said, 'the beautiful woman in a bad-breeding spot'.

Authenticated by Darakutni

THE ISLAMIC CONTEXT

About the man:

وقال:
«إذا جاءكم من ترضوْن دينه وخُلُقه ، فأنكِحوه ، إلاَّ تفعلوه تكنْ فتنةٌ في الأرض وفسادٌ كبير»

أخرجه الترمذي من حديث أبي هريرة

If someone with whose godliness and moral character you are satisfied comes to you as suitor, give him the girl under your care. If you do not do so, there will be trouble and great corruption in the land.

Authenticated by al-Tirmidhi

Social considerations
- As stated before, the financial ability of the husband is a prerequisite, otherwise marriage is postponed.
- Responsible parenthood (i.e. the ability to raise children in the Islamic way and to satisfy the social responsibilities of families) is required of both husband and wife.
- Social and economic compatibility (*kafa'ah*) is highly recommended. If two socially or economically different candidates accept or reconcile their differences then there is no problem.

Marital competence
Puberty and physical maturity are required, hence marriage at a very young age is not compatible (especially for girls) with good standards of marriage (see above). Impotence can be the basis for marriage annulment.

Pregnancy planning
All Muslim couples at all times and places are advised to space their children since breast-feeding is recommended by the Qur'an, while pregnancy during the lactation period is discouraged by the Prophet (PBUH).

Timing of pregnancy to suitable ages and adjusting the number of children according to health, social and economic capacities of the family are the subject of subsequent juristic discussions.

2

Parent and child: rights of one, obligations of the other

Islam endorses the natural child–parent relationship by specifying the rights and obligations of one to the other. Parents are to command tender loving care and respect throughout their lives, and should receive special care in old age. Children have rights to genetic purity, to life, legitimacy and good name, breast-feeding, shelter and maintenance, independent sleeping arrangements, future security, religious training, education, equitable treatment, and a wholesome source for their care. The ability to fulfil these rights should be considered in planning a family.

RIGHTS OF PARENTS IN ISLAM

Parents are held at the highest position in regard to love and loyalty by their children. In several places, the Qur'an puts tender loving care (*ihsan*) of parents next to belief in Allah. This is repeatedly stated in several Qur'anic verses:

$$\ldots \text{وَاعْبُدُوا اللَّهَ وَلَا تُشْرِكُوا بِهِ شَيْئًا وَبِالْوَالِدَيْنِ إِحْسَانًا} \text{ ﴿٣٦﴾}$$

النساء(٤)

And serve Allah, ascribe nothing as partner unto Him, and bestow tender loving care unto your parents.

al-Nisa' (Sura 4:36)

$$\text{قُلْ تَعَالَوْا أَتْلُ مَا حَرَّمَ رَبُّكُمْ عَلَيْكُمْ أَلَّا تُشْرِكُوا بِهِ شَيْئًا وَبِالْوَالِدَيْنِ إِحْسَانًا} \text{ ﴿١٥١﴾} \ldots$$

الأنعام(٦)

Say: Come, I will recite unto you that which your Lord has prohibited

THE ISLAMIC CONTEXT

you from; ascribe none as partner unto Him and bestow tender loving care unto your parents.

وَقَضَىٰ رَبُّكَ أَلَّا تَعْبُدُوٓا۟ إِلَّآ إِيَّاهُ وَبِٱلْوَٰلِدَيْنِ إِحْسَٰنًا ...

الإسراء(١٧)

al-An'am (Sura 6:151)

Your Lord has decreed that you worship none save Him, and that you bestow tender loving care unto your parents.

al-Isra' (Sura 17:23)

This last verse goes on to address the important problem of elderly parents. With the increasing life expectancy in societies in the twentieth century, the problem of the elderly is a growing concern. The over-nuclearization of the family and the unduly exaggerated independence of children from their parents, mean that many parents in western societies find themselves alone in old age without the material or emotional support and companionship of their children. Many end up in sanitaria or homes for the aged which can never replace family care. Islam has tackled this problem at the grassroots level by securing a continued relationship with, and support of the elderly. The previous verses continue:

إِمَّا يَبْلُغَنَّ عِندَكَ ٱلْكِبَرَ أَحَدُهُمَآ أَوْ كِلَاهُمَا فَلَا تَقُل لَّهُمَآ أُفٍّ وَلَا تَنْهَرْهُمَا وَقُل لَّهُمَا قَوْلًا كَرِيمًا وَٱخْفِضْ لَهُمَا جَنَاحَ ٱلذُّلِّ مِنَ ٱلرَّحْمَةِ وَقُل رَّبِّ ٱرْحَمْهُمَا كَمَا رَبَّيَانِي صَغِيرًا

الإسراء(١٧)

Whether one or both of them attain old age with you, say not 'Fie' unto them, nor repulse them, but speak to them graciously.

And bestow kindness, humility and submission unto them and say: 'My Lord! Have mercy on them both as they did care for me when I was little'.

al-Isra' (Sura 17:23, 24)

Dr Abdel Aziz Kamel (1975)¹ finds in this verse several dimensions for treating parents when they become old:

- To be correctly addressed by their children
    'Say not "Fie" unto them.'
    'Speak to them graciously.'

PARENT AND CHILD: RIGHTS AND OBLIGATIONS

- To have their viewpoints respected
  'Nor repulse them.'
- To be treated with kindness and submission
  'And bestow kindness, humility
  and submission unto them.'
- To pray for them in recognition of their earlier favors.
  'And say "My Lord, have mercy on them
  as they did care for me when I was little".'

If parents are of different faith and try to persuade their children away from Islam, the children should not obey them in that regard but should none the less maintain their loving care for them. The Qur'an says

وَإِن جَٰهَدَاكَ عَلَىٰٓ أَن تُشْرِكَ بِى مَا لَيْسَ لَكَ بِهِۦ عِلْمٌ فَلَا تُطِعْهُمَا وَصَاحِبْهُمَا فِى ٱلدُّنْيَا مَعْرُوفًا وَٱتَّبِعْ سَبِيلَ مَنْ أَنَابَ إِلَىَّ ... ۝ لقمان(٣١)

But if they strive with you to get you to ascribe unto ME as partner that of which you have no knowledge, then obey them NOT: yet consort with them in this life kindly, and follow the path of those who turn to ME [for guidance].

Luqman (Sura 31:15)

The above verse follows one which reminds us of the care for parents:

وَوَصَّيْنَا ٱلْإِنسَٰنَ بِوَٰلِدَيْهِ حَمَلَتْهُ أُمُّهُۥ وَهْنًا عَلَىٰ وَهْنٍ وَفِصَٰلُهُۥ فِى عَامَيْنِ أَنِ ٱشْكُرْ لِى وَلِوَٰلِدَيْكَ إِلَىَّ ٱلْمَصِيرُ ۝ لقمان(٣١)

And we have enjoined upon man to be good to his parents – his mother bears him in weakness upon weakness and his weaning is in two years. Lo! Give thanks unto Me and unto your parents. Unto Me is the final goal.

Luqman (Sura 31:14)

The Prophet (PBUH) considered repulsion (*'uquq*) of parents one of the greatest sins. He said

«ألا أنبئكم بأكبر الكبائر : الشرك بالله وعقوق الوالدين»

رواه البخارى

Let me tell you which the greatest of sins are: Ascribing to Allah partners and repulsion of parents.

Authenticated by al-Bukhari

On special care of mothers in particular:

«الجنة تحت أقدام الأمهات»
روى نحوه النسائي

Paradise lies at mothers' feet.

Authenticated by al-Nassa'i

«إن الله حرّم عليكم عقوق الأمهات»
رواه البخاري

Allah has forbidden for you repulsion of mothers.

Authenticated by al-Bukhari

«جاء رجل إلى الرسول صلى الله عليه وسلم يسأل: أيُّ الناس أحقُّ بصحابتي؟ قال : أمك . قال : ثم من ؟ قال : أمك . قال : ثم من ؟ قال : أمك . قال : ثم من ؟ قال: ثُمَّ أبوك»
رواه الشيخان

A man asked the Prophet (PBUH) 'Who deserves my companionship most?' The Prophet said 'your mother.' He asked 'And who next?' The Prophet said 'your mother.' He asked 'And who next?' The Prophet said 'your mother.' He asked 'And who next?' The Prophet said 'then your father.'

Agreed upon by al-Bukhari and Muslim

RIGHTS OF CHILDREN IN ISLAM

Introduction
Children are considered a joy, an adornment as well as a way to continue one's descent. Islam enjoins us to have children, but it insists at the same time that they should be good and righteous which requires an intensive effort to raise them correctly. The ability to raise children correctly is an inherent requirement of marriage in Islam.

Value of children in Muslim societies
Children are highly valued in many societies, but particularly so for the Muslims. There are religious, economic, socio-psychological and child survival related rationales for this phenomenon.

The religious rationale or value
Muslims believe that children are gifts of Allah. The Qur'an says

وَاللَّهُ جَعَلَ لَكُم مِّنْ أَنفُسِكُمْ أَزْوَاجًا وَجَعَلَ لَكُم مِّنْ أَزْوَاجِكُم بَنِينَ وَحَفَدَةً ... ﴿٧٢﴾ النحل(١٦)

And Allah has made for you mates from yourselves and made for you, out of them, children and grandchildren.

al-Nahl (Sura 16:72)

Many Muslims believe that it is their religious duty to multiply and populate the earth. They refer to the Prophet's saying

«تناكحوا تناسلوا تكثروا ، فإني مباهٍ بكم الأمم يوم القيامة»
رواه أبو داود

Marry and multiply for I will make a display of you on the Day of Judgement.

Authenticated by Abu Dawoud

The economic rationale or value
Children are economic assets to parents particularly in traditional societies where the cost of raising children is very modest. Children in these societies may also work at an early age and add to the family's income. The picture is changing now with university education and vocational training for technical jobs. Children constitute an in-built social security system for parents in old age, in crippling sickness and in the case of unemployment.

Socio-psychological rationale or value
This includes the following:

- Having children is a joy for parents, satisfying the instincts for motherhood and fatherhood.
- Pride in having a large family is a feature of traditional societies where numbers are equated with power. This stems from tribal beliefs that having many children, particularly sons, was a prerequisite for protecting family wealth, property, honor and social functions.
- Children are proof of a wife's fertility and a husband's virility.

Child survival related rationale
Until the mid-twentieth century, Muslim societies experienced high infant and child loss. It was logical to expect, therefore, that women would bear

upwards of eight children in the hope that a few might survive. Referred to as the 'child survival hypothesis' in demography, the motivation for high pregnancy rates may be due to the following:

- Compensation for actual loss of children in the family (*the compensatory motivation*).
- Fear of child loss even though there is no child death in the family. Pregnancy in this case is to ensure enough children (*insurance motivation*).
- Adopting the common pattern in the society at large where child loss rates are high (*societal motivation*).
- Child loss by lactating mothers stops breast-feeding which in turn shortens the post-partum infertility period; thus the woman becomes more susceptible to falling pregnant sooner when an infant dies than when the child survives (*biological motivation*).[2]

In recent times, however, child survival has progressively improved in Muslim societies with no corresponding change in the procreation pattern. This is because women are still caught psychologically in the traditional trap of 'high child loss–high fertility'. It will take time to change this pattern.

Children's rights and parents' obligations

Against this long list of rationales for a high procreation pattern, there is a longer list of children's rights; rights that were given them by Allah and the Prophet, and rights that should make parents think of adjusting their procreation patterns to their 'religious' obligations to their children.

The ten cardinal rights of children are listed in Figure 2.1. What follows is a brief explanation of each of the rights accompanied by traditions in its support.

Figure 2.1 The ten cardinal rights of children in Islam

1. The right to genetic purity.
2. The right to life.
3. The right to legitimacy and good name.
4. The right to breast-feeding, shelter, maintenance and support, including health care and nutrition.
5. The right to separate sleeping arrangements for children.
6. The right to future security.
7. The right to religious training and good upbringing.
8. The right to education, and training in sports and self-defense.
9. The right to equitable treatment regardless of gender or other factors.
10. The right that all funds used in their support come only from legitimate sources.

PARENT AND CHILD: RIGHTS AND OBLIGATIONS

1. The right to genetic purity
Muslim children have the right to be born with no actual or potential genetic disorders. The Prophet (PBUH) says

«تخيّروا لنطفكم فإن العرق دسّاس أو نزاع»

رواه ابن ماجة .

Choose where you deposit your sperm, for the line of descent is conducive.

Authenticated by Ibn Maja

They have also to be protected from repeated consanguinity especially in families with a tendency to genetic aberration. Furthermore, children should not be exposed during pregnancy or birth to diseases transmissible from parents. In cases of such diseases, contraception becomes mandatory.

2. The right to life
Islam prohibits killing a child for any reason whether it is poverty, threat of poverty or exaggerated zeal about 'honor'. In the pre-Islamic era (called *Jahiliyya* or age of ignorance), some young girls or girl children were buried alive out of poverty or to protect the family from the risk of misbehavior and shame. The Qur'an detested that most strongly.

وَلَا تَقْتُلُوٓا۟ أَوْلَٰدَكُم مِّنْ إِمْلَٰقٍ نَّحْنُ نَرْزُقُكُمْ وَإِيَّاهُمْ ... ﴿١٥١﴾ الأنعام(٦)

Kill not your children, on a plea of want, we provide sustenance for you and for them.

al-An'am (Sura 6:151)

وَلَا تَقْتُلُوٓا۟ أَوْلَٰدَكُمْ خَشْيَةَ إِمْلَٰقٍ نَّحْنُ نَرْزُقُهُمْ وَإِيَّاكُمْ إِنَّ قَتْلَهُمْ كَانَ خِطْـًٔا كَبِيرًا ﴿٣١﴾ الأسراء(١٧)

Kill not your children for fear of want, we provide sustenance for them and for you. Their killing is a great sin.

al-Isra' (Sura 17:31)

وَإِذَا ٱلْمَوْءُۥدَةُ سُئِلَتْ ﴿٨﴾ بِأَيِّ ذَنۢبٍ قُتِلَتْ ﴿٩﴾ التكوير(٨١)

And when the girl-child who was buried alive is asked 'For what sin she was slain'?

al-Takwir (Sura 81:8, 9)

Even an unborn fetus has the right to life especially after taking shape or 'ensoulment' (40–42 days according to some jurists and four months according to others) and hence should not be aborted beyond that time. Some jurists prohibit abortion from the time of conception throughout. The exception supported universally by all jurists is when continued pregnancy endangers the life of the mother – then abortion is permissible at any stage of pregnancy since the mother is the origin. Jurists differ regarding other reasons (see Chapter 10).

3. The right to legitimacy and good name

Legitimacy is central to family formation in Islam. Every Muslim child has the right to legitimacy, i.e. to be called after a known father. This differs from pre-Islamic times when some children were denied their birth right. There are lengthy juristic discussions on this subject. The yardsticks used are several.

The child, unless challenged, belongs to the family in which he or she is born. The Prophet (PBUH) gives a general rule:

«الـولد للفـراش»

The child belongs
to the marital bed.

There is a decree that a minimum period of six months must elapse between the time of marriage and that of birth of the first child if legality is to be recognized.

Disowning a child requires that the husband proves the infidelity of the mother beyond any shadow of doubt by providing four honest witnesses. If he fails to produce witnesses, which is not uncommon, he may resort to a process called 'li'an' (see Chapter 3).

The child has also the right to a good name. The Prophet said

«مِنْ حقَّ الولد على الوالد أن يحسن أدبه ويحسن اسمه»

رواه البيهقي

The right of a child on his parent is to be given good breeding and good name.

Authenticated by al-Baihaqi

4. The right to breast-feeding, shelter, maintenance and health care

While these are self-explanatory, one issue that must be specified is the child's right to breast-feeding. The Qur'an says

PARENT AND CHILD: RIGHTS AND OBLIGATIONS

وَٱلْوَٰلِدَٰتُ يُرْضِعْنَ أَوْلَٰدَهُنَّ حَوْلَيْنِ كَامِلَيْنِ لِمَنْ أَرَادَ أَن يُتِمَّ ٱلرَّضَاعَةَ

... ﴿٢٣٣﴾ البقرة(٢)

And mothers shall suckle their children two full years, for those who wish to complete breast-feeding.

al-Baqara (Sura 2:233)

5. The right to separate sleeping arrangements for children

The child has the right to have an independent or separate sleeping arrangement. This comes from the Prophet's saying

«مُروا أولادكم بالصلاة وهم أبناء سبع ، واضربوهم عليها وهم أبناء عشر، وفرِّقوا بينهم في المضاجع»

أخرجه أحمد في مسنده عن عمرو بن شعيب عن أبيه عن جده

Instruct your children in prayer at age seven, punish them if they fail [to practice it] at age ten; and LET THEM SLEEP SEPARATELY FROM ONE ANOTHER.

Authenticated by Ahmad Ibn Hanbal

This is quite a restriction on continuous and unplanned procreation. The sleeping arrangement will be a separate room, a separate corner, a separate bed or a separate mat for each child (especially during adolescence).

There is a dilemma in this regard that has to be mitigated. The average size of a Muslim family is 6–7 children. How many families can afford to provide separate sleeping arrangements for them? Certainly spacing of children and adjusting their numbers to the family's means are a part of the solution as well as improving the houseing situation of the family.

6. The right to future security

The Prophet says

«لَأَنْ تذر ورثتك أغنياءَ ، خير من أن تذرهم عالةً يتكففون الناس»

أخرجه البخاري عن سعد بن أبي وقاص

To leave your heirs rich is better than leaving them dependent upon people's charity.

Authenticated by al-Bukhari

7. The right to religious training and good upbringing

Parents are responsible for instilling in their children the religious beliefs of Islam. They are also to train them for prayer, fasting, honesty and avoidance of evil practices such as alcohol, drug abuse, and sexual promiscuity. They should make them aware of their history and heritage. In Muslim societies, these tasks should not be left entirely to schools since it is the primary responsibility of Muslim parents. In non-Muslim societies or in societies where Islamic teachings are not correctly followed, the task of Muslim parents becomes even more grave.

The Qur'an relates the advice of Luqman to his son as follows:

يَٰبُنَىَّ أَقِمِ ٱلصَّلَوٰةَ وَأْمُرْ بِٱلْمَعْرُوفِ وَٱنْهَ عَنِ ٱلْمُنكَرِ وَٱصْبِرْ عَلَىٰ مَآ أَصَابَكَ إِنَّ ذَٰلِكَ مِنْ عَزْمِ ٱلْأُمُورِ ۩ لقمان(٣١)

O my son! Establish regular prayer, enjoin what is just and forbid what is wrong, and bear with patient constancy whatever betide you, Lo! that is of the steadfast heart of things.

Luqman (Sura 31:17)

As to good breeding and character, the Prophet says

«ما ورَّث والدٌ ولداً خيراً من أدب حسن»
رواه الطبراني في الأوسط

There is nothing better for a parent to leave for his child [in inheritance] than good breeding.

Authenticated by al-Tabarani

8. The right to education and training in sports and self-defence

Parents are responsible for the proper education of their children. They are made directly responsible for teaching their children how to read and write. This is clear in the Prophet's instruction below. Parents are also responsible for the sex education and moral guidance of their children in collaboration with public schools and mosque schools.

It is most interesting that the Prophet (PBUH) instructed parents to teach their children how to read and write along with preparation for *jihad* (taking arms in defense of one's religion) and sports. The Prophet says

«عن ابي سلمان مَوْلى أبي رافع قال : قلت يارسول الله : للولدِ علينا حقٌّ كحقنا عليهم ؟ قال نعم . حق الولد على الوالد أن يعلِّمه الكتابة والسباحة والرماية ، وألاَّ يرزقَه إلا طيبا»

رواه البيهقي

The right due to the child from his parent is for the parent to teach him *writing, swimming, archery* and to provide him with nothing but what is wholesome.

Authenticated by al-Baihaqi

9. *The right to equitable treatment regardless of gender*

Children in Islam have the right to equitable treatment regardless of sex, age or any other consideration. The Prophet says

«اعدِلوا بين أولادكم ، كما تحبون أن يعدلوا بينكم»
أخرجه السيوطي في الجامع الكبير

Be equitable in dealing with your children just as you would like them to be equitable in dealing with you.

Authenticated by al-Suyuti

Preference of sons and suppression or negligence of daughters are denounced by Islam. Of course the pre-Islamic burial of girls has been absolutely prohibited in Islam. Equitable treatment is illustrated by an example from the *Sunnah*.

«عن أنس بن مالك : كان رجل عند النبي صلى الله عليه وسلم ، فجاء ابنٌ له فقبله وأجلسه على فخذه ، وجاءت بنتٌ له ، فأجلسها بين يديه ، فقال الرسول صلى الله عليه وسلم : ألاَ سوَّيتَ بينهما؟»
رواه البزار

It is related by Anas Ibn Malik that a man was sitting with the Prophet (PBUH) when a son of his came in; the man kissed him and put him in his lap. Then a daughter of his came in, he let her sit in front of him. The Prophet said 'Shouldn't you have treated them equitably?'

Authenticated by al-Bazzar

10. *The right that their support comes only from legitimate sources*

As presented in the *hadith* in item 8 the Prophet ruled that all funds and resources used for child support should come from legitimate/wholesome sources. This is a most pervasive right to protection against those who might resort to illegitimate means (accepting bribes, stealing, embezzlement, dishonesty, drug pushing, etc.) under the pressure of supporting too many children.

THE ISLAMIC CONTEXT

The enormity of the responsibility

In order to institutionalize these rights, the Prophet (PBUH) emphasized that people who start a family have to bear the attached responsibilities.

« عن ابن عمر عن النبي صلى الله عليه وسلم أنه قال :
كلكم راع ، وكلكم مسئول عن رعيته ، الرجل في بيته راع ومسئول عن رعيته والمرأة في بيت زوجها راعية ومسئولة عن رعيتها»

متفق عليه

Everyone of you is a guardian, and everyone of you is responsible for his flock: the father is in charge of his household, and is responsible for those in his charge; and the wife is in charge of her husband's household, and is responsible for those in her charge.

Authenticated by all sources

In order to give a visual measure of the enormity of the task of caring for a child, Figure 2.2 depicts the most important and vulnerable phases of child development. It can be seen that parents are responsible from the preconcep-

Figure 2.2 The human life cycle

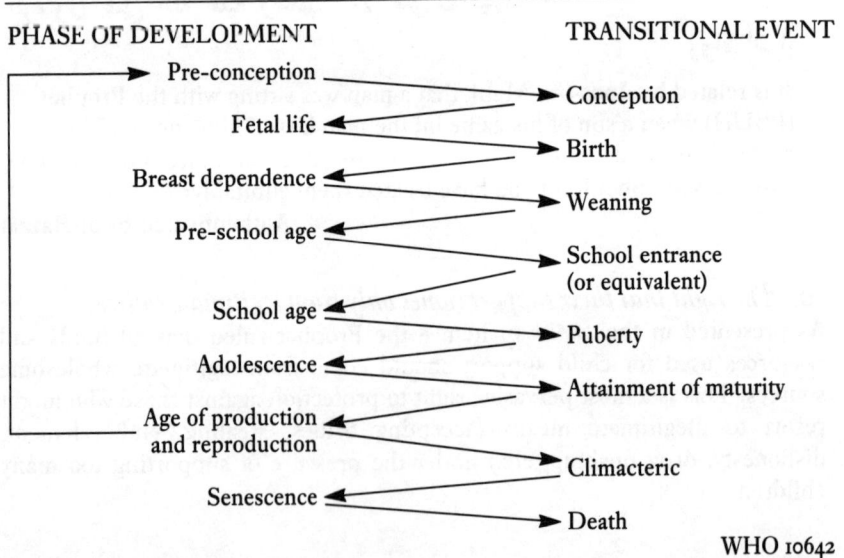

Source: *WHO*, techn. Rep. Ser. 1972, No.485, p.8.

tion phase through the phase of adolescence and even through university education.

The need for planning

In earlier times, life was simpler and family life was less of a burden than it is today. Religious education was the norm through which the community augmented the efforts of parents whose child-rearing responsibility was also shared by other members of the extended family.

Under the current status of Muslim communities, it is not easy for parents to fulfill their obligations towards large families and the increasing demands of growing children. Some Muslim families have looked to the five 'capabilities' of the nuclear family in trying to determine the number of their children. These are as follows:

- Physical (health) capability of the parents especially the mother.
- Economic capability to support the family and safeguard the future of the children, and provide independent sleeping arrangements for them.
- Cultural capability to give the child proper education, religious training as well as training in self-defense and sport.
- Time availability for child care and companionship including verbal investment to stimulate their intellectual development.
- Community support in the area of schooling, health care, day care, housing, etc.

The latter is becoming more difficult; it is hard now to depend on the community. Quite the reverse, communities in many areas of the world are a source of bad influence on children and detract from good behavior including neglect of religious practices, drug abuse, promiscuity, repulsion of parents as old-fashioned, etc. That is why the later Hanafi jurists found it quite permissible to avoid pregnancy (even without the spouse's consent) in situations and circumstances that militate against properly raising a child in a manner that would do honor to the Prophet (PBUH).

3

The status of women in Islam

Islam championed all movements to improve the status of women, at a time when societies were overtly traditional and socially underdeveloped. The woman is considered equal to man in religious, social and patriotic responsibilities but defers to the husband in family affairs. She cannot be forced into marriage by her family or guardian; she has to give her consent. In marriage, she can keep her maiden name. She is completely independent financially and can do with her money as she pleases while the husband (or the father or brother) is responsible for providing for her and her children. In inheritance, she, as a daughter, gets half of her brother's share, but under other circumstances she gets as much as or even more than other men in the family. As a mother she is placed ahead of her husband in regard to the children's loyalty and affection. She is given the privilege to speak up for her rights (within the decency of Islamic tradition) and she did, even to the Prophet (*PBUH*).

INTRODUCTION

The status of women in Islam is seriously misunderstood for many reasons. It is wrongly implied that the behavior of individual Muslims and Muslim communities invariably reflects the laws and orthodoxy of Islam. This is compounded by misconceptions about the status of women in Islam or gross abuse of Islamic family laws among some uninformed Muslim groups. We should also not discount the factor of underdevelopment in some countries, a situation commonly associated with the low status of women in not only Muslim but also in many non-Muslim countries of the Third World.

On the other hand, some Muslim writers are guilty of reverse bias. In their zeal to prove Islam's modernity, they select only the components that would parallel western systems. This distortion presents only a part of the totality which is the Islamic culture. Contrary to common beliefs, Islam raised the status of women and gave them human, civil, social and economic rights never previously given to women. The Muslim woman has an independent personality, equal to man in religious duties, in the right to education, in reward for her deeds as well as in defending her beliefs. She has complete and total control of her possessions. She is free to choose her marital partner, and has the right to demand the power of divorce plus the power at the time of the marriage contract to disallow polygyny by her husband. Furthermore, she can keep her maiden name after marriage, if she so wishes. She is also responsible for her family but the man has the primary responsibility.

WOMEN PERSONALITIES IN THE QUR'AN

The following are but a few examples of women who played crucial roles in the lives of the Prophets.

Adam and Eve

Little needs to be said on the role of Eve in the life of Adam except that Muslims do not follow the common belief that Eve was the one who persuaded Adam to eat the forbidden fruit, and thereafter was expelled from Eden. It was Satan who whispered evil to Adam or to both Adam and Eve. The Qur'an says

فَوَسْوَسَ إِلَيْهِ ٱلشَّيْطَٰنُ قَالَ يَٰٓـَٔادَمُ هَلْ أَدُلُّكَ عَلَىٰ شَجَرَةِ ٱلْخُلْدِ وَمُلْكٍ لَّا يَبْلَىٰ ۝ فَأَكَلَا مِنْهَا فَبَدَتْ لَهُمَا سَوْءَٰتُهُمَا وَطَفِقَا يَخْصِفَانِ عَلَيْهِمَا مِن وَرَقِ ٱلْجَنَّةِ ۚ وَعَصَىٰٓ ءَادَمُ رَبَّهُۥ فَغَوَىٰ ۝ ثُمَّ ٱجْتَبَٰهُ رَبُّهُۥ فَتَابَ عَلَيْهِ وَهَدَىٰ ۝

طه(٢٠)

But the devil whispered evil to him saying 'O' Adam! Shall I show you the tree of immortality and the kingdom that wastes not away'. Then they twain ate thereof, so that their nakedness appeared to them; they began to heap upon them leaves from the garden [to hide their nakedness]. Thus Adam disobeyed his Allah, allowed himself to be seduced. But Allah chose him [for his grace] and relented toward him and guided him.

Taha (Sura 20: 120–22)

In another Sura, the whispering is for both Adam and Eve:

فَوَسْوَسَ لَهُمَا ٱلشَّيْطَٰنُ ... ۝ الأعراف(٧)

Then Satan whispered evil to them.

al-A'raf (Sura 7:20)

THE ISLAMIC CONTEXT

Thus Eve is exonerated of the evil persuasion of Adam. Of course she shares the sin equally with him since both of them ate the forbidden fruit. The first quotation dismisses Adam's (and Eve's) sin after they repented. Thus, *no sin* was transmitted to their progeny.

Moses

Four women figured predominantly in the life of Moses: his mother, his sister, the wife of the Pharoah (who raised him) and the daughter of Shoi'b who later became his wife. An excerpt from the Qur'an reads

وَأَوْحَيْنَا إِلَىٰ أُمِّ مُوسَىٰ أَنْ أَرْضِعِيهِ فَإِذَا خِفْتِ عَلَيْهِ فَأَلْقِيهِ فِى ٱلْيَمِّ وَلَا تَخَافِى وَلَا تَحْزَنِى إِنَّا رَآدُّوهُ إِلَيْكِ وَجَاعِلُوهُ مِنَ ٱلْمُرْسَلِينَ ۝

القصص (٢٨)

And we sent this inspiration to the mother of Moses: 'Suckle him, and when you fear for him, then cast him into the river and fear not nor grieve. Lo! We shall restore him to you and We shall make him one of our Messengers.'

al-Qasas (Sura 28:7)

Mary and Jesus

The story of Mary (*Maryam*) is told in the Qur'an in the most beautiful and compassionate terms depicting her anguish on conceiving immaculately and her fear of facing her people, and her raising the child to become a messenger of Allah.

فَأَتَتْ بِهِۦ قَوْمَهَا تَحْمِلُهُۥ قَالُوا۟ يَـٰمَرْيَمُ لَقَدْ جِئْتِ شَيْـًٔا فَرِيًّا ۝ يَـٰٓأُخْتَ هَـٰرُونَ مَا كَانَ أَبُوكِ ٱمْرَأَ سَوْءٍ وَمَا كَانَتْ أُمُّكِ بَغِيًّا ۝ فَأَشَارَتْ إِلَيْهِ قَالُوا۟ كَيْفَ نُكَلِّمُ مَن كَانَ فِى ٱلْمَهْدِ صَبِيًّا ۝ قَالَ إِنِّى عَبْدُ ٱللَّهِ ءَاتَىٰنِىَ ٱلْكِتَـٰبَ وَجَعَلَنِى نَبِيًّا ۝

مريم (١٩)

At length she brought [the baby] to her people, carrying him [in her arms]. They said 'Oh Mary! Truly an amazing thing have you brought. O sister of Aaron! Your father was not a man of evil, nor your mother a woman unchaste!'

But she pointed to him [the baby]. They said 'How can we talk to one who is a child in the cradle?' He [the baby] said 'I am indeed a servant of Allah: He gave me the book and made me a prophet'.

Maryam (Sura 19: 27–30)

In most references to Jesus in the Qur'an, he is called the son of Mary. Muslims love both of them dearly but they do not see Jesus as God or a son of God.

Mohammad

Two women in particular played crucial roles in the life of the Prophet Mohammad. Their stories come from his *sira* (biography). They are Sayyida Khadija and Sayyida A'isha. Khadija was his first wife and fifteen years his elder. It was crucial to the Prophet in the formative years of his message (*da'awa*) to have a mature and loyal wife. When he received the first revelation of the Qur'an he was terrified; seeing an angel filling the heavens all around him and instructing him repeatedly to 'Read!' while he would reply repeatedly 'But I do not read.' He was perplexed and thought that he was going out of his mind. He went home shaking to Khadija. She comforted him, reassured him and later took him to her cousin Waraqa Ibn Nawfal, a learned man, who explained to him that this must be the same angel who came to Moses and predicted that he (Mohammad) would be a prophet. Khadija died years later.

A'isha, a younger wife with a scientific mind and unusually good memory, was crucial during the maturation phase of the *da'awa*. Beside being a comforting wife, she became learned in religion, social relations, the history of the Arabs, language and interpretation of the Qur'an and *hadith*. She witnessed the day-to-day life and teachings of the Prophet. The Prophet said about her 'Take half of your religion from this lady.' After the Prophet's death, she became a major reference and counselor for the celebrated Companions until her death.

A note is in order here on Mohammad's pattern of marriage. He spent 54 of his 63 years either single or in monogamous marriage. He married at age 25 a woman 15 years his elder, and stayed with her for 29 years until she died. For the next 6 of his remaining 9 years he took more than one wife.

THE QUESTION OF EQUALITY

The human partnership

Men and women were made equal; the only difference in their worth is related to piety not gender. The Qur'an says

THE ISLAMIC CONTEXT

$$\text{يَا أَيُّهَا النَّاسُ إِنَّا خَلَقْنَاكُم مِّن ذَكَرٍ وَأُنثَىٰ وَجَعَلْنَاكُمْ شُعُوبًا وَقَبَائِلَ لِتَعَارَفُوا ۚ إِنَّ أَكْرَمَكُمْ عِندَ اللَّهِ أَتْقَاكُمْ} ...\; \text{۞}$$

الحجرات (٤٩)

O mankind. We created you from a male and a female, and made you into nations and tribes that you may know one another. Lo! The most favored of you are the most righteous.

al-Hujurat (Sura 49:13)

And in the Prophet's *hadith*

«إنَّما النساء شقائقُ الرجال»

رواه أحمد وأبو داود

Men and women are equal halves.
Authenticated by Ahmad and Abu Dawoud

Equality in religious duties
Islam is meant for men and women equally. Women are equal in worship, in carrying the message of Allah and in fulfilling other religious requirements. The Qur'an says

$$\text{وَالْمُؤْمِنُونَ وَالْمُؤْمِنَاتُ بَعْضُهُمْ أَوْلِيَاءُ بَعْضٍ ۚ يَأْمُرُونَ بِالْمَعْرُوفِ وَيَنْهَوْنَ عَنِ الْمُنكَرِ وَيُقِيمُونَ الصَّلَاةَ وَيُؤْتُونَ الزَّكَاةَ وَيُطِيعُونَ اللَّهَ وَرَسُولَهُ ۚ أُولَٰئِكَ سَيَرْحَمُهُمُ اللَّهُ} ...\; \text{۞}$$

التوبة (٩)

And the believers, men and women alike, are protectors, one of another: they enjoin the right and forbid the wrong, they observe regular prayers, pay the poor-due, and obey Allah and his Messenger. On them will Allah have mercy.

al-Tawba (Sura 9: 71)

Women's share in the Islamic revolution
Some of the women, at the time of the Prophet (PBUH) were concerned that men might take a larger share in building Islam's moral and social order. For one thing, men used to go to the Prophet and take the oath of fealty or allegiance (*al-bai'a*) to him. The women asked if they could share this right. The Prophet made a special day for them and the Qur'an gave them equal right:

يَـٰٓأَيُّهَا ٱلنَّبِىُّ إِذَا جَآءَكَ ٱلْمُؤْمِنَـٰتُ يُبَايِعْنَكَ عَلَىٰٓ أَن لَّا يُشْرِكْنَ بِٱللَّهِ شَيْـًٔا وَلَا يَسْرِقْنَ وَلَا يَزْنِينَ وَلَا يَقْتُلْنَ أَوْلَـٰدَهُنَّ وَلَا يَأْتِينَ بِبُهْتَـٰنٍ يَفْتَرِينَهُۥ بَيْنَ أَيْدِيهِنَّ وَأَرْجُلِهِنَّ وَلَا يَعْصِينَكَ فِى مَعْرُوفٍ فَبَايِعْهُنَّ وَٱسْتَغْفِرْ لَهُنَّ ٱللَّهَ ... ﴿١٢﴾ الممتحنة (٦٠)

O Prophet! When believing women come to you to take the oath of fealty to you, that they will not associate in worship anything with Allah, that they will not steal, that they will not commit fornication, that they will not kill their children, that they will not utter slander, intentionally forging falsehood, and that they will not disobey you in any just matter, then do receive their fealty [bai'a], and pray to Allah for their forgiveness.

al-Mumtahana (Sura 60: 12)

Men and women are treated equally in regard to reward and punishment for their deeds.

فَٱسْتَجَابَ لَهُمْ رَبُّهُمْ أَنِّى لَا أُضِيعُ عَمَلَ عَـٰمِلٍ مِّنكُم مِّن ذَكَرٍ أَوْ أُنثَىٰ بَعْضُكُم مِّنۢ بَعْضٍ ... ﴿١٩٥﴾ ال عمران (٣)

And their Allah has responded to them: never shall I cause to be lost the work of any of you, be they male or female. You are [the same] one of another.

al-Imran (Sura 3:195)

وَمَن يَعْمَلْ مِنَ ٱلصَّـٰلِحَـٰتِ مِن ذَكَرٍ أَوْ أُنثَىٰ وَهُوَ مُؤْمِنٌ فَأُو۟لَـٰٓئِكَ يَدْخُلُونَ ٱلْجَنَّةَ وَلَا يُظْلَمُونَ نَقِيرًا ﴿١٢٤﴾ النساء (٤)

And whosoever does good deeds, whether male or female, and he or she is a believer, such will enter paradise and they will not be wronged the dint in a date-stone.

al-Nisa' (Sura 4:124)

In order to show the religious independence of the females from a related male (e.g. a husband), the Qur'an relates the stories of two 'bad women' who were the wives of the two Prophets, Noah and Lott and who did not follow

THE ISLAMIC CONTEXT

their path. Both were punished. On the other hand there is the good wife of the Pharoah who was saved (see al-Insan (Sura 66: 10–11).

Equality in education
Learning and scholarship are central to Islamic faith and culture. The first verse in the Qur'an is a direct instruction for learning. The Prophet considered the learned as the successors of the Prophets. To him the 'ink of scholars is worth more than the blood of the martyrs'. At the time when the Arabs were still confined to their peninsula Muslims were instructed to seek knowledge, 'even in China'.

The woman was equally required to learn as much as men. The Prophet said

«العلم فريضة على كل مسلم»

رواه البخاري

Learning is a duty [*farida*] for every Muslim, [male and female].
Authenticated by al-Bukhari

The opinion of a learned Muslim woman is valued and respected. A prominent example is that of Caliph Omar. Noting the exaggeration in the amount of dowry at the time, he pronounced in the mosque that it should be limited. After the prayer, a woman came to him and reminded him that his opinion was antagonistic to Allah's instruction in the Qur'an and she referred to Sura 4 verse 20.

وَإِنْ أَرَدتُّمُ ٱسْتِبْدَالَ زَوْجٍ مَّكَانَ زَوْجٍ وَءَاتَيْتُمْ إِحْدَىٰهُنَّ قِنطَارًا فَلَا تَأْخُذُوا۟ مِنْهُ شَيْـًٔا ۚ أَتَأْخُذُونَهُۥ بُهْتَـٰنًا وَإِثْمًا مُّبِينًا ۝

النساء(٤)

And if you wish to exchange one wife for another and you have given unto one of them a huge sum of money [*kintaran*], take nothing from it. Would you take it by the way of calumny and open wrong.
al-Nisa' (Sura 4:20)

Omar realised his mistake and said he was in error and the woman was right.¹

Equality in the principle of *jihad* (religious war)
Islam made women equally responsible for the defense of their religion and land (*jihad*). It is justly inferred that women were included in the instruction:

ٱنفِرُواْ خِفَافاً وَثِقَالاً وَجَـٰهِدُواْ بِأَمْوَٰلِكُمْ وَأَنفُسِكُمْ فِى سَبِيلِ ٱللَّهِ ...﴿﴾

التوبة (٩)

Go forth, light-armed or heavy-armed, and strive with your wealth and your lives in the cause of Allah.

al-Tawba (Sura 9:41)

While women were included in this, they were not expected to carry arms and fight battles like men, but they used to accompany men to battle, encourage them, carry the wounded, remove the dead from the field, transport arms and material, etc. In so doing they were equally exposed to death or capture by the enemy. Married women are expected to seek their husband's permission before doing so, whereas unmarried women have no such obligation. However, where the enemy attacks, all women can join the battle freely, and can carry arms and do anything that men do in order to defend their religion and land.

The history of Islam is full of great women, who either participated in battles as second line or even front line troops, or, more commonly, encouraged their sons, husbands, brothers and fathers to go to battle. A well-known example is al-Khansa' who encouraged her children to fight for their religion and lost all four of them in battle. When she was told of their deaths she was grieved and wept with agony but said 'Allah has honored me by their martyrdom '*istishhad*' [death in Allah's cause].

In the battle of '*Uhud*', when the Muslims were being overpowered, the Prophet and his Companions were steadfast in facing the enemy. The Prophet became a target for their arrows and many tried to kill him. There came a Muslim woman, Nasiba bint Ka'b, who defended the Prophet with her sword and arrows. She confronted the enemies face to face screaming 'O my Mohammad' (*Wa Mohammadah!*) until she was injured in the battle and lost much blood. She was taken away, but kept asking about the Prophet to make sure he was safe.[2]

Another example is Ummayya bint Qays al-Ghifariyya who related 'I came to the Prophet (PBUH) with women of my tribe as he was preparing for the battle of Khaibar. We said "O Messenger of Allah: we wish to go with you on this mission. We would take care of the wounded and serve the fighters in whatever way we can." The Prophet said, "Do join us with Allah's blessing".'[3]

Still another example is al-Rabi' bint mo'awwaz who related 'We took part in the combat missions of the Prophet (PBUH). Our task was to carry water to the fighters and serve them, to retrieve the wounded and the dead and send them to Medina.'[4]

There is also Ku'aiba bint Sa'ad al-Aslamiyya, the first nurse in Islam.

Besides treating the wounded on the battlefield, a tent was pitched for her in the mosque where she treated the sick and wounded men. Among her patients was Sa'd Ibn Mu'adh, the great Companion, who suffered a spear wound in the battle of Khandaq. She took good care of him but his injuries were terminal.[5]

Another example of equality in relation to battle is that men used to feel that it was their privilege to speak for captured enemies and ask for their release. However, the Prophet gave the same privilege to Muslim women starting with Um-Hani' and others thereafter.[6]

أجارت أم هانئ بنت أبي طالب رجلين من أحمائها كُتب عليهما القتل، وذلك مجمل حديثها في ذلك . قالت: «لمَّا نزل رسول الله صلى الله عليه وسلم بأعلى مكة ، فرَّ إليَّ رجلان من أحمائي من بني مخزوم . فدخل عليَّ عليُّ بن أبي طالب أخي فقال :«والله لأقتلنهما». فأغلقت عليهما باب بيتي . ثم جئت رسول الله صلى الله عليه وسلم ، فقال: «مرحباً وأهلاً يا أم هانئ، ماجاء بك؟»، فأخبرته خبر الرجلين وخبر عليّ . فقال :«قد أجرنا من أجرت يا أم هانئ ، وأمَّنَّا من أمَّنتِ ، فلا يقتلنهما.»   رواه البخاري

Umm Hani was a cousin of the Prophet (PBUH) who gave refuge to two men of her in-laws who fought against the Prophet during the Makkah conquest. Her brother Ali Ibn Abi Talib told her that the men should be executed. But she did not give them up, she kept them in her house and went to the Prophet. The Prophet welcomed her, and hearing her story, he said that he would protect those to whom she gave refuge. [Before that, giving refuge was the right of men] The two men were spared.

This story was narrated by al-Bukhari.

Equity in treatment as daughters

Son preference seems to have always been a pan-cultural and international trait. In the pre-Islamic period it was especially important to have sons who were expected to defend their tribe, earn a living and support the other dependants of the tribe. Baby girls were not welcome, to say the least, not only because they were an economic liability but because they were an honor risk in a society where honor was a prime concern.

Islam disallowed preferential treatment and urged equity between males and females from their first day of life.

The Qur'an reprimands

THE STATUS OF WOMEN IN ISLAM

$$\text{وَإِذَا بُشِّرَ أَحَدُهُم بِٱلْأُنثَىٰ ظَلَّ وَجْهُهُ مُسْوَدًّا وَهُوَ كَظِيمٌ ۝ يَتَوَارَىٰ مِنَ ٱلْقَوْمِ مِن سُوءِ مَا بُشِّرَ بِهِ ۚ أَيُمْسِكُهُ عَلَىٰ هُونٍ أَمْ يَدُسُّهُ فِي ٱلتُّرَابِ ۗ أَلَا سَاءَ مَا يَحْكُمُونَ ۝}$$

النحل (١٦)

And when one of them receives tidings of the birth of a female child [for him], his face darkens in sadness and disappointment. He hides himself from the folk because of the disgrace of that of which he has had tidings. [He argues with himself] shall he keep it in contempt, or bury it alive? Verily! Evil is their judgement.

al-Nahl (Sura 16:58, 59)

As to burying girls alive (*wa'd*) this was a common practice in the pre-Islamic period (*Jahiliyya*). Islam categorically prohibited that practice and considered it a great sin. Other forms of killing children are prohibited (see Chapter 2 for Qur'anic rulings). To have female children was blessed by the Prophet:

«لاتكرهوا البنات ، فإنهن المؤنسات الغاليات».

رواه احمد والطبراني

Do not hate having daughters, for they are the comforting dears.
Authenticated by Ahmad and al-Tabarani

«من بركةِ المرأة ابتكارُها بالأنثى، لأنَّ الله قال : يهب لمن يشاء إناثا ، ويهب لمن يشاء الذكور» (سورة ٤٢:٤٩)

رواه مردويه وابن عساكر

It is a woman's blessing to have a girl as her first child, for Allah says 'He bestows female children upon whom he will, and bestows male children upon whom he will'.

al-Shura (Sura 42:49)
Authenticated by Mardaweih and Ibn Asakir

Equality in choosing marital partners

Women have recognized equality in many aspects of marriage. As mentioned earlier, all forms of marriage that had prevailed in the pre-Islamic period, save one, were prohibited. The prohibited forms were considered humiliating to woman's dignity and were rejected by Islam.

In choosing their husbands, women have the same rights as men. There is a difference, nevertheless, between the matron (widow or divorcee) and the virgin.

On the authority of Abu Huraira, the Prophet (PBUH) said

«لا تُنكَح الأيِّم حتى تُستأمر ، ولا تُنكح البكر حتى تُستأذن . قالوا يارسول الله وكيف إذنها . قال أن تسكت»

متفق عليه من حديث أبي هريرة

A matron should not be forced into marriage. She should give her preference explicitly. A virgin should also give her consent. He was asked: How to get her permission? He said: her silence.

Agreed upon

It is sometimes argued that

> a father has no power to give away any of his daughter's property without her consent, provided she is of age and capable of exercising judgement. Then how can he [the father or guardian] *force her* to give herself away in marriage? Obviously, surrendering property is far easier than surrendering oneself.[7]

Islam endorses a woman's consent to the extent that a marriage could be annulled where it has been forced on a woman by her guardian. According to al-Bukhari and Muslim, the Prophet (PBUH) annulled the marriage of Khansa' bint Khudham al-Ansariya because her father forced her to marry someone she did not like. (See also the *hadith* on p. 56).

Right to share in public life

Islam has also guaranteed for women the right to participate in religious and worldly affairs as well as the right to work and be involved in trade and commerce. Historical records show that in the early days, reflecting the true Islam, women appeared at public functions, studied and taught in learning classes and schools, traded in markets, sat on consultative councils and, as already mentioned, participated in battle, mostly as supporting lines but sometimes as first line fighters.

Women's privileges over men

Inequalities do exist, some of which favor the woman and others the man. The women's privileges include the following:

- Keeping her maiden name (if she so wishes) as a token of her personal independence.

- The power, according to the majority of Islamic schools of jurisprudence, to allow or disallow *al-azl* or coitus interruptus in marriage as a method of contraception. (Some jurists levy a fine as a form of punishment on the man who neglects to obtain his wife's permission.)
- The right to greater affection, as a mother, from children.
- Economic independence and equal legal capacity: Islam gives the woman *equal legal capacity* with the man. This means that she has the ability to enter into all kinds of contractual arrangement and to conduct business on her own without the need for her husband's consent. Such a legal right, given in the seventh century, is yet to be completely achieved by the married woman in some contemporary societies where the husband has a certain right to oversee his wife's affairs. French women did not achieve this legal right until 1965.

Men's privileges over women

Men were given a 'degree' in marriage over women. The Qur'an says

وَلَهُنَّ مِثْلُ ٱلَّذِى عَلَيْهِنَّ بِٱلْمَعْرُوفِ وَلِلرِّجَالِ عَلَيْهِنَّ دَرَجَةٌ ... ۝

البقرة(٢)

And women shall have rights similar to those levied on them, but men shall have a degree over them.

al-Baqara (Sura 2:228)

And

ٱلرِّجَالُ قَوَّٰمُونَ عَلَى ٱلنِّسَآءِ بِمَا فَضَّلَ ٱللَّهُ بَعْضَهُمْ عَلَىٰ بَعْضٍ وَبِمَآ أَنفَقُوا۟ مِنْ أَمْوَٰلِهِمْ ... ۝

النساء(٤)

Men are the protectors and maintainers of women, because Allah has given one more (strength) than the other, and because they support them from their means.

al-Nisa' (Sura 4:34)

There is considerable discussion by jurists and interpreters about this 'degree' for men over women and for their *qiwama* or responsibility to protect and maintain their wives. Men are the ones who are responsible for the financial and social welfare of the household; they pay the dowry; they provide for the household members while women have the privilege of keeping their own money. Men are assumed to have larger shares than women in inheritance, but this is not absolute and is linked to greater financial responsibilities. Under certain situations, women have larger shares than men in the family as will be discussed in the following section.

CONTROVERSIES RESOLVED

Inheritance differentials and the status of women

One of the most common misconceptions regarding the status of women in Islam is the sex differential in matters of inheritance. The argument consistently used is that a male has double the share in inheritance as the female. Some critics conveniently conclude from this that women are far from being equal to men in Islam. They cite the Qur'an selectively, quoting a segment of a verse in Sura 4 that says

$$... لِلذَّكَرِ مِثْلُ حَظِّ ٱلْأُنْثَيَيْنِ ...$$

النساء(٤)

To the male, a portion equal to that of two females.

al-Nisa' (Sura 4:11)

This segment should be seen in the light of the rest of the same verse and other verses which constitute a part of the inheritance law in Islam. These verses provide a more realistic view of the law and indicate that females may inherit more, as much, or less than males.

In pre-Islamic times, women were deprived of any inheritance. Instead they were themselves inherited. A son, for example, used to inherit his stepmother. It was Islam that established women's right to inheritance. The Qur'an says

$$لِلرِّجَالِ نَصِيبٌ مِّمَّا تَرَكَ ٱلْوَالِدَانِ وَٱلْأَقْرَبُونَ وَلِلنِّسَاءِ نَصِيبٌ مِّمَّا تَرَكَ ٱلْوَالِدَانِ وَٱلْأَقْرَبُونَ مِمَّا قَلَّ مِنْهُ أَوْ كَثُرَ نَصِيبًا مَّفْرُوضًا$$

النساء(٤)

Unto men [in a family] belongs a share of that which parents and close relatives leave, and unto women [in the family] a share of that which parents and close relatives leave, whether it be little or plenty – a legal share it is.

al-Nisa' (Sura 4:7)

Thus, the principle is already set; the size of the share may differ according to circumstances. In other words there is arithmetic inequality on both sides, according to circumstances and responsibilities.

Now we return to the verses concerning shares in inheritance:

يُوصِيكُمُ ٱللَّهُ فِىٓ أَوْلَـٰدِكُمْ لِلذَّكَرِ مِثْلُ حَظِّ ٱلْأُنثَيَيْنِ فَإِن كُنَّ نِسَآءً فَوْقَ ٱثْنَتَيْنِ فَلَهُنَّ ثُلُثَا مَا تَرَكَ وَإِن كَانَتْ وَٰحِدَةً فَلَهَا ٱلنِّصْفُ وَلِأَبَوَيْهِ لِكُلِّ وَٰحِدٍ مِّنْهُمَا ٱلسُّدُسُ مِمَّا تَرَكَ إِن كَانَ لَهُۥ وَلَدٌ فَإِن لَّمْ يَكُن لَّهُۥ وَلَدٌ وَوَرِثَهُۥٓ أَبَوَاهُ فَلِأُمِّهِ ٱلثُّلُثُ فَإِن كَانَ لَهُۥٓ إِخْوَةٌ فَلِأُمِّهِ ٱلسُّدُسُ مِنۢ بَعْدِ وَصِيَّةٍ يُوصِى بِهَآ أَوْ دَيْنٍ ءَابَآؤُكُمْ وَأَبْنَآؤُكُمْ لَا تَدْرُونَ أَيُّهُمْ أَقْرَبُ لَكُمْ نَفْعًا فَرِيضَةً مِّنَ ٱللَّهِ إِنَّ ٱللَّهَ كَانَ عَلِيمًا حَكِيمًا ۝ وَلَكُمْ نِصْفُ مَا تَرَكَ أَزْوَٰجُكُمْ إِن لَّمْ يَكُن لَّهُنَّ وَلَدٌ فَإِن كَانَ لَهُنَّ وَلَدٌ فَلَكُمُ ٱلرُّبُعُ مِمَّا تَرَكْنَ مِنۢ بَعْدِ وَصِيَّةٍ يُوصِينَ بِهَآ أَوْ دَيْنٍ وَلَهُنَّ ٱلرُّبُعُ مِمَّا تَرَكْتُمْ إِن لَّمْ يَكُن لَّكُمْ وَلَدٌ فَإِن كَانَ لَكُمْ وَلَدٌ فَلَهُنَّ ٱلثُّمُنُ مِمَّا تَرَكْتُم مِّنۢ بَعْدِ وَصِيَّةٍ تُوصُونَ بِهَآ أَوْ دَيْنٍ وَإِن كَانَ رَجُلٌ يُورَثُ كَلَـٰلَةً أَوِ ٱمْرَأَةٌ وَلَهُۥٓ أَخٌ أَوْ أُخْتٌ فَلِكُلِّ وَٰحِدٍ مِّنْهُمَا ٱلسُّدُسُ فَإِن كَانُوٓا۟ أَكْثَرَ مِن ذَٰلِكَ فَهُمْ شُرَكَآءُ فِى ٱلثُّلُثِ مِنۢ بَعْدِ وَصِيَّةٍ يُوصَىٰ بِهَآ أَوْ دَيْنٍ غَيْرَ مُضَآرٍّ وَصِيَّةً مِّنَ ٱللَّهِ وَٱللَّهُ عَلِيمٌ حَلِيمٌ ۝

النساء (٤)

Allah directs you concerning [the inheritance]: for *your children: to the male, a portion equal to that of two females*; if only daughters – two or more – theirs is two-thirds of the inheritance, *and if there be only one [daughter] then the half, and to parents [of the deceased] a sixth each* of the inheritance if he has children. If he has no children and his parents are his heirs, then to his mother appertains the third, and if he has brothers and sisters, then to his mother appertains the sixth; all after any legacy he may have bequeathed, or debt [has been paid] ...

And if a man or a woman has a distant heir, having left neither parent nor child, and he or she has a brother or a sister on the mother's side, then to *each of them twain [the brother and sister] the sixth*, and if they be more than two, then they shall have shares in the third, after any legacy that may have been bequeathed or debt [has been paid].

al-Nisa' (Sura 4:11–12)

THE ISLAMIC CONTEXT

It is quite clear that the shares of the male relative to those of females vary, being more, equal or less, depending on the circumstances:

1. *Higher shares for males*: the son takes twice as much as his sister, if the deceased is their father.
2. *Equal shares for males and females*: the female takes an equal share to that of the male if the deceased is their son who has children of his own: 'And to parents [of the deceased] a sixth *each* of the inheritance, if he has children.'
3. *Equal shares* are given to males and females (*brother and sister*) who are distant heirs: 'to each of them twain [the brother and sister] the sixth.'
4. *Higher shares for the females than males*: the female who is the daughter (with no siblings) of the deceased takes *half* and his father takes one *sixth*. 'And if there be only one (daughter) then the *half*, and to the parents of the deceased a *sixth* each.'

The inheritance law, therefore, cannot be taken to infer the relative status of females and males in Islam, given that there are situations where females have higher and lower shares than males. Indeed higher shares are usually given to those whose needs are greater so that they may discharge their financial responsibility. Consider, for example, a brother and sister. The brother is responsible for all the females in his family including his sister. When he gets married, he pays the dowry and is financially responsible for his wife and children. When his sister marries, she receives a dowry and is financially taken care of by her husband. If she remains unmarried, her brother is responsible for her.

Verses 11 and 12 and also verse 176 of Sura 4 lay down the principles of inheritance. The details were worked out by the Prophet (PBUH). The following tradition shows how these principles of inheritance were put to use immediately after the revelation of the verses.

«جاءت امرأة سعد بن الربيع بابنتيها من سعد إلى رسول الله صلى الله عليه وسلم فقالت : يارسول الله هاتان ابنتا سعد بن الربيع قُتل أبوهما يوم أحد شهيدا ، وإنَّ عمَّهما أخذ مالهما فلم يدع لهما مالا ، ولاتُنْكَحان إلاَّ بمال . قال يقضي الله في ذلك . فنزلت آية الميراث . فبعث رسول الله صلى الله عليه وسلم إلى عمِّهما فقال : أعطِ ابنتَي سعدٍ الثُلثين ، وأعط أمَّهما الثُمن ، وما بقي فهو لك»

رواه الترمذي

The wife of Sa'd Ibn Al-Rabi' came to the Prophet (PBUH) with her two daughters from Sa'd. She complained 'O messenger of Allah, these are the daughters of Sa'd Ibn al-Rabi', their father was killed in the cause of Allah in the battle of Uhud. Their uncle has taken their money and left nothing for them, they cannot get married with no money.' He said 'Allah will give us judgement in that.'

The verses of inheritance were then revealed. The Prophet sent to their uncle and told him 'Give the daughters of Sa'd two thirds [of what he left], and give their mother one eighth and the rest is yours.'

Authenticated by al-Tirmidhi

In this example, each daughter had 1.6 times as much as the uncle (daughters 2/3 ffl 16/24, mother 1/8 ffl 3/24 and uncle 5/24).

Woman as witness

There is a verse in the Qur'an that is frequently interpreted or misinterpreted as demeaning to a woman in that it makes her equal to only one half of a man as witness. The verse (Sura 2: 282) stipulated that when a deal is contracted it should be recorded and witnessed by two men. If two men are not available then a man and two women should give witness. The passage reads

وَٱسْتَشْهِدُوا۟ شَهِيدَيْنِ مِن رِّجَالِكُمْ فَإِن لَّمْ يَكُونَا رَجُلَيْنِ فَرَجُلٌ وَٱمْرَأَتَانِ مِمَّن تَرْضَوْنَ مِنَ ٱلشُّهَدَآءِ أَن تَضِلَّ إِحْدَىٰهُمَا فَتُذَكِّرَ إِحْدَىٰهُمَا ٱلْأُخْرَىٰ

البقرة (٢) ﴿٢٨٢﴾ ...

And call to witness, from among your men, two witnesses. And if two men are not [at hand] then a man and two women of such as you approve as witnesses, so that if one forgets the other would help her recollect.

al-Baqara (Sura 2: 282)

This is resorted to in business matters such as contracts, especially in traditional societies where most women are less interested in such matters than men. The same attitude applies in cases of violence and murder where the community seeks to protect woman's compassionate nature. The verse is actually viewed by some as a concession in favour of women, lightening their burdens rather than curtailing their equal rights.

There are occasions where a woman is considered to be a more competent witness than a man, for example in matters of birth, defloration, and defects and injuries to a woman's body. This holds particularly true in conservative societies.

Furthermore, a woman is equal to man as witness, when a husband accuses his wife of adultery. He is legally required to produce four reliable witnesses who have seen the wife commit adultery. If the husband fails to produce the witnesses, he is required to swear four times before Allah (and witnesses) that he is telling the truth. The wife who denies adultery is given an equal chance of swearing four times before Allah that he is lying. One of the two is lying, of course, and they are separated. But the woman is not punished for adultery because her word is equal to her husband's. This process, called *li'an*, is related in the Qur'an as follows:

وَالَّذِينَ يَرْمُونَ أَزْوَاجَهُمْ وَلَمْ يَكُن لَّهُمْ شُهَدَاءُ إِلَّا أَنفُسُهُمْ فَشَهَادَةُ أَحَدِهِمْ أَرْبَعُ شَهَادَاتٍ بِاللَّهِ إِنَّهُ لَمِنَ الصَّادِقِينَ ۝ وَالْخَامِسَةُ أَنَّ لَعْنَتَ اللَّهِ عَلَيْهِ إِن كَانَ مِنَ الْكَاذِبِينَ ۝ وَيَدْرَؤُا عَنْهَا الْعَذَابَ أَن تَشْهَدَ أَرْبَعَ شَهَادَاتٍ بِاللَّهِ إِنَّهُ لَمِنَ الْكَاذِبِينَ ۝ وَالْخَامِسَةَ أَنَّ غَضَبَ اللَّهِ عَلَيْهَا إِن كَانَ مِنَ الصَّادِقِينَ ۝

النور (٢٤)

As for those who accuse their wives [with adultery] but have no witnesses but themselves; let [the husband] bear witness before Allah four times that he is telling the truth. And a fifth [time] is that the wrath of Allah be upon him if he is lying.

And [the wife] shall avert punishment if she bears witness before Allah four times that her husband's accusation is false. And a fifth [time] is that the wrath of Allah be upon her if he is telling the truth.

al-Nur (Sura 24: 6–9)

WOMEN SPEAK UP FOR THEIR RIGHTS

Islamic jurisprudence has many references to Muslim women of the early period who have spoken for their rights. In 1959 Sheikh Shaltout noted the seeds of a 'women's movement' in the discussion between the Prophet (PBUH) and Hind Bint Utba (wife of Abu Safian) regarding the verse giving women the right to take independently the oath of fealty.[8] Another example was reported in the *Sunnah*:

«عن أبي هريرة قال :
جاءت فتاة إلى رسول الله صلى الله عليه وسلم ، فقالت : إن أبي زوّجني من ابن أخيه ليرفع بي خسيستَه ، قال : فجعل صلى الله عليه وسلم الأمر إليها . فقالت : قد أجزْتُ ما صنع أبي . ولكن أردتُ أن أعلِم النساء أنه ليس للآباء من أمرهِن شئ»

رواه الترمذى

On the authority of Abu Huraira who related that a young woman came to the Prophet (PBUH) protesting that her father had given her in marriage to his nephew to improve his social status, apparently without asking for her consent.

The Prophet (PBUH) gave her the choice to accept or reject that marriage. She answered, 'I condone what my father has done but *I just wanted to tell women that fathers have no such right.*'

Authenticated by al-Tirmidhi

Women were worried that only a few of them could participate in *jihad* or fighting in the way of Allah. A delegation of them came to the Prophet (PBUH) and raised the issue with him, as shown in the *hadith* below.

«أتت النساء إلى رسول الله صلى الله عليه وسلم ، فقلن : يارسول الله . ذهب الرجال بفضل الجهاد في سبيل الله ، فما لنا عملٌ ندرك به عملَ الجهاد في سبيل الله ؟ فقال : مهنة إحداكن في بيتها تدرك عمل المجاهدين في سبيل الله»

رواه أبو يعلي والبزار عن أنس

Women came to the Prophet (PBUH) and said 'O Messenger of Allah, men have taken away all the bounty of *jihad*. What work can we do to earn a bounty equal to *jihad*?' He answered 'Running the household of your husbands will bring each one of you equal reward as that of the warriors in the way of Allah.'

(Authenticated by Abu Ya'ly and al-Bazzar

Likewise, Sallama, the nurse of the Prophet's son Ibrahim, came to the Prophet and raised similar issues. The Prophet (PBUH) sensed that she had been put up to the task by other women. He reassured her that women's work, especially carrying, breast-feeding and rearing a child, has rewards unavailable to men. Such interaction demonstrates the dynamics of delegating a spokeswoman to inquire from the Prophet. To give part of the *hadith*:

«إن سلامةَ حاضنةَ ابراهيم بن النبي صلى الله عليه وسلم قالت : يارسول الله: تبشّر الرجال بكل خير ، ولا تبشّر النساء؟، قال : أصُوَيْحِباتك دَسَسنكِ لهذا ؟

قالت : أجل . هن أمَرنني . . »

إلى آخر الحديث

من حديث رواه الطبراني في الأوسط

Sallamah, the nurse of the Prophet's son Ibrahim said to the Prophet 'O, Messenger of Allah, you brought tidings of all the good things to men but not to women.'

THE ISLAMIC CONTEXT

The Prophet (PBUH) said 'Did your women friends put you up to ask me this question?' She said 'Yes, they instructed me to ask you.'
Authenticated by al-Tabarani

A final note
These rights given justly to women are to be exercised in the decency of Islamic behavior. They are furthermore matched with duties to the husband, to the parents and to the community. They are never to be used (or abused) as a basis for reversing roles with men or changing the prescribed family values.

4

Family planning and the basic precepts of Islam

This chapter reviews some of the basic precepts of Islam and concludes that there is enough in these precepts to lend sanction to the principle of family planning with a view to averting hardships. Fortunately the direct evidence for family planning is quite abundant in the *Sunnah* as will be shown in Chapter 7.

INTRODUCTION

Islam is not merely a religion. It is also a social system, a culture and a civilization. As such, it has values, ideals and goals which it regards as the culmination of human perfection in all aspects of life.

Islamic legislation is most comprehensive. It does not deal exclusively with questions of faith and worship. It also regulates moral behavior, social interaction, and business dealings as well as systems of legislation, taxation, family formation, community development, societal structure and international relations.

Several general precepts of Islam provide a convenient context for the proper formation of the Muslim family in a changing society and lend support to the principle of family planning whenever justified. This is, of course, an endorsement of the specific provisions on family planning in Islamic jurisprudence as will be discussed later.

The following accounts deal briefly with some of the basic precepts or characteristics of Islam that are particularly relevant to our subject.

A RELIGION OF EASE (*YUSR*) NOT HARDSHIP (*USR*)

In all its institutions and regulations, Islam addresses itself to reason and keeps in harmony with man's natural character (*fitrah*). It never fails to demonstrate its great compassion for its people, nor does it ever seek to

THE ISLAMIC CONTEXT

impose undue burdens and intolerable restrictions upon them. The Qur'an states this principle very succinctly:

يُرِيدُ ٱللَّهُ بِكُمُ ٱلْيُسْرَ وَلَا يُرِيدُ بِكُمُ ٱلْعُسْرَ ... ۝

البقرة(٢)

Allah desires for you ease [*yusr*]; He desires not hardship [*'usr*] for you.

al-Baqara (Sura 2:185)

وَمَا جَعَلَ عَلَيْكُمْ فِي ٱلدِّينِ مِنْ حَرَجٍ ... ۝

الحج(٢٢)

And has not laid upon you in religion any hardship [*haraj*].

al-Hajj (Sura 22:78)

يُرِيدُ ٱللَّهُ أَن يُخَفِّفَ عَنكُمْ وَخُلِقَ ٱلْإِنسَٰنُ ضَعِيفًا ۝

النساء(٤)

Allah desires to lighten your burden, for man was created weak.

al-Nisa' (Sura 4:28)

Thus Islam would be sympathetic to family planning if spacing pregnancies and adjusting their number will make the mother more physically fit and the father more financially at ease, particularly since this is not antagonistic to any categorical text (*nuss*) of prohibition in the Qur'an or in the Prophet's tradition (*Sunnah*). In point of fact, there is a basic ruling in Islamic jurisprudence (*Shari'ah*) that states:

« لاضَرَرَ ولا ضِرارَ »

رواه مالك وابن ماجة

'No harm and no harassment'

A part of tradition reported by Malik and Ibn Maja

This is a general ruling that is invoked by jurists in religious judgements particularly in the absence of a categorical text of prohibition. Thus if excessive fertility leads to proven health risks to mothers and children, and/or if it leads to economic hardship or embarrassment to the father, or if it results in the inability of parents to raise their children religiously, educationally and socially, then Muslims would be allowed to regulate their fertility in such a way that these hardships are warded off or reduced. Such was apparently the basis for the legal opinion (*fatwa*) by Sheikh Mahmoud Shaltout, the former Grand Imam of *Al-Azhar* (see Chapter 12).[1]

A RELIGION OF MODERATION

Sheikh Shaltout's *fatwa* is in line also with Islam being a religion of moderation. Pushing Muslims to continue their unregulated fertility in face of hardships is rather harsh, for Islam sponsors moderation and discourages excesses, extremism, rigidity, and undue restrictions. The Qur'an says

لَا يُكَلِّفُ ٱللَّهُ نَفْسًا إِلَّا وُسْعَهَا ... ﴿٢٨٦﴾ البقرة(٢)

Allah tasks not a soul beyond its capacity (or limits).
al-Baqara (Sura 2:286)

The Prophet says

«إن الدينَ يسر ، ولن يُشادَّ الدينَ أحدٌ إلا غلبهُ ، فسدِّدُوا وقاربوا وأبشروا واستعينوا بالغدوة والرَّوحة وشيء من الدُّلجة»

متفق عليه

This religion [of Islam] is a religious of *Yusr* free from narrow restrictions; anyone who tries to be too strict in matters of religion will have his purpose defeated. Therefore be on the right path, as in your morning course, your evening course and during your night journey.
Authenticated by al-Bukhari and Muslim

In matters of using money, even for benevolent causes, Islam asked for moderation:

وَلَا تَجْعَلْ يَدَكَ مَغْلُولَةً إِلَىٰ عُنُقِكَ وَلَا تَبْسُطْهَا كُلَّ ٱلْبَسْطِ فَتَقْعُدَ مَلُومًا مَّحْسُورًا ﴿٢٩﴾ الإسراء(١٧)

And let not your hand [in giving] be chained to your neck, nor yet open it to the extreme, lest you end up in rebuke, in beggary.
al-Isra' (Sura 17:29)

Moderation is also coupled with stamping out any basis for extremism even in worship. Reference has been made in Chapter 1, to the Prophet's angry rejection of extremism even in the form of prayers day and night, continuous fasting, self-imposed celibacy and selection of an isolated and harsh way of life. He reacted to that with anger (see p. 16).

A RELIGION FOR QUALITY

As all other religions, Islam has encouraged its people to increase and populate the earth, but with the proviso that their quality should not be compromised. If it is an either/or question, however, Islam would certainly go for quality.² The Qur'an says

قُل لَّا يَسْتَوِي ٱلْخَبِيثُ وَٱلطَّيِّبُ وَلَوْ أَعْجَبَكَ كَثْرَةُ ٱلْخَبِيثِ ... ﴿١٠٠﴾

المائدة(٥)

Say: the evil and the good should not be valued equal, even though the abundance of evil may dazzle you.

al-Ma'ida (Sura 5:100)

كَم مِّن فِئَةٍ قَلِيلَةٍ غَلَبَتْ فِئَةً كَثِيرَةً بِإِذْنِ ٱللَّهِ ... ﴿٢٤٩﴾

البقرة(٢)

How oft, by Allah's will, has a small host vanquished a numerous host.

al-Baqara (Sura 2:249)

The preference of quality over quantity is evident in Sheikh Shaltout's *fatwa* and in the opinions of many other theologians, for example most of those who attended the Rabat Conference of Islam and Family Planning in 1971.³

It is observed that some other theologians are pushing for an indiscriminate high rate of growth among Muslims even if it is far in excess of their means. They use the argument for 'becoming plenty' as an implicit or explicit discouragement of family planning.⁴ This is an important argument and therefore this issue will be discussed in detail in Chapter 6.

A RELIGION FOR PLANNING

As a religion which aims to organize the life of its people, Islam must foster planning. This is evident in many ways. The Qur'an has always emphasized that *everything in this universe has been created according to a plan or law*:

إِنَّا كُلَّ شَيْءٍ خَلَقْنَاهُ بِقَدَرٍ ﴿٤٩﴾

القمر(٥٤)

We have created everything, according to a LAW.

al-Qamar (Sura: 54:49)

Muslims are repeatedly urged to consider and reflect on the divine plan in

FAMILY PLANNING AND THE BASIC PRECEPTS OF ISLAM

the universe around them and in the miracles of their creation. Believers are described as those who

$$\ldots \text{وَيَتَفَكَّرُونَ فِي خَلْقِ السَّمَوَاتِ وَالْأَرْضِ} \ldots \text{ال عمران(٣)}$$

Reflect on the creation of the heavens and the earth.
al-Imran (Sura 3:191)

They are reminded of the orderliness in everything:

$$\text{لَا الشَّمْسُ يَنبَغِي لَهَا أَن تُدْرِكَ الْقَمَرَ وَلَا اللَّيْلُ سَابِقُ النَّهَارِ وَكُلٌّ فِي فَلَكٍ يَسْبَحُونَ} \quad \text{يس(٣٦)}$$

It is not for the sun to overtake the moon, nor does the night outstrip the day. They all float along, each in its own orbit [according to law].
Yasseen (Sura 36:40)

An orderly universe, from a religious viewpoint, is one of the signs of the existence of Allah.

$$\text{تَبَارَكَ الَّذِي بِيَدِهِ الْمُلْكُ وَهُوَ عَلَى كُلِّ شَيْءٍ قَدِيرٌ الَّذِي خَلَقَ الْمَوْتَ وَالْحَيَاةَ لِيَبْلُوَكُمْ أَيُّكُمْ أَحْسَنُ عَمَلًا وَهُوَ الْعَزِيزُ الْغَفُورُ الَّذِي خَلَقَ سَبْعَ سَمَوَاتٍ طِبَاقًا مَّا تَرَى فِي خَلْقِ الرَّحْمَنِ مِن تَفَاوُتٍ} \ldots \text{الملك(٦٧)}$$

Blessed be He whose hand is in the kingdom, and over everything is He potent, who has created death and life that He may try you, which of you is best in deed, and He is the Exalted and Forgiving.

Who has created seven heavens in harmony, one above the other, no defect can you see in Allah's creation.
al-Mulk (Sura 67: 1–3)

Another demonstration of planning, is the *orderliness, even in the main acts of worship*. Prayers five times a day are a constant reminder of planning and orderliness in everyday life. Fasting is required at a fixed time every year as is pilgrimage with specified orderly rituals. Giving alms (*zaqaat*) follows certain quantitative rulings with specified target recipients etc.

The legality of future material planning is exemplified in the Qur'an by Joseph's design for the potential famine in Egypt following his interpretation of the

THE ISLAMIC CONTEXT

Pharoah's dream. As are all Allah's prophets, Joseph is exemplary to Muslims. His plan is the first seven-year plan in history aimed to safeguard the future of a whole nation. As it is related in the Qur'an:

وَقَالَ ٱلْمَلِكُ إِنِّى أَرَىٰ سَبْعَ بَقَرَٰتٍ سِمَانٍ يَأْكُلُهُنَّ سَبْعٌ عِجَافٌ وَسَبْعَ سُنۢبُلَٰتٍ خُضْرٍ وَأُخَرَ يَابِسَٰتٍ يَٰٓأَيُّهَا ٱلْمَلَأُ أَفْتُونِى فِى رُءْيَٰىَ إِن كُنتُمْ لِلرُّءْيَا تَعْبُرُونَ ۝ قَالُوٓا۟ أَضْغَٰثُ أَحْلَٰمٍ وَمَا نَحْنُ بِتَأْوِيلِ ٱلْأَحْلَٰمِ بِعَٰلِمِينَ ۝ وَقَالَ ٱلَّذِى نَجَا مِنْهُمَا وَٱدَّكَرَ بَعْدَ أُمَّةٍ أَنَا۠ أُنَبِّئُكُم بِتَأْوِيلِهِۦ فَأَرْسِلُونِ ۝ يُوسُفُ أَيُّهَا ٱلصِّدِّيقُ أَفْتِنَا فِى سَبْعِ بَقَرَٰتٍ سِمَانٍ يَأْكُلُهُنَّ سَبْعٌ عِجَافٌ وَسَبْعِ سُنۢبُلَٰتٍ خُضْرٍ وَأُخَرَ يَابِسَٰتٍ لَّعَلِّىٓ أَرْجِعُ إِلَى ٱلنَّاسِ لَعَلَّهُمْ يَعْلَمُونَ ۝ قَالَ تَزْرَعُونَ سَبْعَ سِنِينَ دَأَبًا فَمَا حَصَدتُّمْ فَذَرُوهُ فِى سُنۢبُلِهِۦٓ إِلَّا قَلِيلًا مِّمَّا تَأْكُلُونَ ۝ ثُمَّ يَأْتِى مِنۢ بَعْدِ ذَٰلِكَ سَبْعٌ شِدَادٌ يَأْكُلْنَ مَا قَدَّمْتُمْ لَهُنَّ إِلَّا قَلِيلًا مِّمَّا تُحْصِنُونَ ۝ ثُمَّ يَأْتِى مِنۢ بَعْدِ ذَٰلِكَ عَامٌ فِيهِ يُغَاثُ ٱلنَّاسُ وَفِيهِ يَعْصِرُونَ ۝

يوسف (١٢)

And the King said 'Lo! I saw in a dream seven fat cows which seven lean cows were eating, and seven green ears of corn with another (seven) dry.' He asked 'O notables; expound for me my vision, if you can interpret dreams.'

They answered 'Jumbled dreams. And we are not knowledgeable in the interpretation of dreams.'

And he of the two [prison companions with Joseph] who was released, and now at length remembered, said 'I am going to get you the proper interpretation (from one who knows: Joseph), so send me forth to him.'

[Seeing Joseph] he said 'O Joseph, O the truthful one. Expound for us the seven fat cows which seven lean ones were eating and the seven green ears of corn with another (seven) dry, that I may return unto the people so that they may know.'

He [Joseph] designed 'You shall sow seven years as usual, but that which you reap, leave it in the ears, all save a little which you eat. Then after that will come seven hard years which will devour all that you have prepared for them, save a little of what you have stored. Then, after that will come a year when the people will have plenteous crops and when they shall press [juice and oil].'

Yusuf (Sura 12: 43–9)

About how he came to know of so much interpretation and future forecasting and planning, Joseph emphasized to his two prison companions that it was Allah's inspiration:

ذٰلِكُمَا مِمَّا عَلَّمَنِي رَبِّ ... ﴿٣٧﴾ يوسف(١٢)

This is of that which my Allah has taught me.
Yusuf (Sura 12:37)

The implication of this Qur'anic account is pervasive. It denotes without doubt the legality of planning for the future and taking steps to ward off potential future hardships. There is no hint of antagonism to Allah's power to provide or His predestination.

It is also reported by Imam Zabidi that the Prophet Mohammad stored one year's supply of the dates of Khaibar for future use.[5]

Family formation is no exception. It requires preparation, co-ordination and planning, from the choice of a marital partner, to the timing and spacing of pregnancies, to plans of how to bring up children as good, healthy and useful Muslims, as well as to care of the aged and disabled family members. Some families may desire and are prepared to raise many children, other families may restrict the number to their physical, cultural and socio-economic abilities. Thus family planning is within the general concept of family formation in Islam.

A RELIGION FOR ALL TIMES

Islam is the last of the revealed religions and Mohammad is the seal of the Prophets. Thus Islam is meant for all mankind and was not restricted to a special population in a specified area or to a circumscribed period in history. This means that this religion should cater not only for the time of the Prophet and the Arabs of the seventh century (AD), but should satisfy the requirements of future generations and different population groups until the end of time.

Changing population

Demography reveals that population dynamics differ fundamentally from one period of history to another. Islam should be able to satisfy the requirements of each period. The most distinct demographic differences are those between the old (pre-modern) period, preceding the middle of the eleventh century AH (seventeenth century AD) and the modern period thereafter.[6]

Mortality rates were high for all communities including the early Muslim community during the pre-modern period especially in the periods of epidemics (plagues), famine and war. Child mortality was particularly high. In face of such losses, high fertility was advantageous. The rate of population growth fluctuated from year to year but the net increase was very small.

In Figure 4.1, the world population is represented by an almost straight line showing only small increases until the middle of the seventeenth century. With the advent of the modern period epidemics started to recede as social development led to health and hygiene improvements. Mortality rates began to decline in the more developed countries during the eighteenth and early nineteenth centuries with little change in fertility patterns, and the rate of population growth increased. The ensuing population pressures in European

Figure 4.1 World population growth, past and projected (assuming constant fertility levels as of 1960-70)

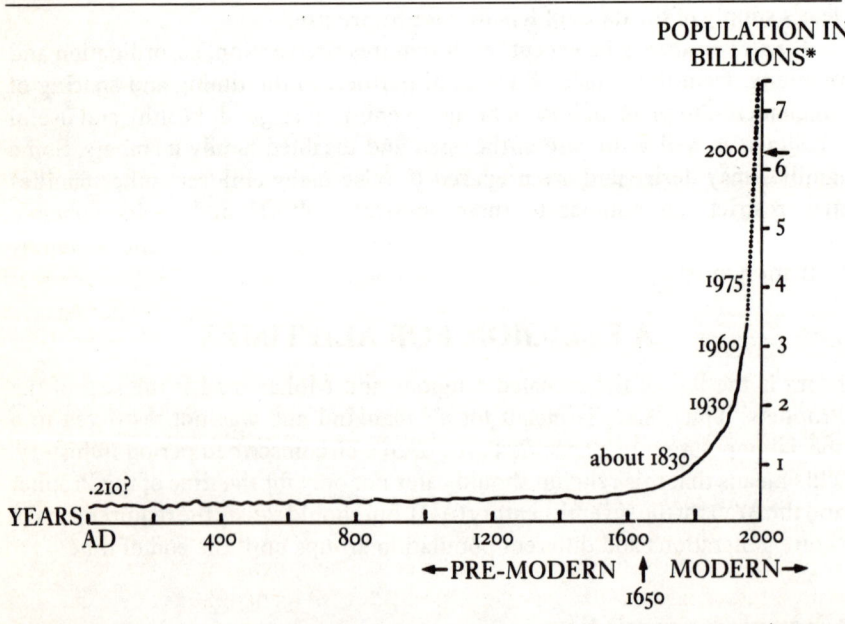

Source: Abdel R. Omran (ed.) *Community Medicine in Developing Countries* (New York: Springer, 1974). p. 102

societies led to massive migration to the United States of America, Canada and elsewhere. This in turn led to relief of the population pressure. In addition family planning became widespread in an effort to adjust the fertility rate to the mortality rate and balance population size. Failure to relieve the population pressures would have impeded economic and social development in Europe.

In Third World countries the delay in social and health developments meant that mortality rates did not begin to decline until the middle of the twentieth century, while fertility rates continued at the pre-modern high level. This reflects the slow pace of social and health development in Third World countries. Population growth rates continued to increase and, in most countries, threatened to outstrip resources and impede economic and social development. Some countries, especially those with limited resources, resorted to community-wide and national family planning campaigns in an attempt to reduce fertility and adjust population growth to levels they could sustain.

As well as these national developments, modernization in such areas as housing, transportation, recreation, schooling, etc, have made changes and new demands at the family level. The cost of raising a child has greatly increased especially in urban areas. Family-size preferences have changed, especially as more women seek education and participation in the labour force. Families are becoming more aware of the reproductive risks associated with unplanned and excessive fertility. In short, families in several developing countries (including a number of Muslim communities) are more willing to consider family planning.

Islam and population change

Islam, being a universal religion, caters for both patterns of family formation, i.e. the patterns of high fertility and large family size (the pre-modern pattern) and the pattern of small family size (the modern pattern). This is depicted simplistically in Figure 4.2. In both patterns there is family planning, the difference being the extent of its use. There is historical evidence that early Islamic societies (including those at the time of the Prophet), used *al-azl* to avoid economic hardship. The extent of contraceptive use in those times, however, was limited compared to the needs of Muslim families in recent times.

The concept of a changing need for family planning over time is implicit in a *fatwa* by Sheikh Hasan Ma'moun, a former Grand Imam of *Al-Azhar*. He explains that in its beginning Islam was a new religion with few followers, whose future mission encouraged a 'multitude' of its people. He continued

> But now we find that conditions have changed. We find that the density of population in the world threatens a serious reduction of the living

THE ISLAMIC CONTEXT

Figure 4.2 Models of growth in Muslim countries

TRADITIONAL MODEL OF MUSLIM COUNTRIES

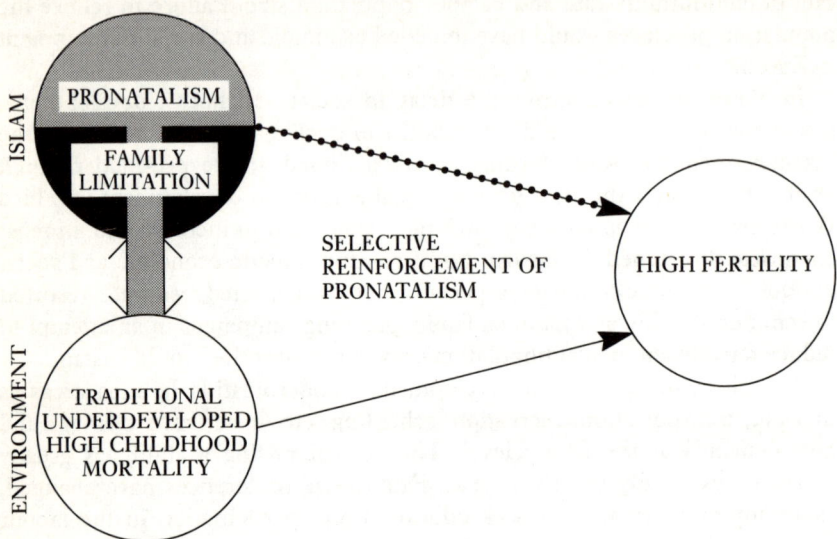

FUTURE MODEL OF MUSLIM COUNTRIES

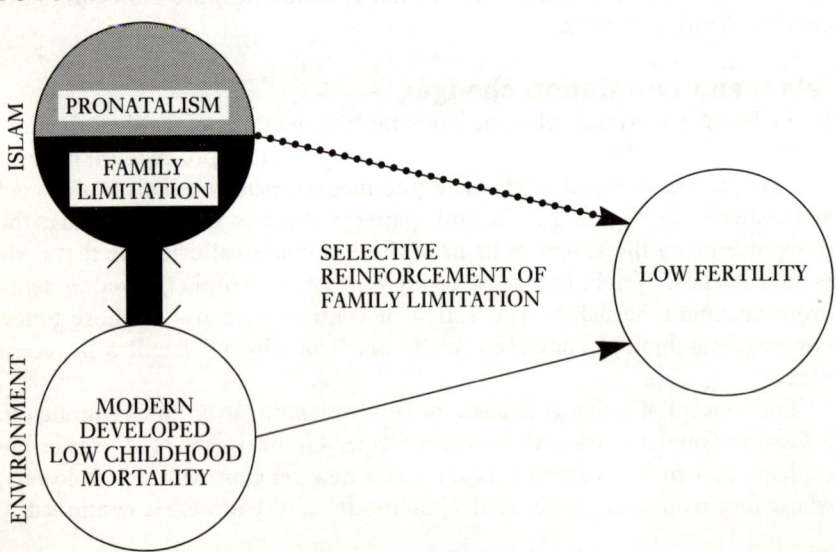

standards of mankind to the extent that many men of thought have been prompted to seek family planning.

He concludes by stating

> I see no objection from the *Shariʿah* point of view to the consideration of family planning as a measure, if there is need for it.[7]

The full text is provided in Appendix II).

PART II

Family Planning in the Qur'an and the *Sunnah*

5

Sources of Islamic jurisprudence

After defining *Sharia‘ah* and *fiqh*, this chapter provides a concise statement on the sources and principles of *Shari‘ah*. The original sources of *Shari‘ah* are two: the Qur'an and the *Sunnah*. Based on these (and subordinate to them) are two more: the Consensus (*ijma‘*) of jurists and Analogy (*qiyas*). Supplementary venues, within the spirit of *Shari‘ah*, are used by different legal schools and include juristic preference (*istihsan*), the example of the residents of Medina, the public welfare (*al-masalih al-mursala*), and rule of concomitance (*istishab*). In addition, there are broad principles such as '*no harm–no harrassment*' and the rule that the *basic nature of things is permissibility unless forbidden by explicit Text (nuss)* from the Qur'an or Prophet's *Sunnah*.

INTRODUCTION AND DEFINITIONS

This chapter states the limits of personal views and the necessity of following the rules of fourteen centuries of Islamic jurisprudence regarding matters that are important to Muslims, especially when dealing with the intricacies of ruling on practices such as child spacing and family planning.

First, some definitions. The two concepts related to Islamic jurisprudence are *Shari‘ah* and *fiqh*.

Shari‘ah refers to the body of institutions, rules and regulations which Allah, the Lawgiver, has ordained to guide the Muslim in matters of worship (*ibadat*) or in his relations with his fellow men (Muslims and non-Mulsims), within the family, the group, the society and the world at large (*mu‘amalat*). The origin of *Shari‘ah* is divine, proceeding directly from Allah who is the only authority to qualify things as *halal* (permissible) or *haram* (prohibited). This is done through the Qur'an or *Sunnah* which is inspired.

Shari‘ah in Arabic means 'the path to be followed'. It is to be followed by Muslims. The Prophet was instructed by Allah to do so:

$$\text{ثُمَّ جَعَلْنَاكَ عَلَىٰ شَرِيعَةٍ مِّنَ الْأَمْرِ فَاتَّبِعْهَا وَلَا تَتَّبِعْ أَهْوَاءَ الَّذِينَ لَا يَعْلَمُونَ}$$

الجاثية (٤٥) ۞

We set you upon a path [*Shari'ah*], so follow it, and not the desires of those who have no knowledge.

al-Jathiah (Sura 45:18)

Fiqh is the science of *Shari'ah*. Literally the term means knowledge, understanding, insight, intelligence. Technically, it is the product of *ijtihad* which is the systematic intellectual search and insight in the analysis, interpretation and development of judgement based on specified sources and following strict procedures and set approaches. *Ijtihad* can be practiced only by a qualified scholar jurist called *mujtahid*.

The difference between *Shari'ah* and *fiqh* is not always recognized. In the minds of many Muslims and in common usage, Islamic law, Islamic jurisprudence and even *Shari'ah* Law encompass two basic components: the divine component (the true *Shari'ah*) and *fiqh* which adds the product of *ijtihad* by qualified jurists, its meticulous nature, notwithstanding.

As a result of differences in interpretations there arose in the second to fourth century AH a number of legal schools of *fiqh* called *madhahib* (singular *madhab*). These schools carry the name of their founder (in the *Sunni* schools), the chosen Imam (in the *Shi'ite* schools) or the character of the school (in the *Kharijite* and *Zahiri* schools). These will be discussed in Chapter 8.

SOURCES AND VENUES OF ISLAMIC JURISPRUDENCE

Islamic laws are derived from specified sources, broad principles and supplementary venues as listed in Figure 5.1.

Group 1: The primary and prerequisite sources

The Qur'an and the *Sunnah* of the Prophet have been designated as the foundation of Islamic *Shari'ah* or law. They are prerequisite in the sense that they are the foremost reference in any *ijtihad*. All judgements or *fatwas* have to be drawn directly from these two sources. If this is not possible, the other sources and venues can be used but have to be based on or fall within the spirit of the Qur'an and the *Sunnah*. This has been repeatedly ordained by the Lawgiver:

SOURCES OF ISLAMIC JURISPRUDENCE

Figure 5.1 Sources and venues of Islamic jurisprudence

Two primary and prerequisite sources (foundation)
- The Qur'an (the Book)
- The Sunnah (The Prophet's tradition)

Two complementary but subordinate sources
- Consensus (*ijma'*) of theologians
- Analogy (*qiyas*) or analogous reasoning

Six supplementary venues
- Juristic Preference: *istihsan*
- The example of Medina residents
- Public welfare/unrestricted interests (*al-masalih al-mursala*)
- Rule of concomitance (*istishab*)
- Blockage of the way (*sadd al-dharai'*)
- Prevailing custom (*urf*)

Four broad principles or rules
- The basic nature of things is their permissibility unless prohibited by a Text (*nuss*)
- The rule of 'no harm and no harassment'
- The rule of 'necessity permits the prohibited' (within limits)
- The rule of 'choosing the lesser harm'

وَمَا كَانَ لِمُؤْمِنٍ وَلَا مُؤْمِنَةٍ إِذَا قَضَى ٱللَّهُ وَرَسُولُهُۥ أَمْرًا أَن يَكُونَ لَهُمُ ٱلْخِيَرَةُ مِنْ أَمْرِهِمْ وَمَن يَعْصِ ٱللَّهَ وَرَسُولَهُۥ فَقَدْ ضَلَّ ضَلَالًا مُّبِينًا ﴿٣٦﴾

الأحزاب (٣٣)

It is not fitting for a believer, man or woman, when a matter has been decided by Allah and His messenger, to have any option about their decision. If anyone disobeys Allah and his messenger, he is indeed on a clearly wrong path.

al-Ahzab (Sura 33: 36)

This is particularly so in regard to things that are prohibited (*haram*). The Qur'an says

... وَقَدْ فَصَّلَ لَكُم مَّا حَرَّمَ عَلَيْكُمْ ... ﴿١١٩﴾

الأنعام (٦)

And he [Allah] has specified to you in detail that
which is forbidden [*haram*] to you.
al-An'am (Sura 6:119)

Therefore, Muslims, including jurists who command our respect and admiration, were solemnly warned against claiming on their own the authority to qualify things as *haram* independently of Allah's teaching:

$$\text{وَلَا تَقُولُوا لِمَا تَصِفُ أَلْسِنَتُكُمُ الْكَذِبَ هَذَا حَلَالٌ وَهَذَا حَرَامٌ لِتَفْتَرُوا عَلَى اللَّهِ الْكَذِبَ إِنَّ الَّذِينَ يَفْتَرُونَ عَلَى اللَّهِ الْكَذِبَ لَا يُفْلِحُونَ}$$

النحل (١٦)

And speak not, concerning the falsehood that which your own tongues admit: this is lawful [*halal*] and this is forbidden [*haram*], inventing a lie against Allah. Lo! Those who invent lies against Allah will not prosper.

al-Nahl (Sura 16:116)

Thus, the authority to legislate *halal* and *haram* has been kept away from man.¹ In Islam there are no rabbis, ministers, priests or pope. The *'ulama'*, jurists, Sheikhs, Mullas or Imams and grand Imams are but interpreters of *Shari'ah* using specified rules and venues. Whosoever transgresses this ordinance and follows jurists who claim to themselves the authority of priests or rabbis will fall within the meaning of the following verse:

$$\text{أَمْ لَهُمْ شُرَكَاءُ شَرَعُوا لَهُمْ مِنَ الدِّينِ مَا لَمْ يَأْذَنْ بِهِ اللَّهُ ...}$$

الشورى (٤٢)

Do they have partners [with Allah] who have prescribed for them in religion that concerning which Allah has given no permission?

al-Shura (Sura 42:21)

The Prophet (PBUH) has equally emphasized the same principle:

«إن الله فرض فرائضَ فلا تضيِّعوها ، وحدَّ حدودًا فلا تعتدوها ، وحرم أشياء فلا تنتهكوها ، وسكت عن أشياء رحمةً بكم غيرَ نسيان ، فلا تبحثوا عنها»

رواه الحاكم والدارقطني وحسَّنه النَّوَوِيّ وقال أبو بكر السمعاني: هذا الحديث أصل كبير من أصول الدين وفروعه.

Allah has prescribed certain obligations for you, so do not escape them; He has defined certain limits, so do not transgress them; He has prohibited certain things, so do not do them, and He kept silent concerning other things out of mercy for you and not because of forgetfulness, so do not probe into them.

Reported by al-Hakim and Darakotny

SOURCES OF ISLAMIC JURISPRUDENCE

This *hadith*, which according to *Sam'ani* is a basic reference in jurisprudence, is in harmony with the broad principle in *Shari'ah* that the basic nature of things is their permissibility unless explicitly prohibited by a text (*nuss*) from the Qur'an or the *Sunnah*.

Dr (Sheikh) al-Qaradawi provided in 1985 a most interesting example of this principle which happened to be related to family planning, when discussing the juristic rules in general. He said that the above principle is supported by what is reported in a sound *hadith* by the Prophet's Companion, Jabir Ibn Abdullah:

«عن جابر قال : كنا نعزل والقرآن ينزل . لو كان شيئا يُنهَى عنه لنهانا عنه القرآن»

رواه مسلم

We used to practise *al-azl* [coitus interruptus] while the Qur'an was being revealed. If the practice were to have been prohibited, the Qur'an would have prohibited it.   Reported by Muslim

According to Sheikh Qaradawi, Jabir has, therefore, implied that if the divine revelation was silent about something, it was permissible and people were free to practice it. Certainly, the Companions have a perfect understanding of the *Shari'ah* including the great principle that no worship can be legislated except by the command of Allah and no practice can be prohibited except by His explicit prohibition.[2]

Group 2: Complementary sources of law: consensus and analogy

Consensus

Consensus is used by all schools of jurisprudence but there are variations in what constitutes consensus. Abu Hanifa and Ibn Hanbal posed no restriction on consensus, but Malik preferred it to be the consensus among the Companions and successors (*tabi'oun*) who have been close to the practice of Islam as it should be. Al-Shafe'i required the consensus of the entire community, which was hardly attainable. Hence al-Ghazali (al-Shafe'i) explained that such was needed for the fundamentals while less important issues require more circumscribed consensus. Shi'ites accept consensus only when it includes the views of Imam Ali or their chosen Imams whom they hold as infallible.

Analogy (qiyas)

Qiyas, in its juristic use, means a parallel. If some practice was previously allowed (or disallowed) by a text or *ijma'* and especially if the reason (*illah*) behind the decision is known, it will be a basis for allowing (or disallowing) a new practice of similar nature especially if it will fulfill the underlying justification or reason (*illah*) or in some cases *hikmah,* i.e. the wisdom for or against such practice. A general example is the prohibition of alcohol because of its intoxicating effect. Other drugs or materials (such as cocaine) that have intoxicating effects or can impair judgement (the underlying *illah*) are by analogous reasoning, prohibited.

The three prerequisites for *qiyas* listed by Muhsinuddin (1986) are as follows:

- The cause must be the idea intended by the *Shariʿah*. It should be apparent and complete in itself.
- The cause must be identical in both the original subject and the subject of analogy. Mere similarities in attributes are not sufficient to justify analogy.
- The rule in the original case should be generally applicable. Thus, analogy is not permissible in the case of a rule which already has a specific reference.[3]

Despite its apparent merits, analogy was the subject of greater differences than *ijmaʿ*, hence it is listed as the fourth source coming after *ijmaʿ*.

Analogy (*qiyas*) is accepted by most of the Companions, by most of the Sunni jurists, particularly Shafeʿis and Malikis. Ahmad Ibn Hanbal accepted analogy in principle but preferred a weak *hadith* to it. The Zaydi Shiʿites accept it, but the Imami Shiʿites frown on it. The Zahiri school rejects it absolutely – one of the reasons why Dawoud Ibn Ali, the founder of the school, split from the Shafeʿi school was because of this difference of opinion on *qiyas*.[4]

These two additional sources were used by the Companions in electing *Sayyidna* Abu Bakr as the first Caliph (successor to the Prophet). Analogy comes from the fact that the Prophet (PBUH) before his death asked Abu Bakr to lead the prayers in his place. Being a leader in religious affairs, he must also be leader in worldly affairs. This was agreed upon by the Companions representing consensus.[5]

Group 3: Supplementary venues
These are procedures found useful by different schools of jurisprudence, as discussed below.

Juristic preference (istihsan الاستحسان)
This was introduced by Imam Abu Hanifa. In his masterful hands and those of others like him the procedure was less subject to arbitrary personal opinion than in other jurists' hands. Hence, it was less frequently used in other schools.

SOURCES OF ISLAMIC JURISPRUDENCE

The example of Medina residents عمل أهل المدينة
This was introduced by Imam Malik who lived in Medina and considered its residents to have lived an exemplary Islamic life.

The public welfare (al-masalih al Mursala المصالح المرسلة)
Literally this procedure means unrestricted (people's) interests, and denotes that the public welfare of the people should be taken into consideration in making laws. This procedure, promoted also by Imam Malik, has a noble intention and involves the broad principle of 'no hardship', thus adding to its legitimacy. However, some jurists felt that this opens the door to arbitrary personal judgement. Malik must have used it within the spirit of the Qur'an and the *Sunnah*. Scholars may, with great care, use it within the spirit of *Shari'ah*. It is actually used in principle by all the Sunni schools.

The rule of concomitance (Istishab الاستصحاب)
This principle is used by the Shafe'i school and is acceptable to other schools. It is defined as relating to the deduction by presumption of continuity which may, at best, be a principle of evidence rather than the source of law. For example, a marriage is presumed to continue until its annulment is pronounced. Ownership based on valid title deeds is presumed valid unless there is proof to the contrary.[6]

Two more procedures are mentioned in the books of jurisprudence:

- *Sadd-al-Dharai (blocking the way* سد الذرائع *)* which can be subsumed under *al-Masalih al-Mursala*.
- *Urf (prevailing custom* العرف *)* in absence of specific rulings from *Shari'ah*. This can be risky and should not be used, especially if the custom is not genuinely Islamic.

Group 4: Broad principles
These principles are as follows:

- The basic nature of things is their permissibility unless prohibited by a text.
- The rule of no harm and no harrassment.
- The rule of necessity permits the prohibited.
- The choice of the lesser harm.

APPLICATION TO FAMILY PLANNING

Let us consider some implications of the above rules to *al-azl* (coitus interruptus) and contraceptive use.

Imam al-Ghazali (d.IIII) in the *Ihya'* found *al-azl* to be permissible. He even rules out its dislike as follows:

«وإنما قلنا لاكراهة بمعنى التحريم والتنزيه، لأنّ إثبات النهى إنما يكون بنصٍّ أو قياسٍ على منصوصٍ، ولا نصَّ ولا أصلَ يقاس عليه.»

We have ruled out its [*al-azl*'s] dislike in the sense of prohibition because, to establish prohibition, one has to have a *text* (from the Qur'an or the *Sunnah*] or resort to analogous reasoning [*qiyas*] based on a precedence for which a text is available. In this case [of *al-azl*] there is neither a text nor a precedent for analogical reasoning.[7]

Sheikh M.S. Madkour, a contemporary jurist, used analogous reasoning to demonstrate the permissibility of the use of the modern mechanical and chemical methods of contraception as follows:

كان الفقهاء لا يكتفون بالبحث عن أحكام الوقائع التي عاصرتهم، وإنما تعدّوا ذلك إلى افتراض المسائل التي لم تقع والتي ربما يصل اليها التطور، والبحث عن أحكامها. يدل على ذلك ما قالوه من أن المرأة تسد فم الرحم منعا من وصول ماء الرجل إليه بقصد منع الحمل، وقولهم يجوز للمرأة استعمال الدواء الذي يؤجل الحمل ويؤخره ولا يجوز لها استعمال الدواء الذي يمنع أصل الصلاحية للحمل، وقولهم: يجوز للمرأة أن تنفض النطفة من الرحم مالم تستقر. والعبارة الأولى يندرج تحتها ما تطورت اليه وسيلة العزل لمنع الحمل، إذ عرفت البشرية وسيلة أخرى هي العجلة التي توضع في فم الرحم تمنع اتصال الحيوان المنوي بالبويضة.

ومن هذا القبيل أيضا الحجاب المانع (الكبوت) الذي يستعمله الرجل ليحول بين الحيوان المنوي الذي يفرزه وبين البويضة. والعبارة الثانية تشمل ما وصل إليه التطور في هذه الوسائل من إيجاد حبوب منع الحمل. فهي وسيلة المنع المؤقت كما هو واضح، وما هي إلا دواء. كما تشمل أيضا الحقن التي نشر عنها وقيل إن مفعولها يستمر عدة شهور كما تشمل كل دواء تهتدى إليه البشرية في سنة التطور ما دام لا يمنع أصل الصلاحية للانجاب سواء أكان بالنسبة للرجل أم بالنسبة للمرأة. والعبارة الثالثة يندرج تحتها ــ فيما أرى ــ وسيلة اللولب لأنه جسم غريب يوضع في الرحم فيحدث تقلصات فيه لا تمكن البويضة الملقحة من العلوق والاستقرار، وإنما ينفضها الرحم.»

The jurists, in this respect, have aimed at something more than simply working out legal formulas to cover contemporary issues: they went beyond that; they even posed hypothetical cases for the purpose of finding legal solutions for them, considering that those cases, although unrealistic so far, are liable to emerge at a later date.

One proof of this assumption, as given by the jurists, is that a woman may resort first to mechanical precautions to block the mouth of the uterus and prevent semen from reaching it; or secondly, may take a drug or a pill to postpone or delay it, without impairing her fecundity. By such methods, a married woman may succeed in either expelling the semen before entry to the uterus, or in destroying the sperm before impregnation.

Translating the above instances into modern terms, we may say that the first mechanical method known as coitus interruptus, *al-azl* in Arabic, used by our ancestors to prevent pregnancy, corresponds to the device used these days by women and known as the diaphragm or ring to block the uterine aperture, or to another device used by men, the condom. Both are designed to prevent the semen from reaching the ovum and fertilizing it.

The second method may be said to correspond to the latest improvement in this respect, for temporary contraception, namely the contraceptive pill. Under this heading may also be included the injectables much advertised and supposed to be effective for several months. Included also is every other beneficial drug which may be discovered by the medical profession for this purpose.

The third instance corresponds, as I see it, to the plastic filament known as the coil (IUD), for it definitely is a foreign body inserted into the uterus, which, by causing contractions, prevents the fertilized egg from attaching itself to the uterine wall, and the uterus expels it instead.[8]

Adaptability of Islamic law

In anticipation of the changing interest and needs of the Muslim community over time and place, an order of flexibility and adaptability was allowed. This of course, applies to social, business and other aspects of personal and communal life called *muʿamalat*. In regard to worship and rituals (*ibadat*) no change is allowed. Fixed rules are also to be respected in regard to established commandments and prohibitions (e.g. murder, alcohol, pork, fornication, stealing, cheating, false witness, etc.).

The adaptability over time is explained eloquently by Ibn Abdin, the Hanafi jurist of the nineteenth century:

«كثيرٌ من الأحكام تختلف باختلاف الزمان ... ... بحيث لو بقى الحكم على ما كان عليه لزم منه المشقه والضرر بالناس ، ولخالف قواعد الشريعة المبنية على التخفيف ، ورفع الضرر ، والفساد ، ولبقاء العالم على أتم نظام وأحسن أحكام. ولهذا نرى مشايخ المذاهب خالفوا مامضى عليه المجتهد فى مواضع كثيرة»

Many laws differ in different times, because customs and conventions of people undergo change in the meantime, or because of necessity. Obviously, if the law were to remain unchanged, hardship and harm to people would be incurred, thereby violating one of the principles of Islamic law which enjoins that people's difficulties are to be relieved and the harm and corruption avoided, and that law and order should prevail in the world. Consequently we observe that religious protagonists of the various schools of jurisprudence have diverged from certain paths outlined by former authoritative interpreters of the law.[9]

Likewise the Maliki jurist al-Qurafi said

«إن الجمود على المنقولات أبداً ضلال فى الدين ، وجهل بمقاصد علماء المسلمين والسلف.»

To observe rigidly the traditional laws forever is to stray away from the true path of religion and to be ignorant of the interests of the learned among the Muslims, and of our ancestors.[10]

An application to family planning of the adaptability of Islamic law was demonstrated by Sheikh al-Sharabassi of Al-Azhar (1974) as follows:

«والملاحظ في الشريعة الغراء ، أن الأمر الذى يتغير أو يتبدل بتغير ظروف الانسان أو الزمان ، أو المكان ، لا تنص الشريعة فيه على وضع موحَّد ثابت، أو نصٍّ صارم قاطع ، بل تَكِلُه إلى اجتهاد البصراء من علماء الأمة، فى نطاق مصادر التشريع الإسلامى ، وفى ضوء قول الله تبارك وتعالى (ولو رَدُّوهُ إلى الرسول وإلى أولى الأمرِ منهُم ، لَعَلِمَهُ الذين يستنبطُونه منهُم) (سورة النساء ٨٣).

ولا شك أن كثرة النسل أو قلته ليست وضعا ثابتاً جامداً مطرداً، وأن معالجة هذا الأمر لا تأخذ شكلا ثابتاً جامداً مطرداً ، بل تتغير وتتبدل حسب الظروف والأحوال. ومفهوم تنظيم النسل يتنقّل تبعاً لتغير الأحوال من أقصى اليمين إلى

أقصى اليسار وما بينهما ، فقد يكون التنظيم فى بعض الأزمنة أو الأمكنة تقليلا من الذرية أو ضبطا لها ، وقد يكون في بعض آخر من الأزمنة أو الأمكنة تكثيراً للذرية ، وإطلاقا لمسيرتها. »

من كلام الشيخ الشرباصى

Islamic law deals with matters that change with the changing conditions of man or with time and place, it does not lay down [for changing matters] a fixed, uniform rule or a rigid, definitive formula but rather leaves this to the opinion of the more discerning scholars of the community within the framework of Islamic jurisprudence ...

There is little doubt that the size of a progeny, large or small, is not a fixed, rigid or uniform position, nor is there any doubt that the manner of dealing with these situations cannot assume a fixed, rigid uniform shape but must change and alter in accordance with conditions and circumstances.

Similarly, birth planning swings from one extreme to the other, taking various positions along the arc of the pendulum only to conform with changing circumstances. At certain times planning may take the form of reduction or control of the number of offspring. At other times and in other places, it may be directed towards increasing progeny and giving childbearing free rein."

REQUIREMENTS OF A NEW RULING OR *FATWA*

In all procedures used to arrive at a ruling or *fatwa*, utmost caution and objectivity should be exercised. Meticulous search and research are needed to be sure that the *fatwa* is within the requirements of Islamic jurisprudence. Examples of these requirements are as follows:

- Any new ruling should be developed by qualified jurists (*mujtahid*). The door of *ijtihad* is open but only for those who satisfy the qualifications of a *mujtahid* (as stated below).
- There should be no categorical text in the Qur'an or the *Sunnah* prohibiting or allowing the proposed practice.
- The proposed practice should not clash with any other text or prior consensus of jurists or prior analogy for which a categorical text exists.
- The proposed practice will not impose undue hardships on Muslims.
- The process of developing the legal background for the proposed practice should follow closely the rules and procedures of *ijtihad*.
- A *mujtahid* should be properly qualified in many theological sciences relating to the Qur'an, *hadith* or *Sunnah*, Arabic language, *fiqh* and *Shari'ah*, *U'sul al-din* (principles of religion), in addition to having research

skills and scientific ability. In matters touching on other areas of knowledge such as medicine, sociology or demography, good jurists should consult experts in these fields when developing a legal opinion or *fatwa*. This, unfortunately, is rarely done.

6

The Qur'an and family planning including the question of multitude

In as much as family planning is concerned and in the light of careful study and consultation there is no verse in the Qur'an (i.e. no explicit text or *nuss*) which forbids the husband or wife to space pregnancies or reduce their number according to their physical, economic, or cultural abilities, i.e. there is no text prohibiting *al-azl* or other methods of contraception. Nevertheless, the proponents and opponents of family planning use the Qur'an to support their arguments and such interpretative use will be discussed in this chapter.

The question of multitude is given special treatment at the end of the chapter because it is central to all arguments about family planning. It draws upon both the Qur'an and the *Sunnah*.

GENERAL STATEMENT

There is no text (*nuss*) of prohibition of birth control in the Qur'an. According to the rules of jurisprudence, the silence of the Qur'an on some issue is not a matter of omission on the part of the Lawgiver for He is All-Knowing; neither can it be because there was no population problem at the time, for Islam is meant for all times. The silence of the Qur'an on family planning has been interpreted by many theologians to mean that the Qur'an does not prohibit its practice. This is evident in the views of the Grand Imam of Al-Azhar, Sheikh Jadel Haq Ali Jadel Haq who stated that:

«وباستقراء آيات القرآن يتضح أنه لم يرد فيه ما يحرِّم منع الحمل أو الإقلال من النسل»

من كلام الشيخ جاد الحق

A thorough review of the Qur'an revealed no text prohibiting the prevention of pregnancy or diminution of the number of children.

Use of the Qur'an

Despite this the Qur'an has been used by both opponents and proponents of family planning in support of their respective opinions. Of course, there is nothing wrong in there being different interpretations, but the problem is that some people in each group start with a preconceived opinion for which support from the Qur'an is sought. Being convinced of their own opinion and failing to find clear supporting text, they sometimes overstate the meaning of verses to give the appearance of support for their view. The correct method is to start with the Qur'an and the major works of its interpretation (*tafsir*) as well as the *Sunnah*, and then formulate opinion.

This chapter portrays the views of those who argue against family planning and consider it prohibited (*haram*) or disfavored and the views of those who defend family planning and consider it permissible (*halal*). The argument of each group is gleaned from many sources. Sources that cannot be categorically classified pro or con have been used as well to illustrate a point on one side or the other.

The chapter is based partly on published reports by both opponents and proponents and takes some of its arguments from conferences and seminars held over the last fifty years.

THE ISSUE OF EQUATING FAMILY PLANNING WITH INFANTICIDE (WA'D)

This is the most crucial issue debated by opponents and proponents of family planning. Its seriousness comes from the fact that infanticide *wa'd* is a cardinal sin (*kabirah*) and not simply (*haram*). It figures in almost all debates on the legality of family planning.

Opponents

Virtually all opponents of family planning argue strenuously that *al-azl* or any practice that prevents pregnancy is infanticide, something that has been repeatedly condemned and prohibited in the Qur'an[1]. They invoke the following quotations:

Allah warns the poor who kill their children:

وَلَا تَقْتُلُوٓا۟ أَوْلَٰدَكُم مِّنْ إِمْلَٰقٍ نَّحْنُ نَرْزُقُكُمْ وَإِيَّاهُمْ ... ﴿١٥١﴾ الأنعام(٦)

Kill not your children, on a plea of want. We provide sustenance for you and for them.

al-An'am (Sura 6:151)

THE QUR'AN AND FAMILY PLANNING

Those who are afraid to become poor are instructed by Allah:

$$\text{وَلَا تَقْتُلُوٓا۟ أَوْلَٰدَكُمْ خَشْيَةَ إِمْلَٰقٍ ۖ نَّحْنُ نَرْزُقُهُمْ وَإِيَّاكُمْ ۚ إِنَّ قَتْلَهُمْ كَانَ خِطْـًٔا كَبِيرًا ﴿٣١﴾ الإسراء (١٧)}$$

Kill not your children for fear of want, We provide sustenance for them and for you, the killing of them is a great sin.

al-Isra' (Sura 17:31)

The condemnation of *wa'd* or burying children alive is given in Sura 81:

$$\text{وَإِذَا ٱلْمَوْءُۥدَةُ سُئِلَتْ ﴿٨﴾ بِأَىِّ ذَنۢبٍ قُتِلَتْ ﴿٩﴾ التكوير (٨١)}$$

And when the girl-child who was buried alive is asked 'For what sin she was slain?'

al-Takwir (Sura 81:8, 9)

In the women's oath of allegiance (*bai'a*) to the Prophet (PBUH), they were asked

$$\text{... وَلَا يَقْتُلْنَ أَوْلَٰدَهُنَّ ﴿١٢﴾ الممتحنة (٦٠)}$$

And they will not slay their children.
al-Mumtahana (Sura 60:12)

Opponents of family planning go further to consider the above quotations as indirect text (*nuss*) of prohibition; they admit however, that there is no explicit text mentioning contraception as such.[2] They support their claim, by referring to a *hadith* narrated by Judama in which the Prophet is reported to have referred to *al-azl* as hidden *wa'd*. (This *hadith* has become the subject of vehement dispute in Islamic jurisprudence and will be discussed in detail in Chapter 7 (see pp. 136–42).

Proponents

Family planning advocates take issue with those who equate contraception with infanticide or *wa'd*. To them *wa'd* occurs *biologically* when a live born child is slain or buried alive or when a formed fetus is aborted, practices that they, as Muslims, detest and forbid. They maintain that contraception merely prevents pregnancy and involves no killing[3].

In support of their claim they cite Imam Ali who, in the presence of Caliph Omar and other Companions denied that *al-azl* is *wa'd*. Imam Ali maintained that *wa'd* could only apply once the fetus reached the seventh stage of creation, i.e. the stage of being 'another creature' (*khalqan'aakhar*). He based his opinion on the verses in Sura al-Mu'minoun explaining the stages of creation:

$$\text{وَلَقَدْ خَلَقْنَا الْإِنسَانَ مِن سُلَالَةٍ مِّن طِينٍ ۝ ثُمَّ جَعَلْنَاهُ نُطْفَةً فِي قَرَارٍ مَّكِينٍ ۝ ثُمَّ خَلَقْنَا النُّطْفَةَ عَلَقَةً فَخَلَقْنَا الْعَلَقَةَ مُضْغَةً فَخَلَقْنَا الْمُضْغَةَ عِظَامًا فَكَسَوْنَا الْعِظَامَ لَحْمًا ثُمَّ أَنشَأْنَاهُ خَلْقًا آخَرَ ۚ فَتَبَارَكَ اللَّهُ أَحْسَنُ الْخَالِقِينَ ۝}$$

المؤمنون (٢٣)

Man We did create from a quintessence of clay;

Then We placed him as (a drop of) sperm [*nutfa*] in a place of rest firmly fixed;

Then We made the sperm into a clot of congealed blood [*alaqa*];

Then of that clot We made a [fetus] lump [*mudgha*];

Then We made out of that lump bones;

And clothed the bones with flesh;

Then We developed of it 'another creature' [*khalqan'aakhar*];

'Blessed be Allah, the best to create.'

al-Mu'minoun (Sura 23: 12, 13, 14)

Caliph Omar agreed with Imam Ali and praised him for his interpretation. There is a similar tradition concerning Ibn Abbas who also denied that *al-azl* is infanticide and practiced it himself. He again based his opinion on the same verses of creation.

As to Judama's *hadith*, proponents of family planning note the following:

- The *hadith* has been considered weak by some *'ulama'*,
- The expression of 'hidden *wa'd*' is like the saying that 'Dissimulation is hidden *shirk* [taking partners to Allah].' Neither expression equates the practice with the actual *wa'd* or *shirk*[4].
- Another expression 'minor *wa'd*' is closer to infanticide than hidden *wa'd*[5], but has nothing to do with *al-azl*. The Prophet himself, denied categorically that *al-azl* is *minor wa'd* (See Chapter 7).
- Imam Ali and Iman Ibn Abbas have denied equating *al-azl* with *wa'd*, as stated above.

- Many Companions practised *al-azl*, if it were *wa'd* (i.e. a cardinal sin) the Qur'an or the Prophet would have prohibited the practice.
- The followers of the companions (*al-tabi'oun*) continued to practice *al-azl* which confirms that the permissibility was not abrogated as Ibn Hazm claimed (Chapter 7).
- Even among opponents, some admit that contraception may be used in individual cases, albeit reluctantly, while vehemently opposing its general introduction as a matter of national policy. This implies that contraception is not *wa'd*.

PREDESTINATION (*QADAR*), PROVISION (*RIZQ*) AND RELIANCE ON ALLAH (*TAWAKKUL*)

Opponents of family planning consider the use of contraception to control one's progeny to be in opposition to predestination, i.e. a mistrust in the ability of Allah to provide for children or simply a negation of basic reliance on Allah. They cite numerous verses from the Qur'an to support their opinion.

Predestination (*qadar*)

They affirm that, if Allah wants a child to be conceived, family planning will not prevent it, because everything hinges upon the will of Allah:

وَمَا تَشَاءُونَ إِلَّا أَن يَشَاءَ ٱللَّهُ رَبُّ ٱلْعَالَمِينَ ﴿٢٩﴾ التكوير (٨١)

But you shall not will except as Allah wills, Master of the Universe.

al-Takwir (Sura 81:29)

قُل لَّا أَمْلِكُ لِنَفْسِي نَفْعًا وَلَا ضَرًّا إِلَّا مَا شَاءَ ٱللَّهُ وَلَوْ كُنتُ أَعْلَمُ ٱلْغَيْبَ لَٱسْتَكْثَرْتُ مِنَ ٱلْخَيْرِ وَمَا مَسَّنِيَ ٱلسُّوٓءُ ... ﴿١٨٨﴾ الأعراف (٧)

Say I have no power to benefit or hurt myself except as Allah wills. Had I knowledge of the unseen, I would have increased my share of good things and adversity would have not touched me.

al-A'raf (Sura 7:18)

Provision (rizq)

$$\text{وَمَا مِن دَآبَّةٍ فِى ٱلْأَرْضِ إِلَّا عَلَى ٱللَّهِ رِزْقُهَا وَيَعْلَمُ مُسْتَقَرَّهَا وَمُسْتَوْدَعَهَا كُلٌّ فِى كِتَابٍ مُّبِينٍ}$$

هود(١١)

There is not a creature on earth, but its sustenance depends on Allah. He knows its habitation and its depository. All is in a clear record [book].

Hud (Sura 11:6)

Thus Allah has granted provision for all His creatures including any conceived children.[6]

Reliance on Allah (tawakkul)

It is a basic concept that the Muslim should rely on Allah for himself and for his children:

$$\text{رَّبَّنَا عَلَيْكَ تَوَكَّلْنَا وَإِلَيْكَ أَنَبْنَا وَإِلَيْكَ ٱلْمَصِيرُ}$$

الممتحنة(٦٠)

[They prayed]: Our Allah! On you we rely, and to you we turn in repentance, and to you is our final journey.

al-Mumtahana (Sura 60:4)

$$\text{وَمَن يَتَّقِ ٱللَّهَ يَجْعَل لَّهُ مَخْرَجًا وَيَرْزُقْهُ مِنْ حَيْثُ لَا يَحْتَسِبُ وَمَن يَتَوَكَّلْ عَلَى ٱللَّهِ فَهُوَ حَسْبُهُ إِنَّ ٱللَّهَ بَالِغُ أَمْرِهِ قَدْ جَعَلَ ٱللَّهُ لِكُلِّ شَىْءٍ قَدْرًا}$$

الطلاق(٦٥)

And he who fears Allah, He will find a way out for him, and He will provide for him from whence he has no expectation, and whosoever relies on Allah, sufficient is Allah for him. Lo! Allah brings his command to pass. Allah has set a measure for all things.

al-Talaq (Sura 65: 2,3)

Family planning proponents as Muslims, have the same beliefs in pre-destination (qadar), i.e. Allah's ability to provide (rizq) and reliance on Allah (tawakkul). They are simply abiding by the rule that 'to have recourse to expedients (al-akhdh bil-asbab) is no negation of reliance on Allah.'

The Prophet was told:

THE QUR'AN AND FAMILY PLANNING

$$\text{فَإِذَا عَزَمْتَ فَتَوَكَّلْ عَلَى اللَّهِ ... ﴿١٥٩﴾}$$
آل عمران (٣)

And when you have made a decision, rely on Allah (for achieving your objective).

al-Imran (Sura 3: 159)

They quote Omar explaining that 'Reliance on Allah means to plant the seeds in the earth, then trust in Allah [for a good crop].' They believe that contraception is only a means the results of which are in the hands of Allah. Contraception can succeed or fail as Allah wills.

The story of Omar when he decided to go to Syria is also recalled. On his way he was told of a serious plague and he wanted to turn back. The celebrated Companion, Abu Obaida Ibn al-Jarrah asked him 'O Omar! Are you running away from Allah's destiny?' Omar soberly replied 'We run from Allah's destiny to Allah's destiny.'

Another example put forward is the threat of a flood: 'Would building dams and fences and establishing new channels to divert the excess water in a flood situation be an opposition to predestination or is that a mistrust in Allah?'7

Proponents also remember a man who asked the Prophet whether to tie his camel or just put his trust in Allah? The Prophet replied

$$\text{« اعقِلْها وتوكَّل »}$$

رواه الترمذي والبيهقي والطبراني

Hobble her and rely on Allah.
Reported by al-Tirmidhi, al-Baihaqi and al-Tabarani

They recall Joseph's interpretation of the Pharaoh's dream and the seven-year plan he devised to help cope with the anticipated bad years. His plan for the 'future' was not considered to be mistrust of Allah or antagonistic to *tawakkul*. After all, it was inspired by Allah.

Islam does not encourage idleness and helplessness in the hope that Allah will provide for man regardless. It is felt that misinterpretation of *tawakkul* and leaving things to heaven with no preparation for the future (i.e. lack of planning) will only contribute to the deterioration of Muslim communities.

In relation to the specific verse (II: 6) about sustenance for all creatures, proponents quote Tafsir al-Manar (interpretation of the Qur'an) as follows:

The verse does not assert that Allah has assured provision for every living creature of every species in the sense that He would create its food and bring it to it whether it sought it by its instinct or by its acquired knowledge. What is meant is that Allah has created for every creature the proper provisions to sustain it. He guided it to how to acquire such provision and has shown it the way to go about it. This is clear in the Qur'an [Sura 20:50].

Our Allah is He who gave unto everything He created its nature, and further guided it aright.

The Tafsir continues:

This disclaims the erroneous views of some poets and men of letters who feel that labour and idleness are one and the same. They see no difference in productivity and absolute inactivity. The right way, according to them, is to place trust in God and thereafter leave it to Him to do the rest. This is shown in the [Arabic] poet's saying:

جرى قلم القضاء بما يكون   فسيّان التحرُّك والسكون
جنون منك أن تسعى لرزق   ويُرزق فى غشاوته الجنين

'The pen of Destiny has written everything that has to happen,
Action and idleness are therefore the same,
It is madness on your part to seek actively for provision,
'God feeds even the fetus in its long sleep.'[8]

Note: this is, no doubt, a gross misinterpretation of the concept of reliance or *tawakkul* in Islam.

PROCREATION

Procreation and the value of children

Family planning opponents emphasize that children have been depicted in the Qur'an as great assets[9]. For example:

ٱلۡمَالُ وَٱلۡبَنُونَ زِينَةُ ٱلۡحَيَوٰةِ ٱلدُّنۡيَا ...

الكهف (١٨)

Wealth and children are the adornment of life.
al-Kahf (Sura 18:46)

وَٱلَّذِينَ يَقُولُونَ رَبَّنَا هَبۡ لَنَا مِنۡ أَزۡوَٰجِنَا وَذُرِّيَّـٰتِنَا قُرَّةَ أَعۡيُنٍ ...

الفرقان (٢٥)

And who say 'O Our Lord. Vouchsafe us comfort of our wives and offsprings. (Make them the joy and apple of our eyes).

al-Furqan (Sura 25:74)

$$\text{هُنَالِكَ دَعَا زَكَرِيَّا رَبَّهُ قَالَ رَبِّ هَبْ لِي مِن لَّدُنكَ ذُرِّيَّةً طَيِّبَةً ۝}$$
$$\text{آل عمران (٣)}$$

There did Zachariah call upon his Lord: 'O my God', said he 'vouchsafe me from myself good descendants'.

al-Imran (Sura 3:38)

Proponents of family planning argue that as the human race exists there must be children, and that children will be or should be the joy of their parents. But this does not translate necessarily into huge numbers of children who cannot be afforded or brought up in the way of Islam. Nor should children and wealth come before good deeds.[10] In support of this argument they cite the full text of verse 46, Sura 18:

$$\text{ٱلْمَالُ وَٱلْبَنُونَ زِينَةُ ٱلْحَيَوٰةِ ٱلدُّنْيَا وَٱلْبَٰقِيَٰتُ ٱلصَّٰلِحَٰتُ خَيْرٌ عِندَ رَبِّكَ ثَوَابًا وَخَيْرٌ أَمَلًا ۝}$$
$$\text{الكهف (١٨)}$$

Wealth and children are the adornment of life, *but* the good deeds which endure are better in your God's sight for reward, and better for hope.

al-Kahf (Sura 18:46)

Thus, begetting children and accumulating wealth will not necessarily satisfy Allah, it is a person's quality and piety that will do this:

$$\text{وَمَا أَمْوَٰلُكُمْ وَلَا أَوْلَٰدُكُم بِٱلَّتِي تُقَرِّبُكُمْ عِندَنَا زُلْفَىٰٓ إِلَّا مَنْ ءَامَنَ وَعَمِلَ صَٰلِحًا فَأُو۟لَٰٓئِكَ لَهُمْ جَزَآءُ ٱلضِّعْفِ بِمَا عَمِلُوا۟ ... ۝}$$
$$\text{سبأ (٣٤)}$$

And it is not your wealth nor your children that will bring you close to Us, but those who believe and do good will, and their reward will be doubled for what they did.

Saba' (Sura 34:37)

The Qur'an goes further to warn that children and wealth may be a temptation (*fitna*) and should not be put before good deeds:

$$\text{وَاعْلَمُوٓاْ أَنَّمَآ أَمْوَٰلُكُمْ وَأَوْلَٰدُكُمْ فِتْنَةٌ وَأَنَّ ٱللَّهَ عِندَهُۥٓ أَجْرٌ عَظِيمٌ ﴿٢٨﴾}$$

الأنفال(٨)

And remember that your wealth and children are but a temptation [fitna], and that with Allah is immense reward.

al-Anfal (Sura 8:28)

Zachariah's prayer (quoted above) was a request to have pious/good children. The Qur'an has many quotations emphasizing the quality of children rather than any children:

$$\text{رَبِّ هَبْ لِى مِنَ ٱلصَّٰلِحِينَ ﴿١٠٠﴾}$$

الصافات(٣٧)

My Lord! Vouchsafe me of the *righteous* [offspring].

al-Saffaat (Sura 37:100)

$$\text{وَإِنِّى سَمَّيْتُهَا مَرْيَمَ وَإِنِّىٓ أُعِيذُهَا بِكَ وَذُرِّيَّتَهَا مِنَ ٱلشَّيْطَٰنِ ٱلرَّجِيمِ ﴿٣٦﴾}$$

آل عمران(٣)

I have named her Maryam, and Lo! I crave your protection for her and for her offspring from Satan, the outcast.

al-Imran (Sura 3:36)

This raises the issue of the ability of a family in the twentieth and twenty-first centuries to raise pious children who are a joy to their parents, an enrichment to their community and a support and defense for their religion. Proponents emphasize the rights of children (see Chapter 2) and doubt that these rights can be fulfilled in the presence of large numbers.

Procreation and marriage

Opponents of family planning believe that procreation is the principal purpose of marriage.[11] They quote the Qur'an:

$$\text{وَٱللَّهُ جَعَلَ لَكُم مِّنْ أَنفُسِكُمْ أَزْوَٰجًا وَجَعَلَ لَكُم مِّنْ أَزْوَٰجِكُم بَنِينَ وَحَفَدَةً وَرَزَقَكُم مِّنَ ٱلطَّيِّبَٰتِ... ﴿٧٢﴾}$$

النحل(١٦)

And Allah has given you wives from yourselves and has given you, from your wives, children and grandchildren and has made provision of good things for you.

al-Nahl (Sura 16:72)

وَلَقَدْ أَرْسَلْنَا رُسُلًا مِن قَبْلِكَ وَجَعَلْنَا لَهُمْ أَزْوَاجًا وَذُرِّيَّةً ... ﴿٣٨﴾ الرعد(١٣)

And verily We sent messengers [to mankind] before you and We gave them wives and children.

al-Ra'd (Sura 13:38)

They also invoke the description of wives in the Qur'an as a tilth to their husbands which implies to them that their continuous cultivation (impregnation) is the norm. They refer to Sura 2:

نِسَآؤُكُمْ حَرْثٌ لَّكُمْ فَأْتُوا حَرْثَكُمْ أَنَّىٰ شِئْتُمْ ... ﴿٢٢٣﴾ البقرة(٢)

Your wives are as tilth unto you, so, Approach your tilth how you wish.

al-Baqara (Sura 2:223)

Proponents of family planning infer that procreation is not the exclusive purpose of marriage[12] (and marital relations) from the following verse:

وَمِنْ ءَايَٰتِهِۦٓ أَنْ خَلَقَ لَكُم مِّنْ أَنفُسِكُمْ أَزْوَاجًا لِّتَسْكُنُوٓا۟ إِلَيْهَا وَجَعَلَ بَيْنَكُم مَّوَدَّةً وَرَحْمَةً ... ﴿٢١﴾ الروم(٣٠)

And one of [Allah's] signs it is that He has created for you mates from yourselves, that you may dwell in tranquility with them. And has ordained between you love and mercy.

al-Rum (Sura 30:21)

As to women as tilth to their husbands, this has been repeatedly interpreted as exactly the opposite from that claimed by the opponents. Ibn Abbas and other Companions explained it to mean 'your tilth, if you wish you can water it, and if you wish you can leave it thirsty'. Some Companions refer directly to *al-azl*. Sa'id Ibn al-Musayyab explains: 'Your tilth: You are free to practice *al-azl* [for contraception] with them if you wish, or do not practice it, if you wish' (see Chapter 7).

ADDITIONAL ARGUMENTS

Opponents refer to children as Allah's gifts

Some opponents try to accumulate additional support for their opinion by referring to children as gifts or provisions of God. Begetting them is *halal*; preventing them is therefore a way of forbidding what God has allowed. This is the argument of Maulana Maudoudi[13] who interprets the following verse to be applicable to pregnancy prevention:

قَدْ خَسِرَ ٱلَّذِينَ قَتَلُوٓاْ أَوْلَـٰدَهُمْ سَفَهَۢا بِغَيْرِ عِلْمٍ وَحَرَّمُواْ مَا رَزَقَهُمُ ٱللَّهُ ٱفْتِرَآءً عَلَى ٱللَّهِ ...

الأنعام(٦)

Losers are those who, from folly, have slain their children, without knowledge, and have forbidden that which Allah bestowed upon them (of *risq* and food), inventing a lie against Allah.

al-Anʿam (Sura 6:140)

Proponents find Maulana Maudoudi's interpretation to be biased. In his zeal to fight the family planning movement (which he felt to be directed against Islam) he tried to use the verse to discourage family planning.

Proponents find evidence for spacing

Proponents try to find indirect evidence from the Qur'an to support their argument and they believe they found it in the issue of breast-feeding and weaning.[14] The Qur'an says

وَٱلْوَٰلِدَٰتُ يُرْضِعْنَ أَوْلَـٰدَهُنَّ حَوْلَيْنِ كَامِلَيْنِ لِمَنْ أَرَادَ أَن يُتِمَّ ٱلرَّضَاعَةَ ...

البقرة(٢)

And mothers shall suckle their children two full years for those who wish to complete breast-feeding.

al-Baqara (Sura 2:233)

In another verse a child's weaning was specified to be in two years:

... وَفِصَـٰلُهُۥ فِى عَامَيْنِ ...

لقمان(٣١)

And his weaning is in two years.

Luqman (Sura 31:14)

If to the two years of weaning is added the minimal six months length of a pregnancy that can produce a viable child under normal circumstances, the result will be 30 months The Qur'an says

$$\text{وَحَمْلُهُ وَفِصَالُهُ ثَلَاثُونَ شَهْرًا ...} \quad \text{الأحقاف(٤٦)}$$

His bearing and weaning is thirty months.
al-Ahqaf (Sura 46:15)

These two verses are taken to be a recommendation for child spacing to enable the mother to breast-feed her child (with supplementary food as the child grows). During this period, a new pregnancy is discouraged. The Prophet (PBUH) warned against a woman getting pregnant in the period of breast-feeding, calling it *al-ghayl, ghaylah* or *gheyal* (assault on the child) (see Chapter 7).

The question is how can a couple avoid pregnancy in the two-year interval after the birth of a child? They can abstain completely from sex, which is an unacceptable hardship for both of them in monogamous marriage, and for the wife, in particular in polygynous marriage. The alternative is to use *al-azl* or other methods to prevent pregnancy.

It seems, therefore, that the principle of child spacing has support from the Qur'an. This was the understanding of Sheikh Shaltout, the former Grand Imam of Al-Azhar. He said in his *fatwa* of 1959:

«والتنظيم بهذا المعنى لايجافي الطبيعه ، ولا يأباه الوعي القومي ، ولا تمنعه الشريعة إن لم تكن تطلبه وتحث عليه ، فقد حدّد القرآن مدة الرضاع بحَولَين كاملين وحذّر الرسول صلوات الله عليه أن يُرضِعَ الطفل من لبن الحامل»

Family planning in this sense is not incompatible with nature, and is not disagreeable to national conscience and is not forbidden by the *Shari'ah* if not prescribed by it and sought after. *The Qur'an* fixed the period of lactation at two full years, and *the Prophet* warned against feeding a baby from the milk of a pregnant mother. This argues in favour of allowing steps to be taken to prevent pregnancy during the period of breast-feeding.

(The complete text of the *fatwa* is given in Appendix 2)

THE QUESTION OF MULTITUDE (*KATHRAH*)

The question of multitude (*kathrah*) or numbers has been a key issue in this debate because its advocates believe that the larger the number of Muslims and the higher their growth rate the greater their power and the closer they are to pleasing Allah and His messenger. They proclaim that multitude is ordained by religion and that failure to achieve it is a deviation from the right path. They find support for their view not only in the Qur'an but also in the

Sunnah. Hence, they oppose family planning especially if the practice is called for by a community, i.e. if it goes beyond individual use. They claim that family planning, having originated in the west, represents a clear conspiracy to reduce the number of Muslims and diminish their power. Advocates of such a view are unlikely to reconcile their position with that of family planning proponents.[15]

Those supporting family planning, on the other hand, believe that the future of today's Muslims has more to do with quality, piety and solidarity than sheer numbers. They do not believe that the Islamic world lacks numbers. They see a need for greater solidarity and co-operation among Muslim countries, as well as for more spiritual, socio-economic and technological training and excellence. They view the rapid population growth in most Muslim countries as the most serious obstacle to the development process.

A case in point is Egypt, where President Nasser was strongly opposed to population programmes during the first decade of his rule. Then, realizing what uncontrolled population growth was doing to his country, he proclaimed:

> Population increase constitutes the most dangerous obstacle that faces the Egyptian people in their drive towards raising the standard of production in their country in an effective and efficient way. Attempts at family planning deserve the most sincere efforts by modern scientific methods.[16]

What follows contrasts the nine points of the argument of the advocates of multitude with the views of the proponents of family planning.

Advocates of multitude

1. Man as Allah's viceroy (khalifa) on earth

Advocates of multitude refer back to the origin of man and his mission on the earth. The Qur'an is quoted:

وَإِذْ قَالَ رَبُّكَ لِلْمَلَٰئِكَةِ إِنِّي جَاعِلٌ فِي ٱلْأَرْضِ خَلِيفَةً ... ﴿٣٠﴾

البقرة(٢)

And when Allah said unto the angels: Lo! I am about to place a viceroy on the earth.

al-Baqara (Sura 2:30)

Man was then reminded that his mission is to inhabit and develop the earth:

$$\text{هُوَ أَنشَأَكُم مِّنَ ٱلْأَرْضِ وَٱسْتَعْمَرَكُمْ فِيهَا} \dots \text{هود(١١)}$$

He brought you forth from the earth and delegated you to inhabit and develop it.

Hud (Sura 11:61)

In order to inhabit and develop the earth, man is ordained to multiply:

$$\text{يَٰٓأَيُّهَا ٱلنَّاسُ ٱتَّقُوا۟ رَبَّكُمُ ٱلَّذِى خَلَقَكُم مِّن نَّفْسٍ وَٰحِدَةٍ وَخَلَقَ مِنْهَا زَوْجَهَا وَبَثَّ مِنْهُمَا رِجَالًا كَثِيرًا وَنِسَآءً} \dots \text{النساء(٤)}$$

O mankind! Be careful of your duty to your Allah who created you from a single soul, and from it created its mate, and from them twain, has spread a multitude of men and women.

al-Nisa' (Sura 4:1)

2. Procreation

Under the above circumstances, to the advocates of multitude, procreation is a most natural approach to, and endorsement of multitude for which marriage was considered the natural way (*fitrah*) in Islam. Procreation is the purpose of marriage.

$$\text{وَٱللَّهُ جَعَلَ لَكُم مِّنْ أَنفُسِكُمْ أَزْوَٰجًا وَجَعَلَ لَكُم مِّنْ أَزْوَٰجِكُم بَنِينَ وَحَفَدَةً} \dots \text{النحل(١٦)}$$

And Allah has made for you mates from yourselves and made for you out of them children and grandchildren.

al-Nahl (Sura 16:72)

The Prophet (PBUH) is reminded that Prophets before him took wives and had children:

$$\text{وَلَقَدْ أَرْسَلْنَا رُسُلًا مِّن قَبْلِكَ وَجَعَلْنَا لَهُمْ أَزْوَٰجًا وَذُرِّيَّةً} \dots \text{الرعد(١٣)}$$

And verily we sent messengers [to mankind] before you, and we gave them wives and offspring.

al-R'ad (Sura 13:38)

Multitude was explicitly blessed in the Qur'an where Sho'ib reminded his people of Allah's reward. If multitude is not the ultimate objective for man, the advocates say, it would not have been considered one of Allah's signs and gifts for pious communities. Says Sho'ib to his people:

$$\text{وَاذْكُرُوٓا۟ إِذْ كُنتُمْ قَلِيلًا فَكَثَّرَكُمْ} ... ﴿٨٦﴾$$
$$\text{الأعراف (٧)}$$

And remember, when you were but few, how did He
help you multiply.

al-A'raf (Sura 7:86)

Besides satisfying Allah's purpose, children are quite a joy in themselves. The Qur'an describes the believers:

$$\text{وَٱلَّذِينَ يَقُولُونَ رَبَّنَا هَبْ لَنَا مِنْ أَزْوَٰجِنَا وَذُرِّيَّٰتِنَا قُرَّةَ أَعْيُنٍ} ... ﴿٧٤﴾$$
$$\text{الفرقان (٢٥)}$$

And who say 'Our Lord! Vouchsafe us comfort of our wives and our offspring' (make them the joy and the apple of our eyes).

al-Furqan (Sura 25:74)

3. *Additional support from the* Sunnah

Advocates of multitude are comfortable with the above Qur'anic support and imply that the Qur'an is in principle against family planning. They claim more direct support from the *Sunnah,* however.

While some of the traditions cited are considered weak, (or less than sound) Shiekh Abu Zahra (1976)[17] claims that they strengthen one another. For example, the prophet says

$$\text{«تناكحوا تكثروا (وفى رواية تناكحوا تناسلوا تكثروا) ، فإنى مباهٍ بكم الأمم يوم القيامة»}$$

$$\text{رواه ابن مردويه فى تفسيره من حديث ابن عمر بسند ضعَّفه العراقى ، رواه كذلك عبد الرازق فى مصنَّفه من حديث ابن أبى هلال مرسلاً بسند ضعَّفه الزبيدى. كذلك رواه أبو داود}$$

Marry and multiply, for I shall make a display of you before other nations on the Day of Judgement.

Authenticated by Ibn Mardaweih with a narration considered weak by
al-Iraqi, and also by Abdel Razik with a narration considered weak by
Zabidi, also reported by Abu Dawoud

Advocates recall with conviction that the Prophet (PBUH) has prayed for Anas Ibn Malik, his aide, that Allah may give him plenty of wealth and children. Prayers of this kind, advocates maintain, can only be for something good and preferred, and since they come from the Prophet (PBUH), such prayers confirm the preference of many children.

Advocates of multitude take these texts as clear invitations from the Prophet for Muslims to increase the number of their offspring so that they can outnumber other nations.

4. Preference of a prolific wife

Advocates argue that in order to sustain these numbers, the Prophet (PBUH) has encouraged marrying a prolific rather than an infertile woman. They cite the following tradition:

»من حديث عن معقل بن يسار قال :
جاء رجل الى رسول الله صلى الله عليه وسلم فقال : يارسول الله أصبتُ امرأة ذات حسب ومنصب وجمال . إلاَّ أنَّها لا تلد . أفتزوجها ؟ فنهاه . ثم أتاه الثانيةَ فنهاه . ثم أتاه الثالثة فقال : تزوجوا الودودَ الولودَ فإني مباهٍ بكم الأمم«

رواه أبو داود والنسائي

A man came to the Prophet (PBUH) to ask his advice about a wealthy woman, who came from a prestigious family but was infertile. He asked the Prophet 'Should I marry her?' The Prophet did not agree with him. He came back twice with the same response. On the third time the Prophet said 'Marry the affectionate prolific woman, for I shall make a display of you before other nations.'

Authenticated by Abu Dawoud and an-Nassa'i

5. Wives as tilth

Advocates also cite the Qur'anic description of wives being as tilth unto their husbands. The expression denotes that the process of cultivation (impregnation) is implicit. The prevention of pregnancy would violate this interpretation of the verse.

These quotations sustain those who advocate procreation as the primary purpose of marriage so that the Prophet (PBUH) can boast of the number of his nation before other nations.

6. Multitude as source of power and development

It is common sense, the advocates say, that multitude is desired by all nations. It is the source of the work force, of military strength, and of those who help in the process of social, spiritual and economic development. To its advocate, the concept of multitude is also the source of genius and philosophers – the wider the population base, the greater the probability of finding people of excellence.

To the advocates, the Islamic world is so vast that it can maintain many times its current population. It has riches of many kinds: some, like oil, minerals, agricultural products, etc. are already being tapped. Great riches remain stored in the good earth and elsewhere in the Islamic world, but need more hands and talents to discover and develop them. By far the most precious wealth in the Islamic world is Muslims themselves.

7. Family planning as conspiracy
Among those who think that the family planning movement is a conspiracy to reduce the number and power of Muslims, Sheikh al-Bahayy al-Kholi believes that the call for family planning pleases the enemies of Islam. He urged instead that the population growth rate should be increased.[18] The views of Sheikh Abu Zahra and Maulana Maudoudi – that support for family planning is a malicious conspiracy against Islam – are also well known.

8. Muslim Minorities
Advocates of multitude maintain that the Muslim minorities would certainly vanish if they were to accept family planning.

9. The Questions of Waʿd and Rizq
Those favoring multitude also question contraception as being a form of *waʾd*, and family planning as being in defiance of Allah's will reflecting mistrust in His ability to provide for His people. Some also deny the permissibility of *al-azl* and consider Judama's tradition (see Chapter 7) as an abrogation of the other traditions that permit *al-azl*.

A point of reconciliation
Despite these arguments, most advocates of multitude accept Jabir's traditions and allow contraception for individual use in presence of a valid reason. Most of the acceptable 'reasons' relate to the mother's health and the needs of a suckling child. However, such provisions must not be the basis for a community or nation-wide campaign or a law coercing people into family planning against their will. Rigorously rejected also are approaches using negative incentives, i.e. punishing parents (and indirectly the child) in situations where a specified quota is exceeded.

Response by proponents of family planning
Proponents of family planning take issue with most of the claims of the advocates of multitude especially if multitude is uncontrolled. They emphasize two simple principles:

1. Multitude can be achieved with few children who are well spaced and conceived by healthy mothers at ages that are not too young or too late according to advice of Muslim physicians.

   Note: some proponents make a demographic error when they claim that having one child will fulfill the ordinance of multitude.[19] In Muslim countries there should be no fewer than two children per family if population is not to decline.
2. The quality of Muslims should not be compromised in favor of sheer numbers. A huge but weak, underdeveloped fragmented Muslim nation with much sickness, poverty, debt, illiteracy and apathy cannot be the subject of pride for the Prophet (PBUH) on the day of judgement.

Proponents fear that rapid population growth with maldistribution of resources are contributing factors to the inevitable situation of Muslim nations today.[20]

Point by point responses to the claims of the advocates now follow.

1. Man as Allah's viceroy on earth

Proponents of family planning accept what is said about man as Allah's viceroy on earth. They add several points, however.

The purpose of creation is to populate and develop the earth, but a supervening objective is to worship Allah as He should be worshipped:

وَمَا خَلَقْتُ الْجِنَّ وَالْإِنسَ إِلَّا لِيَعْبُدُونِ ۝ الذاريات(٥١)

I created the Jinn and humankind only that they might worship Me.

al-Dhariyat (Sura 51:56)

This verse puts the ultimate purpose of man's creation into sharp focus with his duties as viceroy. Man (in this case the Muslim) should be capable physically, spiritually, socially and intellectually to raise the word of Allah on earth. In the beginning of Islam, multitude was unquestioned given the small numbers and the prevalence of disease and disasters plus wars and the human toll exacted by them. Today, multitude continues to be needed but not necessarily in huge numbers. If numbers undermine the quality of Allah's nation in raising His word on earth, then they should be adjusted. A populous Muslim nation that is incapable of raising its children in the Islamic way, representing Allah's religion in a convincing manner, defending its territories and holy shrines against its enemies or commanding the respect of other nations, which is inefficient in keeping its members healthy, literate and united – or a nation such as that is not in conformity with Allah's command and

His Messenger's design. Certainly, such a nation is anything but a subject for the Prophet's pride.

The Prophet predicted:

»يُوشِكُ الأممُ أن تَداعَى عليكم ، كما تَداعَى الأكلةُ إلى قصعتها ، قالوا أوَمِنْ قلَّةٍ نحنُ يومئذٍ يارسول الله ؟ قال : لا . إنكم يومئذٍ لكثير،ولكنكم (كَثرة) كغُثاءِ السيل ولَينزعنَّ الله من قلوب أعدائكم المهابة منكم ، وليقذفنَّ اللهُ في قلوبكم الوَهَن.قالوا : وما الوَهَن يارسول الله ؟ قال : حبُّ الدنيا وكراهيةُ الموت«

رواه أبو داود في السنن

'Nations are about [in the future] to gather together to fall upon you as people would fall upon a trencher to eat.' The Companions asked if that would be because of their small members at the time and the Prophet replied 'No! You will then be of great multitude; but you will be scum like that carried down by a torrent. And Allah will take fear of you from the breasts of your enemy and cast enervation (*wahan*) into your hearts.' He was asked the meaning of enervation and he replied 'Love of the world and dislike of death.'

Authenticated by Abu Dawoud in his Sunan

Thus the multitude that should be promoted is a multitude of quality and not only quantity. Muslim demographers, physicians, social scientists and development specialists warn that rapid population growth in many Muslim countries is an obstacle to spiritual, social, economic and technological development.[21] These facts explain the Prophet's prediction.

The Qur'an also reminds us that the value lies in quality not quantity:

قُل لَّا يَسْتَوِي ٱلْخَبِيثُ وَٱلطَّيِّبُ وَلَوْ أَعْجَبَكَ كَثْرَةُ ٱلْخَبِيثِ ... ﴿١٠٠﴾

المائدة(٥)

Say the evil and the good are not equal, even though the multitude of evil may dazzle you.

al-Ma'ida (Sura 5:100)

كَم مِّن فِئَةٍ قَلِيلَةٍ غَلَبَتْ فِئَةً كَثِيرَةً بِإِذْنِ ٱللَّهِ ... ﴿٢٤٩﴾

البقرة(٢)

How oft, by Allah's will, has a small host vanquished a large host.

al-Baqara (Sura 2:249)

The Qur'an emphasizes that quantity without quality can be risky to the nation. The battle of Hunayn is given as example:

لَقَدْ نَصَرَكُمُ ٱللَّهُ فِى مَوَاطِنَ كَثِيرَةٍ وَيَوْمَ حُنَيْنٍ إِذْ أَعْجَبَتْكُمْ كَثْرَتُكُمْ فَلَمْ تُغْنِ عَنكُمْ شَيْئًا وَضَاقَتْ عَلَيْكُمُ ٱلْأَرْضُ بِمَا رَحُبَتْ ثُمَّ وَلَّيْتُم مُّدْبِرِينَ ﴿٢٥﴾

التوبة (٩)

Allah has given you victory in many battles; but on the day of Hunayn, when you exalted in your multitude, it availed you naught. And the earth, vast as it is, became tight for you, then you turned back in retreat.

al-Tawba (Sura 9:25)

2. Procreation

Proponents of family planning agree that procreation is a purpose of marriage and that marriage is the normal natural way (*fitrah*) in Islam. This in no way antagonizes the keenness to have children of quality.

In the first place, God's messengers pray to Allah that they will have 'good, pious' children, and not delinquent children. Likewise, believers pray for offspring, who would be the apple of their eyes.

The Qur'an illustrates this concern for healthy thriving children as follows:

أَيَوَدُّ أَحَدُكُمْ أَن تَكُونَ لَهُ جَنَّةٌ مِّن نَّخِيلٍ وَأَعْنَابٍ تَجْرِى مِن تَحْتِهَا ٱلْأَنْهَٰرُ لَهُ فِيهَا مِن كُلِّ ٱلثَّمَرَٰتِ وَأَصَابَهُ ٱلْكِبَرُ وَلَهُ ذُرِّيَّةٌ ضُعَفَآءُ فَأَصَابَهَآ إِعْصَارٌ فِيهِ نَارٌ فَٱحْتَرَقَتْ كَذَٰلِكَ يُبَيِّنُ ٱللَّهُ لَكُمُ ٱلْأَيَٰتِ لَعَلَّكُمْ تَتَفَكَّرُونَ ﴿٢٦٦﴾ البقرة (٢)

Would any of you like to have a garden of palm trees and vines, with rivers flowing underneath it, [and] with all kinds of fruit for him therein; and old age has stricken him and he has *feeble offspring*; and a fiery whirlwind strikes it (the garden) and it is all consumed by fire? Thus, Allah makes plain his illustrations unto you in order that you may think them over.

al-Baqara (Sura 2:266)

The Qur'an also questions whether a large number of children is necessarily a sign of Allah's blessing:

$$\text{أَيَحْسَبُونَ أَنَّمَا نُمِدُّهُم بِهِۦ مِن مَّالٍ وَبَنِينَ ۝ نُسَارِعُ لَهُمْ فِى ٱلْخَيْرَٰتِ ۚ بَل لَّا يَشْعُرُونَ ۝}$$

المؤمنون (٢٣)

Do they think that in the wealth and children wherewith we provide them, we hasten unto them with good things? Nay, but they perceive not.

al-Mu'minin (Sura 23:55, 56)

3. Additional support from the Sunnah

The Prophet is reported to have felt that having too many children without the means to take care of them is quite a trial:

$$\text{«جَهْدُ البَلَاءِ كَثْرَةُ العِيَالِ مَعَ قِلَّةِ الشَّيءِ»}$$

رواه الحاكم عن عبد الله بن عمر

The most grueling trial is to have plenty of children with no adequate means.

Authenticated by al-Hakim, on the authority of Abdullah Ibn Omar.

Ibn Abbas, the great exponent in the community of believers, is also reported to have declared that having too many children is an invitation to hardship:

$$\text{قال ابن عباس :}$$
$$\text{«إنَّ كَثْرَةَ العِيَالِ أحدُ الفَقْرَينِ ، وقِلَّةَ العِيَالِ أحدُ اليَسَارَينِ»}$$

رواه القضاعي في مسند الشهاب

A multitude of children is one of the two poverties [or cases of penury], while a small number is one of the two cases of ease.

Authenticated by Quda'ei in Musnad al-Shahab

Of the two cases of poverty, one is that a large number of dependants can overburden the provider to the point of exhaustion; the other is that the lack of pecuniary means can result in the inability to provide adequately for one's family. The two cases of ease are first the availability of comfortable circumstances and the fact that a small number of children can be raised correctly and comfortably within those means. Although the quotation centers on material means, it implicitly suggests that spiritual, intellectual, literary and other needs can be more efficiently met where the family is smaller.[22]

Furthermore, Imam al-Shafe'i finds a reference in the Qur'an to the issue of family size. This is in the third verse in Sura al-Nisa' (4: 3) which instructs Muslims who cannot deal equitably with many wives to be satisfied with only one. Most interpreters read this to mean that being satisfied with one wife is a way to avoid injustice, but Imam al-Shafe'i, an expert in the Arabic language, concluded that the expression:

ذَٰلِكَ أَدْنَىٰ أَلَّا تَعُولُوا ۝

النساء(٤)

Thalika adna alla ta'oulu

al-Nisa' (Sura 4:3)

had a more reaching meaning. He explained it as 'so that you will not have to support too many children'. Reported by Imam Ibn al-Qayyim in his book about the newborn,[23] this interpretation led to a series of linguistic debates concerning the Arabic expression as given below (See also at Sharabassi, 1965):

«فسر الإمام الشافعى قوله تعالى:
«ذلك أدنى ألا تعولوا» بقوله: أى لاتكثر عيالكم.
وهذا القول من الإمام يدل على أن قلة العيال أولى.

وقد نقل هذا القول عن الإمام الشافعى الإمامُ ابن القيِّم فى كتابه « تحفة الودود بأحكام المولود». وإن كان لم يخترِه، وردَّ عليه بردود كثيرة. كما نقلَ هذا القولَ إلإمام القرطبى فى تفسيره «الجامع لأحكام القرآن». وقد شارك الشافعىَّ فى هذا التفسير غيرُه من الأئمة.

وقد ادَّعى الثعلبى أن هذا الرأى لم يقله غير الشافعى، لأنه ــ كما يُدَّعى ــ لايقال: «عال الرجل ، بمعنى كثر أولاده. بل يقال فى ذلك: «أعال الرجل». وردَّ القرطبى عليه بأن هذا التفسير الذى قاله الشافعى قد رواه الدَّارقطنى فى سننه عن زيد بن أسلم، وهو أيضا قول جابر بن زيد، ثم قال القرطبى : «فهذان إمامان من علماء المسلمين وأئمتهم قد سبقا الشافعىَّ إليه».

ولقد ذكر الكسائى وأبو عمر الدروى وابن الأعرابى ــ وهم من العلماء البُصراء باللغة ــ أن العرب تقول: «عال الرجل ، أى كثر عياله». وقال

أبو عمر الدروى: إن هذه لغة حِمْيَر ، واستشهد على ذلك بقول الشاعر:
وإن الموت يأخذ كل حُيٍّ   بلا شك ، وإن أمشى وعالا
أى كثر عياله. ولذلك قال أبو حاتم «كان الشافعى أعلم بلغة العرب منا».

وفوق هذا فهناك قراءة معتمدة تقول: «ذلك أدنى ألا تُعِيلُوا». وهى حجة للشافعى بلا جدال.

ومما يؤكد قولَ القرطبى من أن جابر بن زيد قال بهذا الرأى مارواه شيخ المفسرين ابن جرير الطبرى فى تفسيره المشهور «جامع البيان» ونصه كما يلى:

«حدثنا يونس قال: اخبرنا ابن وهب قال: قال ابن زيد: (ذلك أدنى ألاَّ تعولوا) ذلك أقل لنفقتك ، الواحدة أقل من ثنتين وثلاث وأربع ، ...
... (ألا تعولوا) أهون عليك فى العيال.»

عن الشيخ الشرباصى(٢٣)

This quotation deals with linguistic derivations in Arabic which are difficult to translate. It shows that while some disagree with al-Shafe'i's interpretation the experts in the Arabic language agree with his usage of 'ta'oulu' to mean having children. This was used in this sense even before the time of al-Shafe'i who was an expert in both jurisprudence and the Arabic language.

4. *Preference for a prolific wife*
Family planning proponents, while accepting the preference where possible for a prolific wife who can give her husband the number of children he desires, raise a number of issues:

- They believe that a barren woman should not become an outcast. In the first place, being infertile is not always her fault. The Qur'an says

وَيَجْعَلُ مَن يَشَآءُ عَقِيمًا ... ۝   الشورى(٤٢)

And He (Allah) makes barren whom He will.
al-Shura (Sura 42:50)

While some women (and men) are born infertile, in some situations it may have resulted from acquired diseases. In 40 per cent of cases the reason for infertility lies with the husband not the wife.

- If we have to select the fertile, how can we judge whether or not a virgin is fertile?[24] Judging a woman's fecundity by her sister's is not medically accurate, since her sister's infertility does not necessarily mean she too is infertile.
- No jurist in Islam has judged that a barren woman should not be married, or if she is married and does not carry children, that she should be divorced.[25]
- Some theologians believe that the Prophet (PBUH), in discouraging the man who sought his permission to marry a barren but rich and prestigious woman, may have sensed that the interest of the man lay in the woman's wealth and prestige. These are not primary reasons for marriage in Islam.[26]
- Most of the Prophet's wives, including Sayyida A'isha did not give him children.

Proponents of family planning feel that a barren woman should have a chance to enjoy marital life. Furthermore, they advise strongly that treatment and control of infertility should be an integral part of family planning.

5. *Wives as tilth*
As to wives as tilth upon their husbands, proponents note that this verse was explained by four celebrated Companions (Ibn Abbas, Ibn Omar, Sa'id Ibn al-Mussayyab, and Zayd Ibn Thabit) as follows:

> You are free to practice *al-azl* [for contraception] with them if you wish, or do not practice it, if you wish.

or

> Your tilth, you may water it if you wish or you may leave it thirsty, if you wish [see Chapter 7].

6. *Multitude as source of power and development*
Proponents agree that multitude could be a source of power and development, provided that the following are applied:

1. It is adjusted to the family's or country's needs and means. The family and/or country should have the capacity and means to raise children correctly from the spiritual, physical, social, educational and intellectual viewpoints.

2. The leadership in the community or country should work through a well thought-out development plan and should provide religious direction.
3. The Muslim world is vast indeed and has a wealth of resources, but they are maldistributed. The Muslim world encompasses some of the richest countries in the world side by side with some of the poorest. Will the rich Muslim countries share their wealth with the poor ones? Will the sparsely populated Muslim countries accommodate population surpluses from overcrowded Muslim countries?

    The Muslim world is composed of many sovereign states. Their very sovereignty belies imposing a policy that the countries with small population and vast resources should accept Muslims from poor and populous nations. Similarly, it is not realistic to ask rich Muslim nations to share their resources equitably with the poor Muslim nations. Someday this may happen, but until then we should plan with what *we have now*.

7. Family planning as conspiracy

As to the theory that the family planning movement is a conspiracy against Islam, proponents of family planning advance the following concepts:

- Rather than starting in the west, family planning originated fourteen centuries ago in Islam and the credit to Islam for this should not be denied by zealots of multitude.
- Muslim countries are free to accept or reject outside assistance in health, agricultural and other development programs including family planning.[27] Grants for family planning constitute a small percentage (2 percent) of the aid for development and health from the more to the less developed countries.
- The family planning 'conspiracy' claim advanced by some opponents is not consistent with the much wider prevalence of contraceptive use in western countries than in the rest of the world. A conspiracy means they are calling upon us to do what they do not do in their own countries, a claim that is not demographically correct.
- Furthermore, Muslim countries have the freedom to determine their own population policies in accordance with their own national objectives.

8. Muslim minorities

Proponents of family planning call for Muslim minorities to select the population policies that suit their needs and secure their future. They may choose high fertility with spacing, which is quite plausible for all Muslims. They should also develop their scientific/technical abilities and improve their quality remembering that:

THE QUR'AN AND FAMILY PLANNING

إِن يَكُن مِّنكُمْ عِشْرُونَ صَٰبِرُونَ يَغْلِبُوا۟ مِا۟ئَتَيْنِ وَإِن يَكُن مِّنكُم مِّا۟ئَةٌ يَغْلِبُوٓا۟ أَلْفًا مِّنَ ٱلَّذِينَ كَفَرُوا۟ بِأَنَّهُمْ قَوْمٌ لَّا يَفْقَهُونَ ۝

الأنفال(٨)

If there be of you twenty steadfast they will overcome two hundred, and if there be of you a hundred (steadfast) they shall overcome a thousand of those who disbelieve, because they (the disbelievers) are a folk who do not understand.

al-Anfal (Sura 8:65)

This verse makes it clear that knowledge, technology and the will of a people to fight for a worthy cause are the qualities that make a difference and decide the future of a nation. In the case of minorities, a good balance of numbers and quality is the best policy. They are, however, allowed more leverage with numbers.

9. *The question of* wa'd *and* rizq

Proponents of family planning comment on the issues of *al-azl* as *wa'd*, and the issues of rizq, tawakkul and others in much the same way as they did earlier in this chapter.

Multitude versus harm to the mother: a juristic evaluation

In 1974 Sheikh Mohammad M. Shamsuddin introduced the juristic argument that 'multitude' could be desirable if it caused no harm to the mother. He further argued that the ruling of averting harm is more binding than the one desiring multitude. (His views are detailed on page 166)

A demographic and cultural note

How can multitude be Islamic?

Demographic sciences tell us that societies which have high fertility and declining mortality grow fast. Muslim populations grow faster than other groups as revealed by the following data based on information from the United Nations (1991).

	% growth per year	*Years to double the population*
The Islamic world	3.0	23
The world as a whole	1.7	40
Japan/Europe	0.3	230

The 1991 estimate of the Islamic world is one billion two hundred million and is expected to double to 2.5 billion in twenty-five years. The Muslim world will continue to grow because of the young age structure, large family norms and declining mortality. Even with rigorous family planning, the growth rate will continue to be above the stable population level during the twenty-first Century. Thus, there is no question of continued increase. The question is what quality of Muslim will be produced and how can the multitude be more Islamic.

Requirements of Islamic multitude

You may recall that the Prophet (PBUH) predicted a multitude of Muslims that would be ineffective, vulnerable and no match for its enemies. For the multitude to be more Islamic and acceptable to the Prophet (PBUH), it must satisfy certain requirements strictly and completely. The requirements, given in the Figure 6.1, have been formulated by myself in accordance with the spirit of *Shari'ah*.

Figure 6.1 Requirements of Islamic multitude

1. A multitude of high moral character.
2. A multitude of recognized scientific excellence.
3. A multitude of political prestige that is a deterrent to its enemies.
4. A multitude that produces more than it consumes (no international debts).
5. A multitude that is co-ordinated, if not totally unified (at least no intra-Islamic conflicts or wars).
6. A multitude that is not built on reproductive risks to mothers and children.

7

The Sunnah and family planning

In this chapter an inventory of traditions (*ahadith*) on *al-azl* as a method of birth control is given whereby the traditions are classified into nine categories. Under each category several related traditions are presented. Most of the traditions are unequivocal in the permissibility of *al-azl*; some are viewed as equivocal and the impression of opposition or disfavor according to some interpreters is noted where relevant. Comments of early and later theologians on the traditions are displayed as are the ways they logically reconciled the different traditions and refuted the minority opposing views.

COLLECTIONS OF *HADITH* (TRADITION)

The *Sunnah* is the way or tradition of the Prophet (PBUH). Muslims are asked to follow the Prophet's way or tradition which may take one of these forms (all were committed to memory by companies):

- The sayings (*aqwal*) of the Prophet.
- The deeds (*af'al*) of the Prophet.
- The tacit approval (*taqreer*), or the silence of the Prophet on something that came to his knowledge.
- Information on or from the Companions (*Sahaba*).

In Arabic, a tradition of the Prophet is called *hadith* (plural *ahadith*). The *ahadith* were collected (mostly in the second and third centuries AH) by devoted compilers who spent their lives tracing the sources and authenticating the various reports for which task they traveled to areas such as Hijaz, Iraq, Egypt, Yemen, Syria and Islamic territories in Russia and Spain. Several compilations are in common use. The most authoritative and accepted compilations are called *sahihs* (sound, authentic) of which there are two – one by al-Bukhari and the other by Muslim. Next in authority are the four *Sunan*. The same level of authority is accorded Malik's *Muwatta'* and Ahmad Ibn Hanbal's *Musnad*. Other collections in use include those by al-Baihaqi, al-Seyouti and others. Most of the compilations have authoritative commentaries by leading theologians. The commentary includes explanations of the original texts, additions from other compilations as appropriate and reference to juristic implications.

The nine most authoritative compilations of *ahadith* beginning with the 'six books' are as follows:

1. *Sahih al-Bukhari.*
2. *Sahih Muslim.*
3. *Sunan Ibn Maja.*
4. *Sunan Abu Dawoud.*
5. *Sunan (Jami') al-Tirmidhi.*
6. *Sunan an-Nassa'i.*

} These are the 'six books'.

7. *Malik's al-Muwatta'.*
8. *Ibn Hanbal's Musnad.*
9. *Al-Sunan al-Kubra (al-Baihaqi).*

Although it sounds repetitive, it must be emphasized that these compilations were not restricted to the sayings (*ahadith*); they also include information on the deeds of the Prophet and his *taqreer* or tacit approval as well as information by or on the Companions.

There is a specialty in Islamic theological studies called sciences of *hadith* which covers everything related to the authenticity, comparability and interpretation of *ahadith*. One of these sciences, for example, deals with the narrators, called in Arabic (*ilm asma' al-rijal*). It deals with the life history of the narrators and probes their religiosity, veracity and personal integrity. It concerns over 100,000 narrators and rejects unsubstantiated traditions. Such painstaking research to authenticate the tradition of the Prophet is unique to Islam.

In reporting a *hadith* or tradition in Arabic, the names of reporters in successive generations are systematically listed back to the first person who actually heard and committed to memory what the Prophet said or did. Each name is checked carefully against his/her reputation as a reporter. This investigative process is called narration or *isnad*. The different chains of narration are compared and reconciled by experts. The compilations provide the different narrations verbatim. When a *hadith* or tradition appears in one of the *Sahihs* or *Sunans*, it is routinely acceptable; when it appears in both *Sahihs* it is more acceptable and is termed agreed upon or *muttafaqon alayh*. When it appears in several compilations, it has a high level of authenticity. The wording may differ a little from one compilation to another, but this was something compilers were careful to point out.

It is hoped that this explanation will make the following presentation easier to understand. In it, the Arabic version gives the *hadith* in its entirety for reference, in the English translation parts of the traditions are occasionally condensed. Details on compilations and their compilers are shown in Figure 7.1.

A SURVEY AND CLASSIFICATION OF TRADITIONS CONCERNING *AL-AZL*

The traditions concerning *al-azl* as a contraceptive measure can be conveniently classified into nine major categories:

1. The community of Companions and their experience with *al-azl*.
2. Tacit approval of *al-azl* by the Prophet, accompanied by a reminder of predestination.
3. Sanction of *al-azl* was verbalized by the Prophet.
4. 'Women as tilth' to their husbands.
5. *Al-azl* allowed only with the wife's consent.
6. Equivocal language concerning *al-azl*.
7. *Ghayla* or pregnancy while nursing a child.
8. *Al-azl* as *hidden* infanticide.
9. Denial that *al-azl* is *minor* infanticide.

Category 1. The experience of the Companions with *al-azl* (Jabir's traditions)

There is no doubt that *al-azl* was being practiced by Muslims at the time of the Prophet and that some of the devout Companions did practice it as a contraceptive measure. This was repeatedly mentioned to the Prophet who did not prohibit the practice. The Qur'an was being revealed at the time and no prohibition was pronounced.

Tradition 1.1

«عن جابر بن عبد الله ، قال : كنا نعزل على عهد رسول الله عليه الصلاة والسلام والقرآن ينزل»

أخرجه البخاري ومسلم والترمذي وابن ماجة وأحمد

On the authority of Jabir Ibn Abdullah he said 'We [the Companions of the Prophet] used to practice *al-azl* during the time of the Prophet (PBUH) while the Qur'an was being revealed.

Authenticated by al-Bukhari in his *Sahih*, Muslim in his *Sahih*, Tirmidhi in his *Sunan*, Ibn Maja in his *Sunan* and Ibn Hanbal in his *Musnad*.

Figure 7.1 The common compilations of *hadith*

Sahih al-Bukhari: Imam al-Bukhari (AD 809-69)

Abu Abdullah Mohammad Ibn Ismail famous as al-Bukhari because he was born in Bukhara, is the leading compiler of *hadith*. He traveled everywhere seeking reports of *ahadith*. It took him sixteen years to authenticate 2,762 traditions (7,397 with repetition in various sections since one tradition may be useful in different juristic references). The *Sahih* is organized in 97 'books' (*kitab*) or chapters according to the juristic subjects.

Commentaries include *Fath al-Bari* by Imam Ibn Hajar,
    Omdat al-Qari by Imam al-Ayni,
    Irshad al-Sari by Imam al-Qastallani

Sahih Muslim: Imam Muslim (AD 817-75)

Abul-Hasan al-Hajjaj al-Qusheiri followed the style of al-Bukhari with much overlapping. He actually learned from al-Bukhari and Ahmad Ibn Hanbal. His *Sahih* contains 4,000 traditions (7,275 with repetition).

Commentaries: *Al-minhaj* or *Sharh Sahih Muslim* by Imam al-Nawawi

Sunan Abu Dawoud: Imam Abu Dawoud (AD 817-88)

He is Sulaiman al-Ash'ath al-Sijistani who restricted his compilation to traditions dealing with juristic decisions (*ahadith al-ahkam*). He accepted reporters as long as they were trustworthy. He lived in al-Basra.

Commentaries: *Ma'alim al-Sunan* by al-Imam al-Khattabi

Sunan, (Jami') al-Tirmidhi: Imam al-Tirmidhi (AD 815-92)

Abu 'Iesa Mohammad Ibn 'Iesa was born in Tirmidh near Balkh. He devoted himself to *hadith* and learned from al-Bukhari, Ibn Hanbal and Abu Dawoud. He goes beyond the traditions dealing with *ahkam*.

Commentaries: Imam Ibn al-Arabi (Maliki) and Imam al-'Iraqi (Shafe'i)

Sunan Ibn Maja: Imam Ibn Maja (AD 822-76)

He is Abu Abdullah Mohammad Ibn Yazid. He followed the other *Sunans* and learned from Malik's associates. He has also written books on history and interpretation of al-Qur'an.

Sunan an-Nassa'i: Imam an-Nassa'i (AD 830-915)

He is Abu Abdul-Rahman Ahmad Ibn Shu'ayb. Born in Khurasan, he lived in Egypt, then Syria and died in Makkah. He studied *hadith* with scholars in all these places including Abu Dawoud. His is the *Sunan* with the fewest weak traditions. The *Sunan* was summarized by an-Nassa'i himself in *al-Mujtaba*.

Commentary: Jalal al-Din al-Seyuti

Al-Muwatta' : Imam Malik (AD 710-95)

Malik Ibn Anas lived in Medina and learned from the successors of the Companions (called *al-tabi'oun*). He is the founder of the Maliki school of jurisprudence. His *Al-Muwatta'* is the first compilation of *hadith* anticipating al-Bukhari. *Al-Muwatta'* has been hailed by Imam al-Shafe'i as most authentic. It includes both *ahadith* and rulings based thereupon.

Commentaries: (among others)
>Imam Ibn Abdel Barr,
>Imam al-Baji,
>Imam al-Zurqani

Al-Musnad: Imam Ibn Hanbal (AD 780-855)

Ahmad Ibn Hanbal al-Shaybani founded the Hanbali school of jurisprudence. He is a leading authority on *hadith*. He was a teacher to many of the other compilers. In his *madhhab* he preferred a weak *hadith* to a strong analogy (*qiyas*).

Al-Sunan al-Kubra: Imam Al-Baihaqi (d. AD 1066)

He is Abu Bakr Ahmad Ibn al-Hasan. A later compiler, he based his collections on those preceding him with additions and comments. He has such wide knowledge and expertise in jurisprudence that he could have established a school by himself, but he remained a scholar in the Shafe'i school.

Tradition 1.2

«كنا نعزل على عهد رسول الله عليه الصلاة والسلام فبلغ ذلك رسولَ الله عليه الصلاة والسلام فلم ينهنا»

رواه مسلم عن جابر

Muslim reports another form related to Jabir who said 'We used to practice *al-azl* during the time of the Prophet (PBUH). The Prophet (PBUH) came to know about it, but did not forbid us [doing it].

Tradition 1.3

وفي رواية أخرى لمسلم عن جابر قال : كنا نعزل والقرآن ينزل . زاد سفيان راوى الحديث «ولو كان شيئاً يُنهى عنه لنهانا القرآن».

Muslim reports a third version that Jabir said 'We used to practice *al-azl* and the Qur'an was being revealed.' Sufian, the reporter of the tradition added: 'Had this been something to be prohibited, the Qur'an would have prohibited us [doing it].'

Ibn Hajar, the author of *Blough al-Maram* makes this addition a part of the tradition related to Jabir.

Comments on Traditions 1.1, 1.2, 1.3
These authenticated traditions reveal clearly that the Companions used to practice *al-azl* with no prohibition either from the Prophet or the Qur'an. In these traditions Jabir was not reporting a story but introducing *a ruling* of sanction. This may be made clearer in a form reported by Ibn Hanbal in his *Musnad* that Ata'a heard Jabir being asked about the permissibility of *al-azl* and he (Jabir) said 'We used to do it.'

Rulings or opinions of that sort made by a Companion about a matter known to the Prophet have the same force as those enunciated by the Prophet himself. Says Imam Shawkani in *Nayl al-Awtar*.

جاء في نيل الأوطار للشوكاني ما نصه :
«وقد ذهب الأكثر من أهل الأصول على ماحكاه في الفتح إلى أن الصحابيَّ إذا أضاف الحكم إلى زمن الرسول صلى الله عليه وسلم كان له حكم الرفع قال : لِأنَّ الظاهرَ أن النبي صلى الله عليه وسلم اطّلع على ذلك وأقرَّه لتوافر دواعيهم على سؤالهم إياه من الأحكام.
قال : وقد وَرَدَت عدة طرق تصرّح باطلاعه على ذلكَ ، وأخرج مسلم من حديث جابر قال : كنا نعزل على عهد رسول الله صلى الله عليه وسلم ، فبلغ ذلك نبيَّ الله صلى الله عليه وسلم ، فلم ينهنا»

The majority of scholars concerned with the sources of jurisprudence (*ahl al-usul*) agree with what is stated in Al-Fath, namely, that:

'When a Companion of the Prophet relates an opinion (or ruling) to the time of the Prophet (PBUH), then that ruling acquires the validity of one related to the Prophet, because, he said, the Prophet must apparently have known of it and approved it.'

There are several reports confirming his [the Prophet's] knowledge of *al-azl*. Muslim related on the authority of Jabir who said, 'We used to practice *al-azl* at the time of the Prophet. The Prophet came to know of it and he did not forbid us (doing it)'.[1]

Many authorities (al-Tahawi[2], Ibn al-Qayyim[3], al-Ghazali[4], to mention only a few) used the above traditions (with some others) to conclude the permissibility of *al-azl* for contraception in Islam.

Companions known to have practiced or approved al-azl
The following list of Companions known to have practiced or approved *al-azl* is compiled from several sources including *Al-Muwatta'* by Malik[5], *Al-Omdah* by al-Ayni[6], *Al-Sunan al-Kubra* by al-Baihaqi[7], *Al-Muhalla* by Ibn Hazm[8], *Zad*

al-Ma'ad by Ibn al-Qayyim[9], and *Al-Mughni* by Ibn Qudama[10].

Ali Ibn Abi Talib (son-in-law and cousin of the Prophet),
Sa'd Ibn Abi Waqqas,
Abu Ayyub al-Ansari,
Zayd Ibn Thabit,
Jabir Ibn Abdullah,
Abdullah Ibn Abbas (Prophet's cousin)
Al-Hassan Ibn Ali (Prophet's grandson)
Khabbab Ibn al-Aratt,
Abu Sa'id al-Khudri,
Abdullah Ibn Mass'oud,
Sa'id Ibn al-Mussayyab,*
Tawoos,*
'Ataa',*
Al-Nakhey,*
Alqamah,*
Al-Hajjaj Ibn Amr Ibn Ghaziya,*
Associates of Ibn Abbas,*
Some *ansaars* (Medina dwellers who protected the Prophet after Hijra).
Al-Ayni added: Sa'd Ibn Jubair, M. Ibn Sirin, Ibrahim al-Taymi, Amr In Murrah and Jabir Ibn Zaid.

* tabi'oun ffl followers (disciples) of the Companions

Comment

The fact that the Companions sanctioned and some actually practiced it (with the Prophet's knowledge and approval) is considered by the majority of theologians unequivocal in the permissibility of *al-azl*. Furthermore, the fact that *al-tabi'oun* continued to sanction and practice contraception is unequivocal in continued permissibility after the death of the Prophet. Imam Malik who is a disciple of the *tabi'oun* continued to sanction *al-azl*. This means that *al-azl* was not abrogated as Ibn Hazm claims (see p. 136).

In order to complete the picture I must state that not all the Companions practiced *al-azl* and that some actually disliked it. Those reported to have disliked *al-azl* are as follows:

Abu Bakr,
Omar Ibn al-Khattab (this contradicts the report that Omar agreed with Ali's interpretation of the stages of fetal development, see Tradition 9.5),
Othman Ibn Affan,
Abdullah Ibn Omar (see his interpretation of women as tilth),
Some *muhajiroun* (migrants to Medina).

Even if many more Companions disliked *al-azl*, this does not make it prohibited, because the practice, while allowed, was not mandatory.

Category 2. Traditions denoting tacit approval by the Prophet of *al-azl*

Several of the traditions concerning *al-azl* addressed two components simultaneously: the *behavioral* component which is the act of withdrawal to avoid pregnancy; and the *belief* component which emphasizes predestination, i.e. that the will of Allah has ascendancy over man's will and the results of his action. This means that despite the practice of *al-azl*, pregnancy could occur. This is much like the principle of 'Hobble her and rely on Allah' where the behavioral component is to tie up the camel and the belief component deals with trust in Allah that the camel will not go astray despite hobbling her.

Tradition 2.1

»عن أبي سعيد قال : سئل رسول الله صلى الله عليه وسلم عن العزل ، فقال: ما مِنْ كل الماء يكون الولد ، وإذا أراد الله خلق شئ لم يمنعه شئ«
رواه مسلم

On the authority of Abu Sa'id: The Prophet was queried about *al-azl* and he said 'Not out of all the semen a child is formed,* and if Allah willed to create something nothing would stop him from doing it.'

Authenticated by Muslim

*Modern medicine confirms that only one sperm is needed to fertilize the woman's ovum; more in multiple pregnancy. Each ejaculation contains several million sperm.

Tradition 2.2

روى مسلم عن أبي سعيد أيضا أنه قال :
»ذُكر العزل عند رسول الله صلى الله عليه وسلم فقال: ولِمَ يفعلُ ذلك أحدكم؟ — ولم يقل : فَلاَ يَفْعَلْ ذلك أحدُكم — فإنه ليست نفسٌ مخلوقة إلاّ الله خالقها«
رواه مسلم ، وما تحته خط هو تعليق أبي سعيد

Muslim reported also on the authority of Abu Sa'id who said: *Al-azl* was mentioned to the Prophet (PBUH). He asked 'Why do you do that?' (*He did not say: 'do not do that!'*).* 'No soul fated to be created but will be created.'

*The words between brackets are as such in Sahih Muslim and are an interpretation by Abu Sa'id sanctioning *al-azl*.

Tradition 2.3

عن جابر بن عبد الله قال :
سأل رجلٌ النبيَّ صلى الله عليه وسلم فقال : إن عندي جاريةً وأنا أعزل عنها.
فقال الرسول صلى الله عليه وسلم ، إن ذلك لنْ يمنع شيئًا أراده الله . قال:
فجاء الرجل فقال : يارسولَ الله إن الجارية التي كنت ذكرتها لَك حملت. فقال
رسول الله صلى الله عليه وسلم : أنا عبد الله ورسوله»

رواه مسلم

On the authority of Jabir Ibn Abdullah who said: A man came to the Prophet (PBUH) and said 'I have a mate and I practice *al-azl* with her.' The Prophet said 'This will not prevent something that Allah wills.' The man came back (after a time) and said 'Messenger of Allah! The mate that I mentioned to you has conceived.' The Prophet said 'I am Allah's slave and messenger.'

Authenticated by Muslim*

*In his comment on this tradition, Imam al-Nawawi explains that semen may spill in before withdrawal and cause pregnancy. He uses the argument to defy those who disclaim a child conceived while *al-azl* was consistently practiced.[11]

Comment on Traditions 2.1—2.3

Note that in all these traditions the Prophet did not prohibit *al-azl* but moved directly to the question of predestination. This will be noted as well in the following traditions. Note also that these traditions endorse the first category in revealing contraceptive practice among the Companions; many of the following traditions do the same.

Category 3. Traditions in which sanction was verbalized by the Prophet

In all the preceding traditions, there was neither a prohibition nor verbalized approval. There is at least one authenticated tradition in which the Prophet did specifically mention *al-azl* by name, sanctioning it.

Tradition 3.1

«روى مسلم قال : حدثنا أحمد بن عبد الله بن يونس ، حدثنا زهير ، أخبرنا
الزبير عن جابر قال إنّ رجلاً أتى رسول الله صلى الله عليه وسلم فقال:
إنّ لي جاريةً هي خادمتنا وسانيتُنا في النخل ، وأنا أطوف عليها وأنا أكره أن
تحمل ، فقال ــ اعزلْ عنها إن شئت ــ فإنه سيأتيها ماقُدِّرَ لها . فلبث الرجل

ثم أتاه فقال : إنَّ الجارية قد حبلت ، فقال : قد أخبرتك أنه سيأتيها ما قُدِّر لها،
روى بألفاظ مختلفة في مسلم وابن ماجة
وابن حنبل والدارمي وابن أبي شيبة

Muslim was told by Ahmad Ibn Abdullah Ibn Yunus, who was told by Zuhair who was told by Abu al-Zubair on the authority of Jabir who said 'A man came to the Prophet (PBUH) and said "I have a mate who serves us and waters our palm trees. I consort with her (lawfully) but do not like her to get pregnant".'

The Prophet said '*Practice* al-azl *with her if you so wish*. What is pre-ordained for her will certainly befall her.' After some time the man came back and said 'the mate has conceived.' The Prophet said 'I told you that what is pre-ordained will befall her'.

Authenticated by Muslim, Ibn Maja, Ibn Hanbal, al-Daramy, and Ibn Abi Shaiba. There are other wordings with the same meaning.

This tradition received by far the greatest attention from both the early and late theologians because it is the one tradition in which the Prophet (PBUH) mentions *al-azl* by name in a form denoting sanction. Note that the man did not mention *al-azl* in his question. He merely did not want his mate to get pregnant. The fact that the Prophet mentioned *al-azl* by name spontaneously indicates that the practice was on the minds of the people at the time and he wanted to clarify its permissibility. Sheikh Mohammad al-Madany, commenting on this tradition in *Manbar al-Islam* magazine (June 1965), said

«قال الشيخ مدني : إن هذا الحديث يفيد معنى أعمق في الجواز، والمشروعية
إذ يقرّر أن الرسول هو الذى أشار بالعزل»

This tradition denoted a deep sense of permissibility and lawfulness, since it reveals that the Prophet himself was the one to recommend *al-azl*.[12]

Note also the expression 'if you so wish' indicating that it is voluntary.

Two more traditions are close to the one above and lend more support to the permissibility of *al-azl*.

Tradition 3.2

«روى الكاساني عن رسول الله صلى الله عليه وسلم أنه قال : اعزلوهنَّ أولا
تعزلوهنّ إن الله تعالى إذا أراد خلق نسمةٍ فهو خالقها»

Kasani reported that the Prophet said '*Practice al-azl* with them or do not practice *al-azl* with them, if Allah wants to create a soul, He will create it.'

THE *SUNNAH* AND FAMILY PLANNING

Tradition 3.3

«عن ابي سعيد الخدري أنهم (أى الصحابة) أرادوا أن يعزلوا أيام معركة حنين قال : فسألنا رسول الله صلى الله عليه وسلم عن العزل فقال : اصنعوا ما بدا لكم ، فما قَضَى الله فهو كائن ، فليس من كلِّ الماء يكون الولد»
رواه احمد بن حنبل

On the authority of Abu Sa'id al-Khudri who related that during the battle of Hunayn, they wanted to practice *al-azl*. They consulted the Prophet who said '*Do as you wish!*'* Whatever Allah has ordained will be, and not from all the semen is the child formed.'

Authenticated by Ibn Hanbal

*Note that the Prophet (PBUH) did not say 'Do not do it.'

Category 4. *Al-azl* and 'your wives are as tilth unto you'

Reference has been made before to the Qur'anic verse:

نِسَآؤُكُمْ حَرْثٌ لَكُمْ فَأْتُوا حَرْثَكُمْ أَنَّى شِئْتُمْ ... ﴿٢٢٣﴾ البقرة(٢)

Your wives are as tilth unto you, so approach your tilth how you wish.
al-Baqara (Sura 2:223)

The primary purpose of this verse is to allow various approaches to marital relations except for sodomy which is prohibited. Some, focusing literally on the expression tilth, have taken the verse to mean that, since wives are tilth, they have to be cultivated or impregnated as frequently as possible. The Companions cited below corrected this misconception.

Tradition 4.1 (Ibn Abbas)

«عن زائدةِ بن عُمير : سألت ابن عباس عن العزل ، فقال : إنكم قد أكثرتم فإن كان قال فيه رسول الله شيئا فهو كما قال ، وإن لم يكن قال فيه شيئا فأنا أقول : نساؤكم حرثٌ لكم ، فأتوا حرثكم أنَّى شئتم ، فإن شئتم فاعزلوا وإن شئتم فلا تعزلوا»
رواه الحاكم في المستدرك ، والذهبي والطبري

On the authority of Za'ida Ibn Omayr who said 'I asked Ibn Abbas about *al azl* and he replied 'You have overdone it [repeatedly asking about *al-azl*], if the Prophet has said something about it, it should be as he has

123

ordained. If he hasn't, I say: Your wives are as tilth unto you, so approach your tilth how you will, you are free to practice *al-azl* with them if you wish or do not practice *al-azl* if you wish'.

Authenticated by al-Hakim in *Al-Mustadrak* and by al-Dhahabi and al-Tabari

Tradition 4.2 (Ibn Omar)

«روى أبو بكر الجصّاص عن ابن عمر عن قوله تعالى: «فأتوا حرثكم أنّى شئتم» ... قال: كَيف شئتَ ، إن شئتَ عزلا أو غيرَ عزلَ»
رواه أبو بكر في أحكام القرآن عن أبي حنيفة

On the authority of Abdullah Ibn Omar who explained the verse 'Approach your tilth ...' by saying 'How you wish. You can withdraw [practice *al-azl*] or don't withdraw [do not practice *al-azl*] as you wish.'

Authenticated by al-Jassass through Abu Hanifa

Tradition 4.3 (Ibn al-Mussayyab)

«روى الطبرى عن سعيد بن المسيّب في قوله تعالى ، فأتوا حرثكم أنّى شئتم قال : إن شئتم فاعزِلوا ، وإن شئتم فلا تعزلوا»
تفسير الطبرى

On the authority of Sa'id *Ibn al-Mussayyab* regarding 'Approach your tilth ...' He said 'You are free to practice *al-azl* [for contraception] with them if you wish or you do not practice it if you wish.'

Authenticated by al-Tabari

Tradition 4.4 (Ibn Thabit and Ibn Amur)

«عن الحجاج بن عمرو بن غَزِيَّة ، أنه كان جالسا عند زيد بن ثابت فجاء ابن فهد رجل من اليمن ، فقال : يَا أبا سعيد ، إن عندى جوارى لي ، ليس كلَّهن نسائي التي أكن بأعجب إلى منهن ، وليس كلهن يعجبني أن تحمل مني أفأعزل ؟ فقال زيد بن ثابت : أفتِهِ ياحجاج . قال ، فقلت : يَغفر الله لك إنما نجلس عندك لنتعلم منك . قال : أفتِهِ . فقلت : هو حرثك إن شئت سقيته وإن شئت أعطشته،قال:وكنت أسمع ذلك من زيد . فقال زيد : صَدقت»
رواه مالك في الموطأ

On the authority of al-Hajjaj Ibn Amr Ibn Ghaziyya that he was sitting with Zayd Ibn Thabit when Ibn Fahd (a man from Yemen) came to ask about *al-azl.* 'Zayd Ibn Thabit turned to me and said "Give him the *fatwa.*" I said "May Allah forgive you, we sit with you to learn from you." Zayd insisted "Give him the *fatwa.*" So I said "It is your tilth; if you wish you can water it, and if you wish, you can leave it thirsty. That is what I learned from Zayd." Zayd said "You are right."'

Authenticated by Malik in *Muwatta'*

Tradition 4.5 (Ibn Abbas, using the verse to negate al-azl *being* wa'd*)*

«روى البيهقي عن ابن عباس قال : ما كان ابنُ آدم ليقتلَ نفسا قضى الله خلقها ، حرثُك إن شئت عطشته ، وإن شئت سقيته»

On the authority of Ibn Abbas who said 'Man cannot kill a soul that Allah wished to create: Your tilth if you wish you can leave it thirsty or if you wish you can water it.

Authenticated by al-Baihaqi

All these traditions lend support to the practice of *al-azl.*

Category 5. *Al-azl* is allowed with a wife's consent

Several traditions make it clear that *al-azl* is allowed only with a wife's consent.

Tradition 5.1

«عن أبي هريرة رضي الله عنه قال : قال صلى الله عليه وسلم : "لاَيَعْزَلُ عن الحرة إلا بإذنها"»

أخرجه أبو داود

On the authority of Abu Huraira the Prophet said *al-azl* is not allowed without the consent of the (free) wife.

Authenticated by Abu Dawoud

Tradition 5.2

«عن أبي هريرة عن عمر بن الخطاب رضي الله عنهما أن رسول الله صلى الله عليه وسلم نهى عن العزل عن الحرة بدون اذنها»

أخرجه ابن ماجة وأحمد

Another version on the authority of Abu Huraira quoting Omar Ibn al-Khattab that the Prophet disallowed *al-azl* without the wife's permission.

Authenticated by Ibn Maja and Ibn Hanbal

This means *al-azl* is allowed with the wife's permission. There is a lengthy discussion on this in Chapter 8 in the section on the legal schools, see p. 152.

Category 6. Traditions with seemingly equivocal support for *al-azl*

These traditions contain expressions by the Prophet (PBUH) which can be interpreted by some as sanctioning and by others as frowning upon the practice.

Tradition 6.1

«عن أبي سعيد الخدري أن رسول الله صلى الله عليه وسلم سُئل عن العزل
فقال : لا عليكم ألاّ تفعلوا ذاكم ، فإنما هو القدر»
أخرجه البخاري ومسلم وابن ماجة

On the authority of Abu Sa'id al-Khudri: the Prophet (PBUH) was asked about *al-azl* and he said '*La alaykom alla taf alu*', that is but destiny.'

Authenticated by al-Bukhari, Muslim and Ibn Maja

Tradition 6.2

«عن ابن مُحَيريز أنه قال : دخلت أنا وأبو صِرْمة على أبي سعيد الخدري،
فسأله أبو صِرْمة فقال : يا أبا سعيد هل سمعت رسول الله صلى الله عليه
وسلم يذكر العزل . فقال نعم . غزونا مع رسول الله صلى الله عليه وسلم
غزوة بلمصطق (أي بني المصطلق) ... فأردنا أن نستمتع ونعزل ، فقلنا:
نفعل ورسول الله بين أظهرنا ، ألا نسأله ؟ فسألنا رسول الله صلى الله
عليه وسلم فقال : لا عليكم ألاّ تفعلوا ، ما كتب الله خلق نسمة هي كائنة
الى يوم القيامة، إلا ستكون»

أخرجه مسلم وأبو داود ومالك وأحمد والبخاري
والنسائي وابن ماجة باختلاف في الألفاظ

On the authority of Ibn Muhairiz that Abu Sa'id was asked about whether he heard the Prophet mention *al-azl* and he replied by referring to the battle of Bani al-Mustalaq where some of the Companions wanted to practice *al-azl*. We said 'Do we do that while the Prophet is among us, shouldn't we ask him?' So we asked him (PBUH) and he said '*La alaykom alla taf alu*. No soul fated to come into being till the Day of Judgement but comes into being.'

Tradition 6.3

«فى رواية أخرى لمسلم : جاءت إجابة رسول الله صلى الله عليه وسلم كالآتى:
وإنكم لتفعلون ، وإنكم لتفعلون ، وإنكم لتفعلون ، مامن نسمة كائنة إلى يوم القيامة إلاّ وهى كائنة»

Muslim provides another version in which the answer of the Prophet was as follows: He said 'Surely you do it? Surely you do it? Surely you do it? No soul fated to come into being till the Day of Judgement, but comes into being.'

Tradition 6.4

«فى رواية البخارى ، اختلفت الصيغه إلى تساؤل : أو إنكم لتفعلون؟ ثلاثاً»

Al-Bukhari gives still a form that appears to be slightly different [in Arabic]: He said 'Do you really do it? Do you really do it? Do you really do it?'

Tradition 6.5

«عن أبى سعيد ذُكِرَ العزل عند النبى صلى الله عليه وسلم ، فقال : وما ذاكم؟ قالوا : الرجل تكون له المرأة ترضع فيصيب منها ، ويكره أن تحمل منه، والرجل تكون له الأَمَة فيُصيب منها ويكره أن تحمل.
قال : فلا عليكم ألاّ تفعلوا ذاكم . إنما هو القدر»

رواه مسلم

On the authority of Abu Sa'id who said 'al-azl was mentioned to the Prophet. He asked "Why is that?" They said "A man has a nursing wife and he has relations with her but does not like her to get pregnant, and a man who has a mate and practices [lawful] relations with her but does not want her to get pregnant." He said "*La alaykom alla taf alu*, it is but destiny."'

Authenticated by Muslim

Tradition 6.6

»روى أحمد بن حنبل أن النبي صلى الله عليه وسلم سُئل عن العزل فقال:
أنت تخلُقه ، أنت ترزقُه . أقرَّه قراره ، فإنما هو القدر«

Ibn Hanbal reported that the Prophet (PBUH) was asked about *al-azl*. He said 'Do you create it, Do you provide for it, Put it where it belongs. It is destiny.'

Comment

As can be seen, several of these traditions use the Arabic phrase '*La alaykom alla taf alu*', which stirred considerable linguistic discussion. It is open to two meanings. One supports the practice of *al-azl* as follows: 'There is no disfavor in not doing it', meaning that had it been prohibited, the Prophet would have explicitly prohibited it by saying 'Do not do it.' The other interpretation by Ibn Sirin and al-Hasan al-Basry is that it is closer to a reprimand, with the meaning emerging as 'You have not to do it,' i.e. 'Don't do it.' This interpretation was not accepted by the majority of jurists as Imam Ibn Hajar explains in his *Fath al-Bari Sharh Sahih al-Bukhari*. The exact Arabic text of Ibn Hajar is given first followed by a summary in English.[13]

»روى ابن حجر في الفتح عن ابن سيرين والحسن أنهم فهموا أن التعبير ــ لا عليكم ألا تفعلوا ــ أقرب إلى الزجر أو أنه أقرب إلى النهي ، ثم أورد كلام القرطبي تعليقاً على ذلك ووافقه عليه إذ قال : قال القرطبي كأن هؤلاء فهموا من لا النهي عما سألوه عنه ، فكأن عندهم بعد لا حذفا تقديره «لا تعزلوا وعليكم ألا تفعلوا» ، ويكون قوله وعليكم ألخ تأكيدا للنهي . ونعقب بأن الأصل عدم هذا التقدير ، وإنما معناه «ليس عليكم أن تتركوا» وهو الذي يساوي أن لا تفعلوا ، وقال غيره: قوله لا عليكم ألاَّ تفعلوا أى لا حرج عليكم ألاَّ تفعلوا ، ففيه نفي الحرج عن عدم الفعل ، فافهم ثبوت الحرج في فعل العزل«

Ibn Hajar quotes al-Qurtubi interpreting the phrase as 'you do not have to refrain from it.' Then Ibn Hajar quotes others explaining the phrase as 'there is no dislike in not doing it', which means there may be dislike in doing it.

Thus Ibn Hajar follows his school in attaching disfavor (*karaha tanzihiyya*) to *al-azl* (see Chapter 8). Ibn Hajar went on to rebut those who use the expression to prohibit *al-azl*.

Two more comments are of interest. Imam Malik has reported Tradition

6.2 with the phrase 'La alaykom ...' but he did not consider it against *al-azl* with a wife's consent. Al-Boutti (twentieth century) found that whatever doubt existed because of that phrase has been unequivocally removed by the many traditions in which the Prophet (PBUH) has clearly allowed *al-azl*. As to Tradition 6.6, it was interpreted by Ibn Maja as against *al-azl*, but Ibn Hajar found no prohibition in it.

Category 7. *Al-azl* and *al-ghayla*

The Arabic words *ghayl*, *ghayla* and *gheyal* are used to denote suckling of a child by a pregnant mother or the practice of having relations with a lactating wife. Literally it denotes serious assault (on the child).

Tradition 7.1

«عن أسامة بن زيد أنَّ رجلا جاء إلى النبي صلى الله عليه وسلم فقال : إني أعزل عن امرأتي فقال الرسول صلى الله عليه وسلم : وَلِمَ تفعلُ ذلك؟ فقال له الرجل : أشفق على ولدها (أو على أولادها) . فقال الرسول صلوات الله عليه : لَو كان ضارا ــ أى الغيلة ــ لضر فارس والروم»

رواه مسلم

On the authority of Usama Ibn Zayd who said 'A man came to the Prophet (PBUH) and said "I practice *al-azl* (withdrawal) with my wife." The Prophet asked "Why do you do that?" The man said "Out of consideration for her child" [or her children]. The Prophet said "If it [*al-ghayla*] were harmful, it would have done harm to Persians and Romans."'

Authenticated by Muslim

Imam al-Nawawi considers this to be a form of personal '*ijtihad*' by the Prophet who felt, at the time, that the Arabs fear of *al-ghayla* was exaggerated. Al-Nawawi considers that the main thrust of the tradition is that *al-ghayla* is not prohibited (but is discouraged).[14]

Other traditions, warn against the practice and refer to its dangers to the child.

Tradition 7.2

«عن أسماء بنت زيد بن السكن قالت : سمعت رسول الله صلى الله عليه وسلم يقول: لاَ تقتلوا أولادكم سراً ، فإن الغَيل يدرك الفارس فيدعثره عن فرسه»

أخرجه أبو داود

On the authority of Asma' bint Zayd Ibn al-Sakan who said 'I heard the Prophet (PBUH) say "Do not kill your children unconsciously. For *al-ghayla* will have in the future the same effect as when a horseman is overtaken [by an opponent] and thrown off his horse".'

Authenticated by Abu Dawoud

This tradition strongly discourages *al-ghayla*. It is taken by some as an indirect sanction for contraception. Modern medicine confirms the occurrence of several ill effects from *al-ghayla*.

Category 8. Traditions referring to *al-azl* as hidden infanticide

In this category there is one tradition that instigated considerable discussions in jurisprudence. That is the tradition related to Judama (not Judhama – see al-Nawawi)[15].

Tradition 8.1

«عن جُدامة بنت وهب الأسدية ــ أخت عكّاشة قالت : حضرت رسول الله صلى الله عليه وسلم في أناس وهو يقول : لقد هممت أن أنهي عن الغيْلة. فنظرت في الروم وفارس ، فإذا هم يُغيلون أولادهم ، فلا يضر أولادهم ذلك شيئا. ثم سألوه عن العزل فقال رسول الله صلى الله عليه وسلم : ذلك الوأد الخفي. زاد عبيد الله في حديثه عن المقرىء: وهى ــ إذا الموْءودة سئلت»

أخرجه مسلم وابن ماجة والنسائي وابن حنبل
ولم يرد الجزء الخاص بالعزل في رواية
السنن الأربعة أو في الموطأ

On the authority of Judama bint Wahb al-Asadiyya [sister of Ukkasha] who said 'I was among others in the Prophet's audience while he was saying: "I almost prohibited *al-ghayla* but then I considered the Romans and the Persians and found that they used to suckle their children by their pregnant mothers without ill effects."

Then they asked him about *al-azl* and he said "it is hidden infanticide (*al-wa'd al-khafiyy*)".'

Authenticated by Muslim, Ibn Maja, an-Nassa'i and Ibn Hanbal

Note: The part on *al-azl* was *not* reported in *Muwatta* or the four *Sunans*. This tradition requires special discussion and will be considered in the general

THE *SUNNAH* AND FAMILY PLANNING

comments concerning the *Sunnah* and family planning.

Category 9. Traditions denying that *al-azl* is minor infanticide

Several traditions have denied that *al-azl* is infanticide. It was the Jews (many of whom lived in Medina) who equated *al-azl* with infanticide calling it minor infanticide (*al-maw'udatu al-sughra*). This is because spilling one's seed is against Jewish law: Onan was punished for spilling his seed, hence the expression 'Onanism' for coitus interruptus.

The Jews in Medina tried to convince their Muslim neighbors that *al-azl* was the lesser infanticide. The Prophet categorically denied such a contention.

Tradition 9.1

«عن ابن ثوبان عن جابر قال :
قلنا يارسول الله : كنا نعزل فزعمت اليهود أنها الموءودة الصغرى. فقال:
كذبت اليهود . إن الله إذا أراد أن يخلقه لم يمنعه منه شئ.»
أخرجه الترمذى وأبو داود

On the authority of Jabir; the Companions asked the prophet 'O Messenger of Allah! We used to practice *al-azl* but the Jews claimed that it was minor infanticide.' Such a contention by the Jews was categorically denied by the Prophet who said that the Jews had lied and added that 'if Allah wills its creation nothing could stop Him.'

Authenticated by al-Tirmidhi and Abu Dawoud

Tradition 9.2

«عن جابر بن عبد الله قال : (في رواية أخرى)
... كنا نعزل فقالت اليهود إن تلك الموءودة الصغرى . فسئل رسول الله
صلى الله عليه وسلم عن ذلك. فقال : كذبت اليهود . لو أراد الله خلقه
ما استطعت رده»
أخرجه الترمذى والنسائي

On the authority of Jabir Ibn Abdullah who said 'We practiced *al-azl* and the Jews claimed it was minor infanticide.' The Prophet (PBUH) was asked about this and categorically denied such a contention by the Jews. He added 'If Allah wills its creation, you cannot stop Him.'

Authenticated by al-Tirmidhi and an-Nassai'i

Tradition 9.3

«عن أبي هريرة رضي الله عنه قال :
سئل الرسول صلى الله عليه وسلم عن العزل . قالوا : إن اليهود تزعم أن العزل هو المؤودة الصغرى . قال : كذبت اليهود»

أخرجه البيهقي

On the authority of Abu Huraira, who said 'The Prophet was asked about *al-azl*. They said "The Jews claim that it is minor infanticide."' He categorically denied such a contention by the Jews.

        Authenticated by al-Baihaqi

Tradition 9.4

«عن أبي سعيد الخدري أن رجلا جاء إلى النبي صلى الله عليه وسلم وقال: يارسول الله ، إن لي جارية وأنا أعزل عنها ، وأنا أكره أن تحمل ، وأنا أريد ما يريد الرجال . وإن اليهود تحدّث أن العزل هو المؤودة الصغرى. قال كذبت اليهود . لو أراد الله أن يخلقه ، ما استطعت آن تصرفه»

أخرجه أبو داود وابن حنبل والطحاوي

On the authority of Abu Sa'id, who said 'A man came to the Prophet to ask about the practice of *al-azl* with his mate. He added "I do not like her to get pregnant and I am a man who wants what other men want. But the Jews claim that *al-azl* is minor infanticide."' The Prophet categorically denied such a contention by the Jews and referred to destiny.

    Authenticated by Abu Dawoud, Ibn Hanbal and al-Tahawi

Tradition 9.5

«عن عبيد بن أبي رفاعة الأنصاري قال : تداول أصحاب رسول الله صلى الله عليه وسلم عند عمر بن الخطاب في العزل . فاختلفوا فيه ، فقال عمر: قد اختلفتم وأنتم أهل بدر الأخيار ، فكيف بأناس بعدكم . إذ تناجى رجلان. فقال عمر : ما هذه المناجاة ؟ فقال : إن اليهود تزعم أنها المؤودة الصغرى. فقال علي : إنها لا تكون مؤودة حتى تمر على التارات السبع : تكون سلالة من طين ، ثم تكون نطفة ، ثم تكون علقة ، ثم تكون مضغة ، ثم

تكون عظاما، ثم تكون لحما ، ثم تكون خلقا آخر . فقال عمر : صَدقت .
أطال الله بقاءكَ. فكان أول من قالها في الاسلام»

أخرجه البيهقى والنسائي

On the authority of Obaid Ibn Abi Rifa'a al-Ansari, who related 'A group of the Companions mentioned *al-azl* in the presence of Omar Ibn-al-Khattab and they differed on it. Omar said "You have differed and you are the good people of Badr. What will happen to those coming after you?"

Two men continued to argue. Omar asked about their argument. One of the men said "The Jews claim that *al-azl* is the minor infanticide [*al-maw'udatu al-sughra*]." Ali [Ibn Abi Talib] replied "It cannot be infanticide or *wa'd* until it has passed the seven stages of foetal development: first it is a product of wet earth (the origin of man), then it is a drop of seed [*nutfa*], then it is a clot of congealed blood [*alaqa*], then it is a foetal lump (*mudgha*), then it is bones, which are then clothed with flesh, then it becomes another creature [*khalqan a'khar*]." Omar said [to Ali] "You are right. May Allah prolong your life."'

Authenticated by al-Baihaqi and an-Nassa'i.

Imam Ali inferred these seven stages from the verses in Sura 23 (*al-Mu'minoun*) of the Qur'an referred to earlier.

Tradition 9.6

وفي رواية أخرى

«روى القاضي أبو يعلي بإسناده عن عبيد بن رفاعة عن أبيه قال : جلس إلى عمر كل من علي (إبن أبي طالب) والزبير (ابن العوام) ، وسعد (ابن أبي وقاص).

وتذاكروا العزل . فقال عمر: لا بأس به .

فقال رجل : إنهم يزعمون أنها المؤءودة الصغرى، فرد عليه الامام علىّ قائلا: لا تكون مؤءودة حتى تمر على التارات السبع (وذكر الآيات ...) ، فعجب عمر من قوله ، وقال جزاك الله خيراً»

Another version on the authority of Abu Ya'ly from Obaid Ibn Raifa'a from his father who reported that a group of the Companions, including Ali Ibn

Abi Talib, al-Zubair Ibn al-Awwam and Sa'd Ibn Abi Waqqas were, in the company of Omar, discussing *al-azl*.

'*Omar* said "there is nothing against it?" One of those present said "They claim that it is the minor infanticide [*wa'd*]." Ali replied "It cannot be *wa'd* until it passes the seven stages of development", and he recited the verses from al-Mu'minoun. Omar admired Ali's interpretation and said "may Allah reward you."'

Tradition 9.7

»روى البيهقى وابن رجب في كتابه جامع العلوم والحكم عن ابن عباس أنه قال ، وقد سئل عن العزل : اذهبوا فسلوا الناس ثم ائتونى وأخبرونى فسألوا وأخبروه (وييدو أنَ بعض الناس ذكر المؤءودة الصغرى) ، فتلا هذه الآية «ولقد خلقنا الانسان من سلالة من طين ثم جعلناه ...» إلى آخر الآية. ثم قال ابن عباس كيف تكون موءودةً حتى تمر بهذا الخلق ؟«

Ibn Abbas is also quoted (by al-Baihaqi and Ibn Rajab in his book *Jami al-Ulum Wal-Hikam* as making a similar reasoning to Ali. When he was asked about *al-azl*, Ibn Abbas said 'Go and ask the people and come back and tell me.' They did and came back, and told him (apparently some people mentioned hidden infanticide).

Ibn Abbas recited the verse in al-Mu'minoun Sura dealing with the stages of fetal development until 'And then we made him into another creature.' Then he concluded 'Can a soul die before reaching that stage of creation? (or can it be *wa'd* before reaching that stage?).'

APPRAISAL OF THE EVIDENCE FROM THE *SUNNAH*

This rather lengthy survey is an attempt to classify the majority of the authentic traditions concerning *al-azl*. Each of the traditions cited has already been carefully screened and judged as authentic by the recognized compilers of *hadith*, although the level of authenticity varies a little according to the chain of reporters. (*isnad*).

The permissibility of *al-azl*

The majority of these traditions are straightforward in permitting *al-azl* as a form of contraception. The Companions who were the closest to the Prophet allowed it and some actually practiced it. The Prophet came to know about it and did not prohibit it. The Qur'an was being revealed at that time and its silence on the matter is taken as an added proof of permissibility. Furthermore the Prophet (PBUH) verbalized approval, at least in one tradition.

The majority of jurists and theologians allowed *al-azl* either absolutely (e.g. al-Ghazali and Ibn al-Qayyim) or with a qualification that it is less than impeccable and has an edge of '*karaha tanzihiyya*' (e.g al-Nawawi). A second group, which is in the minority and is represented mainly by Ibn Hazm, prohibited it absolutely basing their opposition primarily on Judama's tradition. Now let us consider the analyses and interpretations by some of the most celebrated jurists.

Abu Ja'afar al-Tahawi (d.933) said, in his *Sharh Ma'ani al' Athar*, after reviewing several traditions, that these and other traditions of the Prophet indicate that *al-azl* is not held in disfavor. He added that when the Prophet was asked about it, he did not command his Companions against it, but said 'There is no disfavor in not doing it, it is destiny.' Al-Tahawi explained that if Allah has willed that a child be created nothing can stand in His way; Allah would then cause some of the semen to reach the correct place and conception would result. If Allah, however, has decreed that no child should be created out of the liquid, then it would not make any difference whether the liquid reached its place or not. This explanation by al-Tahawi is a personal interpretation.[16]

Al-Ghazali (d.1111) who is known as the proof of Islam (*hujjatul-Islam*) concluded that *al-azl* was permitted absolutely (*mubah*). For, prohibition in Islam requires an explicit text (*nuss*) from the Qur'an or *Sunnah*, or analogous reasoning in which case a text on which to base the prohibition must exist. None of these exist for *al-azl*. On the contrary, he said, there is a basis for a different kind of analogy, namely abstention from marriage, or from sexual intercourse after marriage, or from ejaculation in intercourse. All these acts are considered less than meritorious but they are still lawful. All these abstentions, he explained, have the same results, namely avoidance of pregnancy. For pregnancy had four determinants (1) marriage, (2) intercourse, (3) patience until ejaculation, and (4) actual ejaculation allowing the semen to reach the womb. To prevent pregnancy, abstention from the fourth is like abstention from the third (*azl*) which is like abstention from the second, which is in turn like abstention from the first (marriage).[17]

After quoting several of the traditions on *al-azl* in his celebrated work *Zad Al-Ma'ad*, **Ibn al-Qayyim** (d.1350) concluded that 'Now all these traditions of the Prophet (PBUH) are authentic, unambiguous and clear. They show that *al-azl* [withdrawal] is permissible. This view is held by ten of the great companions of the Prophet.' (He cited the names of the first ten in the list given earlier in this chapter.) He also referred to al-Shafe'i as saying 'We have reported on the authority of many of the companions of the Prophet (PBUH) that they have allowed *al-azl* and found nothing wrong about it.'[18]

Ibn Hajar al-'Askalani (d.1449) gave this subject considerable attention in his commentary on *Sahih al-Bukhari* (called *Fath al-Bari*) in which he affirmed the permissibility of *al-azl*. He considered Jabir's traditions binding because the Prophet knew about the matter and did not prohibit it. Also binding was the fact that the Prophet (PBUH) explicitly allowed it (Tradition 3.1). Other traditions make *al-azl* less than impeccable, however.[19]

The views of these jurists were shared by many other theologians who devoted considerable space to discussing *al-azl*. They include **Ibn Al-Humam** of the fifteenth century AD in his *Sharh Fath al-Qadir*,[20] **al-Zabidi** of the eighteenth century AD in his commentary on *Ihya' Ulum al-Din*[21] and **al-Shawkani** of the nineteenth century AD in his *Nayl al-Awtar*[22]. The views of contemporary theologians will be considered in Chapter 12.

Arguments against *al azl* based on Judama's traditions

Opponents of the family planning movement began again in the mid-1950s to cite the traditions forbidding *al-azl* to support their case. This was despite the fact that their interpretation of such traditions had been convincingly refuted by leading theologians over the centuries. The strongest arguments concentrate heavily on the Prophet's qualification of *al-azl* as hidden infanticide in Judama's tradition.

The leading prohibitor of *al-azl* is Imam **Ibn Hazm** who lived in Andalusia (Islamic Spain) and died in AD 1063. Although he failed to convince other theologians of his time, his refutation is cited in several works of Islamic jurisprudence. Ibn Hazm's ideas represent the official opinion of the short-lived Zahiri school and appear in his book *Al-Muhalla*.

Ibn Hazm invoked a fundamental ruling in Islamic jurisprudence that the primary assumption in all things is that they are allowed until they are prohibited by a text. The absence of a prohibiting text is an important argument for those who hold *al-azl* to be permissible and therefore he proceeded to presume the existence of such a text in Judama's tradition.

He argued that the tradition reported by Judama confirms the prohibition of *al-azl* and *must, therefore, be of a later date*, having the effect of abrogating all the other traditions which allow *al-azl*. While he produced no historical proof, he challenged those who claimed otherwise to provide the dated proof. He considered as spurious some of the other traditions.

Ibn Hazm referred also, though briefly, to the dual meaning in Abu Sa'id's tradition and quoted Ibn Sirin as claiming that it was closer to prohibition. Paradoxically, he acknowledged as valid the traditions reporting the permissibilty of *al-azl* by Jabir, Ibn Abbas, Sa'd Ibn Abi Waqqas, Zayd Ibn Thabit and Ibn Mass'oud, but glossed over them without comment. He also listed the names of the Companions he claimed to have disliked or disapproved of *al-azl*. These included Ali Ibn Abi Talib, Ibn Omar, Omar himself, Othman and Ibn Mass'oud, whom he had earlier reported as being among those who approved of *al-azl*.²³ He was, of course, mistaken about Ali and Omar, both of whom are known to have sanctioned *al-azl*.

Refutation of the prohibition

Ibn Hazm's arguments were refuted repeatedly and in some detail by early theologians. Opposing him were al-Ghazali (d.1111) and Ibn al-Qayyim (d.1350). Later came al-Zabidi (d.1790) and Shawkani (d.1830) and, in contemporary times, Madkour (published 1965) and al-Boutti (published 1976).

Attempts at reconciling the traditions and solving any presumed contradictions anticipated Ibn Hazm. For example, more than a century before Ibn Hazm, **Ja'afar al-Tahawi**, (d.933) suggested that the Prophet may have used the phrase 'that is hidden infanticide' early in his mission in congruence with the Jewish law in the absence of any revealed rulings abrogating it. When, however, the Prophet was appraised of the time when the clot was made into another creature (Sura 23: 12–14) he realized that *al-azl* was permissible.²⁴

This is, of course, mere speculation by al-Tahawi. He was challenged by Ibn Rushd and Ibn al-Arabi on the grounds that the Prophet could not have maintained something according to Jewish law and then categorically denied something similar.²⁵

Al-Ghazali (d.1111) was very methodical in dealing with Judama's tradition. He stressed that reliable traditions confirming the permissibility of *al-azl* also existed; that the phrase 'hidden infanticide' in the tradition had the same connotation as in the phrase 'dissimulation is "hidden polytheism"' and that this would presuppose disfavor rather than interdiction. He recalled Imam Ali's rejection of the description of *al-azl* as minor infanticide – based on the seven stages in fetal development before *wa'd* could be claimed. Al-Ghazali added that *al-azl* was not like *wa'd* or abortion because it does not constitute a crime against a being already in existence.²⁶

Al-Nawawi (d.1272) in his authoritative commentary on *Sahih Muslim* championed the concept of reconciling the two sets of traditions. Although the concept was mentioned before by al-Baihaqi (d.1066), al-Nawawi's statement was significant because of his prominence as an ultra conservative. He considered that the 'disallowing' traditions should be taken to mean disfavor (*karaha tanzihiyya*) not prohibition, while the 'allowing' traditions negate prohibition but do not cancel disfavor. That is why he started his summary of the evidence by saying that '*al-azl*, to us, is disfavored [*makrouh*] under all circumstances'. It is because of this statement that some consider that al-Nawawi was opposed to *al-azl* when in fact he allows it with disfavor.²⁷

I should mention here that *disfavor* or failing to do the more meritorious (*karaha tanzihiyya*) means that the act is lawful; it involves no sin and does not invoke reprimand. It is therefore wrong to translate the word as 'blameworthy' as sometimes happens in English language reports. It is disfavored or more simply disliked.

Ibn al-Qayyim (d.1350) refuted the views of those prohibiting *al-azl* and mentioned Ibn Hazm by name. He reviewed theologians attempting to reconcile Judama's and other traditions. One group, for example, take the traditions collectively to mean permissibility with some disfavor. Others maintained that the Jews claimed only that pregnancy could never occur with *al-azl* (a contention that it is similar to curtailing progeny by *wa'd*). Denying this claim, the Prophet said, 'If Allah willed its creation, nothing could stop Him.'

Ibn al-Qayyim then rejected Ibn Hazm's claim that Judama's tradition abrogated several other traditions. For that Ibn Hazm needed dates which were impossible to establish.[28]

Al-Iraqi the father, (d.1404) in his commentary on al-Tirmidhi, took Judama's tradition to mean ejaculation outside the 'womb' of the pregnant woman, thus depriving the fetus of the semen which nourishes it, and may result in its loss (*wa'd*). This is of course a biological error.

His juristic ability is best evidenced in his attempt to differentiate between 'hidden' infanticide (in Judama's tradition) and 'minor' infanticide. Minor infanticide, he explained, refers to killing a live born child, *whereas* hidden infanticide is not actual infanticide. In his opinion, reference to *al-azl* as infanticide amounted to figure of speech meaning only intent to avoid pregnancy.[29]

Al-Baihaqi (d.1066) in his *Al-Sunan al-Kubra* concluded that reporters allowing *al-azl* were greater in number and more trustworthy than those against it. He also concluded that while *al-azl* might have some *karaha tanzihiyya* it was not prohibited.[30]

A detailed account appears in **Ibn Hajar**'s (d.1449) *Fath al-Bari*, a commentary on *Sahih al-Bukhari*. He found that Judama's tradition does not actually prohibit *al-azl*. He affirmed that calling *al-azl* '*hidden* infanticide' was a figure of speech which did not make it *haram*. He also reflected, as did other theologians (*al-Iraqis*), on the distinction between 'hidden' infanticide in Judama's tradition and 'minor' infanticide in the traditions in which the Prophet criticized the Jews. In the latter it denotes an actual murder, while 'hidden' involves no such action. He added that both *al-azl* and *wa'd* have the same intention, i.e. to avoid additional children. While *wa'd* combines both intention and the actual murder, *al-azl* stops at the level of intention which is no crime. That is why it was called 'hidden'.[31]

Al-Ayni (d.1451) considered several possibilities in his *Omdat al-Qari*, another commentary on *Sahih al-Bukhari*. He stated

That Judama's tradition is confused in narration as claimed by Ibn al-Arabi; that Judama's tradition has been counterbalanced by Jabir's tradition; and, that Jabir's tradition has, in turn, been confirmed by two other traditions – those reported by Abu-Sa'id and by Abu Huraira.

He commented further that if it is claimed that Judama entered into Islam only at the time of Makkah's surrender (*fath*), which makes her tradition late, there are also reports that she entered into Islam before *al-Fath* as authenticated by Abdel-Haqq.[32]

In his *Sharh Fath al-Qadir*, **Ibn al-Humam** (d.1457) provided a short but impressive account indicating that *al-azl* has been permitted by the majority of '*ulama*' (theologians) even though some Companions disliked it because of Judama's tradition. Then he pronounced that 'the appropriate conclusion [*al-sahih*] is permissibility'. He found that Judama's tradition had been properly counteracted by the report on the stages of fetal development by Ali in the presence of Omar.[33]

Al-Shawkani (d.1830) in his *Nayl al-Awtar* summarizd previous views and emphasized that Judama's tradition did not entail prohibition; that Jabir's tradition and others like it confirmed tacit approval by the Prophet since he certainly knew about *al-azl* and did not prohibit it; and that Judama's tradition could be weakened because the part on *al-azl* was omitted from the four *Sunan* compilations.[34]

Turning to twentieth-century theologians:

Sheik M.S. Madkour in an Arabic pamphlet on 'The View of Islam on Birth Control' (published in 1965) followed the example of Shawkani in reviewing other theologians' work. In refuting Ibn Hazm's account he made the following points:

- Ibn Hazm needs specific dates to prove that one tradition abrogated another, which is impossible.
- Reconciliation of the two sets is possible by assuming a *karaha tanzihiyya*.
- Ibn Hazm's report on Omar and other Companions as disapproving of *al-azl* conflicts with other more reliable traditions.
- Ibn Hazm's claim that Ali did not practice *al-azl* does not make it prohibited. It is not expected that all Companions would practice something that is merely permissible. Furthermore, there are reliable reports that Ali did practice *al-azl*.
- Ibn Hazm authenticated Jabir's tradition but left it without comment.
- Madkour argued convincingly that 'had the permissibility been abrogated, Companions like Jabir would have reflected that in their traditions and Ali – after the death of the Prophet in the presence of Caliph Omar – would not have negated *al-azl* as being *wa'd*.'[35]

Al-Boutti (Sheikh, Dr Sa'id Ramadan), an opponent of the family planning movement but not of family planning practices, published his book *Birth Control: Preventive and Curative Aspects* in 1976. He selected eight important traditions, corresponding to Traditions 1.1, 6.3, 6.2, 6.1, 2.2, 3.1, 8.1 and 9.2. in this chapter and commented on them as follows:

- If we exclude Judama's tradition, we conclude that *al-azl* is permissible to prevent pregnancy, although the content of the traditions may indicate some *karaha*.
- Jabir's tradition is very convincing, but some traditions with double meaning phrases may cast a shadow on permissibility.
- This shadow is dispelled by the tradition in which the Prophet explicitly allowed *al-azl*.
- In relation to Judama's tradition, he found that theologians had four choices:

    (a) that Judama's tradition implies *karaha tanzihiyya* as al-Nawawi and al-Tahawi indicated;
    (b) that Judama's tradition is 'weak';
    (c) prohibition prevailed in the beginning, then permission came later which requires dates that are not available;
    (d) that prohibition is the right thing, according to Ibn Hazm.

He appraised Judama's tradition and drew the following conclusions:

- There is no reason to infer the weakness of Judama's tradition because the expression 'It is hidden *wa'd*' denotes only disfavor (*karaha tanzihiyya*). It does not denote prohibition.
- There is no evidence for those who claim that *al-azl* was prohibited in the early days of Islam and then allowed. This requires dates for the traditions which are unobtainable.
- There is no basis for Ibn Hazm's claim that Judama's tradition abrogated the traditions that sanctioned *al-azl*. On the contrary Jabir's tradition that the Companions *used to* practice *al-azl* at the time of the Prophet affirms the continuity of permissibility after the death of the Prophet (PBUH). Had the final decision been prohibition, Jabir would have most certainly reported it, yet he did not.
- Judama's tradition is superceded by the other traditions in which the Prophet denied categorically that *al-azl* is minor infanticide.
- It is possible to follow Ibn Hajar and the majority of jurists in reconciling the two traditions by assuming *karaha tanzihiyya* but not prohibition. He, al-Boutti, used the principle of analogous deduction to sanction new methods of contraception.[36]

Finally the head of the council of *'ulama'* in Maghreb, Sheikh **(Dr) M. al-Makki al-Nasiri**, summarized the comments of Judama's tradition is Islamic jurisprudence as follows:

> Regarding the uncertainty occasioned by the tradition reported by Judama, scholars of religion have expressed diverse opinions in their attempt to reconcile it with *al-azl* as a permissible practice. We find those ideas in Murtada al-Zabidi's commentary on al-Ghazali's *Revival of Religious Sciences* and in Shawkani's *Nayl al-Awtar*. One group says that what is meant by Judama's tradition is merely *to point out impeccability (tanzih)*. This group claims that the tradition itself does not explicitly denote prohibition, that calling *al-azl* 'hidden infanticide' does not necessarily imply that it is prohibited. Two elements are present in infanticide according to this group: first, the intention to commit the act; and secondly, the act itself. The act also is concrete and objective, whereas in *al-azl* only the intention is present. This is why it is described as hidden. This is the opinion of Ibn al-Qayyim.

Sheikh al-Nasiri continued

> Another group of scholars solved the problem posed by the tradition of Judama of Asad by suggesting that it is inherently weak, given its conflict with the most familiar traditions or that, Judama's tradition dealing with *al-ghayl*, as related by Sa'id Ibn Abi Ayyub, has a continuation, lacking in the same tradition as related by Abu al-Aswad, and left out by Malik and Yahya in their versions of that same tradition; or that Judama's tradition may be deemed of no force, since its continuation is not mentioned by the four standard collections of the traditions [*Sunan*] and because it conflicts with all the traditions on the same subject which are included in the standard compilations.

He also stated 'al-Tahawi definitely considers Judama's tradition as abrogated.'[37]

In summary
Taking in mind this in-depth analysis by so many theologians, I may venture another kind of classification based on the level of support that each category of traditions lends to *al-azl* as various jurists argued.

(A) Strong unequivocal support for al-azl
Category 3: Traditions 3.1, 3.2, 3.3.
Category 1: Traditions 1.1, 1.2, 1.3.

FAMILY PLANNING IN THE QUR'AN AND THE *SUNNAH*

Category 2: Traditions 2.1, 2.2, 2.3, 2.4.
Category 5: Traditions 5.1, 5.2.
Category 4: Traditions 4.1, 4.2, 4.3, 4.4, 4.5.
Category 7: Traditions 7.1, 7.2.
Category 9: Traditions 9.1, 9.2, 9.3, 9.4, 9.5, 9.6, 9.7.

(B) *Seemingly equivocal support*
Category 6: Traditions 6.1, 6.2, 6.3, 6.4, 6.5, 6.6.

The equivocal nature is *removed* considering other traditions and by considering the linguistic aspects of the statements.

(C) *Disfavorable*
Category 8: Tradition 8.1.

This has been surpassed by the seven traditions included in Category 9.

The majority ruling, given reconciliation by eminent jurists, is permissibility of *al-azl* with *karaha tanzihiyya* (being less than impeccable). This does require, however, a wife's permission. As will be revealed later, where there is justification for avoiding pregnancy (for health or economic reasons or in enemy territory) the ruling is that *al-azl* becomes not only permissible but recommended.

Through further research and use of other sources of jurisprudence, the legal schools formulated detailed positions on *al-azl* and by analogy other forms of contraception. This is the subject of the next chapter.

PART III

Family Planning in Islamic Jurisprudence

8

Family planning in Islamic jurisprudence (legal schools) from the seventh to the nineteenth century

The preceding chapters demonstrate beyond doubt the formidable task undertaken by the jurists and theologians to resolve issues related to contraception and family formation. As Huseyn Atay (1974) puts it:

Muslim scholars, and jurists have done a remarkable job in their attempt to remove the *prima facie* differences and apparent contradictions in the rulings, and in trying to fit them into a consistent system, free from disorder and disarray.[1]

A CHRONOLOGY OF SCHOLARSHIP

From the dawn of Islam to the present day, jurists from various schools of jurisprudence and from various locales, have given considerable attention to the issue of contraception and have documented their views in their texts of *fiqh* or jurisprudence. At no time during a period spanning fourteen centuries did the interest of the jurists wane – each successive group treated the subject with renewed vitality and the zeal of rediscovery. Even in the darkest periods of history when the Islamic Empire started to break up and under the foreign occupation that followed, jurists continued to research the issue and document their views. Islamic jurisprudence flourished against all odds, proving the Prophet's promise:

«إنما يبعث الله لهذه الأمة على رأس كل مائة عام من يجدد لها دينها»
رواه أبو داود عن أبى هريرة

Verily, Allah sends to this nation, at the turn of each century, someone who will regenerate its religion.

Authenticated by Abu Dawoud

Appendix 1 lists the names of theologians who touched upon the subject of contraception (*al-azl*) and/or family formation. They are classified according to the century in which they flourished or died. The list is not comprehensive – many names have been omitted – but it demonstrates continuity. The list does not include twentieth-century jurists whose use of conferences, committees and official *fatwas* to discuss contraception are dealt with in Chapters 11 and 12.

Jurists typically reflect the views of the *legal schools* they represent. Exceptions do occur, of course.

Issues discussed by jurists

Jurists over the centuries did not confine their juristic responsibility to determining the legality of contraception, but went beyond that to an evaluation of the validity of the reason for avoiding pregnancy and such issues as the legal status of children born despite the use of contraception.

SCHOOLS OF ISLAMIC JURISPRUDENCE (AL-MADHAHIB AL-FIQHIYYA)[2]

Distinct schools of islamic jurisprudence evolved over time, each bearing the name of the leading jurist, Imam or founder. These schools are called *madhahib* (singular *madhhab*) which means literally paths or ways. The schools represent different ways of interpretation and are not different religions, denominations or churches as exist in Christianity. Nor is the term 'sect' favored since it connotes a dissenting or schismatic religious body.

All schools of jurisprudence consider the Qur'an and the Prophet's *Sunnah* as their primary sources. Where they differ is in relation to some interpretations, the validity of other sources of jurisprudence and the methodology of formulating a ruling.

The evolution of these schools was necessitated by the increasing secularization of the ruling families (the Umayyads in particular). Instead of devoting time and effort to fulfill their roles as knowledgeable religious leaders, Imams or Caliphs, the rulers of that time kept the prestige of this designation but appointed judges (*qadis*) for the settlement of disputes based on their own opinion (*ra'y*) in the absence of a unifying system of recognized laws or hierarchical supreme courts or councils.

The knowledgeable theologians, called '*ulama*' (for their *ilm* or knowledge), or jurists, called *fuqaha*' (for their *fiqh* or role in providing rulings on some matter), proceeded to systematize Islamic Law through a process of qualified inquiry (*ijtihad*). This effort perpetuated two parallel activities. First, Imam Malik initiated a rigorous collection and authentication of the Prophet's traditions or *ahadith* which was thence carried on by al-Bukhari and the other compilers. Second, a systematic organization and development of Islamic Law was undertaken based on the Qur'an and *Sunnah* as well as juristic sources and approaches. This was led by Abu Hanifa, Malik, al-Shafe'i, Ibn Hanbal and others.

At a time when the Islamic Empire was vast, the schools that were established in different places inevitably reflected some of the local inclinations. For example, scholars in Iraq were upholders of personal or private judgement (this affected Abu Hanifa). In Medina the approaches were more traditional (which affected Malik and Ibn Hanbal). Al-Shafe' was raised in both schools and was able to make use of all the approaches, thus becoming the architect of Islamic jurisprudence.

The Sunni schools

As stated before, these were so called because they adhere to the *Sunnah* of the Prophet, including his sayings, deeds or tacit approval, as well as the example of his Companions. The Sunnis have great affection for the Prophet's descendants and relatives (*ahl al-bayt*), with special regard for Ali and great compassion for his son al-Husayn (grandson of the Prophet) because of his appalling murder at Karbala'. However, they neither revere them nor do they restrict Imamism to them exclusively as do the Shi'ites. There are four Sunni schools named after their founders: Hanafi, Maliki, Shafe'i, and Hanbali.

The Sunnis spread over the Islamic world, with one school or another predominating in some areas. Their method of *ijtihad* centers primarily on the Qur'an and *Sunnah*, followed by consensus, analogy and some of the other sources of jurisprudence.

The Kharijite movement and the Ibaddi school

These were the first to separate themselves from the Community during the Siffin battle (Iraq) between Ali's and Mu'awia's forces in AD 657. When the latter were threatened with defeat, they wanted to force arbitration (*tahkim*) of the word of Allah by raising their Qur'an on their lances. Ali and many of his followers were keen to stop bloodshed among Muslims accepted arbitration too readily. A group of Ali's followers rejected it and walked out on him, hence they were called the *Khawarij* (literally the 'walkers out'); in English they are the Khariji or Kharijites or seceders.

The Kharijite movement began, not as a school of jurisprudence, but as a movement against the Community, formed by rebels who were rigid adherents to their beliefs and puritanical in their practice. They rejected the restriction of Imamism to family lines and accepted any pious Muslim, duly elected, as their more preferred Imam or Caliph. The latter could be deposed (impeached) for the slightest sin. That is why they fought any ruler they deemed to have deviated from the prescribed way. However, in considering sinners (minor or major) as infidels whose blood it was legal to shed, they exceeded the moderate character of Islam.

There were five Kharijite movements: the Sufris, the Najadat, the Azraquis, the Shaybanis and the Ibaddis. All vanished except the Ibaddis, the most moderate, who grew increasingly closer to the Community, until eventually they had the same beliefs but were more uncompromising in their adherence.

The Shi'ites

The Shi'ite movement anticipated the development of the Sunni schools. It started in the first century AH (after Hijra or migration of the Prophet in AD 622 from Makkah to Medina) as a movement which agreed with the Community in every respect except on the political issues of Imamism. During the juristic activities of the second and third centuries AH, the Shi'ites started to develop a body of theology (*fiqh*) of their own.

The Shi'ites (*Shi'ia* means the inclined or partisans) are devoted to Imam Ali (the cousin and son-in-law of the Prophet). They believe that Imamism should be confined to Ali's descendants from Fatima, the Prophet's daughter. Some of their extremists (*ghulat al-shi'ia*) may have even looked upon Imam Ali with reverence and disavowed the Companions who disagreed with him, especially Othman and his cousin Mu'awiyah (head of the Umayyad dynasty). Differences with Sunnis were not always scholarly; politics and rivalries vitiated the relationship. With the passage of time, mysticism (mainly from Persia) because mingled with compassion for the Imams who were held as infallible and whose directives could not be disputed.

Several Shi'ite schools developed over time, some of which have disappeared. The leading contemporary schools are the Zaydis, the Imamis, and the Isma'ilis. The genealogy of the leaders of these schools and their relation to Ali is given in Figure 8.1.

The Shi'ites take also from the Qur'an and *Sunnah*, but they particularly value the traditions related to or reported by Ali whom they consider infallible. They reject traditions related by Companions who disagree with Ali and held some of their later Imams as equal to the Companions. (Some Shi'ites reject the first three Caliphs on the assumption that Ali should have been the one to follow the Prophet immediately.) *Ijma'* to them is restricted to the agreements which include Ali or the consensus of their own community. *Qiyas* was also similarly restricted by them.

Figure 8.2 provides a list of the founders of the schools of jurisprudence and the time when they appeared. Figure 8.3 provides some detail on each school.

Figure 8.1 Genealogy of founders of Shi'ite schools and the Abbasid dynasty

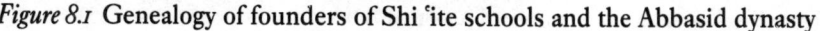

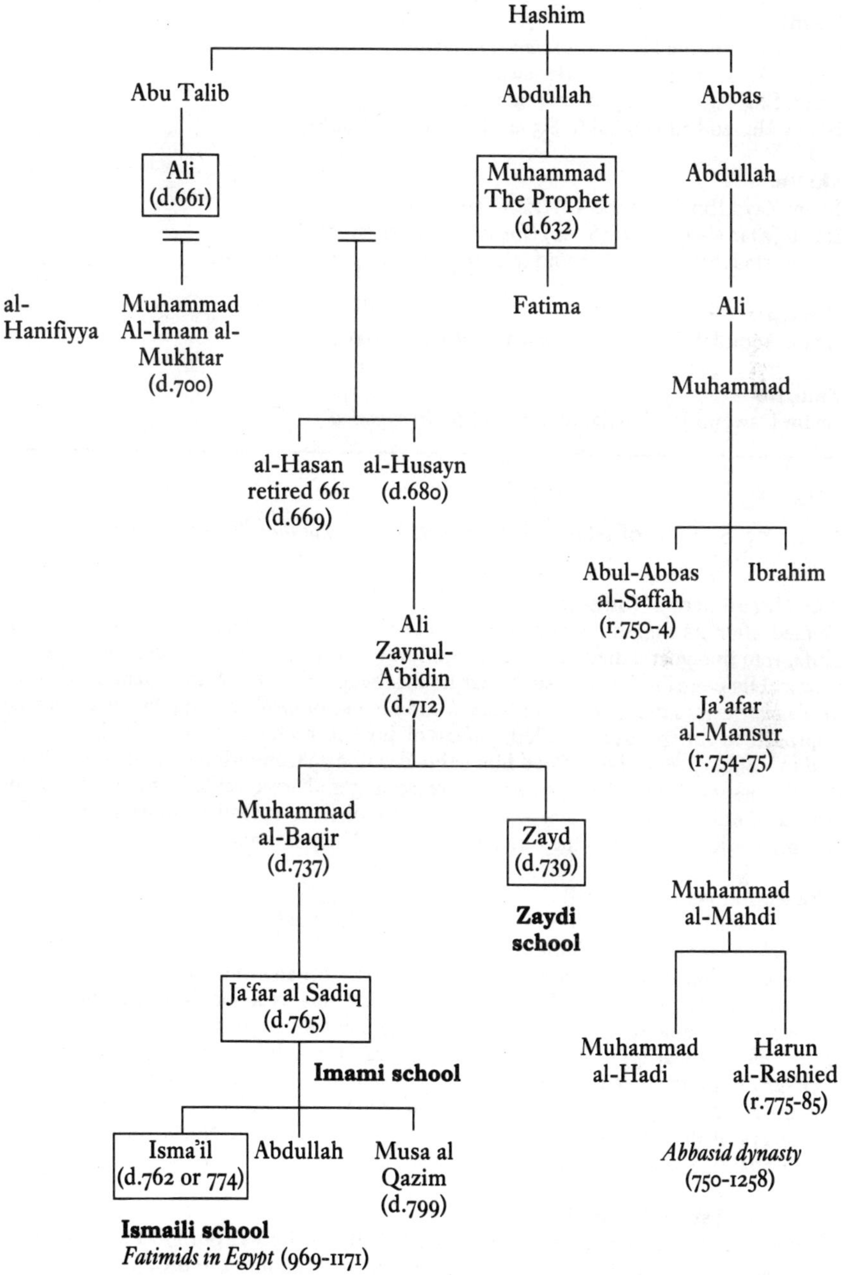

Figure 8.2 Founders of schools of jurisprudence

Sunni
Imam Abu Hanifa (d.767 AD) (*Hanafi madhhab*)
Imam Malik (d.795 AD) (*Maliki madhhab*)
Imam Shafe'i (d.820 AD) (*Shafe'i madhhab*)
Imam Ahmad Ibn Hanbal (d.855 AD) (*Hanbali madhhab*)

Shi'ite
Imam Zayd Ibn Ali (d.700 AD) (*Zaydi madhhab*)
Imam Ja'far al-Sadiq (d.765 AD) (*Imami, Twelvers madhhab*)
Imam Isma'il Ibn Ja'far al Sadiq (eighth century) (*Isma'ili madhhab*)

Kharijite
Imam Abdullah Ibn Ibadd (d.708 AD) (*Ibaddi madhhab*)

Zahirite
Imam Dawoud Ibn Khalaf (d.883 AD) (*Zahiri madhhab*)

Figure 8.3 Schools of Islamic jurisprudence (*al-madhahib al-fiqhiyya*)

The Hanafi school (Sunni)
Named after its founder Imam Abu Hanifa (Nu'man Ibn Thabit) who was born in Kufa, Iraq in 699 and died in AD 767 some seventeen years after the Abbassids came to power. His contribution was such that he has been called the great Imam or *al-Imam al-a'zam*. Besides the Qur'an and *Sunnah* and the use of *ijma'* and *qiyas* he developed an approach to jurisprudence called *istihsan* or juristic preference. Abu Hanifa himself and two of his peers who assisted him (Abu Yusuf, d.798, and Mohammad al Shaybani, d.805) possessed remarkable powers of reasoning and were callled 'the upholders of private opinion'. Followers of the Hanafi school have spread in most parts of the Islamic world. Hanafi was the official way of the Abbassids and the Ottoman Empire.

The Maliki school (Sunni)
Named after Imam Malik Ibn Anas who was born in Medina in 712 and died in AD 795. The school reflects the Medina (Hijaz – now Saudi Arabia) *'ulama'*. He viewed the Medina dwellers from Mohammad to the Companions and their successors (*tabi'oun*) as the example of Muslim living, and developed this as a source of jurisprudence. *'Ulama'* in Medina were known as the 'upholders of the tradition'. To Malik, *ijma'* and *qiyas* refer primarily to the Medina dwellers. He minimized juristic preference (*istihsan*) but introduced the consideration of public welfare, *al-masalih al-mursala*. He composed a comprehensive collection of rules and *ahadith* called *Al-Muwatta'*. Followers of the Maliki school have spread to Egypt, Hijaz, North Africa, Andalus (Arab Spain), and are now predominant also in West Africa and West Sudan.

The Shafe'i school (Sunni)
Named after Imam al-Shafe'i (Mohammad Ibn Idris) who was born in Palestine in AD 767, and raised in Makkah. He is a descendent of Muttalib, the brother of Hashim,

Fig. 8.3 continued

who is the grandfather of the Prophet. He lived in Baghdad before residing in Egypt, where he died in 820. He was a personal student of Malik and studied the concepts of Abu Hanifa and his disciples, as well as those of 'ulama' in Syria, reviewing particularly the teachings of al-Awza'i (d.774) and many others. He was an authority on the Arabic language which gave him an extra edge in the interpretation of the Qur'an and *hadith*. He is considered the chief architect of Islamic jurisprudence. In his own school he struck a moderate path between Abu Hanifa and Malik. He referred everything to the Qur'an and *Sunnah* and would not reject any authenticated *hadith*. He and followers like Imam al-Nawawi and al-Baihaqi developed a talent for reconciling seemingly conflicting *ahadith*. To him *ijma'* means the consensus of the entire community (all centers of Juristic research). Appreciating the difficulty of achieving this, Imam al-Ghazali (also a Shafe'ite) reserved it for fundamental issues; while limited *ijma'* is enough for details. *Qiyas* or analogy is used also for the matter of details provided that a text exists for the precedent ruling which is the basis of *qiyas*. Al-Shafe'i formulated his initial concepts and rulings in Iraq, then moved to Egypt where he developed his final *fiqh*. Followers are spread in most parts of the Islamic world, mainly Egypt, Iraq, Syria, East Africa, the Sudan and parts of Asia.

The Hanbali school (Sunni)

Named after Imam Ahmad Ibn Hanbal al-Shaybani, who was born in Baghdad in AD 780 and died in 855. Unlike the other Iraqi jurists who upheld juristic preference, he adhered strictly to the Qur'an and *Sunnah*. He is one of the compilers of the *hadith* and his *Musnad* is a product of great care and effort in authentication. He allowed only a narrow margin for *ijma'* and *qiyas*. He preferred a weak *hadith* to a strong *qiyas*. As a result of these restrictions the Hanbali school proved to be stricter than the others. Followers are fewer than those of the other Sunni schools but are similarly distributed.

The Zaydi Shi'ite school

Named after Imam Zayd (d.AD 700) a grandson of al-Husayn Ibn Ali (see Figure 8.1). This is closest to the Sunni schools and is actually considered a bridge between the Sunnis and the Shi'ites. Among its intellectual leaders is Imam Yahia Ibn Zayd. Zaydis believe in the hereditary transfer of Imamism. Two geographic clusterings developed (each with its own Imam at times). The larger community inhabits the northern and eastern part of North Yemen (Arab Republic of Yemen); the *madhhab* was popularized in Yemen by Imam al-Qasim al-Rassi. The other clustering is in Iran particularly on the Caspian sea coast.

Imami (Ja'fari) Shi'ite school (also *al-ithna-ashriyya* or The Twelvers)

This Shi'ite *madhhab* is related to Imam Ja'far al-Sadiq (d.AD 765). Imam Ja'far is a great grandson of al-Husayn Ibn Ali. He was an authority on *hadith* and is respected by contemporary and subsequent jurists. This group is called Imamis and Twelvers because they have twelve Imams, the Twelfth of whom it is believed disappeared and will return. This is the largest Shi'ite community based mostly in Iran, Iraq, Syria, South Lebanon, Bahrain, Kuwait, Pakistan, Afghanistan, India and some other parts of Asia and Africa.

Isma'ili Shi'ite school (The Seveners – they have seven Imams)

Related to Imam Isma'il the son of Ja'far al Sadiq (d.eighth century). Isma'ilis restrict Imamism to descendants of Isma'il. Isma'ilis have had historical and political impact

Fig. 8.3 continued

having established several states. Abdullah Ibn al-Mahdi founded the Abidi dynasty in North Africa. Isma'il's descendants include al-Mu'izz Lidinillah al-Fatimi, who founded the Fatimid* dynasty in Egypt and built the city of Cairo and Al-Azhar Mosque in 969. Despite 200 years of Shi'ite rule, Egypt remained Sunni. Al-Azhar has since become the citadel of orthodox Islam, mainly Sunni. In 1817 the Shah of Persia gave the Isma'ili Imam the title of 'Agha Khan'. Followers now cluster in Africa especially Zanzibar and Tanzania, as well as in Iran, Pakistan and India.

Zahiri 'literalist' school
This is related to Imam Dawoud Ibn Khalaf (d.883). He started as a follower of Imam Shafe'i but did not approve the use of analogous reasoning (*qiyas*) as a source of jurisprudence. His preference was to base rules on the exact wording of the texts in the Qur'an and *Sunnah* (*Zahir* in Arabic means literal or apparent since they stuck to the literal meaning of texts). Their ways became known through the writings of Imam Ibn Hazm, especially his book *Al-Muhalla*. It is a minority school with very few followers.

The Ibaddi school
This evolved from a *Kharijite* movement into a juristic school, gradually losing its military character. It is named after Abdullah Ibn Ibadd al-Tamimi (d.AD 708). The movement, the most moderate of all *Kharijite* groups, appeared first in Basra, Iraq, in the middle of the second century AH (eighth century AD). Currently it is a minority school. Followers cluster in Oman, Southern Algeria, Libya (Jabal Island) and Tanzania.

Note: *Fatimid comes from Fatima, Ali's wife and the Prophet's daughter. Al-Azhar comes from Fatima's description as *al-zahra*.

A final note
It should be emphasized that there is nothing in Islam that says explicitly or implicitly that Muslims have to belong to a particular school. Imam Ahmad Ibn Hanbal, founder of one of the schools said 'Do not imitate me, nor imitate Malik or Shafe'i. Draw from where they drew.'[3] In other words, the truth is not the monopoly of any one school and Muslims are encouraged to consider various opinions rather than restricting themselves to one school at all times. Until this happens, however, the views of each individual *madhhab* (on family planning, for example) have to be separately considered.

VIEWS OF LEGAL SCHOOLS ON FAMILY PLANNING

Common or *jumhour* position in Islam
Differences among the schools of jurisprudence on the legality of *al-azl* as a family planning method exist but there is more agreement than disagreement. For example, Sunni and Shi'ite scholars have much in common in their basic

stand on family planning. The majority of theologians (*jumhour al-fuqaha'* or *'aammatul'ulama'* or simply *al-jumhour*) from almost all schools of Islamic jurisprudence agree that '*al-azl* is permissible with a wife's consent.' The prominant dissent to this *jumhour* position comes from the Zahiri *madhhab*. Some dissent exists also inside the schools.

The strength of support for the *jumhour* position can be seen in the views of jurists from the different schools as illustrated in the following passages from Imam Ibn Hajar (d.1449) in *Fath Al-Bari* and al-Baji (d.AH494) in *Al-Muntaqa*.

> Ibn Hajar quoted earlier theologians (Ibn Abdel-Barr) who asserted that there was agreement among jurists ['*ulama*'] that *al-azl* is permissible with a wife's permission because coitus is her right and she can demand it.
>
> Ibn Hajar confirms that such *ijma*' was also reported by Ibn Hubaira.[4]
>
> Imam al-Baji from the Maliki school has a similar statement namely that the *jumhour* are in agreement that *al-azl* is permissible with a wife's consent.[5]

There are still enough honest differences of opinion to distinguish one school from another. Likewise variations exist within schools whereby a minority of theologians may express views different from the majority opinion of their school and cross over to share opinions with other schools. This is a welcome occurrence because all schools stem from the same origin.

In almost every *madhhab* there are a few jurists who disallow *al-azl*. Occasionally opponents of family planning seek out these dissenting views and present them as the representative position of the concerned schools. This is deceptive.

In the following presentation, the majority opinion of each *madhhab* is featured first supplemented by quotations from prominent theologians in the school. Examples are given, where dissenting opinions occur.

The Hanafi school (Sunni)

Majority position
The majority position of the *madhhab* is to permit *al-azl* as a contraceptive measure with differences as to the requirement of a wife's consent. The older and more popular position is that it is not allowed without a wife's consent. Later jurists, however, bypass the wife's (or husband's) permission in times of religious decline 'bad times' (*fasad al-zaman*) and in fear of begetting delinquent children (*al walad al sou'*)

Imam Abu Hanifa and his two disciples Abu Yusuf and Mohammad al-Shaybani represent the old school (eighth and ninth centuries AD) and allowed *al-azl* with a wife's consent. This is reported by al-Khwarizmi (d.AD1572) in his *Jami' Masanid Al-Imam Al-A'zam*.[6]

Al-Tahawi (d.AD933) in his *Sharh Ma'ani Al-'Athar* says that *al-azl* is not held in disfavor. When they asked the Prophet (PBUH) about it, he did not command them against it.[7] Tahawi's interpretation of this statement and his reasoning regarding Judama's tradition have been given in the preceding chapter.

Al-Kasani (d.AD1198) in his *Bada'i Al-Sana'i* reiterated that *al-azl* without the wife's permission is 'disliked', i.e. *yukrah* or subject to *karaha*. (In the Hanafi school *karaha* is closer to prohibition, i.e. *karaha tahrimiyya*.) He explained that ejaculation is the way to get a child and this is the wife's right; *al-azl* deprives her of that right. If she gives her consent, *al-azl* is not disliked (*lam yukrah*).[8]

Al-Marghinani (d.AD1197) in his *Hidayat al-Muhtadi* asserts the position of the old school in requiring a wife's consent.[9] Al-Baberti (d.1384) in his commentary, *Sharh al-Inaya* adds that this confirms the permissibility of *al-azl* and recalls that Ibn Mass'oud was asked about it and replied 'There is nothing wrong with it [*la ba'sa bih*]'.[10]

In a later and more detailed commentary, al-Kamal Ibn al-Humam (d.1457) in his *Sharh Fath al-Qadir* states that *al-azl* has been permitted by the majority of theologians ('*aammat al 'ulama*'); a few dislike it because of Judama's tradition. His refutation of that opinion was detailed in the preceding chapter. After stating the majority position of the school in requiring a wife's consent, he added that her consent can be by-passed in 'bad times' in fear of begetting delinquent children. He confirmed that similar excuses could be taken to justify by-passing her consent.[11]

Ibn Nujaim's (d.AD1562) *Al-Bahr al-Ra'iq* confirmed that the correct theological opinion is permission for *al-azl* with a wife's consent. He endorsed the ruling that consent could be bypassed in bad times and also mentioned that *women can block the mouth of the uterus*, as they used to in his time, to prevent semen from reaching the uterus. Ibn Nujaim considered this practice permissible with the husband's consent. His is a first reference to the use of the pessary in early times.[12]

Ibn Abdin (nineteenth century) in *Radd al-Muhtar* and *Minhat al-Khaliq* reiterated the views of the later theologians of the *madhhab* in allowing *al-azl* with consent of the spouse, a consent that can be cancelled in bad times, including when the couple is undertaking an arduous and lengthy journey. He also referred to 'the changing ruling with changing time'.[13]

Finally, Sheikh Abdel Majeed Saleem, the Grand Mufti of Egypt, pronounced a legal *fatwa* in 1937 summarizing the Hanafi school of law. In it he confirmed that the use of *al-azl* or other measures to prevent pregnancy is allowed with consent of the spouse. Such consent could be bypassed in times of religious decay to avoid having delinquent children (the *fatwa* is reproduced in Appendix 2).[14]

The Maliki school (Sunni)

Majority position
The great majority of Maliki jurists affirm the permissibility of *al-azl* to prevent pregnancy subject to the consent of the wife. Some jurists introduced the concept of compensating the woman for her consent if she so wishes.

Such was the juristic ability of Imam Malik, the founder of the school and a resident of Medina, that a saying became legend in Islamic jurisprudence: 'While Malik is in Medina, no one should venture a *fatwa*' – '*Layufta wa Malik fil Madina*'. His book *Al-Muwatta*' which is a primary collection of *hadith* is highly respected. Imam Shafe'i proclaimed that 'After the holy Qur'an there is no other book on earth that is more authentic than the book of Malik.'[15]

Malik's book, *Al-Muwatta*' authenticated seven traditions:

- One by Abu Sa'id on the Bannul Mustaliq battle when the Companions wanted to practice *al-azl* and the Prophet said '*La alaykom alla taf'alu.*' In Arabic, as discussed earlier in Chapter 7, the expression was the subject of controversy. Apparently Imam Malik did not consider it to forbid the practice of *al-azl*.
- Another tradition reported by Malik contained the *fatwa* by al-Hajjaj Ibn Amr, with permission of Zayd Ibn Thabit, in which he said 'It is your tilth, you can water it if you wish or leave it thirsty if you wish.' Again Malik did not criticize this interpretation.
- Four other traditions were authenticating reports about three of the Companions who did practice *al-azl*: Sa'd Ibn Abi Waqqas, Abu Ayyub al Ansary, Abdullah Ibn Abbas; and one who did not practice *al-azl* and who disliked it, Abdullah Ibn Omar.
- Imam Malik reported also Judama's tradition but only the part of it related to *al-ghayla*. The part of the tradition that made it famous, namely that on *al-azl* was not reported by Malik. With four other major compilations omitting the *al-azl* part, doubts are cast on Judama's tradition.

At the end of the account in *Al-Muwatta*', Imam Malik stated his views very explicitly and this became the position of the Maliki *madhhab*. He ruled that 'No man shall practice *al-azl* without the [free] wife's consent.'[16] This means the practice is permitted with the wife's consent. This is most significant for a number of reasons. Malik lived in Medina and had first-hand knowledge of contraceptive practice among the Companions and their followers (*al-tabiʿoun*). Hence there should not be any doubt that some Companions and their followers practiced *al-azl*. Also, having lived at a time following that of the Prophet and having continued to sanction *al-azl* could only mean that *al-azl* was being practiced at the time of the Prophet's death and was therefore permissible and *not abrogated*. This indirectly refutes the claims that Judama's tradition abrogated the permissibility in the other traditions. Further, Imam Malik submitted *Al-Muwatta'*, including his account on *al-azl*, to seventy jurists in Medina who agreed with it.

Ibn Abdel Barr (fifth century AH) is one of the Maliki jurists who was also an authority on *hadith* and traditions and gave a famous commentary on *Al-Muwatta'* called *Al-Tamhid Lima Fil-Muwatta' Min Maʿany Waʿasanid*. He summarily stated the position of the *madhhab* as follows: 'There is no disagreement between theologians that *al-azl* cannot be practiced with a free wife without the wife's consent.'[17]

Al-Qurtubi (d.AD1272) confirmed this by saying in his *Al-Jamiʿ Liʾahkam al-Qurʾan* that 'the drop of seed is not a thing in actual fact, and therefore no wrong is done by the women if she expels it, unless it is already lodged in the woman's uterus. It is for all purposes as though it is still in the man's loins.' Thus he allows the expulsion of semen subsequent to having reached the uterus, but prior to implantation or lodging in the uterus.[18] This helps explain the practice in early Islamic medicine of prescribing ointments for men and greasy suppositories for women to help the semen seep out of the vagina and not travel up through the cervical canal to the uterus.

Al-Qurtubi, as already mentioned, explains the Arabic expression in some traditions (*La alaykom alla tafʿalu*) as 'you are not obliged to avoid it'; and also agrees with Imam Shafeʿi regarding multitude of children (see Chapter 7).

Al-Baji (d.494AH) in his *Al-Muntaqa* (a four volume commentary on *Al-Muwatta'*), considered the first *hadith* reported by Imam Malik about Ibn Muhairiz (asking Abu Saʿid about *al-azl*) and concluded 'What the knowledgeable *sahaba* used to do in answering inquiries was to resort first to texts. If no text existed, they resorted to *qiyas* and insight. But in the presence of a text, they never look elsewhere.'

Regarding the traditions in *Al-Muwatta'* and other compilations dealing with *al-azl*, Imam al-Baji said that while most jurists are in support of coitus interruptus, some like Ibn Omar disliked it and some others equated it with minor infanticide or *waʾd*. This he rebutted, citing Imam Ali Ibn Abi Talib who asserted that 'it cannot be *waʾd* until it goes through the seven stages of creation', a claim approved by Caliph Omar.

Imam al-Baji then referred to those who disliked coitus interruptus 'basing their opinion on the Prophet's tradition *La alaykom alla taf alu* by which the Prophet may have meant (and Allah knows best) that you would suffer no harm, if you do not do it indicating dislike but not prohibition.' He concluded that the majority of jurists consider *al-azl* permissible (*ja'iz*) with a wife's consent.

Turning to the part of Judama's traditon that deals with *al-ghayl* or *al-ghayla*, al-Baji felt that the statement that the Prophet (PBUH) was about to prohibit *al-ghayla*, until he found it did not harm Persia and Rome, was a sort of *ijtihad* on the Prophet's part in the absence of a Qur'anic text prohibiting the practice. He explained that the Prophet apparently did not want to impose hardship on his people especially those with one wife, by having to abstain for a long period. He did not dismiss the possible danger of *al-ghayla* to children, but assumed that its prevalence was rare while the abstention from marital relations was a more common hardship.

He ended this section on *al-ghayla* by considering the situation of a wet nurse. He emphasized that the wet nurse may be asked to abstain from pregnancy during the period of breast-feeding especially if the child is at risk of suffering ill-health.

Al-Baji concluded by confirming that 'Maliki's ruling that *al-azl* is permissible with a wife's consent is the ruling of all the jurists *jumhour al-fuqaha*'."[19]

Ibn Juzayy (d.AD1340) stated in his *Al-Qawanin al-Fiqhiyya* that *al-ghayla* is not prohibited. As to *al-azl*, its sanction depends on the wife's consent, although al-Shafe'i sanctioned it absolutely. If the semen is 'held by the uterus', it should not be expelled. The prohibition is stronger when the fetus is formed and is the strongest when 'ensoulment' takes place. There is consensus that such action would be killing a living soul.[20]

Al-Zurqani (d.AD1710) in his *Sharh Muwatta' al-Imam Malik*, reviewed other compilations of *hadith* in addition to *Al-Muwatta'*, and provided an interesting account on *al-azl*.

In relation to Ibn Muhairiz's tradition, al-Zurqani suggested that the *sahaba* wanted to ask the Prophet (PBUH) about *al-azl* because they were afraid it would be equivalent to hidden infanticide. He interpreted the Prophet's answer (*La alaykom alla taf alu*) to mean 'there is no harm if you should not practice it [*al-azl*]', i.e. no prohibition.

He recalled Jabir's other tradition about the *sahaba*'s practice of *al-azl* which was not prohibited either by the Qur'an or the Prophet. He confirmed that when a Companion refers a practice to the time of the Prophet, it assumes the same validity as a reliable (*marfou'*) tradition, provided the Prophet knew about it. He also recalled Jabir's tradition in which the Prophet (PBUH) sanctioned *al-azl* by saying 'practice *al-azl* with her, if you so wish.' He did not neglect to mention that some *sahaba* disliked *al-azl*.

Al-Zurqani quoted Ibn Abdel Barr's statement that sanctioning is the position of the great majority (*jumhour*) of theologians and, predictably, he emphasized the need for a wife's consent. He implicitly rejected the assertion that *al-azl* is *wa'd* by recalling the tradition about the meeting (*majlis*) at Omar's and the reference to the Jew's claim that *al-azl* was minor infanticide. He emphasized that Imam Ali rejected that with consent of Omar. In relation to Judama's tradition he provided some details to confirm that *al-azl* is not minor infanticide.

As to abortion, al-Zurqani quoted Ibn Hajar's *al-Fath* that the position on expelling the *nutfa* before 'ensoulment' parallels that on *al-azl*; whoever sanctions *al-azl* sanctions that too. However, al-Zurqani added that the expulsion takes the action further than *al-azl*.[21]

Khalil (d.AD1374) better known as Sidi Khalil became very famous for his summary (*Al-Mukhtasar*) of Maliki law. Called the master of religious law, he achieved a great reputation in Egypt (where he taught *Shari'ah* law and where he became prominent among the 'ulama' of Egypt), in North Africa and later in West Africa.

In his authoritative style, he has this to say on *al-azl* starting with the slave wife:

> The husband of a slave wife may, with his wife's and her master's consent, practice *al-azl* with her. The same with a free wife, provided she consents.[22]

As to abortion:

> It is forbidden for a woman to attempt in any way to procure abortion, even though the husband should consent to it. The same applies in cases where pregnancy is the result of illicit intercourse.

For the rest of the Maliki jurists, there is so much agreement among them, that it is safe to summarize their views without repeating the text from each. They all agree on the permissibility of *al-azl* provided the wife consents. Included are the following selected jurists:

- Al-Hattab (d.AD1547) in his *Mawahib al-Jalil Lisharh Mukhtasar Khalil*.[23]
- Al-Dardir (d.AD1786) in his *Al-Sharh al-Kabir*.[24]
- Al-Dusuqi (d.AD1815) in his *Hashiyat*.[25]
- Eleish (d.AD1881) in his *Fath al-Aliyy al-Malik Fil-Fatwa Ala Madhab Ibn Malik*.[26]

Among texts of the later jurists mention is made of a *monetary arrangement* as compensation for the woman's consent. Al-Dardir, for example says 'The free wife [may] consent to her husband [to practice coitus interruptus] free or for some small or large compensation.'[27]

Finally, Dr al-Makki al-Nasiri, whose comment on Judama's tradition was mentioned in the preceding chapter, says in his 1974 paper on the permissibility of contraception,

> Family planning is in harmony with family formation in Islam if what is involved is rendering parents – men and women – aware of their marital and parental responsibilities and more appreciative of their responsibilities both morally and materially, so that they resist regarding marital life merely as something of pleasure and amusement, and so that they become more concerned about their children's future and keener about bringing up healthy children, able to deal with the problems of life.[28]

The Shafe'i school (Sunni)

Majority position

The characteristic position of the Shafe'i school is that *al-azl* is liberally allowed without the wife's consent. If anything, there is some venial disfavor or *karaha tanziheyya*. Thus when Shafe'is say *yukray* (disliked), they mean it is less than impeccable. They argue that the woman has the right to intercourse (*dhawq ul-usaila*), but not to ejaculation. Several jurists cross over and adopt the *jumhour* position of requiring the wife's consent. A few disallow *al-azl* altogether.

Imam al-Shafe'i (d.AD820), the founder of the school, is known to have had liberal views on family planning. Ibn al-Qayyim quotes him as saying 'We report on several of the Prophet's Companions that they allowed *al-azl* and found nothing wrong with it.'[29] He is also famous for his explanation of the phrase '*Thalika adna alla ta'oulu*' in verse 3, Sura 4 concerning the advisability of having one rather than four wives, as meaning 'you will not have a multiplicity of children'.[30] (See Chapter 6 under multitude.)

Al-Fairouzabadi al-Shirazi (d.1083) was one of the early jurists who crossed over and adopted the common position of allowing *al-azl* only with a wife's consent. His account began with a statement that led some to consider him opposed to *al-azl* – '*Al-azl* is disliked (*yukrah*) because of Judama's tradition'. (We now know that the statement is based on the reconciliation effort as explained in the preceding chapter and means only *karaha tanzihiyya*). He continued, 'In the case of the free wife, if it is with her consent, then *al-azl* is allowed; if not, one view is to allow it because she has the right to intercourse but not to ejaculation. The second view is to disallow it because it prevents progeny.' He did not want to commit himself either way.[31]

Al-Ghazali (d.AD1111) provided the first detailed interpretative account on *al-azl*. Contemporary thinkers find in it all the elements of a modern thesis on the subject.

The account starts with a review of the views on *al-azl* and concludes that the correct (*sahih*) view is liberal permissibility. For those who dislike it, he explains, the disfavor attached to it means it is less than impeccable. He asserts that *al-azl* is not murder and is not like abortion or infanticide where there is a crime against a formed fetus or a born child. After considering the process of fertilization, he lists his famous justifications for *al-azl* (see Chapter 9 p. 168). He then rebuts opponents' views including those who cite Judama's tradition. (see preceding chapter). Finally, he presents some relevant traditions permitting *al-azl*.

Al-Ghazali confirms the legality of contraception by comparing the process of conception to the dynamics of making a legal contract in Islam. For a contract to be valid, there must be an offer (*iejab*) and acceptance (*quboul*). If an offer is made then withdrawn before the other party accepts, there is no violation or breach of contract. In the process of conception according to al-Ghazali's understanding of biology, man's semen represents the offer and the woman's 'fluid' should accept it for the formation of an embryo. He used the term '*iniqad*' for fertilization which is close to '*aqd*', the contract. If the semen is prevented from reaching the woman's 'fluid', this is withdrawing the 'offer' before acceptance, i.e. before a contract is drawn up. This is no violation. If, on the other hand, there is interference after formation, this (abortion) in his view is a violation.

Al-Ghazali allows *al-azl* for health and economic reasons and even to preserve a woman's figure and beauty for the continued enjoyment of her husband (which is legal). He felt that fewer children would protect against economic embarrassment, which in turn, is good for piety. (*Qillatul-haraj mu'inon aladdin*). He found no reason to prohibit *al-azl* or to attach conditions to the practice arguing that if avoidance of marriage is not prohibited, neither should be avoiding a pregnancy.[32]

Al-Ghazali's views were further elaborated in Imam Zabidi's multi-volume commentary almost seven centuries later (d.1790): *Ithaf al-Sada al-Muttaqin Bisharh Ihya' Ulum al-Din*. The commentary also reviews the position of the different Sunni schools on birth control, asserting that these schools approve *al-azl* with a wife's permission. Zabidi maintains that birth control does not contradict reliance on Allah (*tawakkul*). He also endorses al-Ghazali's acceptance of the economic rationale for family planning.

In support of al-Ghazali's refutation of Judama's tradition he provides additional quotations from the *Sunnah* and from the research of other theologians since Ghazali's time. He concludes that there is no basis for equating *al-azl* with *wa'd*. He also comments on Jabir's tradition explaining that the language denotes that *al-azl* was practiced at the time of the Prophet with his approval and continued to be used after his death by the *sahaba* and *tabi'oun*.[33]

The views of Imam al-Nawawi (d.AD1277), another leading figure in the

Shafe'i school, are wrongly perceived as negative because he qualifies *al-azl* as disliked. However, and as related earlier, when Shafe'ites say 'disliked', they mean *karaha tanzihiyya*. In his commentary on *Sahih Muslim*, he says

> *al-azl*, to us, is disliked [*makrouh*] in all circumstances irrespective of whether the woman is consenting or not, for it is a means of limiting procreation. That is why it was designated in one tradition as hidden infanticide because it prevents progeny as actual infanticide does. As to the prohibition, our colleagues [our *madhhab*] said ... if the wife is free and gives her consent, *no prohibition*; otherwise, there are two views, the *more correct of which is no prohibition*. What is stated regarding forbiddance in all these traditions and others should be taken to mean *venial disfavor* [*karaha tanzihiyya*], and what is stated regarding permissibility should be taken to *negate prohibition* but does not cancel disfavor altogether.[34]

Al-Hafez al-Iraqi (d. fifteenth century AD) in collaboration with his father Abdel Rahman Ibn al-Hussein al-Iraqi, made a brief case in *Tarh Al-Tathrib*, for *al-azl*. They reviewed two Shafe'i opinions regarding the free woman, namely 'if she consents, *al-azl* is permitted. If she does *not*, then the *correct way* [*al-sahih*] adopted by al-Ghazali, al-Rafe'i and al-Nawawi is permissibility.' Three Shafe'i theologians who disallowed *al-azl* were named: Ibn Habban, Ibn Yunus, and Ibn Abdel Salam. The Iraqis disagreed with them and rejected Ibn Habban's view, in particular, which was based on Judama's tradition. They did not find any proof in the tradition to support prohibition. They stated that their *madhhab* is to allow *al-azl* liberally with no dependence on a wife's consent.[35] (See also preceding chapter.)

Ibn Hajar al-Asqalani (d.AD1449) in his *Fath al-Bari*, a commentary on *Sahih al-Bukhari*, made it clear that *al-azl* was allowed. His reasoning about Judama's tradition has been discussed in the preceding chapter. In reviewing the works of other theologians both in and outside the Shafe'i school, he noted the condition of a wife's consent in other schools. In the Shafe'i school, the majority including the later theologians believe that the woman has the right to intercourse but not to ejaculation, hence *al-azl* is permitted even if the wife does not consent. The *correct way* is still *permissibility* in Ibn Hajar's view. He, too, did not find Ibn Habban's reasoning a basis for the claimed prohibition.[36]

In another commentary on *Sahih al-Bukhari*, *Irshad al-Sari*, al-Qastallani (d.AD1517) quotes al-Nawawi in establishing the permissibility of *al-azl* with *karaha tanzihiyya* while preferring, though not requring, a wife's consent. *Al-azl* in his view helped ensure that the *number* of children could be afforded economically.[37] This is yet another clear references to the legal use of contraception *to limit the number of children* for economic reasons.

Al-Sha'rani (d.AD1565) introduces in his *Al Mizan (The Balance)* a fresh concept regarding the balance between the liberal attitude of the Shafe'i jurists and the conditional permission in the common position adopted by the other schools. The first opinion, i.e. that Imam Shafe'i allowed *al-azl* without need for a wife's consent is explained by the fact that we do not know if Allah will create a being from the semen. The semen may spoil or alternatively the semen may settle. (That is the balance). In either case, al-Sha'rani agrees with the Shafe'i's liberal attitude.[38]

Finally, a number of Shafe'i jurists did not agree with the majority of the *madhhab* and tended to prohibit coitus interruptus. Among these are al-Imad Ibn Yonis, Ibn Abdel Salam and Ibn Habban, whose arguments, shown earlier, were easily refuted by the Iraqis[39] and Ibn Hajar.[40]

The Hanbali school (Sunni)

Majority position
The great majority in the Hanbali school agrees with the common position that *al-azl* is permissible subject to a wife's consent be she young or old. The consent can be bypassed in certain situations. Some Hanbali jurists made it *mandatory* to practice *al-azl* in enemy territory.

Imam Ahmad Ibn Hanbal (d.AD855) has authenticated in his *Musnad* (one of the original compilations of *hadith*) many traditions on *al-azl*. He allowed *al-azl* but with a wife's consent.[41]

Ibn Qudama (d.AD1223) in his *Al-Mughni* stated that

> *al-azl* is disliked [*karaha tanzihiyya*] ... It was reported that it was disliked by Omar, Ali, Ibn Omar, Ibn Mass'oud and Abu Bakr because it means reduction in progeny and sexual pleasure for the woman. The Prophet (PBUH) advised multitude [marry and multiply]..... If, *however* there is justification, such as being in enemy territory and there is need to have relations, then he can practice coitus interruptus, as stated by Khiraqi [a renowned Hanbali jurist of the fourth century AH] ... If he used *al-azl* with no justification, *it is disliked but not prohibited* [*kuriha walam yuharram*]. The permissibility [of *al-azl*] was reported to have been affirmed by Ali, Sa'ad, Abu Ayyub, Zayd, Jabir, Ibn Abbas, al-Hassan, Khabbab, Sa'id Ibn al-Mussayyb, Tawoos, al-Nakheyi, Malik, al-Shafe'i and those with legal authority [*ashab al-ra'y*].

He also quoted al-Qadi's (another Hanbali jurist) understanding derived from what he understood from Ahmad's statements, that a 'wife's consent was required but may be just preferred, because she has the right to intercourse but not to ejaculation'. Ibn Qudama himself continued to insist on the need for a wife's permission because she has the right to progeny and contraception would harm her.[42]

A later jurist of similar name, is Ibn Qudama al-Maqdisi who died fifty years after the death of Ibn Qudama and agreed with all of Ibn Qudama's views in his commentary on *Al-Muqni* called *Al-Sharh al Kabir*.[43]

In his *Al-Fatawa al-Kubra* (the great *fatwas*), Ibn Taymiya (d.AD1328), the great Mufti and teacher of Ibn al-Qayyim, was asked his views in the case of a woman who uses medicine (a pessary) to prevent semen from reaching her uterus.

> The question put to him was (1) Is this allowed: and (2) If the medicine remains in the body after coitus, would she be allowed to fast and pray after bathing, i.e. *al-ghusl*? He answered that her prayer and fasting were proper even if the medicine remained in her body.* As to *al-azl* itself, he said, it is a matter on which the theologians differed. It may be *safer* [*ahwat*] not to do it.

(Note that he did not prohibit the practice).

He adopted a more positive tone in his Egyptian *fatwas* (*Mukhtasar al-Fatawa al-Masriyya*) where he said 'As to *al-azl*, it was prohibited by some, *but the four Imams [of the Sunni schools] agreed on its permissibility.*'[44]

Ibn Taymiya's views permitting *al-azl* were cited by al-Zabidi as evidence of the whole Hanbali school.[45]

His grandfather, Abul Barakat Abdus-Sallam Ibn Taymiya (d.AD1250) was responsible for a compilation of *hadith* called *Muntaqa al-Akhbar* or selected traditions (of the Prophet). In *Muntaqa*, Ibn Taymiya (the grandfather) devoted a section to the most authentic and pertinent traditions on *al-azl*.[46] The eight traditions cited therein include the following as given in Chapter 7:1.1, 2.2, 3.1, 6.1, 6.2, 6.3, 8.1, 9.2.

Imam al-Shawkani (d.AD1839) wrote an eight-volume commentary on Abul-Barakat Ibn Taymiya's compilation *Nayl al-Awtar Sharh Mutaqal al-Akhbar*. As shown in the preceding chapter, al-Shawkani explained and elaborated on *Al-Muntaqa*, giving a most lucid account on *al-azl* sanctioning it liberally.[47]

Besides Ibn al-Qayyim's (d.AD1350) convincing treatise on *al-azl* in *Zad al-Ma'ad*, his other works on the subject include, for example, *Tuhfat al-Mawdud Fi Ahkam al-Mawloud* (*Rules for the New Born*). In *Zad al-Ma'ad* he treated the subject methodically, first by reviewing several of the authenticated traditions and concluding that they clearly supported coitus interruptus as permissible, a view held by ten Companions, whom he named. (Ali, Sa'ad, Abu Ayyub, Zayd Ibn Thabit, Jabir, Ibn Abbas, Al-Hassan Ibn Ali, Khabbab Ibn al-Aratt,

---

*This is highly relevant to contemporary practices especially the use of IUDs.

Abu Saʿid al-Khudri and Ibn Massʿoud). He then classified the views of theologians either forbidding the practice (e.g. Ibn Hazm) or permitting it, subject to a wife's consent (the majority of jurists). He stated that 'Those who allowed it liberally use the traditions that we mentioned above and hold that the woman has the right to intercourse (*dhawqul ʿusailah*) not to ejaculation.'
In refuting the views of those opposed to the practice of *al-azl* based upon Judama's tradition, he argued as follows:

- There are enough traditions to permit *al-azl*.
- The contention that Judama's tradition abrogated the others requires specific dates which are impossible to establish.
- Imam Ali argued, with the approval of Omar and other Companions, that *al-azl* cannot be *waʾd*.
- There are many traditions in which the Prophet denied the Jew's claim that *al-azl* is minor infanticide.
- Judama's tradition can be reconciled with other traditions on the basis of venial disfavor (*karaha tanzihiyya*).[48]

Later Hanbali Jurists

In contrast to the expansive treatment of *al-azl* by the early Hanbali school the views of subsequent jurists were often conveyed tersely. Some examples follow. Ibn al-Najjar (d.AD1564) stated in *Sharh Muntaha al-Iradat*,

> Prohibited is intercourse in menses, as is *al-azl* without wife's consent, except in enemy territory where it is recommended liberally.[49]

Ibn Abi-Bakr (d.AD1624) reflects the same views but with a stronger and more explicit ordinance of *al-azl* in enemy territory. In his *Ghayat al-Muntaha*, he said

> Prohibited is intercourse in menses by consensus, ... So is *al-azl* without wife's consent ... and *mandatory is al-azl in enemy territory [Yuʿzalu wujuban bidari harb]*.[50]

Al-Bahuti's (d.AD1641) commentary, *Kashshaf al-Qinaʿ*, states

> *Prohibited is al-azl with a free woman without her permission*, because of Omar's tradition ... and Abu Saʿid's ... 'Do as you wish...'; then *Mandatory is al-azl with all women in enemy territory*; so that the child will not be enslaved.[51]

Now, this latter ordinance that *al-azl* is mandatory may not be applicable to contemporary situations since slavery has been abolished in all lands. Still, it has pervasive legal significance since it means that the level of the practice can be raised from the permissible, with venial dislike, all the way up to the mandatory (*wajib*).

The Zaydi school (Shi'ite)

Majority position
The majority position of the Zaydi school is that *al-azl* is permissible as a contraceptive measure with jurists differing as to where permissibility is subject to a wife's consent. The Zaydi views are close to the Shafe'i's.

Ibn al-Murtada (d.AD1437) stated in *Al-Bahr al-Zakhkhar* that *al-azl* is not allowed without the wife's permission, 'because the Prophet (PBUH) prohibited it except with her permission'. Imam Yahya Ibn Zayd is quoted as allowing it on the grounds that it is no more than abstaining from intercourse and because of al-Khudri's tradition in which the Prophet said 'Why would you do that' rather than '*Do not do that.*' Ibn al-Murtada concluded 'There is *no basis for prohibition*; the tradition [Judama's] is counterbalanced by other traditions and, by analogous reasoning, on abstention from intercourse, hence some *karaha* (*tanzihiyya*) is involved.'[52]

A century later Ass'adi wrote *Gawahir al-Akhbar*, a commentary on al-Murtada's statements. He cited a few more traditions and agreed with al-Murtada regarding the permissibility of *al-azl* with a wife's permission.[53]

The Imami (Twelvers) school (Shi'ite)

Majority position
The majority position of the Imami school (almost consensus) is in agreement with the *jumhour* position, i.e. *al-azl* is permissible subject to a wife's consent. The Imami jurists add, however, that consent can be obtained at the time of the marriage contract, once and for all. *Al-azl* is legal thereafter, even if the wife changes her mind. So important is a wife's consent that a few jurists allowed monetary compensation to the wife every time the husband violates this condition, a position very much similar to the Maliki school except that the compensation here is fixed at ten dinars and is called *diya* for *nutfa* (compensation for the sperm). (This payment of ten dinars must have been prohibitive and educational.)

Al-Ajali (d.AD1202) in *Al-Sara'ir Fil Fiqh* stated that it is disliked for a man to practice *al-azl* with his wife, but 'if he did, *he would not be sinning* but just leaving the more meritorious path. He should also pay *diya* [compensation money] of ten dinars for the lost *nutfa*', i.e. for not allowing it to be formed.[54]

Ja'afar Ibn al-Hasan al-Hilli (d.AD1227) in *Shara'i al-Islam Fimas'il al-Halal Wal-Haram* stated that if *al-azl* has not been agreed upon in the marriage contract or if the wife's consent has not been obtained, it is prohibited. In that case the *diya* of ten dinars for the *nutfa* is due. He also referred to another opinion which held that *al-azl* in that situation is only disliked (makrouh) although the *diya* is still due. The same views are found in his summary on Imami jurisprudence *Al Mukhtasar al-Naf i Fi Fiqh al-Imamiyya*.⁵⁵

Al-A'amili (d.AD1558) in *Al-Rawda al-Bahiyya Fi-Sharh al-Lam'a al Dimashqiyya* said '*Al-azl* is not permitted with a free wife without agreement during the marriage contract.... More popular is the view that there is only *karaha* [*tanzihiyya*].' He explains '*Karaha* is not a sufficient basis for prohibition ... In absence of proof of prohibition, we go back to the original permissibility [*al-bara'a al asliyya*].' By this he means that things are originally permitted unless prohibitd by an explicit text (apparently absent in this case). Likewise, he added, the wife should not practice *al-azl* (using pessaries, or medicine, etc.) without the husband's consent.⁵⁶

In considering the lawfulness of birth control and its methods Sheikh Mohammad Mahdi Shamsuddin, one of the current leaders of the Imami Shi'ites stated in 1974, 'It is allowed by *Shari'ah* Law for the couple to restrict their offspring by contraception.' There was no evidence that the practice was prohibited and legal traditions and texts explicitly regard *al-azl* as permissible. 'Clearly this method of coitus interruptus referred to in the legal texts, was the only one available for birth control.'

He affirmed that the lawfulness of birth control is established with the wife's consent. He quoted a tradition indicating that the husband, 'If he wishes he may practice *al-azl*, or if he wishes he may not practice *al-azl*'. He was quick to qualify this by stating that it is disfavored if the husband practices it without his wife's consent unless it was one of the conditions of marriage. He reasoned that, since the purpose of a method is to prevent pregnancy, *then modern methods are by analogy as lawful as al-azl.*

He later considered the question of 'multitude' and found it desirable but conditional upon the couple 'being able to provide well for the offspring and for their righteous upbringing in accordance with Muslim standards'. He pointed out additionally, that the recommended multitude of offspring must also be conditional upon averting harm to the mother.' He considered *the rule of averting harms to be more binding than the one desiring multitude*, stating

> the prohibition of self-inflicted harm, is of *greater weight* than desirability (of multitude) because the former implies a binding ruling; and, as is the standard legal rule, if two pieces of evidence are in conflict, one implying a binding ruling and the other implying a non-binding ruling, the one implying the binding ruling should be operational and given precedence over the other. Hence the evidence for the prevention of self-inflicted harm is made operational against the non-conditional evidence for the desirability of multitude.⁵⁷

The Isma'ili school (Shi'ite)

Majority position
The great majority position of the Isma'ili school is equivalent to the *jumhour* position that *al-azl* is permissible with a wife's consent, with one difference, that the consent can be obtained at the time of marriage contract.

The main source of this school's jurisprudence is the book *Da'a'im al-Islam* by Al-Qadi al-Nu'man (d.AD974) who stated that 'The Prophet (PBUH) has prohibited *al-azl* with a few wife without her consent, because she has the right to get children.' He reported that Imam Ali practiced *al-azl*, so did his son al-Hasan. He quoted Abu Ja'afar Mohammad Ibn Ali who, when asked about *al-azl*, replied, 'I dislike it in case of a free wife unless this has already been agreed upon at the time of marriage contract.' Then al-Qadi goes further to quote Ja'afar Ibn Mohammad as saying 'There is nothing wrong with *al-azl* with a wife's consent. It is advisable to have that agreed upon at the time of the marriage contract. It is also advisable to practice *al-azl* with a nursing woman, lest she should get pregnant and the child may be harmed. Such was reported from the Prophet (PBUH).[58]

The Zahiri school

School's position
Based on Ibn Hazm's views, *al-azl* is prohibited because of Judama's tradition in which the Prophet (PBUH) qualified *al-azl* as hidden *wa'd* and *wa'd* is prohibited. This tradition abrogates all the other traditions in which *al-azl* was permitted.

Ibn Hazm's[59] (d.AD1063) views and their refutation by other theologians have been given in the preceding section (see pp. 136–41).

The Ibaddi school (Kharijite)

Majority position
The majority position of the Ibaddi school coincides with the *jumhour* position, of permitting *al-azl* with a wife's consent.

Atfiyash (twentieth century) presented the school's views in *Sharh Kitab al-Nil Wa-Shifa' Al-Alil* and summarized them as follows: 'He will not practice *al-azl* with her and she will not practice *al-azl* with him without consent.' He added that the permissibility of *al-azl* was reported by al-Ghazali.[60]

9

Justifications for contraception in Islamic jurisprudence

The presence of a valid reason (*udhr*) for preventing pregnancy nullifies the objections to *al-azl* and removes the shadow of disfavor from it. Justifications acceptable to jurists include reasons of health, economics and cultural responsibilities, all of which come under the rule of averting hardship to the child, the mother and the husband, individually or as a family. Under certain circumstances, avoiding pregnancy becomes mandatory.

GENERAL CONSIDERATION

The permissibility of contraception notwithstanding, it is generally assumed that it is practiced for a good reason. Some reasons are more acceptable than others, and some may be so compelling as to cancel the required consent of the wife, remove the disfavor attached to the practice or even make it mandatory. On the other hand, some reasons may not qualify as justified (what al-Ghazali calls *niyya fasida* (bad intention),[1] e.g. practicing *al-azl* to avoid having female offspring. Nevertheless *al-azl* is still legal. Jurists have also considered the practice of contraception for no (obvious) justification. Ibn Qudama in his *Al-Mughni* maintains that if practiced for no justification (*udhr*), *al-azl* is disliked but not prohibited (*kuriha walam yuharram*).[2]

When the various sources of jurisprudence are screened, one can compile an impressive list of reasons for contraception. All are as significant today as they were in the early periods of Islam, although some health reasons have been refined by contemporary jurists in light of modern medical knowledge. The list of reasons as gleaned from various texts of *fiqh* is given in Figure 9.1.

Specified justifications by leading jurists
Al-Ghazali specified five reasons:

- To avoid fathering children who would become slaves (now obsolete).

Figure 9.1 Justifications accepted to jurists (and the key theologians who promoted them)

1. To avoid health risks to a suckling child from the 'changed' milk of a pregnant mother (Ibn Hajar).
2. To avoid maternal health risks to the mother from repeated pregnancies, short intervals or young age (Abdel Aziz 'Iesa).
3. To avoid pregnancy in an already sick wife (Sayyid Sabiq).
4. To avoid transmission of disease to the progeny from affected parents (Shaltout).
5. To preserve a wife's beauty and physical fitness, for the continued enjoyment of her husband and a happier marital life, and to keep the husband faithful (*I'faf*) (al-Ghazali).
6. To avoid the economic hardships of caring for a larger family which might compel parents to resort to illegal means to take care of many children; or exhaust themselves in earning a living (al-Ghazali).
7. To allow for the education, proper rearing and religious training of children which is more feasible with a small rather than a large family size (Tantawi).
8. To avoid the danger of children being converted from Islam in enemy territory (Hanafites, Hanbalites).
9. To avoid producing children in times of religious decline (*fasad alzaman*) (Hanafites).
10. Contemporary jurists refer to a tradition recommending separate sleeping arrangements for children, something that is more feasible with fewer children (Sha'rawi, Tantawi, Abdel-Aziz 'Iesa).

Unwelcome reasons (*niyyah fasidah* i.e. bad intention)
- To avoid begetting female children.
- To avoid (pregnancy because of resentment of) maternity roles.

- To preserve the woman's beauty and health for her husband's continued enjoyment and to safeguard her life from risks associated with pregnancy.
- To avoid economic 'embarrassment' or hardship (*haraj*).
- To avoid begetting female children.
- To avoid maternity altogether out of an exaggerated sense of cleanliness.[3]

It should be noted that it was al-Ghazili who labeled the latter two as *niyyah fasidah*.

Ibn Hajar specified three reasons:

- Fear of fathering slave children (obsolete).
- To avoid having a large number of dependants.
- To avoid risks to the nursing child from a new pregnancy.

He favored the last reason.[4]

Sheikh Sayyid Sabiq in his comprehensive text (*Fiqh Al-Sunnah*) confirmed that contraception (through the use of any one of several medical and barrier methods) is allowed under these conditions:

- When the man already has a large family and cannot properly rear his children.
- If the wife is sickly.
- If the wife gets pregnant too frequently (*mawsulatul haml*).
- If the man is poor.
- The preservation of a wife's beauty, as cited by Imam al-Ghazali.

Sheikh Sabiq adds that some jurists have emphasized that under many such conditions family planning would become not only permissible but mandatory (*mandoub ilayh*).[5]

Sheikh Abdel-Aziz 'Iesa, former Minister of Al-Azhar Affairs in Egypt, recently listed the following reasons for allowing contraception:

- Preservation of the woman's beauty to help her husband stay faithful.
- Protection of the woman's life from the danger of labor especially Cesarian section.
- Avoiding the economic hardship resulting from a large family.
- Avoiding illegal means to support one's children.
- If there is fear of religious decline among children.
- Avoiding the health risks posed for a suckling child by a new pregnancy, especially if the father is too poor to hire a wet nurse or to afford artificial milk.
- The need to abide by the Prophet's tradition requiring separate sleeping arrangements for each child.[6]

Sheikh Shaltout, the former Grand Imam of *al-Azhar*, listed the following reasons as favoring the use of contraceptives:

- Women who get pregnant at close birth intervals.
- Those suffering from diseases liable to be transmitted by heredity (or infection) to progeny.
- Those who are too weak to face up to their economic and social responsibilities.

The Imam added that 'Family planning in situations like these, on an individual basis, is a remedial measure by which certain harms are warded off and through which better and stronger offspring will come into being.'[7]

Sheikh Tantawi (the Mufti of Egypt) in his recent (1988) *fatwa* specified three cases which he finds to be legal:

- A couple with modest means who want to postpone the second child until they can care properly for the first.
- A couple with good means who want to stop procreation temporarily until they can provide a separate room each for their son and daughter.
- A couple with better means and three children who want to use

contraception not because they cannot afford more children but because they live in a country which needs family planning.

COMMENT ON THE ECONOMIC JUSTIFICATIONS

Some people may feel uneasy about economic justifications since they touch upon the area of *tawakkul* (reliance on Allah) and *rizq* (provision by Allah). The jurists found no such relationship and did not hesitate to make the economic reasons duly legal. The legal authority in this regard is al-Ghazali. He expressed these indications most eloquently:

> To escape economic hardship 'embarrassment' (*haraj*) by a large number of children and to guard against overtaxing oneself in earning a living or being tempted to fall into evil ways. This is not forbidden. For, to reduce economic embarrassment and strained circumstances sustains piety [*qillatul haraj mu'enon'ala-ddin*]. True, it is a mark of excellence to place complete trust and confidence in Allah's providence, as declared in the Qur'anic verse: 'There is not a creature on earth, but its sustenance depends on Allah.'
>
> (Sura II: 16)
>
> Nevertheless we allow ourselves to depart from the norm of excellence and leave the worthier course by exercising foresight, and by saving money, although this may seem to contradict the principle of resignation to Allah's will. And, we do not regard this as forbidden.[8]

Ibn al-Jawzi (twelfth century), who is a writer not a theologian, explains eloquently how having a large number of children can lead out of desperation to the pursuit of unlawful ways of earning an income:

> If the young man gets married in destitution, he is preoccupied in finding ways and means for earning a living. Then when he gets children his worries increase and he (may) permit himself to seek other ways of earning until finally he resorts to unlawful means.

And, in another chapter:

> We are facing the worst times. In these days no one is there to whom you can turn for help or from whom you can borrow what you need. One, therefore, is driven to get involved in illicit and improper pursuits and to put oneself into embarrassing situations. Hence, it is imperative that the number of children must be kept small.[9]

FAMILY PLANNING IN ISLAMIC JURISPRUDENCE

The link between having a large number of dependants and the possibility of economic hardship can be found even in the tradition of the Prophet and the Companions, as well as in the views of the founders of the legal schools (*madhahib*).

On the authority of Abdullah Ibn Omar, the Prophet (PBUH) said

»جَهد البلاء كثرة العيال مع قلة الشئ«

ذكره السيوطي والحاكم

The most grueling trial [*jahd al-bala'*] is to have plenty of children with no adequate means.

Authenticated by al-Seyuti and al-Hakim

Sheikh Sharabassi of Al-Azhar has recently explained that the Prophet maintains that man's ordeal grows in magnitude as man's progeny grows in number, for he would then be hard put to provide them with their wants and means. He added that the Prophet was in the habit occasionally of appealing to Allah saying 'I seek refuge in Allah from the most grueling trial: [*jahd al-bala'*]', proving that the stresses and strains of life, whatever their sources, can be avoided by Muslims.[10]

The Companions have also recognized this linkage. Abdullah Ibn Abbas is known to have said

قال عبد الله بن عباس:
»كثرة العيال أحد الفقرين ، وقلة العيال أحد اليسارين«

رواه القضاعي

A multitude of children is one of two cases of poverty, while a few children is one of the two cases of ease.

Authenticated by Quda'ei[11]

Two of the founders of the legal schools had similar advice and concepts. Imam Abu Hanifa counseled his disciple saying

قـال أبو حنيفة:
»كثرة العيال تشوِّش البال«

Multiplicity of dependent children is perplexity to the mind.[12]

Imam al-Shafe'i's explanation of verse 3 in Sura 4 has already been mentioned and provides advice against (but not prohibition of) polygyny in fear of begetting too many dependants. The Shafe'i school is known for its liberal endorsement of contraception. In presence of economic hardship, the endorsement is even stronger.

Economic reasons figure equally in the recent juristic opinions and *fatwas* as shown in those by Sheikh Sayyd Sabiq, Sheikh Shaltout, Sheikh Abdel-Aziz 'Iesa, Sheikh Sha'rawi and most recently Sheikh Tantawi (Chapter 12).

COMMENT ON THE HEALTH JUSTIFICATIONS

Warding off the risks posed to the health of mothers and children by additional pregnancies is the most common reason for accepting contraception in Islamic jurisprudence. These include the following:

- Risks to a suckling child from a new pregnancy.
- Risks to mothers from labor (*talq*).
- Risks of pregnancy at very young age.
- Risks of pregnancy for a sickly woman.
- Risks to mothers from repeated pregnancies.
- Risks to mother (and child) from short birth interval.
- Risks of transmitting hereditary or infectious diseases to the progeny.
- Genetic risks from in-breeding.

Comparison with Islamic medicine (from the earlier Islamic period)

It is interesting to note that the reasons identified in Islamic jurisprudence are wider in scope than those recorded in texts of Islamic medicine (from the earlier Islamic period). Islamic medical texts including those listed in Figure 9.2 characterized the *clinical* justifications. Excerpts from four books of Islamic medicine are given in Figures 9.3–9.6.[13]

Medical justifications for practicing contraception identified by Muslim physicians

- Young age of the wife and inability to sustain a pregnancy because of a small uterus.
- Disease or defect in the uterus.
- Weakness in the bladder and fear of incontinence due to pressure of the head of the fetus during labor.
- Presence of a disease that could be exaggerated by pregnancy or labor, leading to death of the mother.

The early physicians, it can be noted, neglected to mention the dangers to the suckling child from a new pregnancy or the need to preserve the fitness (and beauty) of the wife.

FAMILY PLANNING IN ISLAMIC JURISPRUDENCE

Figure 9.2 Selected tests of Islamic medicine

- *Paradise of Wisdom (Firdwas al-Hikma)* by Ibn Rabban al-Tabari (d.AD 875).
- *The All Inclusive Book (Al-Hawi,* and *Al-Mansuri)* by Abu Bakr al-Razi (Rhazes) (d.AD 929).
- *The Perfect Medical Craft (Kamil al-Sinaʿah al-Tibbiyyah)* by Ali Ibn Abbas (d.AD 994).
- *The Canon in Medicine (Al-Qanoun Fi Tibb)* by Abu Ali Ibn Sina (Avicinna) (d.AD 1036).
- *The Creation of Man (Khalq al-Insan)* by Abul-Hasan al-Tabib (d.1101).
- *The Treasures of Medicine (Al-Dhakhirah Fi Tibb)* by Ismaʾil al-Jurjani (d.AD 1136).
- *The Guide to Health of Body and Soul (Al-Irshad Limasaʾel al-Anfus Wal-Ajsad)* by Hibatullah Ibn Jumaiʾ (d.AD 1193).
- *Selections in Medicine (Al-Mukhtarat Fi Tibb)* by Abul-Hasan Ibn Hubal (d.AD 1213).
- *The Collection of Drugs and Nutrients (Jamʿi Limufradat al-Adwiya Wal-Aghdhia)* by Abdullah Ibn al-Bitar (d.AD 1248).
- *Reminder in Medicine (Al-Tathkira Fi Tibb)* by Ibn Tarkhan al-Suwaidi (d.AD 1291).
- *Reminder of Dawoud (Tadhkirat al-Albab)* by Dawoud al-Antaki (d.AD 1599).

Medical texts written by theologians
- *Culmination of Benefits (Iltiqaʾ al-Manafiʿ)* by Ibn-al Jawzi (d.AD 1201).
- *Prophetic Medicine (Al-Tibb al-Nabawi)* and *Rules of the New Born (Tuhfat al-Mawdud Fi-Ahkam al-Mawloud)* by Ibn al-Qayyim al-Jawziyya (d.AD 1350).
- *Summary of Suwaidi's Reminder (Mukhtasar Tadhkirat al-Suwaidi)* by A. W. al Shaʿrani (d.AD 1565).

Back to jurisprudence

Islamic jurisprudence offers many health-related reasons in support of contraception. In regard to the health of the suckling child, we may recall the Prophet's tradition on *al-ghayla*:

«لا تقتلوا أولادكم سرًّا ، فإن الغيل يدرك الفارس فيعثره عن فرسه»
رواه أبو داود

Do not kill your children unconsciously. For *al-ghayla* will have [in the future] the same effect as when a horseman is overtaken [by an opponent] and thrown off his horse.

Authenticated by Abu Dawoud

The Qur'an has recommended breast-feeding for two years should the parents wish to have complete lactation, and in view of the Prophet's warning against *al-ghayla* or pregnancy during the lactation period, it is inferred that this is an endorsement for child spacing. Rather than avoiding intercourse for two full years (which is a hardship for the couple) they can use contraception.

Al-Ghazali has championed the legalization as a reason for contraception,

Figure 9.3 Excerpt from *Al-Qanoun (The Canon in Medicine)* by Ibn Sina (Avicinna) (Arabic)

من الكتاب الثالث من القانون ٥٧٩

اخرا جا فليك بالضمادات التي تسقط الاجنة فان استعمالها بعد الاجبار اقوى واشد قوة
(فصل في منع الحبل) الطبيب قد يضطر الى منع الحبل في الصغيرة يخوف عليها من الولادة
التي في رحمها علة والتي في مثانتها ضعف فان ثقل الجنين ربما اورث قرحة في المثانة فيسلس البول
ولم يقدر على حبسه الى آخر العمر ومن التدبير في ذلك ان يؤمر عند الجماع ان يتوقى الهيئة
المحبلة التي ذكرناها ويخالف بين الانزالين ويفارق بسرعة وان يؤمر ان تقوم المرأة عند الفراغ
وتثب الى خلف وثبات الى سبع وتسع فربما خرج المني واما الوثب والطفر الى قدام فربما مكن
المني وقد يعين على ازلاق المني ان تعطس ومما يجب ان تراعيه ان تحتمل قبل الجماع وبعده
بالقطران وتمسح به الذكر وكذلك دهن البلسان والاسفيداج وان تحتمل قبل وبعد شحم
الرمان والشب وحمول فقاح الكرنب وبزره عند الطهر وقبل الجماع وبعده ويقوى ذلك
خصوصا اذا جعل في قطران او غمس في طبيخ او عصارة الفوتنج والحمال وورق الغرب بعد
الطهر صوفة وخصوصا اذا كان مع ذلك مغموسا في ماء ورق الغرب وكذلك شحم الحنظل
والهزارجشان وخبث الحديد والكبريت والسقمونيا وبزر الكرنب اجزاء سواء يجمع
بالقطران ويحمل واحتمال الفلفل بعد الجماع يمنع الحبل وكذلك احتمال زبل الفيل وحده او مع
التبخر به في الاوقات المذكورة ومن المشروبات ان يسقى من ماء الباذروج ثلاث اواق فيمنع
الحبل وكذلك دهن الخل اذا طلي به القضيب سيما الكمرة ويجامع فانه يمنع الحبل وكذلك ورق
الدلب اذا احتملته المرأة بعد الطهر منع الحبل

of the preservation of a wife's beauty and health and her protection from the danger of labor (*talq*).[14]

Ibn Hajar (a Shafe'i) favors the protection of a suckling child from the dangers of a new pregnancy.[15] This was also endorsed by al-Qadi al Nu'man (an Isma'ili Shi'ite of the tenth century),[16] Ibn Abdin (a Hanafi of the nineteenth century)[17] and others.

Health risks to the mother were the basis for permitting contraception by the Al-Azhar Fatwa Committee in 1953. The Committee endorsed contraception because 'it helped ease matters for people and relieve them of hardships, particularly if concern is felt for the woman's life or health as a result of too frequent pregnancies.'[18] The Committee provided the following quotations:

FAMILY PLANNING IN ISLAMIC JURISPRUDENCE

Figure 9.4 Excerpt from *Kitab Al-Maliki* by Ali Abbas (Arabic)

Figure 9.5 Excerpt from *The Treasures of Medicine* by al-Jurjani (Persian)

JUSTIFICATIONS FOR CONTRACEPTION

Figure 9.6 Excerpt from *Irshad* by Ibn al-Jami' (Arabic)

ما نفاد الحبل وامساك نعم الحبل بان ينطل الذكر
بعصارة البصل قبل وقت الجماع وكذلك ماء الاحتلت
عصارة النعنع وكذلك الغوطن وبذر الكرات او احتمل
بعد الخمر فان خامس منه الحبل واحتمال المزنج
المتخذ: من المر والحاوشير والـ اب والمزروف مجونة
مرارة ثور بهوقيل: ان الحمت المراة الباذل على الرجل
لم ينزل او يطفئ الذكر بائ بهن كان فعل مثل ذلك.
تذييد الذساء واما امر الرضاع ينبغي ان يصرف
على لبن الام ان امكن والابتذار لك ممن كانت
سن الشباب بما كانت حسنا الخ ونعتد له المزاج سمها
للسم رهيبا الاخلاق ويكون ابها استعد التغدي
ابغ   التعم ويلاثما وان ذبكون زد وتد ولادنا
تربا من زرت ولاد: لا لولا ولحنـ الاندية الروية
والمنا والنحل الند؛ لا تتولا لحل والجبي لم ها

يُرِيدُ اللَّهُ بِكُمُ الْيُسْرَ وَلَا يُرِيدُ بِكُمُ الْعُسْرَ ... ۝ البقرة(٢)

Allah wishes you ease, and wishes not hardship for you.
al-Baqara (Sura 2:185)

هُوَ اجْتَبَىٰكُمْ وَمَا جَعَلَ عَلَيْكُمْ فِي الدِّينِ مِنْ حَرَجٍ ... ۝ الحج(٢٢)

He has chosen you, and has not laid on you any hardship in religion.
al-Hajj (Sura 22:78)

Similar endorsements are found in *fatwas* by Sheikh Shaltout,[19] Sheikh Sayyid Sabiq,[20] and Sheikh Jadel Haq, the Grand Imam of Al-Azhar.[21]

Modern medicine

Modern medicine has documented definite health risks to mothers and children from the following factors:

- Pregnancies too close: short birth interval (less than two years).
- Pregnancies too early: young age (under 18 years) at pregnancy (child brides).
- Pregnancies too late: old age (over 35–40 years) at pregnancy.
- Too many pregnancies: repeated pregnancies (four or over).
- Unwanted pregnancies: in fear of abortion.
- Unattended pregnancies: poor prenatal and natal medical care.
- Pregnancies upon sickness: presence of serious diseases such as heart disease, hypertension, uncontrolled diabetes, severe anaemia and under-nourishment or hereditary disease.
- Pregnancies while breast-feeding: this results in *al-ghalya* which is harmful to the suckling child.

These factors may result in the following risks to the mothers:

- Increased maternal mortality.
- Poor obstetric performance, i.e. difficult labor requiring operative intervention such as Cesarian section and/or blood transfusion.
- Increased gynecological problems such as uterine prolapse and cancer of the cervix.
- Increased diabetes and rheumatism.

The same factors may result in these risks to the progeny:

- Increased fetal loss and still-birth.
- Increased congenital anomalies and low birth weight or prematurity.
- Increased neonatal and infant mortality.
- Poor development and higher susceptibility to infection and malnutrition.

My own studies in several Muslim countries have documented these risks through scientific field surveys conducted in collaboration with national research institutes under the auspices of the World Health Organization.[22]

In the WHO field studies we investigated, among others, 26,000 Muslim women and their 125,000 pregnancies in Egypt, Syria, Lebanon, Iran, Pakistan, Turkey and Muslim communities in south India. Additional maternity studies were also conducted in Egypt, Sudan, Nigeria, Iran, Indonesia and Bangladesh. The risks discovered in these and other studies are summarized in Figure 9.7 under three factors.

For the *birth order* there is some risk for the first child, if the mother is too young. The lowest risks obtain for 2–3 children, then the risk increases

Figure 9.7 Health risks associated with family formation

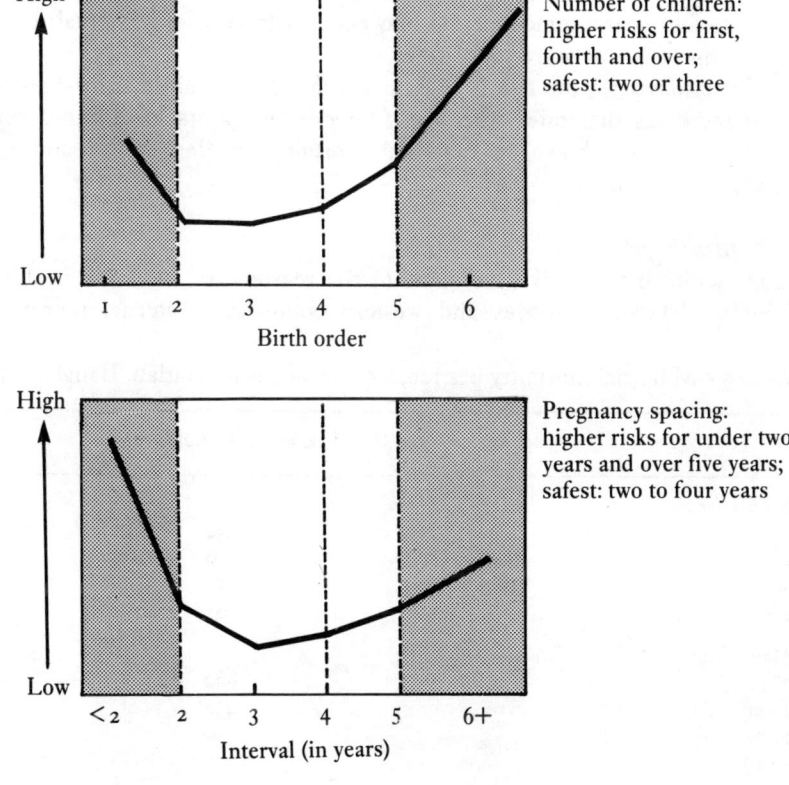

Source: Abdel R. Omran 'Health benefits of family planning for mother and child, *World Health* (January 1974), p.11.

steadily thereafter with the increasing family size.

For the *birth interval*, the risk is extremely high when the interval since the last pregnancy is less than two years. The risk goes down with intervals of three to four years; some increase may occur with very long intervals because the mother is six or more years older.

For *mother's age*, the risk is high under 18 years, is minimal for ages 18–34 then increases thereafter with age. Other investigators have found similar relationships as shown in maternal mortality in Bangladesh and Egypt (Tables 9.1 and 9.2).

The health gap

The factors listed above are some of the reasons for the wide health gap between Islamic countries and western countries. Maternal mortality in

Table 9.1 Maternal mortality per 100,000 live births in Matlab, Bangladesh

	Maternal mortality rate
Birth order	
1–3	254
4–5	456
6–7	558
8+	741
Mother's age	
<20	860
20–29	450
30–39	580
40–49	670

Source: Chen *et al.* 1974

Table 9.2 Maternal mortality per 100,000 live births in Menufia, Egypt

Mother's age	Maternal mortality rate
15–19	250
20–24	160
25–29	160
30–34	150
35–39	300
40–44	270
45–49	340

Source: S. Saleh (1987)

JUSTIFICATIONS FOR CONTRACEPTION

Muslim countries is 400–500 per 100,000 births ranging from 150–740, as shown in Tables 9.1 and 9.2, for a weighted average of 400–500 since the population in the high mortality areas is larger. This is compared to only 20 in Europe, i.e. twenty-five Muslim women die during pregnancy and birth for every one western woman who dies in pregnancy and birth. Likewise Muslim infants die at the rate of 100 or more per 1,000 live births which is 20 times more than in Japan, where infant mortality is only 5 per 1,000.

Can spacing and family planning save lives?

Studies by the World Fertility Survey (1975–84) estimated that in five Muslim countries, maternal mortality can be reduced by up to 72 per cent if family planning is used (see Table 9.3). It is now known the world over that family planning for health improvement saves life.

Intelligence of children also suffers

It is most disquieting to find that the intelligence of children is negatively affected by their number and birth order, as well as when mothers are too young or too old, i.e. when the woman is close to menopause. This is a well-known fact in Europe and the west, and has been recently documented by studies in Muslim countries. The WHO study in Turkey, Iran and Egypt, for example, has documented that the intelligence of children is affected by the following factors:

1. Large number of children in the family. When a child is born in a family

Table 9.3 Maternal deaths that could be prevented

	If all women who say they want no more children use effective contraception[1]	If, in addition, no births occur after age 35[2]
Egypt	28%	43%
Sudan	16%	41%
Tunisia	25%	59%
Kenya	15%	41%
Pakistan	16%	41%
Bangladesh	62%	72%
Mexico	32%	56%

Source: WFS 1975-84

Notes: [1] Women who say they want no more children are usually those who have already the number of children they want, or those who cannot cope with more children physically, economically, or culturally.
[2] Women who become pregnant after the age of 35 are in great danger of losing their own lives or developing serious diseases. They are also at higher risk of having sick children or mentally retarded children.

which already has many children, his or her chances of intellectual development are lower than normal.
2. Teenage pregnancy.
3. When the mother is 35–40 years or older at pregnancy.
4. Poor environment, low education of parents.
5. The limited time parents have to invest in verbalization with their children.

Family formation can be made to avoid these and other reproductive risks through a ten-point program representing the health theme in family planning given in Figure 9.8.

COMMENT ON THE CULTURAL JUSTIFICATIONS

Because the future of Islam depends on the health, intelligence and quality of its children, jurists have emphasized that Muslim children should be born healthy and to healthy mothers, and should be correctly raised, with adequate religious training. The ten rights of children listed in Chapter 2 (p. 32) have to be fulfilled and require considerable parental investment.

These tenets can be met more adequately when the family size is manageable than when it is too large. They can also be more effectively achieved in times of religious ascendancy and within a Muslim community

Figure 9.8 The health theme in family planning: a ten point bill of reproductive health

---

1. Families are planned, even before marriage, through genetic and marriage counseling. Consanguinity is ill-advised.
2. Parenthood is a grave responsibility. Every child is wanted, planned and provided for with social and psychological equity between male and female children.
3. The first child is postponed until the mother is 18-20+, and there are no pregnancies after the age of 40, and preferably after the age of 35.
4. Pregnancies are spaced 3-4 years apart.
5. The optimal number of children varies according to the mother's health and the ability of the family to bring up good, healthy and pious Muslims.
6. High risk pregnancy should be avoided altogether, otherwise specialized care is indicated.
7. Prenatal care and natal care are mandatory for the first pregnancy and highly advisable for all pregnancies.
8. Breast-feeting (with timely supplements) is basic for child heath with no pregnancy throughout breast-feeding.
9. Contraception is chosen after medical counseling with subsequent monitoring.
10. Infertility care is an integral part of family planning.

Source: Omran 1991.

than in times of religious decline and in non-Muslim territory. Jurists, especially of the Hanafi school, considered times of religious decline (*fasad al-zaman*) not only a reason to practice contraception (to reduce the number of children) but also sufficient reason to practice it without the consent of the wife.

An early reference to the use of *al-azl* to ensure that children are correctly raised comes from al-Bijeurmi who maintained that 'If contraception is resorted to for an excuse such as proper upbringing of children, it is not disfavored [*lam yukrah*].[23]

As mentioned earlier, the Hanbali jurists raised the permissibility of *al-azl* from the level of disfavor (*karaha tanzihiyya*) to the point of making it mandatory or *wajib* in enemy territory, lest the children were converted to other religions (*yuʿzalu wujuban bidari harb*). The concept of making contraception mandatory was picked up by other jurists for other reasons, especially health risks. An example is the *fatwa* by Sheikh Shaltout, parts of which were mentioned earlier. After listing the indications, the Grand Imam continued

> [Family] planning in this sense is not incompatible with nature, and is not disagreeable to national conscience, and is not forbidden by the religious law [*Shariʿah*], *if it is not actually required and recommended by it.*[24]

Sheikh Sayyid Sabiq has likewise used the term 'mandatory' (*mandoub ilayh*) for *al-azl* under similar conditions.[25]

Finally, the Muslim nation of today is viewed primarily on the quality of its members, their cultural aspiration, scientific achievement, technological advancement, health and educational level, and economic independence, much more than on its numbers. These qualities should be considered most carefully in family formation and in raising the new Muslim generation.

10

Family planning in Islamic jurisprudence: the more problematical juristic issues

This is an area of pioneering juristic research. The Muslim jurists handled, with great courage and ingenuity, the more problematical issues in family formation and family planning. Early theologians considered, with variation in opinion, the legality of taking medicine that causes permanent infertility; contemporary theologians considered contraceptive sterilization and artificial insemination. Likewise, the issue of abortion was also dissected with variation according to textual and biologic interpretations. Three periods were prominent in this issue according to the period of gestation: less than 40 days, less than 120 days and after 120 days. These were not arbitrary milestones, but were based on texts and perceptions.

Finally jurists considered the problem of repudiating a child born despite consistent use of *al-azl*. They attempted to explain contraceptive failure and to advance juristic judgement on the issue. In the process they explained how *al-azl* can fail.

INFERTILITY AND STERILIZATION

Infertility and artificial insemination

The treatment of infertility is the complement of family planning. Having children is one of the joys of life and those who have no children should be assisted to have some. Services to control infertility should therefore be provided as an integral part of family planning programs.

Infertility is the inability of a woman to conceive or of the man to impregnate a woman (primary infertility) or the loss of such a function after having a child or more (secondary infertility).

Infertility is not uncommon, affecting 10–20 per cent of couples worldwide, with higher rates of 30 per cent or more in some sub-Saharan African countries. No statistics are available for Muslim countries but the rate is estimated to be about 5–15 per cent. The male is responsible for 40 per cent of the infertility cases and the female for 50 per cent with 10 per cent of unknown origin. The causes are generally as follows:

1. Failure of the female to produce a viable egg (due to ovarian failure, imbalance in the sex hormones, infection and radiation).
2. Failure of the male to produce viable motile non-deformed sperms in sufficient quantity. One ejaculation contains millions of sperms. The failure may be due to hereditary insufficiency of hormones (Frohlich's Syndrome) or their imbalance, infection of scrotum or epididymis, complication of mumps or irradiation.
3. Blockage of the uterine or fallopian tubes due to congenital defect or infection. Blockage is more frequent following a complication of septic abortion (secondary infertility).
4. Harmful and thick cervical mucus blocking passage of sperms to uterus.
5. Failure of the fertilized ovum to be implanted on the wall of the uterus.

Modern treatment of infertility can take the following forms:
1. Hormonal or chemical therapy.
2. Surgical treatment, e.g. recanalization of the tubes.
3. Artificial insemination (medically assisted fertility).

Artificial insemination may take many forms. Before discussing the legality of this procedure, some explanations are given:

1. Artificial insemination of wife by husband's semen
   This is performed in the uterus and is therefore called *in vivo* insemination. This method is used when sperms cannot get to the uterus in sufficient quantity because of a hostile mucus plug at the mouth of the cervix or because the motile sperm count is low.
2. Artificial insemination of wife by donor sperm
   This is a method used in the west in which sperm other than the husband's is inseminated.
3. *In vitro* fertilization (test-tube babies)
   This method consists of giving special hormones to the wife to stimulate ovulation. Ova retrieved from her are added to a culture in a petri dish or test-tube. The sperms from her husband (or donors in non-Muslim traditions) are mixed with the ovum. The fertilized ovum is then transferred to the uterus of the wife. Thus the term 'test-tube baby' does not mean the baby is grown in the test tube.
4. Surrogate motherhood
   The fertilized ovum is transferred to the uterus of another woman because of the inability of the wife's uterus to bear a child to term.

5. Genetic cross-engineering
   This entails many forms of experimentation, such as mixing human and animal sperms or ova, and transporting a fertilized human egg to the uterus of an animal.

The legality of infertility control methods

Treatment of infertility is not only allowed but is recommended. There is no problem with chemical or surgical therapy as long as it is performed by honest, experienced specialists. The problem lies, however, with some methods of artificial insemination and genetic engineering. The question was put to Sheikh Jadel Haq in 1980, when he was Mufti of Egypt, by a specialist physician. His response is summarized below.[1]

1. Treatment of ills with legal procedures is mandatory in Islam; infertility in one or the other of the married couple is no exception.
2. Insemination of a wife (*in vivo*) with semen taken from her husband (provided it has not been mixed with other semen) is allowed.
3. Insemination of the wife with semen taken from a donor who is not her husband is forbidden.
4. Artificial insemination *in vitro* (test-tube babies) using the husband's semen only is allowed.
5. Artificial insemination *in vitro* (test-tube) using sperms of donors or mixed sperms (of husband and donors) is forbidden, since it destroys the lineage in the family.
6. Mixing the woman's ovum with semen from a man who is not her husband, then transferring the fertilized ovum to the uterus of the man's wife is forbidden.
7. Sperm banks are against the purpose of lawful family formation and are forbidden.
8. Mixing the wife's ovum with her husband's sperms, and transferring the fertilized ovum to the uterus of an animal (for whatever reason) for a period, then returning it to the wife's uterus is forbidden.
9. The physician is the technical expert in insemination procedures, in its different forms. If he assists in performing illegal procedures (as above), he violates the *Shari'ah* Law.
10. A child resulting from illegal procedures of insemination is illegitimate and cannot claim the husband's name. It should carry the wife's name instead, as does any other product of fornication.

Note: although surrogate motherhood was not specifically mentioned in the *fatwa*, it is understood from other evidence that it is forbidden. Adoption is also forbidden because of the deception involved. Caring for a child and treating him or her as kin is allowed but no false family name is provided.

The question of sterilization

Sterilization is a procedure that results in the permanent or temporary loss of the ability of a man to impregnate a woman or the ability of a woman to conceive. Sterilization in men is performed through dividing or tying the vas (seminal canal) and is called vasectomy. It is different from castration (removal of the testes) since it *does not* impair hormonal function or the ability of men to have complete and normal sex. In women sterilization can be performed by tying the fallopian tubes which are connected to the uterus and which normally pick up the ovum from the ovary and allow the process of fertilization to take place within its cavity. The operation is called tubal ligation. The tubes may also be cut (tubectomy) and then the ends ligated, or the tubes may be blocked with chemicals. These are methods to prevent the ovum from being exposed to the sperms from man's semen and thus pregnancy is avoided. Like sterilization of men, the methods used for female sterilization do not impair a woman's hormonal functions and have no effect on her sexual performance.

It should be emphasized that sterilization operations are performed every day in the Muslim world for medical indications, in which case theologians have no objection because the operations are methods of treatment, and treatment is legal in Islam.

The question becomes more problematical when permanent sterilization is performed for contraceptive purposes. It happens, for example, that a Muslim couple may find that they have enough children and they would prefer for one of them to undergo a sterilization operation than to use contraceptive methods for the rest of the wife's reproductive span. If she is in her thirties, this means 10–15 years of using contraceptive pills, intrauterine devices (IUD) or barrier methods. From their point of view they have the option of using contraceptives (which are costly, worrisome and may fail) or to have a one-time operation that would achieve the same purpose. Some Muslim countries do provide sterilization services to their people Is this option legal?

Before considering contemporary legal opinion, we should remember the following points:

1. The methods of sterilization used today were not known to the early theologians or physicians. There is some vague reference, however, to something taken (apparently by mouth) that stops procreation altogether. This was mentioned by al-Bijeurmi (d.AD1806)[2] and Shubramallissi (d.AH1087),[3] both of whom prohibited the practice. Ironically al-Shawkani (d.AD1839)[4] listed among the permissible practices, coitus interruptus 'to avoid too many children, and also to avoid children altogether', i.e. permanent contraception.

2. Some opponents of sterilization admit that there is *no text of prohibition* of sterilization either in the Qur'an or the tradition of the Prophet (*Sunnah*). For example, Dr Madkour told the Rabat conference in 1971, that 'we have found no text in the Qur'an or *Sunnah* that prohibits permanent sterilization without acceptable justification.'[5]

   Sheikh Jadel Haq was even more specific. He stated in December 1980 that 'If we examine the Qur'an or the *Sunnah*, we find *no text* prohibiting sterilization, i.e. rendering a man or a woman unable to procreate totally and permanently by surgery or chemical or other means.'[6]

   The two theologians were, however, opposed to permanent sterilization based on the general goals of *Shari'ah* which specifies five areas for preservation. These are the preservation of *'self, religion, mind, property* and *procreation'*. It is not clear whether the Sheikhs assumed widespread use of sterilization to an extent that would threaten human existence.

3. There may be a misconception in the minds of some contemporary theologians that surgical sterilization in the male is close to the operation of castration (removal of the testes or *khasy*) which is categorically prohibited. The fact is that removal of the testes will destroy the man's sexual abilities. Dividing or tying the vas (the sperm canal) simply prevents the sperms from mixing with semen that is now made mainly of prostatic fluid and excresions from the vesicle and the two Couper's glands. In other words the man will continue to have normal erection and will ejaculate the same amount of semen. Thus intercourse will be as 'normal' as before, fulfilling the religious requirement of *thawqul' usailah*.

4. Some techniques are now available to 'reverse' sterilization, e.g. to rejoin the canals in the woman in such a way that the ovum can still be transferred to the uterus and pregnancy can occur. However, the degree of success of reversibility is about 60-70 per cent. There is also the possibility of artificial insemination with the husband's sperm.

We pose the question again: Is sterilization permissible as a contraceptive method, for the husband or wife? Opinions differ:

1. The Grand Mufti of Egypt, Sheikh Jadel Haq (March 1980) gave the following opinion. Sterilization is not permissible if it causes permanent loss of fertility, through surgery or through drugs. Sterilization may be used when it is established that a hereditary disease may pass to children or cause pain. In that case sterilization becomes mandatory. This condonation is based on the juristic principle of permitting an injury to avoid a greater injury. This is correct provided that the diseases are incurable, taking into consideration advancing medical technology.[6]

2. Sheikh Shaltout had similar views of disallowing permanent sterilization except for serious reasons of hereditary or transmissible diseases.[7]

3. Dr Madkour is also opposed and quotes the Shafe'i jurist al-Bijeurmi as saying 'It is forbidden to use a device which would cause the elimination of the natural capacity to procreate.'[5]
4. The High Council of Research ruled in 1965 that the use of means which lead to infertility is forbidden.[8] Similar prohibition was made by *fiqh* Council in Saudi Arabia.
5. There was a division of opinion at the Rabat Conference on Islam and family planning. Many participants were opposed, but *a minority* group expressed support for sterilization, since they found no text in the Qur'an or *Sunnah* prohibiting it. Opponents raised the issue that sterilization is a form of changing the form of Allah's creation. Sheikh Bahshati and Sheikh Mohammand Shamsuddin argued for sterilization, however, as did many physicians in attendance. Physicians were afraid that sterilization was confused with castration in the minds of non-medical scholars.[9]
6. It should be emphasized that there is no opposition to temporary sterilization which is equated with *al-azl* and other contraceptives used for a long period. This is provided that sterilization is voluntary with no imposition from anyone.
7. The Imamis sanction permanent sterilization. Sheikh M. Shamsuddin (of the Imami Shi'ites) expressed his sanction at the Rabat conference as follows:

> On examining our legal sources on the subject, we have found that there is nothing preventing the husband and the wife from undergoing such operations [for sterilization], because the preservation of the power to procreate is not a duty prescribed by the Muslim Law, and is not a marital right. Hence, it is legally permissible to undergo a surgical operation (or otherwise) to sterilize man or woman whether it will be possible in the future for both of them to regain their normal state.[10]

This was his personal opinion at the time (1971). The Sheikh has thereafter contacted the leaders of the Imami school of jurisprudence (especially in Iran and Lebanon), a majority of whom sanctioned sterilization (personal communication in 1974).
8. Sheikh Sayyid Sabiq provided a statement that sterilization may be allowed by those who allow *al-azl*.[11]
9. Sheikh Ahmad Ibrahim is a leading theologian of the first half of the twentieth century whose opinions are fully respected by his peers. He researched the question of sterilization before the movement of family planning came to the Middle East and before sterilization became a popular method in several Muslim countries. This account was part of his famous introduction to the dissertation by Dr Al-Sa'id Mustafa al-Sa'id (1936).

The Sheikh declared that it is not forbidden for a person to employ any means at his disposal to destroy the sperms or prevent them from passing through the woman's genital passages or render them ineffective. It goes without saying that the woman may employ, or use anything that would render her infertile for conception. Such is not *haram* (unlawful). He then elaborated saying

> I do not see any religious objection to sterilization because sterilization is a treatment to avoid children by avoiding the element that produces them in a manner generally accepted. This is not a crime against any being already in existence; nor, a crime against a living child. The matter is crystal clear. There should be no hesitation in sanctioning it and blessing it with approval.

The Sheikh then considered some objections and refuted each. He then confirmed that

> In my opinion there is no religious objection to sterilization. Nor is there any objection to temporary birth control as may be the case. This is so after it is thoroughly established that there exists a necessity for either.[12]

Sheikh Ahmad al-Sharabassi commented on this opinion by calling for a re-examination of the legality of sterilization,[13] a view that should be endorsed provided that both theologians and physicians study the issue very carefully. Until then, the majority opinion supervenes, namely, that permanent irreversible sterilization with no excuse is not allowed.

THE QUESTION OF ABORTION

Abortion is a complex problem, charged with emotions and sensitivities related to the unborn fetus, the mother and the society, religion and law. People resort to abortion for different reasons, not all of which are acceptable to religion. The rule of thumb is that prevention (use of contraception) is preferred to control and that even the theologians who find abortion under certain indications allowable do not condone its use as an alternative to contraception. Furthermore, the difference in opinion among theologians should not be taken as a license for indiscriminate use of abortion.

Three tiers of time figure in the theological consideration of abortion:

Before 40 days,
Before 120 days, and
After 120 days.

The 120-days limit is based on the tradition of the 'forties' in which the Prophet (PBUH) informs that the fetus is held as *nutfa* for 40 days, as *alaqa* for another 40 days and as *mudgha* for an additional 40 days. Then (about 120 days) ensoulment takes place.

There is concensus among theologians that abortion after 120 days is categorically prohibited except to save the mother's life. Before 120 days opinions differ as depicted below.

Opinion of legal schools
This account is based primarily on a review by Dr Madkour (1971)[5] and a detailed *fatwa* on abortion by Sheikh Jadel Haq (1980).[6]

The Hanafi School
Abortion is generally allowed before 120 days when the fetus has reached the stage of becoming another creature, i.e. they are referring to ensoulment. Some feel it to be in disfavor without reasonable justification, because once conceived, the fetus has the potentiality of life. One of the most commonly cited indications in the school is when the woman becomes pregnant while she is suckling a child and her milk stops and the father does not have the resource to provide milk. This is justified for preserving the life of the suckling child. Another indication is ill-health of the mother, or if there is a risk of difficult and obstructed labor necessitating operative intervention such as the cesarian section especially if such has occurred in a previous pregnancy. (This latter comment is provided by Dr Madkour). The underlying rule is that a greater risk is warded off by a lesser risk and the mother's life takes precedence over that of the fetus because she is the origin.

The Maliki school
It is not allowed in the Maliki school to expel the product of conception, even before 40 days. (Only al-Lakhim allows before 40 days)

The Shafe'i school
The Shafe'ites are divided on abortion before 120 days. Some such as Ibn al-Imad and al-Ghazali, prohibit it; others, such as Mohammad Ibn Abi Said, allow it as *nutfa* and *alaqa* (80 days), and still others allow it before 120 days.

The Hanbali school
Taking medicine to expel the conceptus before 40 days is allowed. Otherwise it is prohibited.

The Zaydi school
Abortion is allowed before 120 days by analogy with *al-azl*.

The Imami Shi'ites
Abortion is not allowed at any time.

The Zahiri school
Abortion is not allowed before 120 days but is not equated with killing. After 120 days it is like killing.

The Ibaddi school
Abortion is not allowed at any time and the mother should not do anything (such as carrying heavy objects) or take anything that can harm the fetus.

Summary: four classes before 120 days
There are four classes of abortion before 120 days, according to both Sheikh Jadel Haq and Dr Madkour:

1. Unqualified permissibility even in absence of a justification. This is the opinion of the Zaydi school and some of the Hanafi and Shafe'i scholars.
2. Conditional permissibility in the presence of an acceptable justification. If there is no justification it is disfavored. This is the opinion of some Hanafi and Shafe'i scholars.
3. Unqualified disfavor which is the opinion of some Maliki scholars.
4. Categorical prohibition which is the opinion of most Malikis, the Imamis, the Ibaddis and the Zahiris, and the Hanbalis after 40 days.

After ensoulment: 120 days
Abortion after 120 days is prohibited by consensus in all schools except where it is for the protection of the mother's life.

Dr al-Boutti views abortion in an interesting way. In 1976, Dr al-Boutti, Dean of the *Shari'ah* faculty in Damascus, explained this (fifth category) view while differentiating between aborting legitimate and illegitimate pregnancies.

Aborting a legitimate pregnancy
The laws differ concerning abortion of a legitimate as opposed to an illegitimate pregnancy. A legitimate pregnancy, Dr al-Boutti concluded, can be aborted before 40 days. This represents his own interpretation of the Shafe'i and Hanafi schools. He cited the tradition of the 'forties' (see next chapter), and another authenticated tradition that refers to the angel being sent after 42 days to *start* the shape and senses of the fetus. He disagrees with those jurists who permit abortion up to 120 days as well as those who prohibit abortion altogether (e.g. the Malikis). He emphasized that all schools agreed on prohibition after 120 days or 'ensoulment' except in such cases where

compelling reasons exist such as a threat to the mother's life, harming a suckling child, or where the fetus is expected to be deformed. He then explained how abortion *before 40 days* is affected by the three rights:

(1) *Right of the fetus*: Before 40 days the product of conception is still a drop of life germ [*nutfa*] which is still without a shape or soul and is like the semen from which it was formed. After formation especially after 'ensoulment', abortion is prohibited.

2. *Right of parents*: They have the right to continue or terminate pregnancy within 40 days by mutual agreement. However if abortion itself will endanger the health of the mother, then it is disallowed.

(3) *Right of Society*: This relates to the general consequences of abortion. If it becomes prevalent (exceeding limits), the society has the right to intervene.

Aborting illegitimate pregnancy is disallowed according to Dr al-Boutti's juristic research and interpretations.[14]

Views of other theologians

It would be futile to quote other individual theologians, since their views fit into one or another of the above categories. Chapters 11 and 12 and Appendix 2 contain examples of the views on abortion of the following authorities:

Sheikh Abdel Majeed Saleem, Egypt, Chapter 12
Sheikh Abdullah al-Qalquili, Jordan, Chapter 12
Haj Ali Ibn M. Sa'id Saleh, Malaysia, Chapter 12
The President of the High Court of Appeal, Yemen, Chapter 12
Sheikh Ahmad Sahnoun, Morocco, Chapter 11
Sheikh A.R. al-Najjar, Egypt, Chapter 11
The High Council of Islamic Research, Chapter 11
The Rabat Conference, Chapter 11
Sheikh Sayyid Sabiq, Saudi Arabia, Chapter 12
Sheikh Yusuf al-Qaradawi, Qatar, Chapter 12
Dr Huseyn Atay, Turkey, Chapter 12

THE QUESTION OF REPUDIATING A CHILD CONCEIVED DESPITE CONTRACEPTION

How the question arose

Many of the traditions of the Prophet (PBUH) concerning *al-azl* emphasized predestination, i.e. if Allah wills to create a soul, it will be created, with or without contraception (see, for example, Categories 2 and 3, and Chapter 7 p. 000). Thus, jurists were stimulated to explain how contraception, e.g. *al-azl*, could fail. At the same time, a thorny issue arose and had to be resolved, namely: 'Can a man disown or repudiate a child born to him by a woman with whom he has been practicing coitus interruptus [*al-azl*] consistently?

How the jurists prepared themselves

Medical knowledge before the nineteenth century was almost primitive concerning reproductive physiology, fertilization, fetal development, etc. In order to use the best knowledge at the time, the Muslim theologians studied and synthesized, not only the texts of such Muslim physicians as Ibn Sina and Abu Bakr al-Razi and such philosophers as al-Kindi and al-Fakhr al-Razi, but they also drew upon the translated Greek texts. In this way, the jurists augmented their knowledge of biology, physiology and matters dealing with generation. Thus, some Islamic texts, in addition to the usual reference to the Qur'an, the *Sunnah* and other legal schools, might contain references to Hippocrates and Galen with agreement or rejection as appropriate. Notable examples include Ibn al-Qayyim's books on generation (*Tuhfat al-Mawdoud*), Prophetic medicine (*Al-Tibb al-Nabawi*) and *Tibyan Fi Aqsam al-Qur'an*.[15] This style can still be found in the writings of theologians who came later, such as al-Zabidi in his great commentary on al-Ghazali's *Ihya' Ulum al-Din*.[16]

The Jurists' knowledge of reproduction

Through study and logical inferences, jurists advanced the following concepts:

- Just as man has his semen, the woman has also her own fluid that she can feel during orgasm, some actually call it semen as well.[17]
- The semen from the man has to reach and mingle with the woman's fluid in the vagina (*majari al-habal*) or uterus for pregnancy to occur. They did not know of the existence of an ovum or of the process of ovulation and fertilization, but they logically inferred that something from the woman's fluid or menstrual blood played a role in the fertilization (*in'eqad*) process.[18] Some agreed, however, that the substance involved must be of higher quality to contribute to generation. They added that the flow of the woman's fluid is accompanied with pleasure, while the flow of menses is not.[19]
- Some went further and assumed that the man's ejaculation has to coincide with the woman's orgasm for pregnancy to take place.[20]
- They also believed (as the Prophet said) that a drop of semen was enough to cause pregnancy. This is in agreement with what we now know that only one sperm in an ejaculation succeeds (if at all) in penetrating an

ovum. It is only occasional that more than one sperm succeeds in that way resulting in twins or a multiple pregnancy. A drop of semen contains millions of sperm.
- Fetal development goes through sequential stages of development according to the Qur'an (Sura 23: 12–14)
- They believed that 'ensoulment' occurs towards the end of the fourth month of pregnancy after which the fetus becomes 'another' creature or human being – *khalqan a'akhar*. This was based both on the Qur'an (Sura 23: 12–14) and specifically on the tradition of the 'forties' (*hadith al-arba'eenat*) which follows:

«إن أحدكم يُجْمَع خلقُه في بطن أمه أربعين يوما نطفة ، ثم يكون علقةً مثل ذلك ، ثم يكون مضغةً مثل ذلك ، ثم يُرسل إليه الملك فينفخ فيه الروح»
رواه البخاري ومسلم

The germ of everyone of you is concentrated in his mother's womb in the form of a drop or life-germ [*nutfa*] for forty days, then becomes a clot of congealed blood [*Alaqa*] for a similar period, then he becomes a (fetus) lump [*mudgha*] for a similar period; then the angel is sent to him to ensoul him.

Authenticated by al-Bukhari and Muslim

Other than to save the mother's life, all jurists believed that it is murder to expel the fetus once the stage of ensoulment has been reached. This endorses the argument that contraception is neither killing nor *wa'd*, and is in accordance with the interpretation of Imam Ali and Ibn Abbas (with the consent of Caliph Omar and several of the Companions).

Jurists who believed that only after ensoulment could killing occur, allowed induced abortion for acceptable reasons up to 120 days. Those who held that even before 120 days the fetus has the potential to become a complete human being, disallowed or discouraged induced abortion.[21] A third group assumed that the fetus takes some form after 40 days and allowed abortion only before that period.[22] Still others such as al-Ghazali held that, while contraception does not amount to killing since it does not affect a being that exists, abortion does affect a being 'that already exists' and the degree of prohibition and magnitude of crime increases with the progress of pregnancy.[23]

Explaining predestination in the traditions
Many theologians gave a straightforward explanation of predestination. For example, al-Sha'rani (d.AD1565) in *Al-Mizan* (*The Balance*) advanced the following explanation:

- If Allah wills no soul to be created, the semen from the man would spoil or fail to reach the uterus (even without *al-azl*).
- If, on the other hand, Allah wills the creation of a soul, despite *al-azl*, semen may seep into the vagina before withdrawal (pre-emission) and cause pregnancy.[24]

The question of repudiation

Most Muslims practiced *al-azl* with the realization that it could fail; a few believed it was fool-proof and were inclined to repudiate the resulting child. With the exception of the Hanafi school, the majority of jurists disallowed repudiation for two reasons:

- Fatherhood is established by cohabitation of a husband and wife (*al-waladu lilfirash*).
- Contraceptive failure is possible and was not uncommon with *al-azl*.

That failure was not uncommon and was acceptable is evident in Ibn al-Qayyim's reference in *Zad al-Ma'ad* to the common (humorous) saying 'There is no child of mine but was the result of *al-azl*.'[25] Likewise Ibn Qudama (in *al-Mughni*) quoted Abu Sai'id saying that *al-azl* gave him the most beloved child.[26]

Those who believed that *al-azl* was perfect and that it could not result in pregnancy were faced with a dilemma when pregnancy did occur. They had three choices:

- To accept it.
- To reject it and disown the child.
- To divorce the woman, which was rated by al-Zabidi as a better alternative to bad publicity in a conservative society.

Repudiation of the child entails charging the mother with adultery. To sustain this most serious accusation in Islam, the man has to produce four witnesses who will testify to the woman's cohabitation with another man. Should he fail to do this, the man has to resort to the *li'an*, swearing four times in front of a judge or witnesses that his wife has been unfaithful. The woman has an equal right to defend herself, including a counter-swearing that she was faithful.

Most jurists disallow repudiation, explaining the possibility of failure in *al-azl*: pre-emission during withdrawal leading to pregnancy is the most common reason provided in jurisprudence. Ibn Taymiya (d.AD1328), of the Hanbali school, emphasized that withdrawal before ejaculation will not prevent pregnancy if Allah wills it, because there could be involuntary pre-emission.[27] Ibn Juzayy (d.AD1340), of the Maliki school, had similar views[28], as did the Shafe'i scholars Ibn Hajar (d.AD1449)[28], al-Qastallani (d.AD1517)[30], al-Sha'rani (d.AD1565)[31], and al-Zabidi (d.AD1790).[32]

Al-Qastallani reiterates, that whether you withdraw before ejaculation or not, if Allah wants a child to be born, semen will seep out during intercourse (pre-emission) without the man's knowledge. Allah, he reminds us, created Adam with neither a male nor a female, and Eve without a female and Jesus without a male.[33]

Ibn al-Qayyim adds that semen may drop on the woman's genital parts during withdrawal and later gain access to the vagina.[34]

According to the Hanafi school, repeated intercourse without washing will allow remnants of semen on the glans or in the canal to seep to the vagina during the second intercourse. Also, repeated intercourse after urinating (without washing) will also allow remnants of semen driven out by urination to reach the vagina.[35] This is why Imam Abu Hanifa recommended that if coitus is to be repeated, the man should wash the male organ thoroughly, and if he urinates, he should wash again before repeating intercourse. Hanafis are very meticulous about these precautions and therefore the Hanafi jurists allowed repudiation. Ibn Nujaim, however, (d.AD1562) sets three conditions for allowing repudiation:

- That the woman is not *muhsana* (a free woman with impeccable reputation).
- That *al-azl* has been practiced consistently.
- That the man has good reason to suspect that the child is not his own.[36]

Other Hanafi jurists who allowed repudiation, included Ibn al-Humam (d.AD1457)[37] and Ibn Abdin (d.AD1836)[38]. Furthermore, al-Ghazali is reported by al-Ramli to have allowed repudiation because 'if he has been especially careful, he would be as if he did not have intercourse'.[39]

The most vehement opposition comes from the Shi'ite jurists who disallowed repudiation under all circumstances. Al-Ajali (d.AD1202) said in *Al-Sara'ir Fil-Fiqh*: 'He cannot repudiate [the child] on the basis of *al-azl*. If he does, he has to resort to *li'an*.' Such strong opposition to repudiation is to ensure the child's welfare, a concern that is reflected in other schools.[40]

PART IV

Islam and Family Planning in the Twentieth Century

11

Conferences and publications by jurists on Islam and family planning

The twentieth century witnessed a continuation of the juristic activity concerning family planning with new challenges and fresh approaches. A demographic dimension has been added to the issue; communal programmes and population policies are spreading in Muslim countries; new contraceptive methods are periodically introduced and their suitability for use by Muslims is evaluated; public debate ensues on the issue in mass media, in specialized articles and books, as well as in conferences and committees. Official *fatwas* are issued by theologians from time to time. Theologians' opinions are influenced not only by juristic considerations, but by other factors as well. These issues are dealt with in this and the following chapter.

NEW CHALLENGES TO JURISTIC RESEARCH

It may seem that religious opinion has oscillated in the course of this century between the sanctioning of contraceptive practices – even in citadels of Islamic orthodoxy – and hardening attitudes and sometimes hostile opposition to the family planning movement.

Given the undisputed support of family planning by the majority of jurists (*jumhour al-ʿulamaʾ*) belonging to eight out of nine legal schools (*madhahib*), and despite the fact that such support fell short of a clear cut consensus (*ijmaʿ*) of the entire community, the variations in religious opinion suggest the influence of factors that are not primarily juristic, but mostly situational.

Compare, for example, the less positive views coming from some rich countries with those from overpopulated countries, which are, in the main positive. Furthermore, opinions fluctuate in some situations. As reported by W. Ahmad (1974) of Pakistan, leaders of the Debandhi orthodox theological group allowed contraception based on early *fatwas* in the group. Some of these *fatwas*, which emanated from Mufti Mohammad Shafi, Mufti Azizur-Rahman and Maulana Rashid Ahmad Ganguho, are still in current circulation. Yet, says W. Ahmad, present day disciples of these renowned authorities in religious matters have made sharp attacks on the family planning movement in Pakistan.[1]

NEW CHALLENGES TO THE JURISTIC PROCESS

Contraception and family planning have acquired new dimensions that pose serious challenges to the juristic process. Some of the most relevant are now discussed.

A demographic dimension has been added to the family planning issue. Family planning can hardly be discussed today without reference to the problem of overpopulation or what is known as 'the population explosion'. Jurists are told that overpopulation is manifest in several Muslim countries and threatens the basic welfare of the Muslim people, especially in poor countries where it has been hindering the process of economic, social and cultural development. Family planning opponents argue that the overpopulation problem is artifactual and does not exist; it has been fabricated by family planning proponents. The Islamic world, they claim, has enough resources to support many times its current population.[2]

Groups, communities and even governments, including several that are Muslim, have for the first time in history, established communal, subnational or national family planning programs. Jurists are called upon to provide rulings on the legitimacy of such programs.

The strongest indictment of the family planning movement is that it is viewed by some Muslims (including a number of theologians) as an attempt to reduce the Muslim population.[3] New methods of contraception are being periodically introduced and their suitability for use by Muslims will have to be medically and juristically approved. The question of multitude became, under these circumstances, not only a theological but also a political issue. Many Muslims, even in poor countries, believe that multitude is an asset rather than a liability, 'equating number with power'.[4]

The family planning debate has acquired new dimensions. It has extended to public fora, conferences, seminars, newspapers, radio and television – and has been considerably politicized in the process. Nor has the debate been confined to qualified jurists, those classified as '*mujtahidoun*, but has spread to include writers, demographers, economists and health planners, all of whom, though juristically unqualified, use the Qur'an and *Sunnah* in support of their arguments. Adding to the confusion, some bearers of religious titles,

---

*Anyone who leads a group prayer is called 'Imam', but this differs from Muslim use of the title, meaning qualified theological leader.

including Sheikhs and Imams,* pronounce authoritative legal opinion (*fatwa*) in matters of family planning for their communities despite having limited religious training and qualifications. Unfortunately, their views are not seriously challenged by their communities.

What is disquieting is the degree to which opinions for or against family planning are delivered in the name of Islam. Rather than defining an opinion in terms of Islamic jurisprudence, too many statements claim their authority in the phrases 'Islam is for' or 'Islam is against' as if there were two Islams, one for and one against family planning.

The family planning movement has been accused by some of encouraging moral decline in the west. As family planning flourished in Europe and North America, concurrent developments included secularization, the break up of the family structure, and the marriage institution, sexual promiscuity, a rise in illegitimate children, drug abuse, etc. Some of these are uncritically attributed to the consequences of family planning, and jurists are told that this is what they should expect if they allow family planning in their countries.

Some jurists fear that their approval of family planning will be used politically or as basis for laws to be imposed on people to coerce them to follow a certain quota of children prescribed for political purposes. There is an apparent lack of demographic knowledge and training among theologicans who too often equate family planning with depopulation.

THEOLOGIANS WHO OPPOSE FAMILY PLANNING

Despite the accumulating evidence in favor of family planning and in spite of the multitude of articles and books by theologians sanctioning the practice, some theologians continue to be opposed to the practice of family planning by Muslim couples; and/or the family planning movement *per se* and its role in the establishment of family planning services in Muslim countries.

The case of those who oppose *family planning practice* runs along the lines demonstrated in the preceding chapters. They cite the Qur'an in support of their opposition as follows:

- Multitude is highly recommended in Islam.
- Children are the adornment of life.
- Begetting children is the purpose of marriage.
- Contraception is *wa'd* or murder.
- Family planning contradicts the will of Allah (predestination) and doubts His ability to provide for children (*risq*).

In addition, opponents of the *family planning movement* claim the following:

- The movement is a conspiracy against Islam aiming to reduce the

number of its adherents and/or diminishing the majority status in some countries.
- It will bring with it promiscuity, moral decline, secularization and all the evils that they claim it caused in western countries.
- The so-called population problem does not apply to the Islamic world because it has enough resources to sustain several times its present population.

Examples of articles and books written by theologians opposed to family planning and those sanctioning family planning follow.

Sheikh Abu Zahra[5]

Sheikh Mohammad Abu Zahra, Professor of *Shariʿah* at the Law Faculty of Cairo University and author of several books on early theologians, published a bitter critique of family planning in *Liwaʾ al-Islam* magazine in 1962.

He began by referring to the verses in the Qurʾan which deal with killing children out of poverty or fear of poverty.

الأنعام(٦)   ... وَلَا تَقْتُلُوٓا۟ أَوْلَٰدَكُم مِّنْ إِمْلَٰقٍ نَّحْنُ نَرْزُقُكُمْ وَإِيَّاهُمْ ...

Kill not your children, on a plea of want, we provide sustenance for you and for them.

al-Anʿam (Sura 6:151)

وَلَا تَقْتُلُوٓا۟ أَوْلَٰدَكُمْ خَشْيَةَ إِمْلَٰقٍ نَّحْنُ نَرْزُقُهُمْ وَإِيَّاكُمْ إِنَّ قَتْلَهُمْ كَانَ خِطْـًٔا كَبِيرًا

الإسراء(١٧)

Kill not your children for fear of want, we provide sustenance for them and for you.

al-Israʾ (Sura 17:31)

Sheikh Abu Zahra interpreted 'killing' to include both *waʾd* and abortion since what is involved is the slaying of a human being (soul) which Allah has prohibited. This, he claimed, 'indirectly' encompasses birth control because it implies denying Allah's ability to provide (*rizq*). If Muslims really believe in Allah they should leave their progeny and what support they expect for them to Allah. He concludes that the texts of the Qurʾan suggest prohibition of birth control through sterilization or other means 'in fear of poverty or because of it'.

Referring to the two traditions 'marry and multiply' and 'marry the fertile', Sheikh Abu Zahra concluded that multitude is *required* from Muslims and affirmed that the principal purpose of marriage is procreation, according to the consensus of the jurists. Then he related

> We can find that people since old times take the liberty of preventing pregnancy. This happened as well during the time of the Prophet when the Jews used to practice *al-azl* about which the Prophet was queried. He said 'If Allah wills they cannot prevent the pregnancy.'

The Sheikh inferred from that statement the disapproval of the Prophet and claimed that *al-azl* spread from the Jews to some Muslims. Hence, some Muslims reported 'We used to practice *al-azl* at the time of the Prophet.' The Sheikh believed it was logical that they practiced *al-azl* and discussed it among themselves, *but that they kept it from the Prophet.*

He then stated that the jurists should classify *al-azl* in the category of forgivable things and that its permissibility is exceptional *istithna*. Birth control, he concluded, is allowed only for individuals and only for personal reasons. Even then, the Sheikh restricted individual use to specified situations:

- When the woman is too sick to sustain repeated pregnancies, in which case birth control is allowed, provided that a reliable Muslim physician recommends it.
- When the man or wife has a hereditary disease and fears its transmission to progeny in which case he must stop procreation.

He emphasized that children are the human wealth and the source for national development, hence, their numbers should be increased rather than decreased. He concluded that the call for birth control or family planning is 'foreign' in its origin and 'foreign' in its consequences.

Responses by Sheikh (Dr) Madkour[6]

Sheikh (Dr) Mohammad Sallam Madkour, also a Professor of *Shar'ah* at Cairo University, responded to his colleague, Sheikh Abu Zahra, in *The Islamic Look at Birth Control: A Comparative Study of Islamic Schools* published in 1965.

Sheikh Madkour contended that it was incorrect to encompass *wa'd*, abortion and birth control in the interpretation of the two verses about 'killing' children. The verses did not specify *wa'd* and could not apply to abortion unless it were proven that the pregnancy was beyond the four months specified by the jurists for ensoulment. To claim that birth control is similarly implied in this interpretation is *unacceptable and inconsistent* with all the traditions sanctioning *al-azl*, and what had been reported about the Companions and the ruling of the majority of jurists.

Sheikh Abu Zahra's claim that 'birth control' is forbidden by the Qur'an is refuted by the fact that birth control which involves no killing is not contradictory to predestination. This is also borne out in the Prophet's tradition: "Practice *al-azl* with her, if you wish.'

Reference to 'marry and multiply' and 'marry the fertile' is no contradiction to family planning.

It is also an historical error to claim that *al-azl* was a Jewish practice during the Prophet's time and that it was transmitted by them to the Muslims or that the Prophet, when queried, meant the Jews. None of the reporters of *hadith* ever mentioned that the Prophet was being asked about the Jews. Instead, the question was put to the Prophet by Companions who themselves were practicing or wanted permission to practice *al-azl*. His answer 'practice *al-azl* with her, if you wish', was given to a Muslim, not a Jew.

It is also incorrect to claim that Jabir's tradition 'We used to ...' means that they practiced *al-azl* secretly and did not tell the Prophet about it. Sahih Muslim leaves no doubt that 'the Prophet *came to know about it* and did not forbid us (doing it).'

The claim that jurists qualified *al-azl* among the forgivable things and that it is an exception is contradictory to the tradition; it is a fixed ruling in jurisprudence. His restriction of *al-azl* to severe health conditions is too harsh and should be extended to encompass the many other reasons allowed by jurists.

Sheikh Abu Zahra's 'foreign conspiracy' theory of family planning was dismissed by Dr Madkour as strange because 'he knows that our leaders in the Arab and Muslim world are calling for it for the welfare of their people and they are not a part of a foreign plot.'

Maulana Maudoudi[7]

Maulana Maudoudi, a religious leader in Pakistan with significant contributions to Islamic thought, launched a fierce attack on family planning in his book *The Birth Control Movement*. Some Muslim theologians use this book uncritically to support their arguments against family planning. It makes the following claims:

- The birth control movement is a plot against Islam.
- To import birth control into developing countries would be tantamount to ushering in moral malaise ranging from the breakdown of the family to sexual promiscuity and sexually transmitted diseases.
- Women would feel free to join the labor force and abandon their traditional roles.

While he is frequently cited by theologians, the bulk of the Maulana's book is socio-political rather than theological. Furthermore, the Maulana's views provoked a strong reaction to family planning proponents. Wajihuddin Ahmad, a Pakistani colleague of his, makes the point that the Maulana gives little juristic basis for his opposition to the family planning movement:

> The Maulana bases his case against family planning almost entirely on secular grounds, giving the usual pronatalist arguments and supporting them from the writings of Keynesians, of Colin Clark, Dudley Stamp, McCormick, Cole, Pernal and medical anxiety-makers like Sherlieb and Lurand.[8]

The theological part of the Maulana's book, less than one-tenth of its total, is devoted to theological views. While the Maulana concedes that the Qur'an has no clear prohibition of contraception, he argues that those who control their births are no less losers than those who slay their children, invoking the Qur'anic verse:

> Losers are those who besottedly have slain their children without knowledge, and have forbidden that which Allah bestowed upon them [of *rizq*], inventing a lie against Allah.
>
> al-An'am (Sura 6: 140:)

He also argued that birth control falls within the forbidden change of Allah's creation. The Qur'an reports that the devil said

النساء(٤)   ۝ ... وَلَآمُرَنَّهُمْ فَلَيُغَيِّرُنَّ خَلْقَ ٱللَّهِ

And surely I will command them and they will change Allah's creation.
al-Nisa' (Sura 4:119)

He further argued that the verse on 'wives as tilth unto their husbands' is a call for procreation and stands clearly against contraception.

In relation to the *Sunnah*, Maulana Maudoudi's survey of the traditions was not comprehensive. An example is the tradition reported by Abu Sai'd in which the Prophet asked 'Do you really do it' (and he did not say 'Do Not Do It'). Maulana Maudoudi, unintentionally, of course, omitted that part of the tradition in parentheses, although it is reported as such in *Sahih Muslim*. He also claimed that had the Prophet known of the family planning movement he would have prohibited birth control categorically. Some consider this as a trespass on the authority of the Prophet and a violation of a basic precept of Islam, namely, that it is applicable for all times. Furthermore, if the Prophet (PBUH) did not anticipate the family planning movement, the Lawgiver did. Had birth control been something to be prohibited, the Qur'an would have prohibited it, as reported in *Sahih Muslim*.

The book's non-theological arguments by Dr Khurshid Ahmad are accompanied by tables and statistics some of which are informative but it is unfortunate that some of the data and conclusions are not historically based. For example the account is mistaken in concluding that the population explosion in Europe was the determining factor in making it a world power. Had the author checked historical demographic references, he would have realized that mass migrations from Europe to North America and elsewhere played a significant role in relieving population pressure and thus catalyzing the economic success story that subsequently unfolded. As to holding family planning responsible for all moral ills in the west, this is an exaggeration.

The Maulana's high position notwithstanding, it is most interesting that several other scholars in the subcontinent sanction family planning, among them are Maulana Ghulam Murshid, Syed M. Jaffar Khan, Allama Ala'uddin Siddiqui and Maulana Abul-Kalam Azad.[9]

Finally, in fairness to and respect for Maulana Maudoudi, his zeal to defend Islam from the family planning movement made him overprotective and defensively negative. He did admit the permissibility of *al-azl* and quoted traditions and Companions allowing it. Nevertheless, he restricted the practice to individuals only and for compelling health reasons.

Sheikh Ahmad Sahnoun[10]

Sheikh Sahnoun, of Morocco's Ministry of Education, represented the negative minority at the Rabat Conference in 1971, where he presented a paper on 'Abortion and Sterilization' in which he also considered contraception. The paper incorporated many of the arguments against family planning and thus some space is given to it here.

Sheikh Sahnoun conceded that the Companions practiced *al-azl* with the Prophet's full knowledge but charged that a contradictory tradition existed. That tradition (related in al-Bukhari on the authority of Abu Sai'd al-Khudri) reports the Prophet as asking three times, on being told of the practice of *al-azl* by some of the Companions: 'Do you really do it?' According to Sheikh Sahnoun, this indicates that the Prophet was unaware of the practice among his own Companions. The fact that the Prophet reported the question suggests disapproval. This latter tradition is rejected in al-Bukhari which Sheikh Sahnoun gives credence over all other collections, thus the traditions reporting that the Prophet knew about the practice and approved it are less authentic in the Sheikh's opinion (although they were reported in *Sahih Muslim*). In listing some of the reasons why *al-azl* was practiced, he rejected all, save protection of a suckling child. Even that he doubted. He quoted Ibn Hazm and similarly inclined theologians to support his viewpoints.

He characterized sterilization as an alteration of Allah's design and order, a defiance of His will, and a weakening of the strength of the Islamic nation through the reduction of its numbers. Despite the vast difference between abortion and sterilization, he felt that each led to the depletion and eventually, extermination of the human race. He considered abortion to be murder, a horrible and most damnable act, interdicted by Islam in the strongest terms.

Sheikh Sahnoun expressed his suspicion of the Rabat Conference's sponsorship by a non-Muslim agency, the International Planned Parenthood Federation. His claim that the *fatwa* was issued by the Grand Mufti of Egypt in 1936 when Egypt was under British occupation (implying foreign influence) aroused much anger among delegates, given the insinuation that the *fatwa* was foreign-inspired. So outraged was the delegates' response in asserting that Muslim theologians would not change the rules of Allah under such pressure or for earthly rewards that Sheikh Sahnoun apologized publicly and retracted his insinuation.

BOOKS BY THEOLOGIANS ON ISLAM AND FAMILY PLANNING

Several books by theologians have been devoted to the position of Islam on family planning and birth control. Most notable are those by Sharabassi, al-Najjar, Sallam Madkour and al-Boutti. (The two-volume proceedings of the Rabat Conference on Islam and Family Planning will be dealt with in the next section.)

Sharabassi's *Religion and Family Planning* (1965—6)[11]

The Sheikh (Dr) Ahmad al-Sharabassi, Professor at Al-Azhar, was one of the first to write on Islam and contraception. Dr al-Sharabassi was a member of the international committee authenticating the Arabic proceedings of the Rabat Conference. He is the author of several books on *fiqh* including one on the four Sunni schools. The first edition of his book on family planning appeared in 1965, and the second, a year later, was translated into English. Aimed at the general public, the book deals with issues of religion, marriage and family, multitude and size of population, plus views on contraception, abortion and sterilization.

The book makes a case for contraception, presenting a number of traditions on *al-azl*, in addition to its use of analogous reasoning to sanction modern methods. Acceptable reasons for the use of contraception include the following:

- The existence of infectious diseases that may affect progeny.
- Health conditions that could be aggravated by pregnancy.
- Pregnancies at short intervals.

- The preservation of a woman's beauty or fitness.
- Avoiding the economic hardships associated with raising large families.

In dealing with sterilization, the book relies primarily on the views of Sheikh Ahmad Ibrahim who found no juristic objection to sanctioning permanent sterilization. Sheikh Sharabassi, however, was inclined to sanction only temporary sterilization. As to abortion, the author confirmed its prohibition after ensoulment, albeit with no detailed juristic elaboration.

Sallam Madkour's *Islamic Look at Birth Control: a Comparative Study in Islamic Schools* (Arabic, 1965)[12]

Dr (Sheikh) Mohammad S. Madkour, Professor of *Shari'ah* at Cairo University, lists three plausible solutions – all acceptable to Islam – to the population problem: development of resources, emigration and family planning.

The author reviewed juristic opinions and concludes that, with the exception of the Zahiri school, the majority of jurists in each school sanction family planning. As to abortion, he concludes that there is agreement on prohibition after ensoulment, with differences among the legal schools as to its permissibility before that. In cases of compelling danger to a woman's life, abortion is allowed at any time. He disallows sterilization except in cases of hereditary disease or mental illness. Stressing the need to make the views of Islam on family planning known to Muslims everywhere Dr Madkour urged that governments support such a campaign.

Al-Boutti's *Birth Control: Preventive and Curative Approaches* (Arabic, 1970)[13]

Dr Sa'id Ramadan al-Boutti, Professor and Dean of *Shari'ah* in Syria and prolific writer on Islam and contemporary problems, vehemently objects to the family planning *movement* in his book while presenting a solid and well-researched juristic argument in support of family planning *practice* including abortion before 40 days.

In theological terms, the book is well-researched and presented in an innovative fashion, dividing the subject matter into two components: pre-pregnancy, where preventive measures (contraception and sterilization) can be applied, and post-pregnancy where curative measures (abortion) can be applied.

Each measure is discussed from the theological, sociological, and legal point of view. Each measure is also discussed in relation to three rights: the right of the fetus, the right of parents, and the right of society.

Eight traditions are presented and analyzed as detailed in Chapter 7 (p. 140) with the author concluding that to practice *al-azl* is lawful (and, by analogous reasoning, the use of modern contraceptives with only *karaha tanzihiyya*). He explains this sanction of *al-azl* as follows:

- *The right of the fetus* does not apply because the semen in itself does not constitute a fetus and therefore does not command the rights of inheritance or independent personality.
- *The right of parents* is satisfied by exercising their free choice to postpone or limit the number of their children.
- *The right of society* does not apply because society has no claim on the semen before fertilization. But, for the ruler to *force* the people to cease procreation would be an encroachment on society's right.

For Dr al-Boutti's comments on abortion see Chapter 10, p. 192.

Sterilization is disallowed by Dr al-Boutti who equates it with changing Allah's creation, on the grounds that it would affect man's sexual power and woman's ability to bear children.

Demography

There is a demographic section in the book which shows how interested theologians are in population growth. Dr al-Boutti criticized those who claim that the Islamic world is growing faster than more developed countries. He took population density as a measure of population growth and found that Japan grows at a higher rate than Muslim countries. Of course Japan has a very high population density, but its growth rate in 1991 is 0.3 per cent per year which means it would double itself in 230 years. In comparison the Islamic world grows at a rate of 3 per cent per year which is ten times as much as Japan; it will need only twenty-three years to double its population. The way to calculate the growth rate is to find the difference between the birth rate per 1,000 and the death rate per 1,000 (assuming no migration) and divide by ten to get percentage. For example:

The birth rate in the Islamic world is 42 per 1,000.
The death rate in the Islamic world is 12 per 1,000.
The difference is 30 per 1,000.
The natural increase is 30/10 ffl 3 per 100.

The more accurate way is to use the formula in Figure 11.1. Of course, our beloved theologian, Dr al-Boutti has tried and has used the common concept of population density. I am sure he will accept this correction.

A simpler more direct method would be to combine the rate of natural increase (the demographic gap or the difference between the annual birth rate and the annual death rate per 1,000) to the net migration rate per 1,000,

Figure 11.1 How to calculate population growth

$P_t = P_o(1+r)^t 100$

or

$r = \left(t\sqrt{\dfrac{P_t}{P_o}} - 1 \right) \times 100$

where

P_o = the census count for the earlier census
P_t = the census count for the later census
r = the average annual rate of growth (it is usually multiplied by 100 in order that it may be expressed as a percent)
t = the interval in years or decimal fractions thereof between the two censuses.

dividing by 10 to get a percentage. The growth rate is then used in another formula to calculate the years needed to double the population.

Data from the United Nations[14] and the Arab Central Bureau of Statistics plus documentation from the Council of Arab Economic Unity[15], show that the population growth rate in Europe during the period 1980–5 was 0.3 per cent per year. This means that Europe's population will require 230 years to double itself. The Third World as a whole grows at 2.0 per cent per year and needs thirty-five years to double itself, while the Muslim world has been growing at 3.0 per cent per year which means it will need only twenty-three years to double its population. From an economic point of view Europe is giving itself enough time to develop, while the Muslim world is growing at a rate that cannot be matched by economic and service development. Already, Muslim countries have been forced to acquire debts, import food and rely on foreign aid to cope with the needs of their growing populations. The result is a vicious cycle of poverty, ill-health, illiteracy, overpopulation and unemployment being compounded with social frustration, extremism and social unrest.

The only exception is the oil-rich countries which can afford some increase in their population, but their population is only a fraction of the Islamic world.

Al-Najjar's *An Objective Look at the Call for Family Planning* (Arabic, 1982)[16]

This fifty-eight page booklet was written by Sheikh (Dr) Abdel Rahman al-Najjar, Director of Mosques and *Da'wah* in Egypt's Ministry of Religious

Affairs. The booklet includes brief accounts on the family and society, value of children, family planning in Islam, the views of the *Sunni* schools, some of the recent *fatwas* and some questions and answers dealing with multitude, predestination, *tawakkul*, and whether contraception is *wa'd*.

Sheikh al-Najjar sanctions contraception without reservation, but he prohibits sterilization. While he conceded that some jurists allow abortion before ensoulment, he himself finds it safer to prohibit it throughout. He emphatically rules out that contraception is *wa'd* or contradictory to *rizq*, predestination or *tawakkul*. He refutes claims for unrestricted multitude and calls for quality that would make the Prophet (PBUH) proud of his nation.

His booklet offers mosque Imams *a model Jum'a ceremony (khotba)* to follow. The first concept dealt with is the importance of the family in Islamic society, delineating foundations for a good marriage. These are the comforts (*sakan*), the love and friendship (*mawadda*), the mercy (*rahma*) and the responsibility (*masu'uleyya*). Children are valued but Prophets have prayed only for good (*salih*) children. Islam did not specify a number for children, leaving it to the physical, social and economic ability of the parents. Society also has a vested interest in this and its welfare should be considered.

In order to correlate the number of children to needs and abilities, Sheikh al-Najjar's model continues, family planning is allowed. This enables parents to bring up a healthy, pious and well-educated generation that can defend Islam against its enemies. Contraception is particularly relevant in case of existing or *feared* health problems or *expected* economic hardships. Ibn Abbas said 'A multitude of children is one of the two poverties and few children is one of the two forms of ease.'

In the second part of the *khotba* the concept of quality is emphasized as well as the concept of 'no harm and no harassment' emphasizing that Islam is a religion of ease (*yusr*) not hardship (*'usr*).

The Position of Islam on Family Planning, Ministry of Religious Affairs and Ministry of Information, Egypt (1990)

This recent monograph deals with the family in Islam, family planning and breast-feeding. It presents quotations from the *Sunnah* supporting contraception and identifies five justifications for it:

1. Spacing gives the mother a chance uninterruptedly to breast-feed and care for her child.
2. Spacing will allow the parents to take care of their children without economic hardships or having to sustain overwork to 'make ends meet'.
3. Permanent sterilization in case of inheritable serious disease will protect progeny.

4. Developmental efforts should augment family planning.
5. Treatment of infertility is also needed.

The monograph presents views of Muftis and other theologians. Each in his own way sanctions family planning.

The monograph also discusses multitude and quality, and confirms that Islam favors a quality and strong multitude to a weak disorganized one.

Note: There are two more books on the subject: *The Family Planning Movement* by Maulana Maudoudi which was referred to earlier; and the two-volume book on the Rabat conference which will be discussed next.

CONFERENCES ON ISLAM AND FAMILY PLANNING

Introduction

A relatively recent innovation in twentieth-century juristic activity is the convening of conferences and task forces for the collective analysis or exchange of views on current issues. As will be seen, however, it may not be totally without precedence.

Apparently the Companions used to meet and exchange ideas and sometimes discuss a legal issue with a specified conclusion. The tradition, on the authority of Rifa'a Ibn Rafi', relates that a group of the Companions sat with Sayyidna Omar Ibn al-Khattab. The group included Imam Ali, al-Zubeir Ibn al-Awwam, Sa'd Ibn Abi Waqqas and some of the fighters in the battle of Badr (*ahl Badr*). They discussed whether *al-azl* was a form of *wa'd* and Sayyidna Omar said there was nothing wrong with the practice ('*La ba'sa bin*). Imam Ali advanced that *al-azl* could not be *wa'd* before passing through the seven stages of fetal development.... He was commended by Omar and no Companion contradicted Ali's interpretation. This means tacit approval and consensus of those present (see Chapter 7).

In the fourth century AH (tenth century AD) a secret group calling itself *Ikhwan al-Safa'* (The Purity Brotherhood) used to meet and study philosophical, political, theological and other scientific issues. They produced over fifty documents (*rasa'il*) containing syntheses of knowledge at the time. Five members were thought to have been identified but the remainder of the group remain unnamed.

In the twentieth century, group analysis of theological issues takes three forms. The common form is the *Fatwa Committee* which exists in many countries. The most famous is that at Al-Azhar in Cairo. Another is located in the Gaza Strip. Other committees exist in Makkah, Kuwait, Malaysia, etc. Committee members complement one another in research and analysis. The resolutions are usually unanimous.

Another form is the extended committees or *councils* such as the Academy of Islamic Research at Al-Azhar and the *Majmaʿ al-Fiqh al-Islami* in Makkah both of which include theologians from various schools of jurisprudence. Decisions or resolutions take time to be agreed upon and usually the restrictive or orthodox views prevail.

Still another form is *popular conferences* on Islamic issues, which include attendance by theologians, are held for an exchange of views to popularize ideas but are *not* authorized to undertake collective juristic research and *cannot* function as a vehicle for collective *ijtihad.*

Of these we will consider the following:

- The Rabat Conference on Islam and Family Planning, 1971.
- The Banjul Conference on Islam and Family Planning, 1979.
- The Dakar Conference on Islam and Family Planning, 1982.
- The Aceh Congress on Islam and Population Policy, 1990.
- The Mogadishu Conference on Islam and Child Spacing, 1990.

Fatwa Committees and Councils

The Academy (High Council) of Islamic Research[17]

The Academy first met in 1964 to agree upon conference objectives and procedures. The actual conference, held in 1965, discussed matters related to family formation and family planning and made the following resolutions:

1. Islam regards it as desirable to increase the number of offspring and multiply on the consideration that multitude is calculated to give strength to the Islamic nation, 'socially, economically and militarily and enhance its prestige and render it stoutly invulnerable.'
2. Where personal need makes family planning imperative, spouses are free to act according to individual conscience and sense of religion.
3. *Shariʿah* law forbids enacting ordinances by which people are compelled to stop childbearing in any form whatsoever.
4. Abortion for the purpose of limiting childbearing, or the use of means which lead to infertility for this purpose, is forbidden in *Shariʿah* law to the two spouses or to anybody else.

The conference recommended that citizens should be made aware of such cases, and be given assistance in all matters covered by the foregoing decisions in connection with family planning.

The Councils of Islamic fiqh *in Makkah (Saudi Arabia)*[18]

While this eminent group of scholars sanctions family planning in a restricted and individual sense, it considered as unacceptable its practice for economic reasons of hardship and was resolutely opposed to national family planning campaigns.

The council concluded its deliberations as follows:

> [The council] *Majmaʿ al-Fiqh al-Islami* decides with consensus of opinion [of its members] that family planning is unlawful. Contraception is prohibited if it is because of the fear of want because Allah provides sustenance or on account of other factors prohibited by Islamic Law. But if contraception is due to any risk or danger to a mother such as she cannot deliver her child in an ordinary manner and is subjected to operation; in such cases there is no harm in contraception.
>
> Therefore, a call to family planning or contraception in general is not allowed in *Shariʿah* for the causes mentioned above; rather it is a grave sin.
>
> *Al-Iqtisad al-Islami* magazine, March 1987

The Rabat Conference[19]

In 1971, a conference was held in Rabat, Morocco to review the Islamic position on family planning and exchange information on population problems in the Muslim world. In that meeting, Muslim scholars from religious and scientific institutions, representing Muslim communities in the Middle East, Asia, the Far East and Africa, discussed these issues at length. Some forty-five research papers were presented by participants. Members agreed initially that no resolution should be passed because of the nature of the issues discussed. However, the press release issued at the conference's conclusion was subsequently interpreted as the conference's resolutions.

The proceedings were published in 1974 as *Islam and Family Planning* (Nazer, Karmi and Zayid (eds)). An international committee of ten members (including myself) was formed to review and authenticate the entire content of the original Arabic edition of the book. A summary of the proceedings in Arabic appeared thereafter (1979) and was prepared by four members of the committee (I. Nazer, H. Karmi, A. Omran and M. Zayid).

While the conference was sponsored by the International Planned Parenthood Federation, it was made clear by participants and organizers alike that the IPPF had nothing to do with the papers or discussions. The following is a summary of the conference's view:

> That Islamic *Shariʿah* law, by virtue of its rules on the family, adequately provides for its being taken care of and for its safety and the regularity of its affairs in such a way as not to leave room for disintegration or infirmity in its structure.
>
> That the Islamic law, through its provisions, whether recorded in the Qur'an or the traditions or inferred from other provisions according to the principles of inference and *ijtihad*, ensures that the Muslim family will be

able to tackle successfully any new situation and have it under control, with correct and sound solutions and measures.

That the Islamic law allows the Muslim family to be able to look after itself as regards the procreation of children, whether this is in the sense of having many or few of them. It also gives it the right to deal with sterility and to plan suitably spaced pregnancies, and to have recourse, when needed to safe and lawful contraceptive methods.

The conference considered the question of sterilization and felt that the findings of the Academy of Islamic Research at Al-Azhar are worth following in this matter, namely, that the use of means which may lead to sterility is not allowed by the law to the married couple or to anybody else.

On the subject of abortion, i.e. the expulsion of the fetus from the uterus, the conference reiterated the opinion that it is forbidden after the fourth month except for such extreme personal necessity as saving the mother's life. For the period before the end of the fourth month, and although there are numerous different opinions among the scholars in jurisprudence, the correct view tends to forbid it at any stage unless for extreme personal necessity to save the mother's life (or in the case of there being no hope for the life of the fetus).

The conference took cognizance of the intention of Al-Azhar to carry out extra scientific studies in the field of demography in the Islamic world in co-operation with the United Nations. The undertaking of this task by Muslim men of science, in commitment to the Islamic law and its rules, redounds to the actual benefit for the Islamic world.

The Banjul (sub-Saharan) Conference[20]

In 1979, a Conference on Islam and Family Planning for sub-Saharan Africa was held in Banjul, The Gambia. Because of the particular significance of this conference to Africa, selected excerpts of its discussions are quoted from the final report as reported by Milas, Nabwiso and Dossou-Youo (1979) (mimeograph):

> The papers and discussions brought out the fact that family planning is not new in African culture, nor in Islamic practices. Family planning in the context of birth spacing has been an aspect of African culture from time immemorial. Islam also places value on birth spacing through the Qur'anic recommendation of two full years of breast-feeding for the child. (p. 13).

> Other Africans think that Islam is against family planning. In this regard, the Guinean delegation cited a statement of the Constitutional Council of the Islamic World League which described family planning as 'an aggression against the Muslim religion, personal liberty and human rights', adding that consequently 'The Guinean Party and Government

were opposed to generalized family planning and would never adopt any law favourable to this so-called family planning.' The same delegates said that their government's policy was to encourage increased natality and to provide to each and every person the opportunity to live in freedom and dignity. They further claimed that Africa has limitless resources which need to be exploited by a larger population and that according to the Qur'an, anyone who fears Allah always receives from Him the means of resolving his problems.

Many participants expressed serious reservations about the above-mentioned conceptions. It was pointed out that although many African countries have been under the influence of Islam for several centuries, there have not been serious conflicts between Islam and family planning. Islam is not against family planning and is a dynamic and progressive religion which has sought to improve the cultural and moral lives of its followers and to accelerate the development of Muslim nations. (p. 14)

It was shown that where family planning (birth spacing) is needed in terms of the health of mother and child, it is encouraged by Islam. (p. 14)

The participants discussed thoroughly the various papers presented and the relevant references from the Holy Qur'an and the *Sunnah* and found ample evidence to support the acceptability of family planning in Islam. *They then recommended that family planning should be encouraged in all Muslim societies in Africa and explained within the teachings of Islam with emphasis on responsible parenthood.*

The Dakar Seminar[21]

Still another African interchange of views on Islam and family planning took place in Dakar, Senegal, in April 1982. More than 200 participants attended, among them eminent Islamists, religious leaders and key members of the Senegalese government. During the seminar, the following points were made:

1. Islam considers the family to be the basic unit of society and the foundation of all nations. For this reason, marriage is placed at the first order of duties to be fulfilled by every Muslim, because without marriage there could be no Muslim nation in quantity and quality.
2. As accepted in Islam, family planning or the planning of births enhances the family's well-being.
3. Furthermore, family planning is seen in Islam from the viewpoint of protecting the rights of children and sheltering them from poverty, ignorance and sickness, and attending to their physical, moral and religious education.

ISLAM AND FAMILY PLANNING

All the authors of papers agreed on conditions under which family planning could be practiced by the Muslim family.

There was agreement that family planning is authorized in the following situations:

- If the woman is not able to carry closely-spaced pregnancies to term.
- If she suffers from a contagious disease which could be passed on to her children.
- If the parents are afraid of not being able to protect their progeny and provide for their needs.
- To avoid pregnancy while breast-feeding a child.

There was, however, some disagreement in regard to *national programs*. One author suggested that Islam permits family planning on an individual basis, but does not tolerate the imposition of family planning on a society. Others were more tolerant and suggested that governments are responsible for the welfare of their people, including family planning. The seminar participants expressed the desire that Senegal adopt a family planning system which takes into consideration the teachings of the Muslim religion and the necessity to protect the happiness and prosperity of the Senegalese family.

The Aceh Congress

The following text is taken from the declaration which resulted from the international congress convened in Aceh, Indonesia in February 1990 by the Government of Indonesia in collaboration with Al-Azhar University International Islamic Center for Population Studies and Research.

> [The Congress] has come to a concensus to issue this Declaration for all Muslim Communities the world over to initiate and/or promote a concerted and coordinated effort in the fields of population policies and population programmes. The Congress therefore
> - **Starts** with the conviction that Islam which has its sources in the Al Qur'an and *Sunnah* provides guidance for all aspects of life, including issues of population and family welfare.
>
>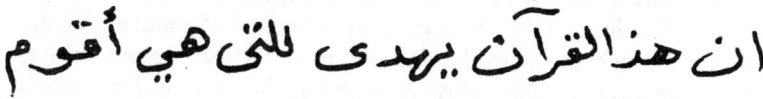
>
> and affirms that it is within this context that this Declaration is made;
> - **Emphasizes** the responsibilities towards future generations, in particular in the field of population, where the decisions and actions of one generation influences to a significant degree the quality of life of future generations;

- **Acknowledges** that population, resources and the environment are inextricably linked and stresses our commitment to bringing about a balanced and sustainable relationship among them;
- **Expresses concern** that while some Muslim countries may afford to increase their population, for most countries, rapid population growth, unplanned migration and urbanization, increasing degradation of the environment threaten the process of their development and the welfare of their people;
- **Recognizes** that Muslim women are crucial to the process of the development in Islamic societies and that the improvement of their status and the extent to which they are informed and participate in making family decisions will be essential in determining the future quality of life and growth rates of the Islamic population;
- **Recognizes** further the need to consolidate the expertise, knowledge and experience in Muslim countries in forms that are more amenable to practical application at all levels, and through appropriate mechanisms that will bring about sustained self-generating efforts in Islamic communities;
- **Underscores** the fact that the improvement of the quality of life can best be achieved through integrated and balanced efforts which encompass the social, economic and spiritual dimensions of development within the context of Islam;
- **Acknowledges** that for the successful realization of these development measures, the initiative should come from the Muslim community itself, and, in this regard, Islamic leaders and scholars are entrusted with the profound responsibility of providing the leadership which must now be rendered with the deepest sense of humility and selfless dedication;
- **Recognizes** the sovereign right of each country to establish in the context of Islam its own population policies and programmes responding to country-specific needs while mindful that national action or inaction in population may have effects that extend beyond national boundaries;
- **Notes** that the progress made by population programmes in the past decades, notably the increased awareness of population issues throughout the world, and throughout Muslim communities, yet access to proper information and quality services for maternal and child care and family planning, including management of infertility, is still lagging and needs to be strengthened.

With these considerations in mind, and recognizing that the conclusions and recommendations emanating from the Congress offer an excellent opportunity to reflect on past activities and to chart an optimal course of action for the immediate future and the remainder of the 15th century after Hijrah, the Congress hereby issues this Declaration.

Islamic values on population issues

Emphasizing the firm conviction that Islam is a religion of the present and the future, and cognizant that Population Issues are both related to the present as well as the future, the Congress stresses the relevance of Islamic guidance to population issues to the extent that these are aimed towards the betterment of human life, and the elimination of hardships to Muslim countries and communities.

Specific immediate action to be taken therefore is the propagation of Islamic values on population issues among and within countries and communities through information, education and communication including the eradication of misconception of Islamic attitudes towards population issues.

Islam and the quality of life

Reaffirming that Islam teaches optimism in viewing life in general, and that Islam also emphasizes human responsibility towards current world problems as these determine one's destiny in life and hereafter. Specific recommended actions to be taken are as follows:

The Congress appeals to all Muslim communities throughout the world to assume their responsibilities to seek appropriate ways and means within the realm of the Religion of Islam to enhance and improve the quality of life both for the present and future generations.

The demographic conditions of Islamic world

The Congress notes with concern the unfavourable demographic conditions of Muslim countries and communities.

The Congress urges all Muslim countries to immediately initiate and/or intensify firm policies and programmes to rectify these adverse conditions.

The Congress further urges all Muslim countries to formulate population policies according to country-specific needs, and integrate these policies into development plans and giving them high priority.

The status and role of women in Islamic societies

The congress reaffirms that an improvement in the role and status of women is central to the development of their own potential in society, as well as that of their families.

In this interest the Congress therefore endorses the following actions to be taken:

1. To provide adequate illiteracy eradication and education programmes for women.
2. To provide accessible Mother and Child Care throughout with emphasis on rural and disadvantaged areas, especially for the high risk groups, with a view to ensure safe motherhood and child survival.
3. To provide accessible family planning and counselling services available and accessible without coercion, and endorse effective and safe contraceptive methods which are not antagonistic to Islamic *Shariʿah*.
4. To motivate and educate rural and disadvantaged women in income generating activities, and to provide training opportunities to uplift their economic conditions and to provide them with supportive infrastructure for child care, including breast-feeding.
5. To strenghten women organizations and networks, and to organize special seminars and conferences to consider issues of concern to Muslim women.

The role of ʿulamaʾ and Islamic institutions in population programmes

The Congress firmly believes that the 'ulamaʾ of Islam' are instrumental to the formation of norms and the shaping of attitudes in Muslim communities.

The Congress therefore calls for increased efforts of the ʿulamaʾ to help the development process and to achieve a happy family.

Muslim communities in non-Muslim countries

The Congress notes the sizeable number of Muslims living in non-Muslim countries, and recommends that the population-related issues of these communities should be examined to determine practical solutions and addressed immediately to the extent possible.

Cooperation and collaboration among Muslim nations and communities in population policies and programmes

The Congress reaffirms that although national and community characteristics dictate a diversity in the actions taken to deal with population issues, in the interest of 'Ukhuwah Islamiah' (Islamic brotherhood), strong international and national commitment towards cooperation and collaboration must be intensified and institutionalized.

The Congress finally urges the formation of follow-up committees to promote propagation and implementation of this Aceh Declaration.

(Printed by permission of the Al-Azhar University International Islamic Center for Population Studies and Research)

The Mogadishu Conference

The following recommendations and suggestions were issued by the National Conference on 'Islam and Child Spacing' held in Mogadishu, Somalia in July 1990 in collaboration with Al-Azhar University International Islamic Center for Population Studies and Research.

1. The Conference confirms and endorses what the Somali Government declared about the great importance of child spacing for the Somali family and the future of family planning in Somalia.
2. The conference recommends having a system for demographic and health studies on a national and local level so as to assess the population problems in Somalia, including migration from villages to cities and the inclusion of the demographic factor in the Somalia Development Plan.
3. The Conference confirms, without sensitivities, the conviction that the population problems should be faced in the context of the Islamic Shari'ah so as to improve the Somali spiritual, social, cultural, health and scientific standards. The Conference, likewise, recommends that no effort should be spared in developing natural resources in the country as means of overcoming population problems.
4. The Conference endorses the care of the Muslim child such that he is brought up and educated in the Islamic way, and that his rights are duly regarded from the time of its inception in his mother's womb.
5. The prevention and treatment of infertility is the way to make the Muslim family happy. The Conference was informed about the *fatwas* by Al-Azhar *'ulama'* and those of the *fiqh* councils in Makkah and Jiddah, confirming the legality of the 'assisted' medical fertilization (artificial insemination and in-vitro fertilization) provided that there are indications for such procedures, that the cells used therein come form the spouse of the patient and that the procedure is performed by an experienced and just Muslim physician.
6. The Conference was informed that the Companions (*sahabah*) of the Prophet (PBUH) used to practice *al-azl* (or coitus interruptus) at the time of the Prophet while the Qur'an was being revealed (from Jabir's tradition reported in the two Sahihs i.e. agreed upon); had it been something to be prohibited, the Qur'an would have prohibited its practice. Further and according to another tradition reported by Muslim, the Prophet (PBUH) came to know about it (*al-azl* by his Companions) and he did not forbid them (practicing it). The Conference agreed that by analogous reasoning (*qiyas*), other methods of contraception (such as the methods used in these days) are likewise lawful provided they are temporary, safe and legal and that they are

used without compulsion of either spouse.
7. Based on the above knowledge, the Conference assures that there is no contradiction between the Islamic *Shari'ah* and child spacing as decreed by Muslim Jurists and on the account of its benefits to the health and welfare of the mother and child. Such is within the sphere of planning which is one of the basic principles of Islam in matters of religion and daily life.
8. The Conference recommends the continuity of cooperation between Al-Azhar, represented by its International Islamic Center for Population Studies and Research, and the Family Health Care Society in Somalia. As a start, the conference called upon Al-Azhar to publish and disseminate the papers, proceedings and recommendations of the Conference as soon as feasible. Al-Azhar is also called upon to hold similar future meetings on subnational levels and disseminate the results at the grass root level throughout the country.

(Printed by permission of the Al-Azhar University International Islamic Center for Population Studies and Research)

12

Fatwas and opinions of other twentieth-century jurists

Besides the books discussed and conference reports, there are two more aspects of twentieth-century jurisprudence. The first is the *fatwas* pronounced by a recognized jurist or an official Mufti in response to an inquiry. The second refers to the researched opinion of leading theologians and jurists working individually or in groups.

A COMMENTARY ON *FATWAS* ON FAMILY PLANNING

A *fatwa* is a legal opinion in Islamic jurisprudence. In this century it characterizes most of the 'official' or formal opinions issued by jurists who, because of their fame or because of their official appointment to the office of *ifta'*, in which case they are called *Muftis*, respond to questions about juristic problems.

This section will review several of the *fatwas* on family planning which have come from different parts of the Islamic world, including fourteen twentieth-century *fatwas* which will be discussed (mostly) in chronological order. The texts of these *fatwas* are given in Appendix II. The following section will also present earlier *fatwas* from the Indian subcontinent.

Sheikh Abdel Majeed Saleem (Egypt, 1937)[1]

The *fatwa* by Sheikh A.M. Saleem (the Grand Mufti of Egypt) which sanctions family planning has special relevance because of the following:
1. It is the first of its kind in this century, thus it served as a bridge to the knowledge of earlier jurists.
2. It preceded what is called the family planning movement in Egypt and other Islamic countries. (The Egyptian family planning program was established twenty-eight years later in 1965.)

3. It has the signs of *ijtihad* at a time when pronouncements of this sort were expected to be within the ultra-conservative milieu that characterized the post-Ottoman era in Muslim territories.

The *fatwa* was made in response to a specific question that contained several of the health, social and economic indications for family planning. The Grand Mufti referred to the textual statements of the Hanafi scholars of jurisprudence and sanctioned the use of family planning through *al-azl*. He used the principle of analogy to sanction new methods of contraception. He required the usual consent of the spouse. He also reiterated the Hanafi views on abortion allowing it before ensoulment where there is justification.

Fatwa from the *Fatwa* Committee of Al-Azhar (1953)[2]

This *fatwa* was issued in 1953. What caught my attention is that the *Fatwa* was in response to the same question asked of Sheikh Saleem, sixteen years earlier. According to Sheikh Shaltout, then a professor in a *Shari'ah* college, the earlier *fatwa* caught the conservative theological community by surprise and came under attack by those who considered it to be unduly permissive, this despite its being based on the Hanafi views made centuries earlier. Sheikh Shaltout came to the defence of the *fatwa* and emphasized the permissibility of contraception for health and other indications, not only by the Hanafi school but by the majority of the early (*salaf*) and following (*khalaf*) jurists.

Interestingly, the *Fatwa* Committee confirmed the permissibility of contraception, based this time on the Shafe'i school of jurisprudence. The Committee disallowed permanent sterilization.

Fatwa of Sheikh Mahmoud Shaltout (Al-Azhar, 1959)[3]

After rejecting the idea of enforcing family planning by promulgation of a national law committing the whole nation to restrict childbearing, Sheikh Shaltout, former Grand Imam of Al-Azhar endorsed strongly the use of contraception, on an individual basis for health, social and economic reasons. He also recognized that under certain conditions contraception becomes mandatory: 'Planning in this sense is not incompatible with nature, and is not disagreeable to national conscience, and is not forbidden by *Shari'ah*, if not prescribed by it.'

Fatwa of Tuan Haji Ali M.S. Saleh (Singapore 1955)[4]

Tuan Haji Saleh, chief Qadi of Singapore adopted the views of the *Fatwa* Committee of Al-Azhar and ruled that steps taken to space births in order to safeguard the health of mothers is not contrary to Islam. He disallowed sterilization and abortion after the fourth month of pregnancy.

Fatwa of the Advisory Council on Religious Matters (Turkey 1960)[5]

The Council allowed contraception with the wife's consent, a consent that can be bypassed in case of war or turmoil or if it becomes hard to bring up children because of such difficult conditions.

Fatwa by Sheikh Hasan Ma'moun (Al-Azhar, 1964)[6]

This is a very important *fatwa* in which Sheikh Ma'moun, former Grand Imam of Al-Azhar talked about two thorny issues: the problem of multitude and the legality of national programs. He explained that Islam in its early days needed a lot of followers, hence the emphasis on multitude which may still be needed under certain circumstances. However, we are faced with overpopulation which threatens human welfare to the extent that some thinkers *introduced family planning in their country to enable governments to provide services for its people*. Islam, he concluded, is never against human welfare. Family planning in this sense without compulsion, is sanctioned and quality is preferred to quantity.

Fatwa by Sheikh Abdullah Al-Qalqili (Jordan, 1964)[7]

This is a lengthy *fatwa* by Sheikh Qalqili, then the Mufti of Jordan, in which he reviews some of the traditions on *al-azl* and concludes that there is clear indication that contraception is definitely allowed. He also argued that it is allowable to take drugs to cause abortion before quickening, basing his view mainly on those in the Hanafi school.

Fatwa of Ayatollah Baha'eddin Mahallati (1964)[8] and Sheikh Shamsuddin's view on sterilization (1971)[9] (both Imami Shi'ites)

There is a very short *fatwa* by Sheikh Mahallati of Iran sanctioning contraception provided it will not impair the fertility of the female and make her sterile.

This represented at the time the Shi'ite view, but Sheikh Mohammad Shamsuddin of Lebanon, collected views of the leaders of Imami Shi'ites in Lebanon, Iran, Iraq and elsewhere, the majority of whom agreed to the acceptability of both temporary and permanent sterilization. The views of Sheikh Shamsuddin have been given in the preceding chapters.

Fatwa of Haji Abdel Jalil Hassan (Malaysia, 1964)[10]

This brief *fatwa* by Haji Abdel Jalil, the assistant Mufti of Jahore, Malaysia permitted contraception but disallowed sterilization.

Fatwa of Al-Sayed Ali Al-Zawawi (Malaysia, no date)[11]

This is a longer *fatwa*, also from Malaysia, in which Sheikh al-Zawawi, Mufti of Ragganu reviewed some traditions on the subject and made the following ruling:

1. Contraception for health reasons is definitely allowed.
2. Abortion is prohibited after the fourth month; (opinions vary to how much earlier).
3. Sterilization is not permitted.

Fatwa of President of High Court of Appeals (Yemen Arab Republic, 1968) (Zaydi)[12]

This is a short *fatwa* which was in response to a question on abortion and pointed out that abortion is allowed by the *Shariʿah* before the fifth month of pregnancy (based on the *Zaydi* school).

Fatwa by Sheikh Jadel Haq (Al-Azhar, 1979, 1980)[13]

Sheikh Jadel Haq is the Grand Imam of Al-Azhar. He issued this *fatwa* (presented at the beginning of the book) when he was the Mufti of Egypt. After reviewing some of the juristic views he pronounced sanction for family planning (using modern methods) provided such would not result in permanent infertility. He also argued that contraception is not murder and is not antagonistic to trust in Allah, neither is it contradiction of the will of Allah. As to abortion, he reviewed the various schools, and explained that some allowed it before 120 days (Hanafi and Zaydi), some before 40 days (Hanbali), while the Zahiri and Maliki disallowed it at any time. All of the schools disallowed abortion after the fourth month except to save the mother's life.

Sheikh Jadel Haq is known to oppose there being *a law* to force people to practice family planning.

Opinion of Sheikh Shaʿrawi (1980)[14]

Sheikh Shaʿrawi is an eminent scholar with a sizable following all over the Arab world. Conservative as he may be, he sanctioned family planning like other theologians. His only reservation and warning was to be careful not to confuse planning with predestination or guarantee of *rizq* by Allah. Nevertheless he listed among the acceptable indications (a) preservation of a wife's health and beauty, and (b) limited space in the family's house.

Fatwa by Sheikh Tantawi (Egypt, 1988)[15]

Sheikh Sayyid Tantawi, the current Mufti of Egypt, issued a *fatwa* on family planning in 1988. The *fatwa* was comprehensive, well-researched, very assertive and frank. In it, the Mufti sanctioned family planning liberally for economic, cultural or health reasons. He actually approved contraception by a rich couple with three children who wanted to use contraception not because they cannot afford more children but because they live in a country which needs family planning.

He ruled that new methods are as lawful as *al-azl* and contraception is not murder or contradiction of predestination or *rizq*. Abortion is disallowed. He emphasized that nations now boast of their technical and scientific abilities not their size.

Comment on *Fatwa* above by the *Fatwa* Committee of Al-Azhar (1988)

Shortly after Sheikh Tantawi issued his *fatwa*, the *Fatwa* Committee of Al-Azhar met to examine the *fatwa*. After deliberation, the Committe unanimously endorsed the *fatwa*, its progressive nature notwithstanding. This was published with Tantawi's *fatwa*.

FATWAS FROM THE INDIAN SUBCONTINENT

It is interesting to note that important *fatwas* on family planning were issued prior to the twentieth century in the Indian subcontinent.

Shah Abdel Aziz (d.1864)[16]

A nineteenth-century *fatwa* from Shah Abdel Aziz was included in his famous *Tafsir* of the Qur'an which states

> *Al-azl* is lawful on the basis of authentic and well-known traditions of the Prophet (PBUH). The use of medicines before or after coitus for preventing conception is as lawful as *al-azl*. Imam Shafe'i interpreted the Qur'anic verse [Sura 4: 3–4] as a counsel to monogamy as the best way to avoid too many children.
>
> *Tafsir Aziz* pp. 77–8

A consensus in seventeenth-century India[17]

A consensus of 500 religious scholars who codified Islamic law during the time of the Moghul Emperor of India, Aurangzeb Alamgir (1670), allowed contraception with the consent of the partner.

Leading contemporary ʿ*ulama*ʾ in the subcontinent

Dr Anwarul-Haq[18] in his booklet *Family Planning in the Light of Islam* (1967), related that:

Contemporary notable '*Ulama*' like Maulana Ghulam Murshid, Syed M. Jaffar Khan, Allama Ala'uddin Siddiqui and the late Maulana Abul-Kalam Azad, are in favour of the judicious practice of contraceptive measures even for reasons other than health. Others like Maulana Maudoudi permit it, but only as a health measure, while still others ban it altogether.

OPINIONS OF OTHER TWENTIETH-CENTURY SCHOLARS ('ULAMA')

Views on family planning from prominent twentieth-century '*ulama*' were published as articles or parts of books. The following selection of these views will complete the picture.

Sheikh Ahmad Ibrahim (Egypt, 1936)[19]

The opinion of Sheikh Ahmad Ibrahim (then professor of Islamic *Shari'ah* in Cairo University) was written in 1936 as an introduction to a doctoral dissertation by Dr al-Sa'id Mustafa al-Sa'id who studied under him. The dissertation was entitled 'The Extent of Family Rights'. This opinion anticipated by one year the famous *fatwa* by Sheikh Abdel Majeed Saleem, but did not match the *fatwa* in popularity because of the limited distribution of the dissertation. Like Sheikh Saleem's *fatwa*, this opinion was made twenty-eight years before the family planning program in Egypt.

The opinion has two main thrusts:

1. The permissibility of contraception.
2. The lawfulness of sterilization.

It must be noted that Sheikh A. Ibrahim is one of the leading jurists and a recognized *mujtahid* of this century, who has been quoted by other theologians.

On contraception, Sheikh Ibrahim found it unequivocally permissible to use contraception and provided evidence for this from Islamic jurisprudence. He argued that this is not a contradiction to Allah's design. On the issue of sterilization, Sheikh Ibrahim argued skillfully and scholarly for its permissibility in Islam. Some details of his opinion were given in Chapter 10 (see p. 189).

Sheikh Nadim Al-Jisr: Mufti of Tripoli (Lebanon, 1964)[20]

In his research paper presented to the first conference of the Academy For Islamic Research, Sheikh Nadim al-Jisr, said

> Islam's position on birth control does not go beyond the freedom we have

just ascertained: namely that the married couple has the complete freedom in limiting their progeny *or stopping it altogether*, as long as they are in agreement with one another. If one of them disagrees, then the other loses that freedom since it violates the other's right.

As to what came in the *Sunnah* encouraging multiplication, this is not mandatory [*wajib*] as it takes away the freedom of the couple: it is only a form of encouragement of those who possess the health and economic means. If not, such as those with hereditary diseases, or the poor who may become poorer with multiplicity of children, the decision is theirs. All that is in harmony with the concept of freedom in Islam.

Note: In case of hereditary diseases, the couple have no choice but to prevent pregnancy.

Sheikh Sayyid Sabiq (Saudi Arabia, 1968)[21]

In his popular encyclopedia, *Fiqh al-Sunnah*, Sheikh Sabiq allows the use of contraception especially if the husband already has a large family, if he cannot bring up his children correctly, if his wife is weak or sick or has repeated pregnancies, or if the husband is poor. He explained further that in some of these situations, jurists not only allow contraception but make its use mandatory *mandoub ilayh*. To support this view, he cites some of the traditions on *al-azl*.

He declared categorically that abortion is disallowed after ensoulment (120 days) but found abortion before that to be permissible when justifiable. However, if no justification exists abortion is disliked (*yukrah*). He quoted the author of *Subul al-Salam* (al-San'ani) as saying

> The permissibility of a woman using treatment to abort a *nutfa* before 'ensoulment' varies in permissibility along the same lines as *al-azl*: those who permit *al-azl* allow abortion, and those who prohibit *al-azl* prohibit it. The same exists with taking or using what may prevent pregnancy permanently.

The latter reference is apparently to sterilization. Sheikh Sabiq referred also to al-Ghazali's views on abortion, to demonstrate differing opinion on the subject.

Sheikh (Dr) al-Ahmadi Abonnour (Al-Azhar, 1970)[22]

Sheikh al-Ahmadi Abonnour, then an instructor at Al-Azhar, wrote his dissertation, 'The Way of *Sunnah* in Marriage' prior to joining the Faculty of Jurisprudence. Until a few years ago he was Minister of Religious Affairs in Egypt.

His twenty-page account on contraception, entitled 'Fruits of Marriage' begins with a discussion of multitude, including the usual affirmation of its desirability in Islam but with the qualification that it should not impair the quality of the people. The author argues that if the Prophet (PBUH) will make a display of Muslims, they should be healthy, well-educated, correctly trained, industrious, pious and above all unified in *one nation* with one aim.

إِنَّ هَٰذِهِۦٓ أُمَّتُكُمْ أُمَّةً وَٰحِدَةً وَأَنَا۠ رَبُّكُمْ فَٱعْبُدُونِ ۞ الأنبياء(٢١)

Verily, this nation of yours is a single nation, and I am your LORD, so worship Me.

al-Anbiya' (Sura 21:92)

He then quoted some of the Qur'anic verses which favor quality:

قُل لَّا يَسْتَوِى ٱلْخَبِيثُ وَٱلطَّيِّبُ وَلَوْ أَعْجَبَكَ كَثْرَةُ ٱلْخَبِيثِ... ۞ المائدة(٥)

Say: The evil and the good are not alike, even though the multitude of the evil may dazzle you.

al-Ma'ida (Sura 5:100)

Muslims should not bear unhealthy children and the way to do so is to impregnate a woman while she is lactating. An additional child means poorer nutrition for both the suckling child and the new fetus. Pregnancy hormones, progesterone and estrogen increase during pregnancy and impair the quality of breast milk with some inadequacy in fats and proteins. This makes the suckling child vulnerable to malnutrition and infection. That is why the Prophet (PBUH) warned against *al-ghayla*. Sheikh Abonnour emphasizes spacing of about three years (allowing 30 months for bearing and weaning).

He points strongly to the traditions asserting that the Companions did practice *al-azl*; when they asked the Prophet about it, neither he nor the Qur'an forbade the practice. In one tradition, the Prophet suggested it to the inquirer.

Considering the question of 'your wives as tilth unto you', he quotes the Companions who interpreted the verse as a choice between practicing *al-azl* or not practicing it. He asserts that *al-azl* is not *wa'd* by quoting some of the relevant traditions where the Prophet denied the allegation of the Jews that *al-azl* is minor infanticide.

He also considered some of the traditions that have equivocal language (in Arabic) and could be interpreted either way. He was inclined to interpret them as supporting *al-azl* in view of the traditions cited by Abu Sa'id in which the Prophet (PBUH) said 'Why do you do that?' rather than 'Do not do that'. (Coming from an expert in the sciences of *hadith*, this is most reassuring.)

Quoting Dr Mustafa Suefi, a psychologist, he explained that the larger the family the less instructive the interaction between parents and children. If parents can at most devote eight hours to their offspring and have four children, each will receive two hours of their time. But since large families usually make parents impatient and physically overworked, the net time for interaction is even less and cannot be compensated for by interaction with the older siblings.

Sheikh Yusuf al-Qaradawi (Qatar, 1980)[23]

Sheikh al-Qaradawi, Professor of Islamic Studies at Qatar University, devoted a special section to contraception in his popular book *Al-Halal Wal-Haram Fil-Islam*, which has been translated into English as *The Lawful and the Prohibited in Islam* and is widely used in Muslim countries as well as in Europe and the USA. He began by saying that:

> The preservation of the human species is unquestionably the primary objective of marriage, and such preservation of species requires continued reproduction. Accordingly, Islam encourages having many children and has blessed both male and female progeny.
>
> However, it allows the Muslim to plan his family due to valid reasons and recognized necessities. The common method of contraception at the time of the Prophet (PBUH) was coitus interruptus, or withdrawal ... The Companions of the Prophet (PBUH) engaged in this practice during the period when the Qur'an was being revealed to him.

He then proceeded to quote some of the traditions on *al-azl*, after which he specified the valid reasons as follows:

- Fear that the progeny or delivery may endanger the mother's health.

البقرة(٢)   ﴿١٩٥﴾ ... وَلَا تُلْقُوا بِأَيْدِيكُمْ إِلَى التَّهْلُكَةِ

And do not be cast into ruin by your own hands.

al-Baqara (Sura 2:195)

- Fear that the burden of children may strain the family's means to the extent that one might accept or do something *haram* to satisfy their needs.

ISLAM AND FAMILY PLANNING IN THE 20th CENTURY

يُرِيدُ ٱللَّهُ بِكُمُ ٱلْيُسْرَ وَلَا يُرِيدُ بِكُمُ ٱلْعُسْرَ ... ﴿١٨٥﴾

البقرة(٢)

Allah desires ease for you, and He desires not hardship for you.
al-Baqara (Sura 2:185)

- Fear that the children's health or upbringing may suffer.
- Fear that the new progeny may harm a suckling child.

Sheikh Qaradawi confirms that modern contraceptive methods are similar in purpose to *al-azl* and are allowed by analogy. He also quoted Ahmad Ibn Hanbal as requiring the consent of the wife. As to abortion, he objects to it especially after the fetus is completely formed.

Hajj Nasiruddin Latif (Indonesia, 1974)[24]

In his address to the Rabat Conference on Family Planning, Hajj Latif, of the Ministry of Religious Affairs in Indonesia, considered the legality of family planning and made the following points:

1. In the light of our studies and knowledge so far, we can affirm that there is no verse in the Qur'an or any explicit text forbidding the wife or husband to practice family planning.
2. There are two verses in the Qur'an (Sura 6: 151 and Sura 17: 31) relating to killing of children, but the reference is to the slaying of a person or a being that has a soul. These verses cannot be taken to forbid family planning for the simple reason that family planning is not designed to destroy the fetus which is already animated; it simply prevents pregnancy.
3. If we search the *Sunnah*, which ranks as the second source of Islamic law next to the Qur'an, we still fail to find any reliable tradition in which the Prophet prohibited his companions from practicing *al-azl*.
4. Muslims practice family planning with the full realization that the will of Allah has ascendancy over man's will. This situation is exactly the same as that of ill-heath or disease. True, Allah has pre-ordained the final result or outcome of disease and yet He has allowed, even urged us to treat illness.
5. While having children is encouraged, the responsibility of raising them has to be qualified.

He referred to the *fatwa* by the *Fatwa* Committee of *Al-Azhar* and the *fatwa* by Sheikh Abdel Majeed Saleem, both of which support his opinion. He concluded that 'I, for one, do not feel that Islam interdicts family planning to ward off hardship in Muslim married life.'

Dr Huseyn Atay (Turkey, 1974)[25]
Dr Huseyn Atay, Professor of (Islamic) Theology at the Faculty of Theology, Turkey, researched the legality of family planning.

He considered the issue of multitude and concluded that Islam prefers the multitude of quality. He added that the Muslim world today is not suffering from a lack of people, but from a lack of great industrious Muslims.

Reviewing the Prophetic traditions on *al-azl*, he found that several traditions sanctioned it while a few others were equivocal. He provided examples of each and refuted Ibn Hazm's views. He actually praised theologians who were able to reconcile Judama's tradition with the others.

In considering abortion and the stages of fetal development, he introduced an intriguing concept. *Al-azl* in Arabic, as already indicated, means isolation or separation. In seeking to extend the meaning beyond its customary use, he drew an analogy between the act of separating sperm from ovum (*al-azl*) and the act of preventing the early 'product' of conception from ever reaching the stage of ensoulment. He recognized that the jurists were divided on the issue; confirming that they all forbid abortion after ensoulment, i.e. after the fetus becomes a complete human being.

He then turned to sterilization and tried to differentiate between it and castration. Castration is forbidden and entails the destruction of the power of getting children. Sterilization, on the other hand, allows the individual to resume his natural functions. He suggested that the issue of sterilization should, at least, be discussed.

Sheikh (Dr) Abdel Aziz al-Khayyat (Jordan, 1985)[26]
Sheikh (Dr) al-Khayyat, Minister of Religious Affairs in Jordan, deals with family planning in his book *The Cooperating Society in Islam* (1985). He explains that family planning in Islam starts with the choice of the wife (to avoid genetic problems) and puts a great emphasis on raising children physically, educationally and spiritually. That is why quality is favored to quantity. He agrees with al-Ghazali in supporting family planning and is inclined to support individual rather than national use. He sanctions the use of the contraceptive pill because like *al-azl*, it is not murder or crime against a being.

Dr Isma'il Balogun (Nigeria, no date)[27]
Dr Balogun, Professor of Religion at the University of Ilorin, Nigeria, prepared an interesting paper on Muslim attitudes to family planning. An important problem in Nigeria, he states, is that many Muslims there believe that polygyny is required in Islam. He argues that such is contrary to the nature of Islam which makes monogamy the rule, but accepts polygyny only

as an exception based on the ability of man to maintain justice and strict impartiality among the wives.

He unequivocally endorses family planning to improve the quality of Muslims. He states that Muslim supporters of the practice argue that since all lives up to the day of resurrection have already been created, it must stand to reason that lives which are prevented by family planning measures were not among those already created and, therefore, they are not destined to come to the world.

He quotes the debate in the early 1960s between Sheikh M. al-Sharqawi of Jordan (a supporter of family planning) and other theologians. The debate went along the usual lines (as discussed earlier in Chapter 6), as evidenced by this passage from Sheikh Sharqawi:

> The consideration, therefore, for the happiness of the individual, the security of the family, the safety, strength and comfort of the government is not in 'how many' but in 'how well'. According to a UN report, the country with the highest rate of birth in the early 1960s was the Ivory Coast, and the one with the lowest rate was Sweden. It cannot be said that the individual persons, the families or the government of the first country were happier, more secure, more satisfied, stronger and more comfortable than the second.

Sheikh Abdel-Aziz Iesa (Al-Azhar, 1987)[28]

Sheikh Iesa, former Minister of Al-Azhar Affairs in Egypt and a member of the Academy of Islamic Research, compiled a booklet on family planning in Islamic jurisprudence based on lectures he delivered to physician trainees at Al-Azhar University. His presentation is summarized below.

One of the directions of the Prophet (PBUH) was to form a family through marriage with a view to secure tranquility and to beget children. If a youth cannot afford marriage, however, it should be postponed.

Family planning is far from population control either on a general or individual basis. The foremost objective is to produce offspring who would worship Allah, and who would populate the earth. And yet, marrying a barren woman is not prohibited.

Islam looks for high quality offspring, not hopeless masses that are weak despite their multitude. The rights of children on their families should be fulfilled to produce good, able and well-instructed offspring, a goal that cannot be achieved except by regulating procreation. 'The multiplication of the human race should neither be fearful nor an economic burden on the society.' The Muslims should be such that the Prophet will boast of them. One of the children's rights stressed by the Prophet is for them to have separate sleeping arrangements, something poor families with too many children can hardly afford.

Some people refer to the verse 'Kill not your children for fear of want', but this is different from family planning in which there is no killing.

Family planning is religiously permissible and it is for the family to choose the time. The indications are like those given by al-Ghazali (health, beauty and fear to deviate from the Prophet's path in order to seize money unlawfully to meet expanding family needs following a new delivery).

Abortion after ensoulment is categorically prohibited except for compelling medical reasons. Before ensoulment (four months) it is a matter of controversy.

Some people think of birth control policy as a common law enjoining every couple to restrict births to a specified limit. This is unimaginable and is rejected.

Birth regulation becomes unequivocally permissible, if not obligatory, when a woman has a quick conception capability, or when people suffer from (incurable) contagious diseases, or when individuals do not have the means to meet such responsibilities.

According to the Qur'an a mother should suckle her infant for two full years and the Prophet warned against pregnancy during the lactation period.

> Not because *Shari'ah* requires multiplication, should we produce offspring unmindfully. Birth should be immune from weakness, and no harm is accepted or sanctioned by *Shari'ah*.
>
> Following this rule, the jurists allow contraception either temporarily or permanently according to the merits of each case. And this principle is to be unanimously and generally agreed to by everybody.

A GRAND FINALE:
THE GRAND IMAM OF AL-AZHAR RECONFIRMS IN 1991 HIS VIEWS OF 1979—80

Just before this book went to press, Sheikh Jadel Haq Ali Jadel Haq, the Grand Imam of Al-Azhar, published in 1991 a monograph, *Laws of Shari'ah and Gynecological Problems*.[29] The monograph included, among other things, consideration of contraception, abortion, sterilization and methods of infertility control. The Grand Imam confirmed, in all these issues, his *fatwas* produced earlier when he was the Mufti of Egypt in the 1970s and 1980s. Such a confirmation is of the greatest significance, because the 1980s witnessed some revival of opposition to reproductive control by a few jurists.

These *fatwas* and opinions are the same as those given in the prologue to this book. The part on infertility control and genetic engineering is found in the Imam's *fatwa* reproduced in Chapter 10. In order to ascertain the Iman's views, please refer back to the Prologue.

In both the early and the recent documentation the Grand Imam ruled that:

1. There is no text (*nuss*) in the Qur'an prohibiting prevention of pregnancy or diminution of the number of children. *But* there are several traditions of the Prophet that indicate its permissibility.
2. Pregnancy prevention is not killing (*wa'd*) or contradictory to provision (*rizq*) or reliance on Allah (*Tawakkul*).
3. Modern methods are, by analogy, permissible.
4. Temporary sterilization is permissible, but permanent sterilization is not, except for health reasons.
5. Abortion after 120 days is prohibited except to save the mother's health. Before that opinion differs.
6. Artificial insemination with the husband's sperm is allowed. Donor sperm and sperm banks are prohibited.
7. No law should coerce people to use contraception or to fix the number of children.

Epilogue

A poem on family planning by Sheikh Abul-Fath M. Khattab, Imam of the Abul-Makarim Mosque, Menufia, Egypt

خاتمة شعرية

قصيدة عن تنظيم الأسرة في الإسلام للشيخ أبو الفتح مختار خطاب
امام وخطيب مسجد أبو المكارم ، شبين الكوم «المنوفية» *

في كل أمر شأنـه التقـويم	عصب الحيـاة وروحهـا التنظيـم
سنن قضاء الله وهـو حكيـم	فالكائنـات جميعهـا تجـرى على
هل جائـز أم شأنـه التحريـم	تنظيـم نسل النـاس مـاذا حكمـه
أو تعتـريـك متـاعـب وهموم	هـو جائـز إن لم تصبك مضرة
فأجـاب مـن بالمؤمنيـن رحيم	طلب الصحابة حكم عزل نسائهم
ولكـل حتى حظـه المقسوم	«إن شئت فاعزل» والقضاء محكم
لكـن ربك بالأمـور عليـم	قد تنتج الأسباب ما هـو ضدهـا
ومن الرجـال أو النسـاء عقيـم	يهب الذكور أو الإنـاث لمن يشا
في الملك تأخيـر ولا تقـديـم	والله قد أحصى الوجود فما لنـا
والـرزق مكفول لنـا مقسوم	إيمانـنـا باللـه يـوجب سعيـنـا
ان التـواكـل شأنـه مذمـوم	لكنـه بالسعـى وهـو عبـادة
ولكـل زرع مـوسـم معلـوم	والنسل مثل الـزرع في تكوينـه
والأم تنجب والبنـاء سليم	وصلاح تربيـة عليـه نجاحـه
لكـن سكرتـه لها تحتيم	ونساؤنا حرث لـزرع مليكنـا
تغنى الحبـوب ولولب معلـوم	ومثال عزل الناس فيما قد مضى
يختـار مـا هـو للبنـاء سليم	لكنـه بمشورة الـطب الـذى

* مع تعديل في ترتيب الأبيات

241

EPILOGUE

Planning is the core of life and its soul,
    In everything which is right and designed.

All creatures are subject to God's wisdom and law
    And God is indeed most wise.

Planning man's offspring, what is God's rule?
    Is it allowed or prohibited?

It is allowed as long as it is harmless, and causes no distress or burden.

The Companions of the Prophet asked about withdrawal as contraception.
    And He with compassion for believers replied
'You may withdraw, if that be your wish, but fate is inevitable
    Each living being has his fortune.'

Causes may bring about adversaries, but God is omniscient
    He bestows males and females as he wills,
    And it is his will that some men and women are sterile.

God determines everything, we have no choice
    But our faith in God compels us to endeavour.
Our fortune is secure and guaranteed
    And endeavour is a form of worship, and laziness blameworthy.

Progeny is like plant, and each plant has a known season.
    Its success depends on good upbringing,
    mother gives birth, and the child is sound.

Our women are cultivated by us, but there is a limit to everything.

In the past, our method was to practice 'withdrawal' and today it is the pill or the IUD
    By consulting medicine, we choose what is good for our body.

Appendix 1
A Chronology of theologians cited in this book

A chronology of religious texts and jurists delineating the legal position of *al-azl* in Islam from the first to the thirteenth century AH (seventh to nineteenth century AD) compiled by the author. For details see Bibliography.

THE FIRST TO THIRD CENTURY AH (SEVENTH TO NINETH CENTURY AD)

The Holy Qur'an
No specific statement (text ffl *nuss*) prohibiting the prevention of pregnancy or limiting the number of children.

The Prophet's tradition (*al-Sunnah*)
Major compilations:
Sahih al-Bukhari
Sahih Muslim
Sunan Ibn Maja
Sunan Abu Dawoud
Sunan (Jami') al-Tirmidhi
Sunan an-Nassa'i
Muwatta' Malik
Musnad Ibn Hanbal
Al-Sunan al-Kubra (*Baihaqi*)

Companions and *Tabi'oun* approving *al-azl*
Imam Ali Ibn Abi Talib
Sa'd Ibn Abi Waqqas
Zayd Ibn Thabit
Abu Ayyub al-Ansari
Jabir Ibn Abdullah

Abdullah Ibn Abbas
al-Hasan Ibn Ali
Khabbab Ibn al-Aratt
Abu Saiʿd al-Khudri
Abdullah Ibn Massʿoud
Saiʿd Ibn al-Mussayyab
Omar Ibn Al-Khattab
Zubair Ibn Al-Awwam
Tawous
Ataʿa
al-Nakhʿey
al-Qama
al-Hajjaj Ibn Amr Ibn Ghaziya
associates of Ibn Abbas
some Ansar (Medina supporters of the Prophet)
see also al-Ayni's addition, Chapter 7

Companions disliking *al-azl*
Abu Bakr al-Siddique
Othman Ibn Affan
Abdullah Ibn Omar
?Abdullah Ibn Massʿoud (as reported by some)

Founders of schools of jurisprudence

Sunni
Imam Abu Hanifa (d.767 AD)
Imam Malik (d.795 AD)
Imam Shafeʿi (d.820 AD)
Imam Ahmad Ibn Hanbal (d.855 AD)

Shiʿite
Imam Zayd Ibn Ali (d.700 AD) (Zaydi *madhhab*)
Imam Jaʿfar al-Sadiq (d.765 AD) (Imami, Twelvers *madhhab*)
Imam Ismaʾil Ibn Jaʿfar al-Sadiq (eighth century) (Ismaʾili *madhhab*)

Kharijite
Imam Abdullah Ibn Ibadd (d.708 AD) (Ibaddi *madhhab*)

Zahirite
Imam Dawoud Ibn Khalaf (d.883 AD) (Zahiri *madhhab*)

Compilers of Traditions see Table 7.1

Other jurists and their works
al-Kadi Abu Yusuf
Mohammad al-Shaybani } Associates of Abu Hanifa
Ibn Qutaiba
- *Taʾawil Mukhtalifh al-Ahadith*
- *Uyun al-Akhbar*

JURISTS OF THE FOURTH CENTURY AH (TENTH CENTURY AD) AND THEIR WORKS

Abu Jaʿafar al-Tahawi
- *Mushkil al-ʾAthar*
- *Sharh Maʿani al-ʾAthar*

M. Ibn Yaʾkub al-Razi
- *Al-Furuʾ Min al-Kafi*

al-Qadi al Nuʿman
- *Daʿaʿim al-Islam*

Ahmad Ibn Ali al-Razi
- *Ahkam al-Qurʾan*

JURISTS OF THE FIFTH CENTURY AH (ELEVENTH CENTURY AD) AND THEIR WORKS

Abul Hasan al-Basri al-Mawirdi
- *Al-Ahkam al-Sultaniyyah*

Ibn Hazm (Zahiri)
- *Al-Muhalla*

al-Tusi
- *Al-Mabsout* (Imami *fiqh*)

al-Shirazi
- *Al-Muhadhab Fi Fiqh Al-Imam al-Shafeʿi*

al-Ghazali (see twelfth century)

Ibn Abdel Barr
- *Al-Tamheed Lima Fil-Muwattaʾmin Maʿani Waʾasanid*

JURISTS OF THE SIXTH CENTURY AH (TWELFTH CENTURY AD) AND THEIR WORKS

Al-Ghazali, Abu Hamid
- *Ihyaʾ Ulum al-Din*
- *Al-Wajiz Fi Fiqh al-Imam al-Shafeʿi*

- *Al-Mustasfa*

al-Baghawi
- *Maʿalim al-Tanzil*

al-Zamakhshari
- *Al-Kashshaf aʿn Haqaʾiq Ghawamidd al-Tanzil*

Ibn al-Arabi
- *Ahkam al-Qurʾan*

al-Marghinani
- *Al-Hidayah Sharh Bidayat al-Mubtadi*

al-Kasani
- *Badaʾi ʿal-Sanaʾiʿ Fi Tartib al-Sharaʾiʿ*

Ibn al-Jawzi
- *Zad al-Musafir*
- *Al-Mawduaʿat*
- *Iltiqaʾ al-Manfiʿ*

al Ajali
- *Saraʾir al-Hawi Fi Tahrir al-Fatawi*

JURISTS OF THE SEVENTH CENTURY AH (THIRTEENTH CENTURY AD) AND THEIR WORKS

Ibn Qudama
- *Al-Mughni Ala Sharh Mukhtasar al-Khiraqi*
- *Al-Muqniʿ Fi Fiqh Ibn Hanbal*

al-Khwarizmi
- *Jamiʿ Masanid al-Imam al-Aʿzam Abi Hanifa*

al-Qurtubi
- *Al-Jamiʿ LiʾAhkam al-Qurʾan*

al-Nawawi
- *Rawdat al-Talibin*
- *Sharh Sahih Muslim*

Jaʿfar al-Hilli
- *Al-Mukhtasar al-Nafi Fi Fiqh al-Imamiyah*
- *Sharaʾi al-Islam Fi-Masʾil al-Halal Wal-haram*

Ibn Qudama al-Maqdisi
- *Al-Sharh al-Kabir*

Ibn Taymiya (the grandfather)
- *Muntaqa al-Akhbar*

JURISTS OF THE EIGHTH CENTURY AH (FOURTEENTH CENTURY AD) AND THEIR WORKS

Ibn al-Mutahar al-Hilli
- *Sharh Tabsirat al-Mutaʿallimin*

Ibn Taymiya (Taqiyyuddin)
- *Al-Fatawa al-Kubra*
- *Al-Fatawa Almisreya*
- *Mukhtasar Majmouʿ Fatawa Ibn Taymiya*

Ibn Juzayy
- *Al-Qawanin al-Fiqhiyya*
- *Al-Tasheel Li Ulum al-Tanzil*

al-Khazin
- *Lubab al-Taʾaweel Fi Mʿani al-Tanzil*

Ibn al-Qayyim al-Jawziyya
- *Zad al Maʿad*
- *Badaʾiʿ al-Fawaʾd*
- *Tuhfat al-Mawdoud Fi Ahkam al-Mawloud*
- *Al-Tibb al-Nabawi*

al-Dimashqi
- *Rahmat al-Umma Fikhtilaf al Aʾimmah*

al-Baberti al-Roumi
- *Sharh al-Inaya*

al-Shatbi
- *Al-Muwafaqat*

Ibn Rajab
- *Al-Dhailʿ Ala Tabaqat al-Hanabila*
- *Al-Qwaʾid Fil Fiqh al-Islami*
- *Jamiʿ al-Ulum Wal-Hikam*

al-Iraqis (Abdel Rahman Ibn al-Hussein and his son al-Hafiz, fifteenth century AD)
- *Tarh al-Tathrib Fi Sharh al-Taqrib* (by both father and son)
- *Sharh al-Tirmidhi* (by Iraqi the father)
- *Takhreej Ahadith al-Ihyaʾ* (the son)

JURISTS OF THE NINETH CENTURY AH (FIFTEENTH CENTURY AD) AND THEIR WORKS

Ibn al-Murtada
- *Al-Bahr al-Zakhkhar*

Ibn Hajar al-Asqalani
- *Fath al-Bari Sharh Sahih al-Bukhari*
- *Blough al-Maram*

al-Ayni
- *Ramz al Haqa'iq*
- *Omdat al-Qari Sharh Sahih al-Bukhari*

al-Kamal Ibn al-Humam
- *Sharh Fath al-Qadir*

al-Iraqi, al Hafez (the son)
- see above

al-Minhaji al-Assiuti
- *Jawahir al-Sunna al-Mohammadiya*

JURISTS OF THE TENTH CENTURY AH (SIXTEENTH CENTURY AD) AND THEIR WORKS

al-Qastallani
- *Irshad al-Sari Li Sharh Sahih al-Bukhari*

al-Hattab
- *Mawahib al-Jalil Li Sharh Mukhtasar Khalil*

al-Halabi
- *Multaqa al-Abhor*

al-ʿAmili (Zein al-ʾAbidin)
- *Masalik al-Afham Sharh Sharaʾiʿ al-Islam*
- *Al-Rawda al-Bahiyya*

Ibn Nujaim
- *Al-Bahr al-Raʾiq Sharh Kanz al-Daqaʾiq*

Ibn al-Najjar
- *Muntaha al-Iradat*

al-Shaʿrani
- *Kashf al-Ghummaʾ An Jamiʿ al-Umma*
- *Al-Mizan*
- *Mukhtasar Tadhkirat al-Suwaidi Fi Tibb*

Abu al-Soʿud
- *Irshad al-Aql al-Saleem Ila Mazaya al-Kitab al-Karim*

al-Ramli
- *Nihayat al-Muhtaj Fi Sharh al-Minhaj*

al-Saʿdi
- *Jawahir al-Akhbar*

JURISTS OF THE ELEVENTH CENTURY (SEVENTEENTH CENTURY AD) AND THEIR WORKS

Ibn Abi Bakr
- *Ghayat al-Muntaha*

al-Bahuti
- *Kashshaf al-Qina' An Matn al-Iqna'*

al-Najdi
- *Hidayat al-Raghib*

al-'Amili (al-Hurr)
- *Wasa'il al Shi'ah*

JURISTS OF THE TWELFTH CENTURY AH (EIGHTEENTH CENTURY AD) AND THEIR WORKS

al-Zurqani
- *Sharh Muwatta' al-Imam Malik*

al-Wazzani
- *Al-Mi'yar al-Jadid*

al-Dardir
- *Al-Sharh al-Kabir*

al-Zabidi
- *Ithaf al-Sada al-Muttaqin Fi Sharh Ihya' Ulum al-Din*

JURISTS OF THIRTEENTH CENTURY AH (NINETEENTH CENTURY AD) AND THEIR WORKS

al-Bijeurmi
- *al-Iqna'*

al-Dusuqi
- *Hashiyat al-Dusuki*

al-Tahtawi
- *Hashiyat al-Durr al-Mukhtar*

al-Shawkani
- *Nayl al-Awtar*

Ibn Abdin (M. Amin)
- *Minhat al-Khaliq*
- *Radd al-Muhtar*

Eleish
- *Fath al-A'liyy al-Malik*

Ibn Abdin (Ala'uddin)
- *Al-Hidiya al-Ala'iyyah*

Appendix 2
Text of the Fatwas

FATWA BY SHEIKH ABDEL MAJEED SALEEM THE MUFTI OF EGYPT

Issued from Dar el-Eftwa', no. 81, regd: 43, on 25 January 1937, published in journal of the Egyptian Medical Association, vol. 20, no. 7, July, 1937, pp. 55.

Question

A married man has a child. He fears if he gets many children that he may be embarrassed by becoming unable to bring them up and take care of them, or that he may suffer ill-health and a nervous breakdown from the inability to fulfill his duties and responsibilities towards them; or that his wife's health may be affected from repeated pregnancies and deliveries without having intervals for her to rest and regain her strength and compensate for what her body lost during pregnancy.

Does a man or his wife have the right to take some scientific measures based on medical advice to lengthen the intervals between pregnancies, so that the mother can have rest and regain her health, and the father would not be under health, economic or social stress?

Answer

According to the Hanafi school of jurisprudence, it is permissible to take some measures to prevent pregenancy under the circumstance cited, either by ejaculating outside the vagina, or by the woman inserting something to shut off the opening of the uterus to prevent entrance of the seminal fluid.

The basic position in the school is that it is not the right of the man to ejaculate outside the vagina except with the permission of his wife and that it is not for the woman to shut off the opening of her uterus except with the permission of the husband.

But it may be allowed (according to later Hanafi scholars) for the man to ejaculate outside the vagina without permission of the wife if he is afraid of having aberrant offspring, e.g. due to times of religious decline. The author of al-Muqni' indicated that other excuses may be found such as when the husband plans to go on a lengthy journey and being afraid for the child.

By analogy, it may be allowed for the woman to shut off the opening of her uterus without the husband's permission if she has reasons for that.

To sum up: either husband or wife, with the permission of the partner, is allowed to take measures to prevent entrance of the seminal fluid into the uterus as a method of birth control and either of them may take such measures without permission of the partner if there are reasons such as those cited or similar ones.

Is it permissible to abort a fetus before ensoulment?

The Hanafi scholars differed somewhat on this but they are inclined to allow a pregnant woman to terminate pregnancy in the early months before fetal movements occur, if there is a valid reason [udhr]. They mentioned among the excuses that the woman becomes unable to breast-feed the child while the husband is too poor to buy a replacement for breast milk from the mother. After ensoulment abortion is prohibited [end].

The same question was answered by the *Fatwa* Committee of Al-Azhar in 1953

The use of medicine to prevent pregnancy temporarily is not forbidden by religion (according to the Shafe'i school of jurisprudence, which is adopted by the Committee), especially if repeated pregnancies weaken the women due to insufficient birth intervals for her to rest and regain her health. The Qur'an says 'Allah desires for you ease. He desires not hardship for you' (2:185), 'And has not laid upon you in religion any hardship' (22:78). But the use of medicine to prevent pregnancy absolutely and permanently is forbidden by religion.

FATWA OF SHEIKH MAHMOUD SHALTOUT, GRAND IMAM OF AL-AZHAR

Issued from Al-Azhar Press, Cairo in 1959

As regards birth control in the sense of regulating births for women who get pregnant too soon, for those suffering from diseases liable to be transmitted by heredity, or infection, and for a small number of individuals whose nerves are too weak to face up to manifold responsibilities, unhelped as they are by their governments or by the well-to-do in their community to the extent of being able to bear such responsibilities.

Family planning in some way like that, on an individual basis, is a remedial measure by which certain harms are warded off and through which better and stronger offspring will come into being.

Planning in this sense is not incompatible with nature, and is not disagreeable to national consciousness, and is not forbidden by the *Shari'ah*, if it is not sought after and prescribed. The Qur'an fixed the period of lactation at two full years, and the Prophet warned against feeding a baby from the milk of a pregnant mother. This argues in favor of allowing steps to be taken to stop pregnancy during breast-feeding.

If *Shari'ah* requires that the multitude of children should be strong and not feeble, it is only trying to safeguard the offspring against weakness and poor health, and to fend off harm which may befall man during lifetime; one of its rules being: harm is to be obviated with every possible means.

This is why doctors of religion decided to allow temporary or permanent prevention of childbearing between the two spouses, if there is in both, or either of them, a disease which is apt to be transmitted to the children or grandchildren.

FATWA OF TUNAN HAJI ALI BIN MOHAMMAD SAID SALEH, CHIEF QADI, SINGAPORE

Issued on 25 April 1955 in Utusan Melayu

The Chief Qadi is in agreement with Sheikh Mohammad Abdul Fattah al-Ainani, Chairman of the *Fatwa* Committee at Al-Azhar who rules that steps taken temporarily to space out births or for family planning are not forbidden in Islam, particularly for such mothers as are liable to suffer physically on account of the exhausting continued childbearing.

From the explanation given by the Chief Qadi it appears that there is no objection to Malay and Muslim mothers joining the Family Planning Association or seeking advice from it if they are among those who have been bearing children continuously and whose health has suffered in consequence.

But the Chief Qadi warns that to practice abortion in order to destroy a child in pregnancy of four months and over is *haram* (unlawful) in the Islamic faith.

FATWA BY ADVISORY COUNCIL ON RELIGIOUS AFFAIRS, TURKEY

Issued on 19 December 1960

Although coitus interruptus which could be considered as a means of birth control was condemned by certain of the Prophet's disciples, and by those scholars who followed them, it was considered lawful by the scholars among the disciples (including sages such as Hazret Ali, Saʻd Ibn Abi Waqqas, Zayd Ibn Thabit, Abu Ayyoub al-Ansari, Abdullah Ibn Massʻoud) and, in deference to their views, by all subsequent scholars.

We can go so far as to say that, while the woman's consent is normally a necessary condition, if the proper raising of children is made impossible by conditions of the time, such as the state's being a state of war or disorder or similar circumstances, then this condition will also not apply.

FATWA OF SHEIKH HASAN MA'MOUN', RECTOR OF AL-AZHAR

Published in *Akhbar al-Yum* newspaper, 22 August 1964

The view of Islam on family planning is clear and frank. But perhaps what gives rise to wonderment on your part and on the part of many others is the traditional impression that Islam calls for procreation and multiplication, urges those young men who are to get married to do so and favors that man should take unto himself as wife the woman who is prolific of offspring and affectionate of heart, and such other impression which would put into the minds of some people that this whole idea is the idea of Islam, and nothing else.

But we can deal with the subject from another angle, namely, the wisdom underlying the legal ruling and the legitimate good to be aimed at and to be realized; in our subject, the wisdom and the good required at the time that there should be procreation and multiplication to be urged.

This is because Islam, in its initial stage, was something of an intruder, a stranger in the polytheistic society before Islam, and its early followers were few and weak in the midst of a vast majority of aggressive and oppressive people, by reason of their wealth and social standing and influence. The good of the Muslims then required that there should be a call for the multiplication of their number, in order that they might be able at the time to fulfill their responsibilities in defending the mission of Islam and protecting the true religion of Allah against the powerful and multitudinous adversaries threatening it.

But now we find that conditions have changed. We find that the density of population in the world threatens seriously to reduce the living standards of mankind to the extent that many men of thought have been prompted to seek family planning in every country, so that the resources may not fall short of ensuring a decent living for its people to provide public services for them.

Islam, as the religion of pristine nature, has never been opposed to what is good to man. Indeed it has been always ahead in the effort towards the achievement of this good so long as it is not in conflict with the purposes of Allah's law.

I see no objection from the *Shariʿah* point of view of the consideration of family planning as a measure, if there is need for it, and consideration is occasioned by the people's own choice and conviction, without constraint or compulsion, in the light of their circumstances, and on condition that the means for effecting this planning is legitimate.

FATWA BY SHEIKH ABDULLAH AL-QALQILI, THE GRAND MUFTI OF JORDAN

Issued in December 1984

Marriage has been one of the Islamic ways and procreation has been one of its desirable and gratifying aims. Even the Lawgiver views multiplicity with favor, for multiplicity implies power, influence and invulnerability. This is why, in one of the traditions of the Prophet, marriage with an affectionate prolific woman, is strongly urged. The tradition says 'Marry the affectionate prolific woman, for I shall be making a display of you among the nations.'

Nevertheless, the Lawgiver made marriage with a prolific woman and marriage for procreation *conditional upon* the availability of means and the ability to bear the costs of marriage and meet the expenses of child education and training, so that children may not go to the bad and develop anti-social ways. And according to the Islamic religious rule (laws change as conditions change), marriage should be disallowed if the would-be husband is incapable of meeting the expenses of married life. To this, reference is clear in the Qur'an and in the traditions.

Moreover, there are genuine traditions which allow methods for restricting procreation, such as coitus interruptus. For instance, in the two most reliable compilations of traditions, Abu-Saʿid is reported to have said that in one of the military missions, he and others wanted to practice al-Azl with their women, and they asked the Prophet about that and the Prophet said 'Indeed, do that', and repeated it three times, and continued 'No creature to be created from now till the Day of Judgement will not but be created.' Another report has it that a man said to the Prophet 'I have a young wife, I hate that she should be pregnant, and I want what men want; but the Jews claim that coitus interruptus is minor infanticide.' The Prophet replied, 'The Jews lie. If Allah wishes to create the child, you will not divert Him from that.' In the two reliable collections of traditions, it is stated that Muslims used to practice coitus interruptus during the life time of the Prophet and during the period of the Qur'anic revelation. It is also reliably reported that Muslims used to practice coitus interruptus during the lifetime of the Prophet, the Prophet knew of this, but he did not prohibit it.

In these genuine traditions there is definitely permission for the practice of coitus interruptus which is one of the ways of contraception or restricting procreation, even without excuse. Permission for this practice was reported by a number of the Prophet's Companions and followers of the Companions, and is the position in the four Sunni schools. A corollary of this is the permissibility of the use of medicine for contraception, or even for abortion before the embryo or the fetus is ensouled. The Hanafi allow that if for an excuse.

The jurists gave examples to illustrate the meaning of the excuse for abortion, as in Ibn Abdin who says 'Like the mother who has a baby still unweaned and who becomes pregnant and thus her milk ceases, and the father is unable to hire a wet nurse to save the life of his baby.'

The jurists also state that it is permissible to take the medicine for abortion so long as the embryo is still unformed in the human shape. The period of this unformed state is given as 120 days. The jurists think that during this period the embryo or the fetus is not yet a human being. A report says that Omar (the second Caliph) does not regard abortion as infanticide unless the fetus is already past the limit.

Malik, the founder of the Maliki Sunni school, says that the husband should not practice coitus interruptus with his wife unless she permits it. Al-Zurqani, in his comment on this, says that the practice is lawful if the wife allows it. Permission or prohibition of coitus interruptus may serve as a guide in deciding the question of abortion before the fetus is ensouled.

All this shows that there is agreement among the founders of the four Sunni schools that coitus interruptus is allowed as a means of contraception. Religious savants inferred from this that contraceptives might be used, and even medicines might be used for abortion.

Accordingly, we hereby give our judgement with confidence in favor of family planning.

FATWA ISSUED BY HIS EXCELLENCY AYATOLLAH HAJJI SHEIKH BAHA'EDIN MAHALLATI, OF IRAN

Issued on 12 November 1964 in response to question from Dr Mohammed Sarram

Question
Would you permit and is it religiously lawful that a physician, temporarily, prescribe drugs or contraceptive devices for excessive human reproduction?

Answer
In the name of God: From the standpoint of the divine law, the utilization of

drugs or contraceptive devices, especially if it is temporary, to control human fertility does not seem illegal if this practice does not lead to damage of the female's fecundity and make her barren.

FATWA BY ASSISTANT MUFTI, JOHARA MALAYSIA, HAJI ABDUL JALIL BIN HAJI HASSAN

Issued on 21 November 1965

Birth control using oral or contraceptive devices is permitted providing they do not cause permanent sterility.

Sterilization by use of oral drugs or contraceptive devices is forbidden except in cases where a certificate can be obtained from two doctors confirming that another pregnancy will be dangerous or might even result in death.

FATWA OF AL-SYYID YOUSOF B. ALI AL-ZAWAWI, MUFTI OF TRENGGANU, MALAYSIA (summarized)

In short, I feel inclined to see three aspects to this question:

- If it is necessary to resort to contraception for reasons of health, in respect of the husband, the wife or the baby-to-be, there are no laws in religion against it at all, as proved by the Qur'anic verse: 'A mother shall not beget harm because of her child, nor should a (father) because of his child' (Sura 2:233), the implication also is that this is applicable for a certain period of time, limited in duration, and for special cases.
- The opinions of jurists on the question of pregnancy and childbearing vary as to whether contraception is to be regarded as allowed before animation (which takes place in the fourth month of pregnancy). They are, however, agreed that it is forbidden after the expiry of four months. If this happens and abortion is included, those who are responsible for the operation, namely, the doctor, the midwives, etc. must pay the blood-money to the parents.
- It is categorically forbidden to stop childbearing completely or to cause permanent sterility without good reasons approved by religion, even if it is done voluntarily.

    All this shows clearly the extent to which Islam attaches importance to the question of family planning. It is, therefore, the duty of bodies and societies established for this purpose to act according to what is allowed by the Islamic laws, as expounded in the *fatwa* issued by Sheikh Abdul-Fattah al-Inani. (see above under the *Fatwa* Committee of Al-Azhar.)

APPENDICES

FATWA OF THE PRESIDENT OF THE HIGH COURT OF APPEAL, YEMEN ARAB REPUBLIC

Question
May we have if you please, your considered opinion, within the framework of religion, as to a married woman with a number of children, who in her ignorance of the modern devices of contraception, has now got pregnant again, and is seeking to be aborted. Do your *Shariʿah* Laws sanction the operation for abortion, considering that it is to be performed with her consent and that of her husband?

Answer
The faultless *Shariʿah* does not forbid that with the husband's consent, provided it is performed before quickening. The *Shariʿah* decides that animation takes place as from the beginning of the fifth month of pregnancy.

OPINION BY SHEIKH SHA'RAWI, 1980

See Chapter 12.

FATWA BY SHEIKH JADEL HAQ

See Prologue.

FATWA BY SHEIKH SAYYID TANTAWI, MUFTI OF EGYPT

Published in al-Wafd newspaper 8/9 September 1988 (condensed)

Preamble
Certain facts have to be made clear from the start:

- Heavenly religions are for the welfare of humanity.
- Speaking about religion should be based on correct knowledge and familiarity with jurisprudence. The opinion (by qualified persons) should be objective, without hiding the truth or fear of intimidation.
- We are living in a time when nations do not boast of their numbers or the size of their territory but of technical ability, invention and scientific achievements in such a way that other nations will be dependent on you rather than you on them.
- One of the characteristics of Islamic jurisprudence is that a decisive text is given for things that do not change. But in cases where the welfare of people changes over time, leeway is given for the knowledgeable thinkers

APPENDICES

  of the people to adjust rules to their welfare within the general principles and objectives of *Shari'ah*.
- The need for family planning varies; some nations need it more than others, while some may wish to increase their population growth.
- Children are the apple of our eyes but they are the responsibility of their parents who should provide them with adequate care physically, educationally, culturally and economically.

The *fatwa*

First: Family planning means that the husband or wife use, with mutual agreement between them, a method to space pregnancies or to stop procreation temporarily with a view to reduce the size of the family in a way to enable the parents to take good care of their children without physical hardship or economic embarrassment. It is different from sterilization or abortion both of which are not permitted.

Second: Contraception is lawful both religiously and logically for justifiable reasons. This has been approved by early jurists like al-Ghazali and by contemporary jurists like Sheikh Sayyid Sabiq. [He reiterated and confirmed the reasons listed by Sheikh Sabiq (see Chapter 9). He later added three cases presented to him that he found to be legal]:

- A couple with modest means who want to postpone the second child until they can care for the first.
- A couple with good means who want to stop procreation temporarily until they can provide each of their son and daughter a separate room.
- A couple with better means and three children who want to use contraception not because they cannot afford having more children but because they live in a country which needs family planning.

Third: Family planning is not the only way to face the overpopulation problem. A parallel way to face the problem is that people get united, industrious and perform their duties as best as they can in order to build up their society.

Fourth: This *fatwa* complements previous *fatwas* on this subject by Sheikh Saleem (1937), The *Fatwa* Committee of Al-Azhar (1953), Sheikh Shaltout (1959) (and Sheikh Jadel Haq, 1980).

Fifth: It is not advisable that the state issues a law forcing family planning on all the people. The state can, however, communicate proper information to the populace on the country's situation, the rights of children, and religious aspects of family planning.

Sixth: Family planning is not killing or *wa'd*, it does not contradict predestination or reliance on Allah [*tawakkul*] or ability of God to provide for His people [*rizq*]. Neither is family planning a contradiction to the call for multitude [*kathrah*]. It is quality not quantity that makes the Prophet proud of us. The Prophet has mocked at an inefficient, disorganized multitude.

Seventh: Islam approves of all methods of contraception provided they are safe, legal and approved by Muslim physicians. *Al-azl* was the method available in the early period of Islam. Now we have the pill, the loop, the injectables and other methods discovered by modern medicine.

And Allah knows best.

Thus, Dr Tantawi's *fatwa* was endorsed by the *Fatwa* Committee of al-Azhar and published by it (1988).

Notes

CHAPTER 1 FAMILY AND MARRIAGE IN ISLAM

1. Al-Ghazali *Ihya'*, vol. 2., p. 53.
2. Al-Ajali 'Sara'ir (Kitab al-Nikah)', manuscript, p. 155.
3. Al-Hilli 'Shara'i', Marriage (al-Nikah)', manuscript.
4. Abu Hanifa, cited in al-Sa'ih *Rabat Proceedings*, vol. 1, pp. 171–2.
5. Sayyid Sabiq *Fiqh*, vol. 6, pp. 227–31 and Al-Qaradawi *Al-Halal*, pp. 178–80.
6. Abdullah Yusuf Ali, translation of the *The Qur'an* with commentary, p. 179.
7. Sayyid Sabiq *Fiqh*, vol. 6, pp. 231–2.
8. Al-Ghazali *Ihya'*, p. 41.

CHAPTER 2 PARENT AND CHILD: RIGHTS OF ONE, OBLIGATIONS OF THE OTHER

1. Abdel Aziz Kamel in 'Al-Umouma, Fil-Islam', conference proceedings, pp. 84–109.
2. Omran *Health Theme*, pp. 115–32.

CHAPTER 3 THE STATUS OF WOMEN IN ISLAM

1. Al-Qurtubi *Al-Jami'*, vol. 5, p. 99 and Shaltout *Al-Qur'an Wal-Mar'ah*, p. 386.
2. Ibn Kathir *Al-Bidayah*, vol. 42, pp. 34,35.
3. Afifi *Al-Mar'ah*.
4. Reported by al-Bukhari.
5. Afifi, op.cit.
6. Reported by al-Bukhari.
7. See e.g. Shaltout, op.cit., p. 396.
8. ibid, p. 381.

CHAPTER 4 FAMILY PLANNING AND THE BASIC PRECEPTS OF ISLAM

1. Shaltout *Fatwa*, 1959.
2. Khalaf Ali and Mar'i in *Rabat Proceedings*, vol. 2, pp. 117–44.

3. See *Rabat Proceedings*, 2 volumes.
4. Sheikh Abu Zahra *Tanzim al-Usrah*, pp. 102–4.
5. Al-Zabidi *Ithaf*, p. 382.
6. Omran 'The Epidemiologic Transition', *Milbank Journal*, p. 509–38.
7. Ma'moun *Fatwa*, 1964.

CHAPTER 5 SOURCES OF ISLAMIC JURISPRUDENCE

1. Al-Qaradawi *Al-Halal*, pp. 22–30.
2. ibid, p. 25.
3. Muhsinuddin *Philosophy*, p. 136.
4. See the endnote, p. 34 in Madkour *Nazrat*.
5. Muhsinuddin op.cit., pp. 68, 135.
6. Doi *Shariʿah*, pp. 83–4.
7. Al-Ghazali *Ihya'*, vol. 2, p. 53.
8. Madkour *Rabat Proceedings*, vol. 1, pp. 294–5.
9. Ibn 'Abdin cited in Madkour, ibid, vol. 1, p. 297.
10. Al-Qarafi in Madkour, ibid, vol. 1., p. 301.
11. Al-Sharabassi in Madkour, ibid, vol. 2, p. 8.

CHAPTER 6 THE QUR'AN AND FAMILY PLANNING INCLUDING THE QUESTION OF MULTITUDE

1. See e.g. Maudoudi *Harakat*, p. 79 and Abu Zahra '*Tanzim al Nasl*', *Liwa*' 1962.
2. Maudoudi, op.cit., pp. 138–43.
3. See e.g. Sheikh al-Najjar *Ru'yah*, p. 30; Sheikh Jadel Haq *Fatwa* and al-Ghazali *Ihya'*, vol. 2, p. 53.
4. Al-Ghazali, ibid., p. 54.
5. Cited in al-Iraqis *Tarh*, vol. 7, p. 59.
6. See e.g. Jadel Haq, op.cit. and Al-Najjar, op.cit., pp. 28–9.
7. Madkour *Nazrat*, pp. 94–5.
8. *Tafsir al-Manar*, vol. 12, p. 13.
9. Abdel-Wahid *Al-Usrah*, p. 82.
10. Al-Sharabassi *Al-Din*, pp. 123–4.
11. Abu Zahra 'Tanzim al-Usra', pp. 103, 104.
12. Al-Najjar, op.cit., pp. 9, 10.
13. Maudoudi, op.cit., p. 79.
14. Shaltout *Fatwa*, 1959.
15. Al-Kholi 'Tahdid' in *Manbar al Islam*, 1965.
16. President Nasser 'National Charter' in *Speeches*, p. 335.
17. Abu Zahra 'Tanzim al-Usrah', op.cit. pp. 103, 104.
18. Al-Kholi, op.cit.
19. Al-Sharabassi op.cit., p. 113.
20. Al-Makki al-Nasiri *Rabat Proceedings*, vol. 2, p. 67.
21. Abonnour *Manhaj*, pp. 409–12.
22. Al-Mubarak Abdullah *Rabat Proceedings*, pp. 152, 153.
23. Al-Shafe'i cited in Ibn al-Qayyim *Tuhfat*, p. 8. The Arabic text is from al-Sharabasi, op.cit. See also al-Baqouri *Al-Usrah*, pp. 41, 42.
24. Dr Anwarul-Haq *Family Planning*, p. 50.
25. Al-Najjar, op.cit., pp. 34, 35.

NOTES

26. Atay *Rabat Proceedings*, vol. 2, pp. 173, 174.
27. S. Huzayyin *Rabat Proceedings*, vol. 2, pp. 274, 275.

CHAPTER 7 THE SUNNAH AND FAMILY PLANNING

1. Al-Shawkani *Nayl*, vol. 5, pp. 197–374.
2. Al-Tahawi *Mushkil*, vol. 1, pp. 370–4.
3. Ibn al-Qayyim *Zad*, vol. 4, pp. 16–18.
4. Al-Ghazali *Ihya'*, vol. 2, p. 54.
5. Malik *Al-Muwatta'*, vol. 2, pp. 595, 596.
6. Al-Ayni: *Omdat*, vol. 20, p. 195.
7. Al-Baihaqi *Al-Sunan*, vol. 7, p. 230.
8. Ibn Hazm *Al-Muhalla*, vol. 10, p. 71.
9. Ibn al-Qayyim, op.cit., p. 16.
10. Ibn Qudama *Al-Mughni*, vol. 8, p. 133.
11. Al-Nawawi *Sharh*, vol. 10, pp. 11, 13.
12. Madani in *Manbar*, 1965.
13. Ibn Hajar *Fath*, vol. 9, p. 247.
14. Al-Nawawi, op.cit., pp. 16, 17.
15. ibid.
16. Al-Tahawi *Sharh*, vol. 3, p. 34.
17. Al-Ghazali, op.cit., p. 53.
18. Ibn al-Qayyim, op.cit., pp. 16–18.
19. Ibn Hajar, op.cit., pp. 245, 246.
20. Ibn al-Humam *Sharh*, vol. 2, pp. 494, 495.
21. Al-Zabidi *Ithaf*, vol. 5, pp. 379–84.
22. Al-Shawkani, op.cit., vol. 6, pp. 346–50.
23. Ibn Hazm, op.cit., pp. 70, 71.
24. Al-Tahawi *Mushkil*, vol. 2, pp. 372–4.
25. Ibn Rushd and Ibn al-'Arabi cited in Ibn Hajar *Fath*, vol. 9, p. 248.
26. Al-Ghazali *Ihya'*, vol. 2, p. 53.
27. Al-Nawawi, op.cit., pp. 9, 10.
28. Ibn al-Qayyim, op.cit., pp. 17, 18.
29. Cited in al-Iraqis *Tarh*, vol. 7, p. 59.
30. Al-Baihaqi, op.cit., p. 232.
31. Ibn Hajar, op.cit., pp. 248, 249.
32. Al-Ayni *Omdat*, vol. 20, p. 195.
33. Ibn al-Humam, op.cit., p. 203.
34. Al-Shawkani, op.cit., vol. 6, pp. 346–50.
35. Madkour *Nazrat*, pp. 68, 69.
36. Al-Boutti *Mas'alat*, pp. 20, 22, 23, 24.
37. Al-Makki al-Nasiri in *Rabat Proceedings*, vol. 2, pp. 53–4.

CHAPTER 8 FAMILY PLANNING IN ISLAMIC JURISPRUDENCE FROM THE SEVENTH TO THE NINETEENTH CENTURY

1. Atay in *Rabat Proceedings*, vol. 2, p. 183.
2. See for example: (a) Al-Sharabassi *The Four Imams*; (b) Muhsinuddin *Philosophy*, Chapter 7, pp. 67–81; (c) Doi *Shari'ah*, Chapter 5, pp. 85–112.

NOTES

3. Madkour *Rabat Proceedings*, vol. 1, p. 299.
4. Ibn Hajar *Fath*, vol. 9, p. 247.
5. Al-Baji *Al-Muntaqa*, vol. 4, pp. 141–3.
6. Al-Khwarizmi *Jamiʿ*, vol. 2, pp. 118–9.
7. Al-Tahawi *Mushkil*, vol. 2, pp. 370–4 and *Sharh*, vol. 3, pp. 34, 35.
8. Al-Kasani *Badaʾi*, vol. 2, pp. 234, 335.
9. Al-Marghinani *Al-Hedayah*, vol. 2, pp. 494, 495.
10. Al-Baberti *Sharh*, vol. 2, pp. 494, 495.
11. Ibn al-Humam *Fath*, vol. 2, pp. 494, 495.
12. Ibn Nujaim *Al-Bahr*, vol. 3, pp. 214, 215.
13. Ibn ʾAbdin *Radd*, p. 586 and *Minhat*, vol. 3, pp. 214, 215.
14. Saleem *Fatwa*, 1937.
15. Al-Shafeʿi comment in *Al-Muwattaʾ*, edited by M. Abdel Baqui, front page.
16. Malik *Al-Muwattaʾ*, vol. 2, pp. 594–6.
17. Ibn Abdel Barr cited in Ibn Hajar *Fath*, vol. 9, p. 247.
18. Al-Qurtubi *Al-Jamiʿ*, vol. 12, p. 8.
19. Al-Baji, op.cit.
20. Ibn Juzayy *Al-Qawanin*, p. 212.
21. Al-Zurqani *Sharh*, vol. 3, pp. 75–8.
22. Khalil *Al-Mukhtasar*, (English), p. 103.
23. Al-Hattab *Mawahib*, vol. 3, pp. 476–7.
24. Al-Dardir *Al-Sharh*, vol. 2, p. 266.
25. Al-Dusuqi *Hashyat*, vol. 2. p. 266.
26. Eleish *Fath*, vol. 1, pp. 341–3.
27. Al-Dardir, op.cit.
28. Al-Makki al-Nasiri in *Rabat Proceedings*, vol. 2, pp. 39–67.
29. Ibn al-Qayyim *Tuhfat*, pp. 8, 9.
30. Al-Shafeʿi cited in al-Sharabassi *Al-Din*, pp. 104–6.
31. Al-Shirazi *Al-Muhadhdhab*, vol. 2, p. 66.
32. Al-Ghazali *Ihyaʾ*, vol. 2, pp. 53, 54.
33. Al-Zabidi *Ithaf*, vol. 5, pp. 378–84.
34. Al-Nawawi *Sharh*, vol. 10, pp. 9, 10 (summary), and pp. 10–18.
35. Al-Iraqis *Tarh*, vol. 7, pp. 59–63.
36. Ibn Hajar, op.cit., pp. 244–9.
37. Al-Qastallani *Irshad*, vol. 8, pp. 99, 100.
38. Al-Shaʿrani *Al-Mizan*, vol. 2, pp. 124, 125.
39. Al-Iraqis, op cit., pp. 61, 62.
40. Ibn Hajar, op cit., p. 249.
41. Ibn Hanbal quoted in *Masaʾil*, by Abu Dawoud, p. 168.
42. Ibn Qudama *Al-Mughni*, vol. 8, pp. 132–4.
43. Ibn Qudama al-Maqdisi *Al-Sharh*, vol. 8, pp. 132–4.
44. Ibn Taymiya *Al-Fatawa al-Kubra*, vol. 1, p. 71, No.35 and *Mukhtasar al-Fatawa al-Masria*, p. 426.
45. Al-Zabidi, op.cit., p. 379.
46. Ibn Taymiya (the grandfather) *Muntaqa*, vol. 6, pp. 346–50.
47. Al-Shawkani *Nayl*, vol. 6, pp. 346–50.
48. Ibn al-Qayyim *Zad*, vol. 4, pp. 16–21.
49. Ibn al-Najjar *Muntaha*, vol. 2, pp. 227.
50. Ibn Abi Bakr *Ghayat*, vol. 3, p. 91.
51. Al-Bahuti *Kashshaf*, vol. 5, p. 149 and *Sharh*, vol. 3, p. 96.

NOTES

52. Ibn al-Murtada *Al-Bahr*, vol. 3, p. 81.
53. Ass'adi *Gawahir*, vol. 3, p. 81.
54. Al-Ajali *Al-Sara'ir*, p. 155.
55. Al-Hilli *Shara'i*, vol. 2, (*Al-Hikah*) and *Mukhtasar*, p. 172.
56. Al-'Amili *Al Rawda*, p. 156.
57. Shamsuddin in *Rabat Proceedings*, vol. 2, pp. 281–5.
58. Al-Qadi al-Nu'man *Da'a'im*, vol. 2, p. 212.
59. Ibn Hazm *Al-Muhalla*, vol. 2, pp. 70, 71.
60. Atfiyash *Sharh*, vol. 3, p. 298.

CHAPTER 9 JUSTIFICATIONS FOR CONTRACEPTION IN ISLAMIC JURISPRUDENCE

1. Al-Ghazali *Ihya'*, vol. 2, pp. 53, 54.
2. Ibn Qudama *Al-Mughni*, vol. 8, p. 133.
3. Al-Ghazali, op.cit., p. 53.
4. Ibn Hajar *Fath*, vol. 9, p. 247.
5. Sabiq *Fiqh*, vol. 7, pp. 132, 135.
6. Abdel-Aziz 'Iesa *Muhadarat*
7. Shaltout *Fatwa*, 1959.
8. Al-Ghazali, op.cit.
9. Ibn al-Jawzi quoted by al-Naciri in *Rabat Proceedings*, vol. 2, pp. 63, 64.
10. Al-Baqouri *Al Usrah*, pp. 41, 42.
11. Al-Mubarak Abdullah *Rabat Proceedings*, p. 152.
12. Imam Abu Hanifa *Husn al-Taqadi*, p. 79.
13. Ibn Sina, Ali Ibn Abbas, al-Jurjani, Ibn al-Jami', Excerpts; see also Himes *Medical*, pp. 155, 169.
14. Al-Ghazali, op.cit.
15. Ibn Hajar, op.cit.
16. Al-Qadi al-Nu'man *Da'a'im*, vol. 2, p. 212.
17. Ibn Abdin *Radd*, p. 587.
18. *Fawta* Committee Al-Azhar *Fatwa*, 1953.
19. Shaltout, op.cit.
20. Sabiq, op.cit., p. 133.
21. Sheikh Jadel Haq *Fatwa*, 1980.
22. Omran, *et al. Family Formation*, 1976. Omran, *et al. Further Studies*, 1981. Omran *Studies in Africa*, 1985. Omran *The Arab Population*, 1988 (English), 1988 (Arabic).
23. Al-Bijeurmi *Al-Iqna'*, vol. 3, p. 40.
24. Shaltout, op.cit.
25. Sabiq, op.cit.

CHAPTER 10 FAMILY PLANNING IN ISLAMIC JURISPRUDENCE THE MORE PROBLEMATICAL ISSUES

1. Jadel Haq '*Fatwa* on infertility' in *Al-Fatawa al Islamiyya*, vol. 9, 1980.
2. Al-Bijeurmi *Al-Iqn'a'*, vol. 3, p. 40.
3. Al-Shubramallissi *Hashyat* cited by Madkour.
4. Al-Shawkani *Nayl*, vol. 6, p. 349.

5. Madkour *Nazrat*, pp. 94–5 and *Rabat Proceedings*, vol. 2, pp. 286–311.
6. Jadel Haq *Fatwa* on abortion, 1980.
7. Shaltout *Fatwa*, 1959.
8. Academy (or High Council) of Islamic Research *Resolutions*, 1965.
9. 'Abortion and Sterilization' in *Rabat Proceedings*, vol. 2, p. 279ff.
10. Shamsuddin 'Tahdid', in *Rabat Proceedings*, vol. 2, p. 281.
11. Sabiq *Fiqh*, vol. 7, pp. 132–5.
12. Ahmad Ibrahim 'Introduction to a Dissertation', 1936 in al-Sharabassi.
13. Al-Sharabassi *Al-Din*, 1965.
14. Al-Boutti *Mas'alat*, especially pp. 73–6 and pp. 89–100.
15. Ibn al-Qayyim *Tuhfat*, p. 148.
16. Al-Zabidi *Ithaf*, vol. 5, p. 148.
17. Al-Ghazali *Ihya'*, vol. 2, p. 53 and Ibn Taymiya *Ilm al-Sulouk*, pp. 26, 27.
18. Al-Ghazali, op.cit.
19. ibid. and Al-Zabidi, op.cit., vol. 5, p. 381.
20. Al-Zabidi, ibid.
21. Al-Baqouri *Al-Usrah*, Chapter 5, pp. 45–56.
22. Al-Lakhmi in Eleish *Fath*, p. 343 and Al-Boutti, op.cit.
23. Al-Ghazali, op.cit.
24. Al-Sha'rani *Al-Mizan*, vol. 2, pp. 124, 125.
25. Ibn al-Qayyim *Zad*, vol. 4, p. 18.
26. Ibn Qudama *Al-Mughni*, vol. 8, p. 134.
27. Ibn Taymiya, *Ilm al-Subouk*, pp. 26, 27.
28. Ibn Juzayy *Al-Qawanin*, p. 212.
29. Ibn Hajar *Fath*, vol. 9, p. 247.
30. Al-Qastallani *Irshad*, vol. 8, p. 100.
31. Al-Sha'rani, *al-Mizan*, vol. 2, pp. 124, 125.
32. Al-Zabidi, op.cit.
33. Al-Qastallani *Irshad*, vol. 8, p. 100.
34. Ibn al-Qayyim *Miftah*, vol. 2, p. 271
35. Al-Tahtawi *Hashyat*, vol. 2, p. 77.
36. Ibn Nujaim *Al-Bahr*, vol. 3, pp. 214, 215.
37. Ibn al-Humam *Sharh*, vol. 2, p. 495.
38. Ibn Abdin *Radd*, p. 587.
39. Al-Ramli *Nihayat*, vol. 7, p. 107.
40. Al-Ajali *Al-Sara'ir*, p. 162.

CHAPTER 11 CONFERENCES AND PUBLICATIONS BY JURISTS ON ISLAM AND FAMILY PLANNING

1. Wajihuddin Ahmad 'Al-Mujtama'' in *Rabat Proceedings*, vol. 1, p. 337.
2. Al-Boutti *Mas'alat*, p. 34.
3. Abu Zahra *Tanzim al Usrah*, pp. 101, 102.
4. Al-Maudoudi *Harakat*, p. 22, 23.
5. Abu Zahra 'Tanzim al-Nasl', *Liwa' al-Islam*, 1962.
6. Madkour *Nazrat*, pp. 70–3.
7. Maudoudi *Harakat*, p. 209.
8. W. Ahmad, op.cit., vol. 1, pp. 337–339.
9. Anwarul-Haq *Family Planning*, p. 45.
10. Sahnoun 'Nazrah' in *Rabat Proceedings*, vol. 2, pp. 402–17.

NOTES

11. Sharabassi *Al-Din*, especially pp. 57–80.
12. Madkour, op.cit, especially pp. 49–57.
13. Al-Boutti, op.cit, especially pp. 15–26 and 45–57.
14. United Nations *World Population Prospects*, No. 8, table A–2.
15. Arab central bureau of statistics and documentations *Year Book* 1984, Tables 48, 49, 50 and Population Reference Bureau, 1991.
16. Al-Najjar *Ru'yah*.
17. Academy of Islamic Research *Proceedings of Conferences*, 1964, 1965.
18. Council of Islamic Fiqh 'Report' in *Al-Iqtisad*, 1987.
19. 'Islam and Family Planning' in *Rabat Proceedings*, 2 volumes.
20. Banjul Conference *Report*, 1979.
21. Dakar Conference *Report*, 1982.

CHAPTER 12 FATWAS AND OPINION OF OTHER TWENTIETH CENTURY JURISTS ON ISLAM AND FAMILY PLANNING

1. Saleem *Fatwa*, 1937.
2. *Fatwa* Committee of Al-Azhar *Fatwa*, 1953.
3. Shaltout *Fatwa*, 1959.
4. Saleh, Tuan Haji Ali *Fatwa*, 1955.
5. Advisory Council, Turkey *Fatwa*, 1960.
6. Ma'moun *Fatwa*, 1964.
7. Qalqili *Fatwa*, 1964.
8. Mahallati *Fatwa*, 1964.
9. Shamsuddin in *Rabat Proceedings*, vol. 2, pp. 281–5.
10. Abdel Jalil Hassan *Fatwa*, 1964.
11. Al-Zawawi *Fatwa*, no date.
12. High Court of Appeals, Yemen *Fatwa*, 1968.
13. Jadel Haq *Fatwa*, 1980; and additions, 1987.
14. Sha'rawi *Opinion*, no date.
15. Tantawi *Fatwa*, 1988.
16. Shah Abdel Aziz *Fatwa*, 1864.
17. Seventeenth century, India *Consensus*.
18. Anwarul-Haq: *Family*, p. 45.
19. Ahmad Ibrahim 'Introduction to a Dissertation', 1936.
20. Nadim al-Jisr 'Hurriyyat' in *Proceedings of... High Academy of Islamic Research*.
21. Sayyid Sabiq *Fiqh*, 8 volumes.
22. Abonnour 'Nazrah' in his dissertation, 1976.
23. Al-Qaradawi *Al-Halal*.
24. Latif 'Nazrat' in *Rabat Proceedings*, vol. 2, pp. 29–38.
25. Atay 'Takhtit' in *Rabat Proceedings*, pp. 160–89.
26. Al-Khayyat *Al-Takaful*, pp. 125–8.
27. Balogun 'Muslim Attitude to Family Planning', Mimeograph.
28. 'Iesa *Tanzim al-Usrah, 1987*.
29. Jadel Haq Laws of Shari'ah, 1991.

Bibliography

al-ʿAmili, Zein al-ʿAbidin Ibn Ali (d.1558), *Al-Rawda al-Bahiyyah Fi-Sharh al-Lam'a al-Dimashqiyya*, Matbaʿat al-Adab, Najaf.
— *Masalik al-Afham Sharh Sharaʾiʿ al-Islam*, Tehran (AH1283).
Al-Hurr Al-'Amili, Mohammad Ibn al-Hasan (d.1621), *Wasa'il Al-Shiʿah Ila Tahsil Masa'il al-Shariʿah*, Tehran (AH1388).
Abdel Aziz, Shah, (d.1864), *Fatwa*, cited in Ahmad, *Rabat Proceedings*, vol. 1, IPPF (1974) p. 334.
Abdel-Wahid, Mustafa, *Al-Usrah Fil-Islam*, 3rd edition, Darel-Iʿtisam, Cairo (1980).
Abdullah, Sheikh M. al-Mubarak, 'Al-Islam Watanzim al-Walidiyya' in *Rabat Proceedings* vol. 2, IPPF. (1974), pp. 145–55.
Abonnour, M. Al-Ahmadi (written 1976), 'Thamarat al-Zawaj' in 'Manhaj al-Sunnah Fil Zawaj', a dissertation on *hadith* under Sheikh M. Abu-Zahra, College of Usul Al-Din, Al-Azhar, manuscript.
Abu Dawoud, Sulaiman Ibn al-Ashʿath al-Azdi al-Sijistani (d.888), *Sunan Abu Dawoud*, Al-Siada, Cairo (AH1369). Also printed in margin of al-Zurqani.
— *Masa'il al-Imam Ahmad*, Al-Manar, (AH1353).
Abu Hanifa, Imam Abu Hanifa Al-Nuʿman, *Husn al-Taqadi*, p. 79. Cited also in Sharabassi, *Al-Din*, p. 102.
Abu Zahra, Sheikh Mohammad, 'Tanzim al-Nasl' *Liwaʿ al-Islam* magazine, vol. 16, no.11, Nov. (1962).
— *Tanzim al-Usrah Wa Tanzim al-Nasl*, Dar al-Fikr al-Arabi (1976), 119pp.
Academy (High) of Islamic Research (Al-Azhar), *Proceedings of Conferences* 1964, 1965, Cairo.
Advisory Council on Religious Affairs, Turkey, *Fatwa* issued on 19 December 1960.
Afifi, Abdullah, *Al-Marʾah al-Arabiyah Fi Jahiliyyatiha Wa Islamiha*, Cairo.
Ahmad, Wajihuddin, 'Al-Mujtamaʿ Wattanmiyah al-Ijtimaʿiyyah' in *Rabat Proceedings* vol. 1, IPPF (1974), pp. 328–41.
Al-Ajali, Mohammad Ibn Idris (d.1202), *Al-Sara'ir Fil Fiqh*, manuscript, Al-Azhar Library.
— *Saraʾir al-Hawi Fi-Tahrir al-Fatawi*, Tehran (AH1270).
Ali, Abdullah Yosuf, *The Holy Qurʾan: Text, Translation and Commentary*, Darel-Arabiyah Littibaʿah, Beirut (1968).
Anwarul-Haq, *Family Planning in the Light of Islam*, Darsi Printing Press, Gujarat (1976), 150pp.

BIBLIOGRAPHY

Arab Central Bureau of Statistics and Documentations, *Statistical Year Book*, Amman (1984).
Ass'adi, Mohammad Ibn Yahia Bahran, *Gawahir al-Akhbar Wal' athar*, derived from and printed with *Al-Bahr al-Zakhkhar* by Ibn al-Murtada.
Atay, Dr Huseyn, '*Takhtit al-usrah kama warada fil-qur'an wal-sunnah*' in *Rabat Proceedings*, vol. 2, IPPF (1974), pp. 160–89.
Atfiyash, Mohammad Ibn Yusuf (d.1914), *Sharh Kitab al-Nil Wa-Shifa' al-'Alil*, Al-Matabi'h al-Amiriyya, Cairo.
Al-Ayni, Badrel Din Mahmoud Ibn Ahmad (d.1451), *Omdatul-Qari Sharh Sahih al-Bukhari*, Cairo, (AH1348).
al-Baberti, Mohammad Ibn Mahmoud al-Baberti al-Roumi (d.1384), *Sharh al-Inaya Alal Hidayah*. On margin of Ibn Al-Humam, *Sharh*.
al-Baghawi, Abu Mohammad al-Husein Ibn Mass'oud al-Farra' (d.1122), *Ma'alim al-Tanzil*. On the margin of *Lubab al-Ta'wil* by al-Kazim, Cairo (1955).
al-Bahuti, Mansour Ibn Yunis (d.1641), *Sharh Muntahal Iradat*, Ansar al-Sunnah al-Mohammadiyyah (AH1366).
—— *Al-Rawd al-Murbi Sharh Zad al-Mustanqi*, al-Matba'ah al-Salafiyya, Cairo (AH1380).
—— *Kashshaf al-Qina' An Matn al-Iqna'*, Ansar al-Sunnah al-Mohammadiyyah (AH1366).
al-Baihaqi, Abu Bakr Ahmad Ibn al-Hasan Ibn Ali (d.1066). *Al-Sunan al-Kubra*, Da'irat al-Ma'arif al-Islamiyyah, Haidar Abad (AH1353).
al-Baji, Al-Kadi Abul Walid Sulaiman Ibn Sa'd Al-Baji al-Andalusi (d.AH494),*Al-Muntaqa Sharh Muwatta' Imam Darel Hijrah Sayyedna Malik*, Matba'at al-Sa'ada, Cairo.
Balogun, Ismail, 'Muslim Attitudes to Family Planning' mimeograph from Department of Religion, University of Ilorin, Nigeria (no date).
Banjul Proceedings,*Islam and Family Planning* (for sub-Saharan Africa), report by Milas, Nabwiso and Dossou-Youo, Banjul, The Gambia (1979).
al-Baqouri, Ahmad Hasan, *Al-Usrah Fil Islam*, Kitab al-Yawm (1983).
al-Bijeurmi, Sulaiman Ibn Mohammad (d.1806), *Al-Iqna' Ala Sharh Abi-Shuja'*, Cairo (AH1294).
al-Boutti, M. Sa'id Ramadan, *Mas'alat Tahdid al-Nasl, Wiqayatan Wa'ilajan*, Maktabat al-Farabi, Damascus (1975).
al-Bukhari, Abu Abdullah M. Ibn Isma'il (d.869), *Sahih al-Bukhari*, Tab' Abdel Rahman Mohammad (AH1348). Also printed on the margin of *Fath al-Bari* by Ibn Hajar. English translation by Dr M. Muhsin Khan, Darel-Arabia, Beirut.
Chen, et. al, 'Maternal Mortality in Rural Bangladesh' in *Studies in Family Planning*, vol. 5, no. 11, November 1974, pp. 334–41.
Council of Islamic *Fiqh*, Makkah, 'Report on Meeting on Family Planning', *Al-Iqtisad* (1987).
Dakar Proceedings, *Islam and Family Planning* (for Africa), mimeographed report. Population and Development Policy Program, Battelle Human Affairs Research Center (1983).
al-Dardir, Ahmad Ibn M. Abul-Barakat (d.1786), *Al-Sharh al-Kabir*, on the margin of *Hashiat al-Dusuqi*, Mustafa Mohammad (AH1355).
al-Dimashqi, Mohammad Ibn Abdel Rahman (Al-Khatib al-Othmani) (d.1378), *Rahmat al-Umma Fikhtilaf Al'a'Immah*, Al-Matb'ah al-Bahiyya (AH1304).
Doi, Abdur-Rahman, *Shari'ah: The Islamic Law*, Taha Publishers, Lebanon (1984).
Al-Dusuqi, M. Ibn Arafa (d.1815), *Hashiyat al-Dusuki* with *Al-Sharh Al-Kabir* by al-

Dardir, Mustafa Mohammad, Cairo (AH1355).
Eleish, M. Ibn Ahmad (d.1881), *Fath Al-A'liyy al-Malik Fil-Fatwa Ala Madhab Malik*, Dar al-Fikr (1937).
Fatwa Committee, Al-Azhar University, Abdel Fattah El-Enani, Chairman, *Fatwa* (10 March 1953).
Fatwa Committee, Al-Azhar University, *View on family planning* endorsing Taulaw's *Fatwa* and published with it 8 September 1988 by the Al-Azhan Int. Islamic Center.
Fatwa Committee, Gaza Strip (Palestine) *Fatwa* (Ramadan AH1384).
al-Ghazali, Abu Hamid M. (d.1111), *Ihya' Ulum al-Din (Revival of Religious Sciences)*, al-Babi al-Halabi, Cairo, with an authentication of the *Ahadith* by al-Hafiz al-Iraqi on the margin.
— *Al-Wajiz Fi Fiqh al-Imam al-Shafe'i*, al-Adib, Cairo (AH1317).
Ghorbal, *et. al*, *Al-Mawsou'ah al-Arabiyyah al-Muyassarah*, 2nd edition, Dar al-Sha'b, Cairo (1972).
al-Halabi, Ibrahim Ibn Mohammad (d.1550), *Multaqa al-Abhor*, Darel-Tiba'ah al-Masriyyah, Cairo (AH1363).
Hassan, Haji Abdel-Jalil Bin Haji Hassan of Malaysia, *Fatwa* (21 November 1965).
al-Hattab, M. Ibn M. al-Maghrabi (d.1547), *Mawahib al-Jalil Li Sharh Mukhtasar' Abi Dya' Sidi Khalil* with *Al-Taj Wal-Iklil* by Mawwaq; Matba'at al-Sa'ada, Cairo (AH1328).
High Court of Appeal, Yemen Arab Republic, *Fatwa* issued by the President of the Court.
al-Hilli (Ibn al-Mutahhar), Hasan Ibn Yusuf Ibn al-Mutahhar (d.1325), *Sharh Tabsirat al-Muta'allimin Fi Ahkam al-Din*, Najaf (1962).
al-Hilli (Ja'far), Ja'far Ibn al-Hasan (d.1277), *Shara'i al-Islam Fi-Mas'il al-Halal Wal-Haram*, manuscript, Al-Azhar Library.
— *Al-Mukhtasar al-Naf'i Fi Fiqh al-Imamiyyah*, Darel-Kitab al-Arabi, Cairo.
Huzayyin, Sulaiman, 'Discussion' in *Rabat Proceedings* vol. 2, IPPF (1974) pp. 274, 275.
Ibn Abbas (The Physician), Ali (Hali Abbas in the west) (d.994), *Kamil al-Sina'ah al-Tibbiyyah*, Bulaq, Cairo (AH1294).
Ibn Abdin, M. Amin Ibn Omar (d.1836), *Minhat al-Khaliq*. On margin of *Al-Bahr al-Ra'iq* by Ibn Nujaim.
— *Radd al-Muhtar Aladdur al-Mukhtar Fi Sharh Tanwir al-Absar, Tab'* Bulaq, Cairo (1870).
Ibn Abdin (Ala'), Ala'uddin (d.1889), *Al-Hidaya al-Ala'iyyah*, Damascus (1965).
Ibn Abi Bakr, Mar'i Ibn Yusuf al-Karmi, famous as Ibn Abi Bakr, *Ghayat al-Muntaha Filjam' Bayn al-Iqna' Wal-Muntaha*, Damascus (AH1378).
Ibn al-Arabi, Abu Bakr M. Ibn Abdullah (d.1148), *Ahkam al-Qur'an*, Cairo (1957).
Ibn Hajar, Ahmad Ibn Hajar al-Asqalani, famous as Ibn Hajar or al-Hafiz (d.1449), *Fath al-Bari Sharh Sahih al-Bukhari*, al-Matab'ah al-Bahiyyah al-Misriyyah, distributor Dar Ihya' al-Turath al-Arabi, Beirut (1985), vol. 9, pp. 250–5. Earlier edition: al-Matba'ah al-Khayriyyah, Cairo, (AH1325), vol. 9, pp. 244–9.
— *Blough al-Maram Min Adillat al-Ahkam*, Eve Littiba'ah Beirut.
Ibn-Hanbal, Imam Abu Abdullah Ahmad Ibn M. Ibn Hanbal Ibn Hilal Al-Shaybani, Founder of Hanbali School (d.855), *Al-Musnad al-Imam Ahmad*, Iasa Al-Halabi, Cairo (AH1313).
Ibn Hazm, Ali Ibn Ahmad (d.1063), *Al-Muhalla* (authenticated by M. Munir al-Dimashqi), al-Tiba'ah al-Muniriyya, Cairo (1352).
Ibn al-Humam, Kamaluddin M. (d.1457), *Sharh Fath al Qadir*, Bulaq, Cairo (AH1315).

BIBLIOGRAPHY

The set contains also: *Nata'ij al-Afkar* by Qadi Zadeh; *Al-Hidayah* by Marghinani; *Sharh al-Inaya* by al-Baberti; *Hashyat* by Sa'id Ibn Halabi (see note below).*

Ibn al-Jawzi, Abul-Faraj Abdel-Rahman Ibn Ali (d.1201), *Saydul-Khatir*, Damascus (1960).

— *Zadel-Masir Fi Ilm al-Tafsir*, Al-Matba'ah al-Islamiyyah Damascus, Beirut (1965).

Ibn Jumi', Hibatullah (d.1193), *Al-Irshad Li Masa'il Al-Anfus Wal-Ajsad*, Cairo.

Ibn Juzayy, M. Ibn Ahmad (d.1340), *Al-Qawanin al-Fiqhiyyah*, Matba'at al-Nahda, Fez (1935).

Ibn-Kathir, Abul-Fida' Ismail Ibn Kathir al-Qurashi al-Dimashqi, *Tafsir al-Qur'an*, Dar Ihya' al-Kutub al-Arabiyya. It has a summary edition by al-Saboni. Dar al-Qur'an al-Karim, Beirut.

— *Al-Bidayah Wannihayah*, Darel-Sa'ada, Cairo.

Ibn Khaldoun, Abdel Rahman (d.1406), *Muqaddimat (Prolegomena)*, Darel-Sha'b, Cairo.

Ibn Maja', Abu Abdullah M. Ibn Yazid Ibn Maja al-Ri'i al-Qazwini (d.876), *Sunan Ibn Maja*, Iasa al-Halabi, Cairo (1313).

Ibn al-Murtada, Ahmad Ibn Yahya (d.1437), *Al-Bahr al-Zakhkar al-Jami' Li Madhahib 'Ulama' al-Amsar* with its summary *Jawahir al-Akhbar* (by Sa'di) with comments by al-Garafi, Cairo (1948).

Ibn al-Najjar, Taqiyyudin M. Ibn Ahmad (d.1564), *Muntaha al-Iradat* (ed. Abdel-Ghani Abdel Khaliq), Maktabat Darel-'Uruba, Cairo.

Ibn Nujaim, Zeinel-'Abidin Ibn Ibrahim Ibn-Nujaim al-Masri, known as the second Abu Hanifa (d.1562), *Al-Bahr al-Ra'iq Sharh Kanz al-Daqa'iq* with *Minhat al-Khliq Ala al-Bahr al-Ra'iq* by Ibn Abdin printed on the margin, al-Matba'ah al-Ilmiyyah.

Ibn al-Qayyim, M. Ibn Abi Bakr Ibn Qayyim al-Jawziyya (d.1350), *Zad al-Ma'ad Fi Hady Khayr el-'Ibad*, Matba'at al-Halaby (1950).

— *Tuhfat al-Mawdoud Fi-Ahkam al-Mawloud*, al-Maktabah al-Qayyima, Cairo.

— *Al-Tibb al-Nabawi*, Cairo.

— *Miftah Dorel-Sa'adah*, Cairo, Beirut.

Ibn Qudama, Abu Abdullah Ibn Ahmad (d.AH630), *Al-Mughni Ala Sharh Mukhtasar al-Khiraqi*, with *Al-Sharh al-Kabir* (see below).

— *Al-Muqni' Fi Fiqh Ibn Hanbal*, al-Matba'at al-Salafiyyah.

Ibn-Qudama, al-Maqdisi, Shamsuddin Abul-Faraj Abdel-Rahman (d.AH682), *Al-Sharh al-Kabir*, a commentary on Ibn Qudama's *Al-Muqni'*, printed with *Al-Mughni* as above.

Ibn Qutaiba, Abdullah Ibn Muslim Ibn Qutaiba al-Dinawari (d.889), *Ta'awil Mukhtalif al-Ahadith*, Cairo (AH.1326).

---

*The six book collection was written chronologically as follows:

1. Al-Marghinani (d.AH593) wrote the first book, *Bidayat al-Mubtadi*.
2. Al-Marghinani wrote a commentary on his own book, *Hidayat al-Muhtadi*.
3. Al-Baberti (d.AH786) wrote another commentary on *Bidayat* called *Al-Inaya Sharh al-Bidayah*.
4. Then Ibn al-Humam (d.AH861) wrote a commentary on *Al-Hidayat* calling it *Fath al-Qadir*.
5. This was completed by Qadi Zadeh (d.988) in a supplement called *Nata'ij al-Afkar Fi Qashf al-Rumouz Wal-Asrar*.
6. Finally Sa'id Halabi wrote a commentary on both *Al-Hidayah* and *Al-Inayah* calling it *Hashyat*.

All six books are printed with *Fath al-Qadir*.

BIBLIOGRAPHY

— *'Uyun al-Akhbar*, Cairo (1963).
Ibn Rajab, Abul-Faraj Abdel-Rahman (d.1393), *Jami' al-'Ulum Wal-Hikam*, Cairo (1969).
Ibn-Rushd (The Physician), M. Ibn Ahmad (d.1198), *Al-Kulliyyat*, Morocco (1939).
Ibn Rushd (The Theologian), Abul-Walied M. Ibn Ahmad Ibn-Rushd al-Qurtubi (d.AH595), *Bidayat al-Mujtahid Wa Nihayat al-Muqtasid*, Darel-Ma'rifah, Beirut (AH1405).
Ibn Sina, Avicinna Abu Ali Al-Husain Ibn Abdullah (d.1036), *Al-Qanoun Fi Tib*, al-Halabi, Cairo.
Ibn Taymiya, Taqiyyuddin Ahmad Ibn Abdel Halim (d.1328), *Al-Fatawa al-Kubra*, Darel-Kutub al-Hadithah, Cairo (1966).
— *Mukhtasar al-Fatawa al-Misriyya*, Tab' al-Sunnah al-Mohammadiyyah (1949).
— *'Ilm al-Sulouk* in *Majmou' Fatawa Ibn Taymiya*, al-Ryad (AH1381).
Ibn Taymiya (the grandfather), Abul-Barakat Abdus-Salam (d.1250), *Muntaqa al-Akhbar Min Ahadith Sayyid al-Akhyar*, included in *Nayl al-Awtar* by Al-Shawkani al-Matba'ah al-Othmaniyyah, (AH1357).
Ibrahim, Sheikh Ahmad, Introduction to dissertation, '*Kalimah Fi Taqlil al-Nasl' aw Man'ih Wa Ta'qim*'. The dissertation, Fi Mada Isti'mal *Huquq al-Zawjiyyay*', by al-Sa'id M. al-Sa'id, Cairo University (1936).
'Iesa, Sheikh Abdel-Aziz, *Tanzim al-Usrah Fil Fiqh al-Islami*, translated and printed as *Family Planning in Jurisprudence*, Matba'at al-Ahram, Cairo (1987).
— *Muhadarat on Islam and Family Planning*, Mimeograph.
Indian Muslim Jurists (*'ulama'*) (seventeenth century), 'collective *Fatwa*' cited in Ahmed, *Rabat Proceedings*, vol. 1, IPPF (1974) p. 334.
Ikhwan Al-Safa' (The Purity Brotherhood), a secret organization of writers in the tenth century, *Rasa'il Ikhwan Al-Safa*', Beirut (1957).
al-Iraqi (the father), Abdel Rahman Ibn al-Iraqi (d.1404), *Tarh al-Tathrib Fi Sharh al-Taqrib*, a commentary on *Taqrib al-Asaneed Wa Tartib al-Masaneed*, completed by his son (see below).
— *Sharh*, a commentary on Tirmidhi, Jam'iyyat al-Nashr Watta'alief al-Azhariyya (AH1354).
al-Iraqi (the son), Waliyyuddin Abu Zar'ah known as al-Hafiz al-Iraqi (d.1430), *Tarh al-Tathrib* (with his father).
— *Al-Mughni Fi Haml al-Asfar Fi Takhriej Mafil Ihya' Min 'Athar*, printed on the margin of *Ihya'* by al-Ghazali, al-Babi al-Halabi.
Jadel Haq, Sheikh Jadel Haq ali Jadel Haq, the Grand Imam of Al-Azhar, 'Ra'y al-Din Fi Tanzim al-Usrah' in *Al-Tasawwuf al-Islam* magazine, no. 21 (December 1980).
— 'Interview with the Grand Imam', published in a booklet by the National Population Council, Egypt and translated by Al-Azhar International Islamic Center for Population Studies and Research.
— 'Fatwa on Family Planning, 11 February 1979' in *Al-Fatawa al-Islamiyah*, vol. 29, High Council of Islamic Research (1983), pp. 3087–92.
— 'Fatwa on Family Planning, 29 December 1980' in *Al-Fatawa al-Islamiyah*, vol. 29, pp. 3110–13.
— 'Fatwa on Abortion' in *Al-Fatawa al-Islamiyah*, vol. 29, pp. 3093–109.
— 'Fatwa on Infertility Control' in *Al-Fatawa al-Islamiyah*, vol. 29, pp. 3213–28.
— *Laws of Shari'ah and Gyneocological Issues*, Al-Azhar International Islamic Center for Population Studies and Research, Cairo (1991).
Al-Jurjani, Isma'il (d.1136), *Al-Dhakhirah Fi Tib*, Cairo.
Kamel, Dr Abdel Aziz, 'Al'Umouma Fil Mujtama' al-Islami', paper presented at the

BIBLIOGRAPHY

Pan Islamic Conference on Motherhood, Al-Azhar University (December 1978), pp. 84–109.

Al-Kasani, Ala'uddin Abu Bakr Ibn Mass'oud (d.1191), *Bada'i al-Sana'i' Fi Tartib al-Shara'i'*, Shirkat al-Matabou'at al-'Ilmiyya, Cairo (1327).

Khalil, Khalil Ibn Ishaq Musa, known as Sidi Khalil, (the master of religious law) and Sheikh Khalil (d.1374), *Al-Mukhtasar Fi Madhab al-Imam Malik, Imam Dar al-Tanzil*, (Arabic) published within the various commentaries e.g. *Mawahib al-Jalil* by al-Hattab, Matba'at Darel Sa'ada, Cairo (AH1328) and *Jawahir al-Iklil* by al-Azhari, Darel-Ma'rifa, Beirut. (English) (quoted in this text) called *The Maliki law* being a summary of French translation of the *Mukhtasar of Sidi Khalil*, by F. Ruxton of Nigeria, London (1914).

Khattab, Sheikh Abul-Fath, 'A Poem on Family Planning' (1970).

al-Khayyat, Sheikh (Dr) Abdel Aziz, *Al-Mujtama' al-Mutakafil Fil Islam*, Dar al-Salam, Cairo, Beirut, Aleppo (1985).

al-Kholi, Sheikh al-Bahayy, 'Tahdid al-Nasl' in *Manbar al-Islam* magazine, no. 1 (May 1965).

al-Khwarizmi, M. Ibn Mahmoud Ibn M. (d.1257), *Jami' Masanid al-Imam al-A'zam Abi Hanifa*, Tab' Haider Abad (AH1322).

Latif, Haj Nasiruddin, 'Nazrat al-Islam Ila Tanzim al-Usrah' in *Rabat Proceedings*, vol. 2. IPPF, (1974), pp. 29–38.

Ma'moun, Sheikh Hasan, Rector of Al-Azhar, *Fatwa*, Al-Azhar (1964).

al-Madani, Sheikh Mohammad, Tanzim al Nasl *Manbar al-Islam* magazine (June 1965).

Madkour, Dr M. Sallam, *Nazrat al-Islam Ila Tanzim al-Nasl*, Dar al-Nahda al-Arabiyyah, Cairo (1965).

— '*Al-Islam Wal-Mujtama' Wattatawwur*' in *Rabat Proceedings*, vol. 1, IPPF (1974), pp. 289–311.

— Al-Ta'qim wal Ijhad, Ibid., vol. 2, pp. 287–308.

Mahallati, Ayatollah Hajji Sheikh Baha'eddin of Iran, *Fatwa* issued on 12 November 1964 in reponse to a question from Dr Mohammad Sarram.

Majma' al-Fiqh al-Islami, Makkah, 'Report' in *Al-Iqtisad al-Islami* magazine (March 1987).

Malik, Imam Malik Ibn Anas al-Asbahi al-Madani (d.795), *Al-Muwatta' Al-Imam Malik*, Riwayat Yahia Ibn Yahia al-Laithy Madba'at al-Babi al-Halabi, Cairo (1384). Arabic/English printing (translated by M. Rahimuddin), Eve Littiba'ah, Beirut (1985).

al-Maqdisi: See Ibn Qudamah al-Maqdisi.

al-Mardawi, Ali Ibn Sulaiman (d.1480), *Al-Tanqih al-Mushbi' Fi Tahrir Ahkam al-Muqni'*, Al-Maktabah al-Salafiyah, Cairo (1962).

al-Marghinani, Ali Ibn Abi Bakr (d.1197), *Al-Hidayah* (*Hidayat al-Muhtadi Sharh Bidayat al-Mubtadi*) with *Sharh Fath al-Qadir*, Bulaq, Cairo (AH1315).

Maudoudi, Maulana Aboul-A'ala, *Harakat Tahdid al-Nasl* (Arabic), Mu'assasat al-Risalah, Beirut (1982).

al-Mawirdi, Abul-Hasan Ali Ibn M. Ibn Habib al-Basri al-Bughdadi, known as al-Hasan al-Basri (d.AH450), *Al-Ahkam al-Sultaniyyah*, Tab' al-Halaby, Cairo (1966).

Muhsinuddin Dr M., *Philosophy of Islamic Law and the Orientalists*, Taj Company, New Dehli (1986).

Muslim, Abul-Hasan al-Hajjaj al-Qusheiri (d.875), *Sahih Muslim* (with commentary by Nawawi), Dar Ihya' al-Turath al-Arabia.

Nadim al-Jisr (Mufti of Tarablus), 'Hurriyyat Tahdid al-Nasl' in *Proceedings of the First Conference of The High Academy of Islamic Research*, Mu'assasat Akhbar al-Yaum (1964).

Also in *Nour al-Yaquin* magazine, Gaza Strip, (AH1385).
al-Najdi, Othman Ahmad (d.1688), *Hidayat al-Raghib Li Sharh Omdat al-Talib*, Cairo (1960).
al-Najjar, Sheikh (Dr) Abdel Rahman, *Ru'yah Mawdou'iyyah Fi al-Da'Wah Ila Tanzim al-Usrah*, al-Hay'ah al-'Ammah Lil-Isti'lamat, Cairo (1986).
al-Nasiri, Sheikh (Dr) M. al-Makki, 'Nazrah Ilattakhtit Al-a'ily Ala Daw' al-Tashrie' al-Islami' in *Rabat Proceedings*, vol. 2, IPPF (1974), pp. 39–67.
an-Nassa'i, Abu Abdel-Rahman Ibn Ali Ibn Shu'ayb al-Khurasani (d.910), *Sunan an-Nassa'i*, al-Matba'ah al-Azhariyyah.
Nasser: President Jamal Abdel-Nasser of Egypt, 'Proclamation of the National Charter' in *Nasser's Speeches and Press Interviews*, Information Department, Cairo (1962).
al-Nawawi, Abu Zakariyya Yahya Ibn Sharaf (d.1277), *Sharh Sahih Muslim (al-Minhaj)*, Dar Ihya' al-Turath al-Arabi, al-Matba'ah al-Misriyyah al-Azhariyyah. Commentaries on al-Minhaj by al-Ramli, and others.
—— *Al-Majmou' Sharh al-Muhadhab*, Matba'at al-'Asima, Cairo.
Nazer, *et al.*: see *Rabat Proceedings*.
Omran, Dr Abdel Rahim, 'The Epidemiologic Transition: a Theory of the Epidemiology of Population Change', *Milbank Memorial Fund Quarterly*, vol. 49, (1971), pp. 509–38.
—— *The Health Theme in Family Planning*, Monograph 16, Carolina Population Center, Chapel Hill, North Carolina (1971).
—— 'Health Consequences of High Risk Pregnancy in Muslim Women: a Cross-national Maternity Center Study', presented at the Pan Islamic Conference on Motherhood, Al-Azhar University (December 1978).
—— *Population Problems and Prospects in the Arab World*, a UN monograph published for the World Population Conference in Mexico (1984).
—— *Family Planning for Health in Africa*, monograph published by Carolina Population Center, Chapel Hill, North Carolina (1985).
—— *Fertility and Health: The Latin American Experience*, monograph published by WHO, Washington, DC (1985).
—— *The Arab Population: Present and Future* (Arabic), UNFPA publication, al-Qabas Press, Kuwait (1988).
—— and Fan, *Family Formation and Health in Taiwan*, monograph published by the Institute of Maternal And Child Health, Taipeh, Taiwan (1985).
—— and Standley, C.C., (eds), *Family Formation Patterns and Health: an International Collaborative Study in India, Iran, Lebanon, Philippines, and Turkey*, WHO, Geneva (1976).
—— —— *Further Studies on Family Formation Patterns and Health: an International Collaborative Study in Colombia, Egypt, Pakistan and Syria*, WHO, Geneva (1981).
al-Qadi al-Nu'man, Abu Hanifa al-Nu'man Ibn M. Ibn Mansour al-Tamimi, known as al-Qadi al-Nu'man (d.974), *Da'a'im al-Islam Wa Dhikr al-Halal Wal-Haram Wal Qadaya Wal Ahkam An Ahl Bayt Rasoul Allah, Alayhi Wa Alayhim Afdal Ussalam*, second edition, Darel-Ma'arif, Cairo.
al-Qalqili, Sheikh Abdullah, the Grand Mufti of Jordan, *Fatwa* (December 1964).
al-Qaradawi, Sheikh (Dr) Yusuf, *Al-Halal Wal-Haram Fil Islam*, al-Maktab al-Islami, Beirut, Dimashq, 325pp. Translated as *The Lawful and the Prohibited in Islam*, American Trust Publications, Indianopolis (1980).
al-Qastallani, Ahmad Ibn M. (d.1517), *Irshad al-Sari Li Sharh Sahih al-Bukhari*, Bulaq, Cairo (AH1305).

al-Qurtubi, Abu Abdellah M. Ibn Ahmad al-Ansari (d.1272) *Al-Jami˚ Li' Ahkam al-Qur'an*, Cairo (1967).
Rabat Proceedings, Al-Islam Wa Tanzim al-Usrah (editors: I Nazer; M.Y. Zayid; Y.G. al-Najjar) 2 vols, IPPF (1974). (The Conference itself took place in 1971.)
al-Ramli, Ibn Shahab al-Din (d.AH1987), *Nihayatal-Muhtaj Fi Sharh al-Minhaj*, al-Babi al-Halabi (1938).
al-Razi, M. Ibn Y'qub (d.940), *Al-Furu' Min al-Kafi*, Tehran.
al-Razi, al-Fakhru (d.1209), *Al-Tafsir al-Kabir* (or *Mafatih al-Ghayb*), Cairo (1962).
al-Sa˚di, M. Ibn Yahya Bahran (d.AH957), *Jawahir al-Akhbar Wal-'Athar al-Mustakhrajah Min Lujjat al-Bahr al-Zakhkar* by Ibn al-Murtada. Both printed together, al-Sunnah al-Muhammadyya, Cairo (1948).
al-Sa'ih, Sheikh Abdel-Hamid, 'Nazrat al-Islam Ila al-Usrah Fi Mujtama' Mutatawwir', in *Rabat Proceedings*, vol. 1, IPPF (1974), pp. 166–82.
Sabiq, Sheikh Sayyid, *Fiqh al-Sunnah*, Darel-Bayan, Kuwait (1968).
Sahnoun, Sheikh Ahmad, 'Nazrat al-Islam Ila al-Ijhadd Watta'qim' in *Rabat Proceedings*, vol. 2, IPPF (1974), pp. 402–17.
Saleem, Sheikh Abdel-Majeed, the Grand Mufti of Egypt, *Fatwa*, no. 81, Regd:43, (25 January 1937). Published also in *Journal of the Egyptian Medical Association*, vol. 20, no. 7, (July 1937), pp. 55.
Saleh, Saniyya, *Maternal Mortality in Menufia*, Social Research Center, American University of Cairo, Egypt (1987).
Saleh, Tuan Haji Ali Bin M. Said, Chief Qadi in Singapore, *Fatwa*, Uustan Malaysia, 25 April 1955.
al-San˚ani, M. Ismail al-Yamani, known as al-Amir al-San˚ani (d.AH1182), *Subul al-Salam Sharh Blough al-Maram*, Darel-Fath al-Islami, Alexandria, Egypt.
al-Seyuti, Jalaluddin Abdel-Rahman Ibn Ali Bakr (d.1505), *Al-Durr al-Manthour Fittafsir Bil-Ma'thour* (commentary on the Qur'an), Beirut.
— *Al-Jami˚ al Saghir* (*hadith*), Cairo.
— *Al-Ashbah Wannaza'ir*, Mustafa Mohammad (AH1357).
— *Sharh Sunan an-Nassa˚i*, summarized in *Al-Mujtaba*, Cairo.
al-Sha˚rani, Abdel Wahhab (d.1565), *Al-Mizan*, al-Matba˚ah al-Azhariyyah (1955).
— *Mukhtasar Tadhkirat al-Suwaidi* (Medicin), printed on the margin of *Kamil al-Sina˚ah al-Tibbiyyah* by Ali Ibn Abbas, Bulaq, Cairo (AH1294).
al-Shafe˚i, Imam M. Ibn Idris (d.820), *Al-Umm*, Matba˚at al-Kulliyyah al-Azhariyyah, Cairo (1961).
Shaltout, Sheikh Mahmoud, the former Imam of Al-Azhar, *Fatwa* issued from Al-Azhar Press, Cairo (1959).
— *Al-Qur'an and the Woman* (*Al-Qur'an Wal-Mar˚ah*), reprinted by Al-Azhar International Islamic Center for Population Studies and Research, Cairo in *Makanat al-Mar'ah Fil-Usrah al-Islamiyyah*, pp. 335–426.
Shamsuddin, Sheikh M. Mahdi, '*Nazrat al-Islam Ilal-Usrah Fi Mujtama' Mutattawwir*' in *Rabat Proceedings*, vol. 1, IPPF (1974), pp. 13–23.
— 'Al-Islam Wa Tanzim al-Usrah', ibid, vol. 2, pp. 68–95.
— 'Tahdid al-Nasl: Mashrou'iyatuh Wa Wasa'iluh', ibid, vol. 2, pp. 281–5.
al-Sharabassi, Sheikh (Dr) Ahmad, *Al-A'Immah al-˚Arba˚ah* (*The Four Imans*), Darel-Hilal, Cairo (1964).
— *Al-Din Wa Tanzim al-Usrah*, Dar Matabi˚ al-Sha˚b, Cairo (1965).
al-Sha˚rawi, Sheikh Mohammad Mitwalli, 'Opinion on Family Planning' *Alexandria* newspaper (1980).
— 'Al-Islam Wa Tanzim al-Usrah' in *Rabat Proceedings*, vol. 2, IPPF (1974), pp. 5–28.

BIBLIOGRAPHY

al-Shawkani, M. Ibn Ali Ibn M. (d.1839), *Nayl al-Awtar Sharh Mutaqal Akhbar Min Ahadith Sayyid al-Akhyar*, Al-Matbaʿah al-Othmaniyya (AH1357).

al-Shirazi, Abu Ishaq Ibrahim Ibn Ali al-Fairouzabadi (d.1083), *Al-Muhadhab Fi Fiqh al-Imam al-Shafeʿi*, with a commentary, *Al-Nazm al-Mustaʿdhab Fi Sharh Gharib al-Muhadhab* by al-Rakbi, Matabaʿat al-Halabi.

al-Shubramallissi, Abuddia' Noureddin Ali Ibn Ali (d.AH1087), *Hashyat al-Shubramallissi Ala Nihayat al-Mihtaj'*, Cairo.

al-Sijistani, Abu Dawoud, see under Abu Dawoud.

al-Tabari, Abu Jafar M. Ibn Jarir (d.923), *Jamiʿ al-Bayan ʿAn Taʾwil Aʾay Al-Qurʾan* (ed. M. Mahmoud Shakir), Dar Ihya' al-Kutub al-Arabiyya (al-Halabi).

al-Tahawi, Abu-Jʿafar Ahmad Ibn Mahmoud al-Masri al-Azdi (d.933), *Mushkil al-'Athar*, Majlis Da'irat al-Maʿarif al-Nizamiyya, India (AH1333).

— *Sharh Maʿani al-'Athar*, Cairo.

— *Al-Mukhtasar Fil-Fiqh*, Darel-Kitab al-Arabi (AH1370).

al-Tahtawi, Ahmad Ibn M. (d.1816), *Hashiyat al-Durr al-Mukhtar*, Cairo (1838).

al-Tantawi, Sheikh Sayyid, the current Mufti of Egypt, *Fatwa*, Published in *al-Wafd* newspapers, Cairo (8, 9 September 1988). Also by Al-Azhar Int. Islamic Center.

al-Tirmidhi, Abu Iasa M. Ibn Iasa (d.892), *Jamiʿ (Sunan) al-Tirmidhi*, Cairo.

al-Tusi, Abu Jaʿfar M. Ibn al-Hasan al-Tusi (d.1067), *Al-Mabsout Fi Fiqh al-Imamiyyah*, Tehran (AH1387).

United Nations, *World Population Prospects: Estimated and Projected as Assessed in 1984*, Population Studies No. 8, New York (1986) UN Data Chart 1990, Demographic Yearbook 1991.

al-Wazzani, Al-Mahdi Ibn M. (d.1730), *Al-Miʿyar al-Jadid al-Muʿrib An Fatwa al-Muta'akhkhirin Min ʿUlama' al-Maghrib*, Fez (AH1318).

al-Zabidi, M. Ibn M. al-Murtada (d.1790), *Ithaf al-Sadah al-Muttaqin Fi Sharh Ihya' Ulum al-Din*, Dar Ihya' al-Turath al-Arabia, Beirut.

al-Zamakhshari, Mahmoud Ibn Omar (d.1144), *Al-Kashshaf ʿAn Haqaʾiq Ghawamidd al-Tanzil*, Beirut (1947).

al-Zawawi, Al-Sayyid Yousof B. Ali of Malaysia, *Fatwa* (n.d.).

al-Zurqani, Abu Abdillah M. Abdel-Baqi (d.1710), *Sharh Muwatta' al-Imam Malik*, Matabaʿat al-Kulliyya al-Azhariyyah (with *Sunan Abu Dawoud* on the margin).

Index

Does not include names of surahs (chapters) of the Qur'an or the names of the narrators of the tradition.

Abassid dynasty, the 149–50
Abdel Aziz, Shah 229
Abidi dynasty, the 151
Abonnour, Sheikh Al-Akmadi 231–3
abortion 3, 7–9, 34, 137, 158, 160, 178, 184, 190–3, 204–5, 208–10, 213, 215, 217, 226, 228–9, 231, 234–5, 237–8, 251–2, 255–7; septic 185
abstention: from intercourse 165; from marital relations 157; from marriage 135
Abu Bakr (al-Siddiq), Sayyidna 78, 119
Abu Dawoud, Sulaiman Ibn al-Ash'ath 17, 31, 44, 78, 101, 104, 116, 125, 127, 130–2, 145, 174
Abu Hanifa, Imam Abu Hanifa Al-Nu'man 19, 77–8, 124, 147, 151, 153, 172, 197
Abu Huraira, Sayyedna 57, 125, 131, 139, 153
Abu Zahra, Sheikh Mohammad 100, 102, 204–6
Academy (Council) of Islamic Research 2, 214–15, 217, 230
Aceh Congress on Islam and Population Policy 1990 215, 219–22
Adam 41–2, 197
adolescence 35
adoption 186
adultery 55–6, 196

Advisory Council on Religious Matters, Turkey 227, 252–3
Afghanistan 151
Africa 152, 216–18
Agha Khan, the 152
agriculture: products 102; programs 110
Ahmad, Dr Khurshid 208
Ahmad, Wajihuddin, 'Al-Mujtama' 21, 44, 49, 202, 207
A'isha, Sayyida 43, 109
Al-'Ajali, Mohammad Ibn Idris 18
alcohol: prohibition of 78
Ali, Abdullah Yosuf 20, 77, 87–8, 150
anaemia 178
analogy (*qiyas*) 73, 75, 77–8, 83, 135, 147, 151, 166, 191, 226, 234
Andalus (Arab Spain) 150
animal sperm 186
animal, the uterus of an 186–8, 250–51
al-Ansar, Ibn Abi Rifa'a Obaid 133
an-Nassa'i, Abu Abdel-Rahman 30, 101, 116, 126, 130–1, 133
annulment 26, 79
Anwarul-Haq 229
apathy 103
Arab Central Bureau of Statistics 212
Arabia 15
artificial insemination 184–6, 223; *see also* in vitro fertilization
Asia 51, 216

276

INDEX

al-Aslamiyya Kuʿaiba bint Saʿd 47
al-Asqalani, Ibn Hajar 161
Assʾadi, Mohammad Ibn Yahia Bahran 165
al-Aswad, Abu 141
Atay, Huseyn 145, 235
Atfiash, Mohammad, 167
Avicina (Ibn Sina) and others 175-7
al-Ayni, Mahmoud Ibn Ahmad 116, 119, 238
Azad, Maulana Abdul Kalam 208, 230
Al-Azhar Fatwa Commitee, the 175
Al-Azhar University 2, 4
Al-Azhar University International Islamic Center for Population Studies and Research 219, 222-4
al-Azl *see* coitus interruptus
Azraquis, the 148

al-Baberti, Mohammad Ibn Mahmoud 154
Baghdad 150-1
Bahrain 151
al-Bahuti, Mansour 164
al-Baihaqi, abu Bakr Ahmad 8, 34, 37, 91, 114, 117-18, 125, 132-4, 137-8
al-Baji, Al-Kadi Abul Walid 117, 153, 156-7
Balogun, Dr Ismaíʾl 235-6
Bangladesh 18, 178, 180-1
Banjul Conference on Islam and Family Planning 1979 215, 217
Bannul Mustaliq battle, the 155
Barakah, Sheikh Abdel Fattah 2
barrier methods 169, 187; *see* the coil; the condom; intrauterine devices; the loop
Basra, Iraq 152
battle of Badr, the 214
battle of Bani al-Mustalaq, the 126
battle of Hunayn, the 105, 123
battle of Khaibar, the 47
battle of Khandaq, the 48
battle of Siffin 147
battle of Uhud, the 20, 47, 55
birth control 9, 85, 113, 139, 60, 166, 190, 204-7, 209-10, 230, 237, 251, 256; prohibition of 204
birth planning 1, 83
birth rate, the 211

birth spacing 217, 219; *see also* child spacing
bladder, the 173
blood transfusion 178
al-Boutti, M. Saʿid Ramadan 129, 137, 140, 192-3, 209-11
breast-feeding 9, 26, 32, 57, 96-7, 57, 174, 178, 182, 213, 217, 219, 222, 252; *see also* lactation; weaning; wet nursing
al-Bukhari, Abu Abdullah M. 16, 30, 35, 46, 48, 50, 61, 113, 115-16, 126-7, 146, 208

Cairo 152, 214
Cairo University 204-5, 210
Canada 66
Cancer of the cervix 178
Caspian Sea, the 151
castration 16, 187-9, 235
celibacy 16, 61
cervical canal, the 156
cervical cancer 178
cervical mucus 185
cervix, the 185
cesarian section 170, 178, 191
chemical therapy 185-6
child care 220, 222
child spacing 96, 174, 181, 213, 223-4
child survival 31-2
childbearing 83, 215, 226, 252, 256
children, illegitimate 203
China 46
Christianity 146
chromosomes: X 34; XX 23; XY 23
coil, the (IUD) 7, 81; *see also* intrauterine devices
coitus interruptus (*al-azl*) 1-4, 6-8, 18, 51, 67, 77, 79-81, 85-6, 88-9, 95, 97, 102, 109, 111, 113, 115, 117-42, 146, 152-68, 183-4, 187, 189, 191, 193, 196-7, 205-6, 208-11, 214, 223, 226, 229, 231-5, 252, 254-5, 259; prohibition of 255; *see also* withdrawal
Companions of the Prophet 1, 16, 43, 47, 77-8, 87, 89, 95, 104, 113-16, 118-21, 123, 126, 131, 133-6, 139-41, 148, 150, 155-6, 159, 164, 172, 205, 208, 214, 223, 232, 255
conception 7, 135, 160, 190, 193, 229
condom, the 81
congenital anomalies 178
congenital defects 185

277

INDEX

consensus (*ijma'*) 73, 75, 77–8, 147
Constitutional Council of the Islamic World League 217
contagious diseases 219, 237
contraception 1, 3–4, 6–9, 18, 33, 51, 81, 85–7, 89, 91, 95, 109, 118–19, 124, 130, 134, 140, 142, 145–6, 156, 159–60, 162–3, 166, 173, 187, 190, 193, 201–3, 207–10, 212–13, 215–16, 223, 226–33, 235, 237–8, 255–9; cultural justifications for 182–3; economic justifications for 171–3; health justifications for 173–82; in Islamic jurisprudence 168–83; with modern mechanical and chemical methods 80; *see also* birth control; birth planning; birth spacing; child spacing; coitus interruptus; family formation; population control; withdrawal
contraceptive injection, the 81
contraceptive pill, the 7, 81, 187, 235, 259
contraceptives 15, 170, 189, 255–6; *see* barrier methods; the coil; the condom; the contraceptive injection; the contraceptive pill; intrauterine devices (IUDs); the loop
contractions 81
Council of Arab Economic Unity 212
Council of Islamic fiqh in Makkah 215–16
Couper's glands 188
Cultivation (impregnation) 95, 101
cultural aspiration 183
cystic fibrosis 23–4

Dakar Conference on Islam and Family Planning 1982, 215
Dakar Seminar, the 218
Day of Judgement 31, 100, 103, 126–7, 254
Debandhi orthodox theological group, the 201
debt 103
demography 65, 84, 211, 217; *see also* population
destitution 171
development programs 110
diabetes 178
diaphragm, the 81
diseases: contagious 219, 237; diabetes 178; genetic 23, 33; of the heart 178; hereditary 8, 170, 173, 178, 188, 205, 210, 213, 231, 251; infectious 173, 209, 251
divorce 15, 17–18, 20–1, 23, 41
donor sperm 186; *see* sperm banks
drugs 39, 188, 253–4; abuse of 203; prohibition of 78
drugs abuse 203

East Africa 151
economic conditions 10, 222
economic development 67, 101
economic independence 183
education 67, 221; in religion 39, 218
Egypt 2, 61, 98, 113, 150–2, 158, 170, 178, 180–1, 201, 208
ejaculation 120, 135, 138, 154, 159, 161, 163–4, 185, 196–7
embryo, the 160, 255
emigration 210
ensoulment 157–8, 191–3, 205, 210, 213, 226, 231, 235, 237, 251
environment, the 220
epidemics 66
epididymis 185
equality 43–58; choosing marital partners 49–50; education 46; inheritance differentials 51–5; the principle of Jihad 46–8; religious duties 44; women's share in the Islamic revolution 44-6
estrogen 232
Europe 111, 181, 203, 211, 233
Eve 41–2, 197
extremism 61, 212

fallopian tubes 185–6; *see also* in vitro fertilization
family formation 13, 15, 145–6, 179, 182–4, 215
Family Health Care Society, Somalia 224
family in Islam, the 13–26; cultural considerations 23–6; marital competence 26; pregnancy planning 26; social considerations 26
family planning 1–4, 6, 79, 170–1, 181–3, 201–26, 228–30, 234–7, 252–6, 258–9; the basic precepts of Islam 59–69; in Islamic jurisprudence 145–67, 184–97; and the Qu'ran 85–112; and the Sunnah 113–42; *see* contraception
Family Planning Association 252
Family Planning Program, Egypt 225, 230

278

Far East, the 216
fasting 16, 18, 61, 63
Fatima 148, 152
al-Fatimi, al-Muʿizz Lidinillah 151
Fatimid dynasty, the 152
fertility 7–8, 18, 31–2, 60–1, 66–7, 109–11, 188, 226, 256
fertilization 9, 160, 187, 211
fetus, the 9, 34, 138, 157, 191, 193, 211, 234; the expulsion of 217, 254; *see also* the embryo
First World War 19
foreign aid 212
fornication 186; *see also* sexual intercourse
Frohlich's Syndrome (hereditary insufficiency of hormones) 185

Gambia, the 217
Gaza Strip, the 214
genetic cross-engineering 185–6, 238
genetic diseases 23, 33; *see* cystic fibrosis; phenylketonuria (PKU); sickle cell anaemia; thalassemia
genetic risks from in-breeding 23, 173
gestation period 184
al-Ghazali, Imam Ulum al-Din 6–9, 18, 23, 77, 79, 118, 135, 137, 141, 151, 159–61, 167–71, 174, 191, 197, 231, 235, 237, 258
al-Ghifariyya, Ummayya bint Qaya 47

Hassan, Abdel-Jalil 227, 254
Hanafi jurists 7, 39, 182, 197
Hanafi school, the 7, 147, 150, 153–5, 182, 191–2, 196–7, 226, 228, 248; *see also* Abu Hanifa
Hanbali jurists 9, 162, 164, 183
Hanbali school, the 7, 21, 117, 147, 151, 162–5, 191–2, 196, 228
al-Harbi, Ibrahim 23
health programs 110
health risks 170
heart disease 178
hereditary diseases 8, 170, 173, 178, 188, 205, 210, 213, 231, 249; *see also* genetic diseases
hidden infanticide 115, 136–8, 141, 157, 161
High Council of Research 189
High Court of Appeal (Yemen) 228, 257
Hijaz (now Saudi Arabia) 113, 150
al-Hilli, Jaʿfar Ibn al-Hasan 18, 165
hormonal therapy 185–6

hormones, sexual 185
housing 67
al-Husayn, Ibn Ali 151
hypertension 178

Ibaddi school, the 147–8, 152, 167, 192
Ibaddis, the 148
Ibn Abbas, Ali 88, 95, 106, 109, 119, 123, 125, 134, 136, 155, 162, 172, 213
Ibn Abdel-Barr, Imam 117, 153, 156–7
Ibn Abdin, M. Amin Ibn Omar 81, 136, 154, 197, 255
Ibn Abdullah Ibn Yunus, Ahmad 122
Ibn Abdullah, Jabir 7, 102, 115, 117–19, 121–2, 131, 136, 139–40, 157, 160, 162, 206, 223
Ibn Abi Ayyub, Saʾid 141, 162, 164
Ibn Abi Bakr 164
Ibn Abi Talib, Ali *see* Oman, Caliph
Ibn Abi Waqqas, Saʿd 119, 134, 136, 155, 214, 251
Ibn al-Khattab, Sayyidna Omar *see* Omar, Caliph
Ibn Ali, Abu Jaʿafar Mohammad 167
Ibn Ali, Imam Zayd 150
Ibn Amr, al-Hajjaj 155
Ibn al-Arabi, Imam 116, 137, 139
Ibn al-Awwam, al-Zubair 134
Ibn Ghazziyya, al-Hajjaj Ibn Amr 119, 124
Ibn Hajar, Ahmad 16–17, 128–9, 135, 138, 140, 151, 153, 158, 162, 169, 175, 197
Ibn Hanbal, Imam Abu Abdullah Ahmad 35, 77–8, 113–18, 122–3, 125, 127–8, 130, 132, 147, 150, 152, 162, 234; *see also* al-Shaybani
Ibn Hazm, Ali Ibn Ahmad 89, 119, 135–40, 152, 164, 167, 208, 235
Ibn al-Humam, al-Kamal 139, 154, 197
Ibn Ibadd, Imam Abdullah 150, 152
Ibn Juzayy, M. Ibn Ahmad 157, 196
Ibn Khalaf, Imam Dawoud 150, 152
Ibn al-Khattab *see* Oman, Caliph
Ibn al-Mahdi, Abdullah 151
Ibn Maja, Abu Abdullah 17, 21, 25, 33, 60, 115–16, 122, 125–7, 129–30
Ibn Mohammad, Iaʿfar 167
Ibn Muʿadh, Saʿd (the great Companion) 48
Ibn al-Mussayyab, Saʾid 95, 109, 119, 124, 162

INDEX

Ibn al-Najjar, Taqiyyuddin 164
Ibn Nawfal, Waraqa 43
Ibn Nujaim, Zeinel-'Abidin Ibn Ibrahim 154, 197
Ibn Omar, Abdullah 106, 119, 124, 134, 136–7, 155, 158, 162, 164, 172, 232–3
Ibn Omayr, Za' 123
Ibn al-Qayyim, M. Ibn Abi Bakr 21, 107, 118–19, 135, 137–8, 141, 159, 163, 196–7
Ibn Qudama Abu Abdullah Ibn Ahmad 119, 162–3, 168, 196
Ibn Quddama al-Maqdisi *see* al-Maqdisi
Ibn Al-Rabi', Sa'd 54–5
Ibn Rajab Abul-Faraj Abdel-Rahmad 134
Ibn Rushd, Abul-Walid 137
Ibn al-Sakan, Asma' bint Zayd 130
Ibn Sirin, Mohammad 119, 128
Ibn Taymiya, Abul Barakat Abdus-Sallam 163, 196
Ibn Taymiya, Taqiyyuddin 163, 196
Ibn Thabit, Zayd 109, 119, 124–5, 136, 155, 164, 251
Ibn Zayd, Imam Yahia 151, 162, 165
Ibn Zayd, Usama 129
Ibrahim, Sheikh Ahmad 57, 189, 210, 230
'Iesa, Sheikh Abdel-Aziz 2, 169–70, 173, 236
ignorance 218
Ijma' *see* consensus
illegitimate children 203
illegitimate pregnancy 192–3
illiteracy 103, 212
Imami jurisprudence 166, 189
Imami school, the 148, 151, 165–6, 192
immaculate conception, the 42
impotence 26
in vitro fertilization (test-tube babies) 185–6, 223
in-breeding: genetic risks from 23, 173
incontinence 18, 173
India 151–2, 178
Indian Ulama' of the seventeenth century 229
Indonesia 178
Indonesian government, the 219
infanticide (*wa'd*) 49, 86–9, 102, 111, 125, 130–4, 137–8, 140, 158, 160–1, 164, 167, 203–5, 212–13, 253, 257; hidden 115, 136–8, 141, 157, 161; minor 115, 131–4, 138, 156, 164, 232, 254

infection 178, 232; of the scrotum 185; *see also* contagious
infectious diseases 173, 209, 251
infertility 4, 32, 108–9, 182, 184–90, 213, 215, 220, 223, 228, 238; primary 184; secondary 184–5; *see also* sterility
injection, the contraceptive 81
insemination *see* artificial insemination
intercourse, sexual 18–19, 135, 158–9, 161, 163–4, 174, 188, 197
International Planned Parenthood Federation (IPPF) 209, 216
intrauterine devices (IUDs) 163, 187; *see* the coil; the loop
Al-Iqtisad al-Islami Magazine 216
Iran 151–2, 178, 181, 189
Iraq 113, 147, 151
al-Iraqi, Abdel Rahman Ibn al-Hussein 100, 161
al-Iraqi, Al-Hafez 116, 138, 161
Islamic jurisprudence 3, 87, 136, 141–2, 202, 225, 236; contraception in 168–83; family planning in 145–67, 184–97; sources of 73–84; *see also* Islamic law; Islamic legislation
Islamic Empire, the 145, 147
Islamic law 81–3, 146–7, 216, 229, 234, 257
Islamic legislation 59; community development 59; family formation 59; international relations 59; moral behavior 59; social interaction 59; societal structure 59; taxation 59
Islamic medicine, comparison with 173–4
Isma'il, Imam Isma'il in ja'far al-Sadiq; *see* al-Sadiq
Isma'ili school, the 148, 151, 167
Ivory Coast, the 236

Jadel-Haq, Sheikh Jadel Haq Ali 2, 85, 177, 186, 188, 191–2, 228, 238, 256
Japan 111, 181, 211
Jesus 42–3, 197
Jewish law 131, 137
Jews, the 131–3, 138, 158, 164, 205–6, 232, 254
al-Jisr, Naddim; *see* Omar, Calip
Joseph 91
Judama 87–8, 102, 130, 135–41, 154–61, 164–5, 167, 235
juristic research 201–2, 215

280

Kamel, Dr Abdel Aziz 28
Karbala 147
Karmi, H. 216
al-Kasani, Ala'uddin Abu Bakr Ibn Mass'oud 122, 136, 154, 162, 164
Kenya 181
Khadija, Sayyida 43
Khaibar 65
Khalil, Sidi 158
Khan, Sayyid M. Ja'far 208, 230
Kharijite movements 147–8, 152; the Azraquis 148; the Ibaddis 148; the Najadat 148; the Shaybanis 148; the Sufris 148
Kharijite school, the 74
Khattab, Sheikh Abul-Fatth 4
al-Khayyat, Sheikh Abdel Aziz, 235
al-Khattabi, al-Imam 116
al-Kholi, Sheikh al-Bahayy 102
al-Khudri, Abu Sa'id 9, 119–20, 123, 126–7, 132, 136, 139, 155–6, 164–5, 208
al-Khwarizmi, M. Ibn Mahmoud Ibn M. 154
Kuwait 151, 214

labor (*talq*) 6, 173–4, 178, 191
lactation 26, 174, 232, 237, 252
Latif, Hajj Nasiruddin 234
Lebanon 151, 178, 189
legitimate pregnancy 192
Libya (Jabal Island) 152
life expectancy 28; *see also* child survival; mortality
Liwa al-Islam Magazine 204
loop, the 257
Lott, the Prophet 45
low birth weight 178
lust 18

al-Madany, Sheikh Mohammad 122
al-Manar, Tafsir 90
al-Mawirdi, Hasan al-Basri 128
Madkour, Sheikh M. S. 80, 137, 139, 188, 191–2, 205–6, 209–10
Mahallati, Ayatullah Baha'eddin 227, 253-4
Makkah 139, 148, 150, 214
Makkah conquest, the 48
Malaysia 214
Malik, Imam Malik Ibn Anas 37, 60, 77, 79, 00, 113–14, 116, 118–19, 125, 127–8, 141, 146–7, 150–1, 155–6, 162, 253
Maliki jurists 9, 78, 155, 158
Maliki school, the 7, 117, 147, 150, 152–3, 155–9, 165, 191–2, 196, 228, 253
malnourishment 178
malnutrition 178, 232; *see also* malnourishment
Ma'moun, Sheikh Hasan 67, 227, 251-2
Manbar al-Islam Magazine 122
al-Marghinani, Ali Ibn Abi Bakr 154
marriage 94–5, 99, 101, 105; 209, 218, 233, 252; age at 18–19; cultural considerations 23–6; in Islam 13–26; marital competence 26; pregnancy planning 26; social considerations 26; *see also* the marriage contract
marriage contract, the 165–7
Mary (*Maryam*) 42–3
maternal care 220, 222; *see also* prenatal care
Maudoudi, Maulana 96, 102, 206–8, 214, 230
medical technology 8
medicine, modern 23, 177–82, 257
Medina 47, 73, 75, 79, 116, 131, 147–8, 150, 155–6
menopause, the 181
mental illness 210
Mexico 181
Middle East 189, 216
migration 66, 220, 223
minerals 102
Ministry of Information, Egypt 213
Ministry of Religious Affairs, Egypt 212–13
minor infanticide 115, 131–4, 138, 156, 164, 232, 254
mixed sperm 186
modern medicine 23, 177–82, 257
Mogadishu Conference on Islam and Child Spacing 1990 215, 223–4
Mohammad, the Prophet 43, 47, 65, 150
monetary compensation 165
monogamy 15, 20–1, 229, 235
moral decline 204
mortality 66–7, 111–12; of children 66, 178, 181; maternal 178, 180–1
Moses (*Mousa*) 42–3
Muhsinuddin, M. 78

INDEX

multitude of children (*kathrah*) 3, 85–112, 156, 162, 166, 172, 202–4, 209, 212–15, 232, 235–6, 252, 259
Murshid, Maulana Ghulam 208, 230
Muslim, Abul-Hasan al-Hajjaj al-Qusheiri 16, 30, 51, 61, 115–16, 120–2, 126–7, 129–30, 223
Muslim jurists 184, 224
Muslim Law 189
mysticism 148

Nadim al-Jisr 230
Najadat, the 148
al-Najjar, Sheikh (Dr) Abdel Rahman 212–13
al-Nasiri, Sheikh (Dr) M. al-Makki 141, 159
Nasser, President 98
natural resources 223
al-Nawawi, Abu Zakariyya 116, 121, 129–30, 135, 137, 140, 151, 161
Nazer, Isam 216
Nigeria 18, 178, 235
Noah, the Prophet 45
North Africa 50–1, 158
North America 203, 208
North Yemen (Arab Republi of Yemen) 151
Al Nu'man, al-Qadi 167, 175

oil 102
Oman 152
Omar, Caliph Sayyidna Omar Ibn al-Khattab 8, 22, 46, 87–8, 91, 119, 125, 133, 139, 156, 162, 214, 253
Omran, Abdel Rahim 5, 66, 179, 182, 216
Onan 131; 'Onanism' 131
Ottoman Empire, the 19, 150
Ottoman Family Law 19
ova 185–6
ovarian failure 185
ovary, the 187
overpopulation 202, 212; *see also* population
ovulation 185
ovum, the 9, 81, 120, 185–8, 235

Pakistan 151–2, 178, 181, 201–2, 206
Palestine 150
parent and child, the rights and obligations of 27–39; repulsion of parents 29–30, 39
Persia 148, 157
pessaries 163, 166; *see also* suppositories
phenylketonuria (PKU) 23–4
polyandry 19
polygamy 19
polygyny 15, 19–22, 41, 172, 235
population 65–7, 102–3, 110–12, 180, 204, 209–10, 216, 218–23; density 211, 253; European societies 66; explosion in Europe 208; growth 67, 98, 102–4, 112, 211–12, 220, 258; issues 221; policies 110, 201; pogrammes 98; of the world 66–7
population control 236
poverty 9, 103, 06, 172, 204, 212–13, 218; *see also* destitution
precepts of Islam and family planning, the basic 59–69
predestinaton (*qadar*) 1, 9, 89–91, 115, 120–1, 193, 206, 212–13, 228–9, 259
pre-emission 196–7
pregnancy 6–7, 9, 18–19, 26, 32, 34, 39, 81, 86–7, 96–7, 101, 115, 120–1, 135, 138, 140, 142, 146, 154–5, 157–8, 160, 166, 168–9, 173–5, 178, 181–2, 187–8, 191–3, 196, 205, 209, 219, 226, 228, 231–2, 234, 237, 248–50, 256–7; illegitimate 192–3; legitimate 192
prematurity 178
prenatal care 178, 182
primary inertility 184
procreation 14–15, 92, 94–5, 99, 101, 105, 161, 170, 187, 205, 207, 211, 216, 236, 251–3, 256; *see also* reproduction
progeny 42, 159, 161–3, 170, 172–3, 178, 204–5, 209, 213, 219, 231, 233–4
progesterone 232
prohibition (*haram*) 6, 35–7, 139–41, 154, 157, 161, 166, 189, 192, 207–10; of alcohol 78; of birth control 204; of coitus interruptus 255; of drugs 78
promiscuity, sexual 18, 39, 203–4, 206
property 188
prostatic fluid 188
provision by Allah (*rizq*) 89–92, 95, 102, 111, 171, 203–4, 207, 213, 228–9, 257
public welfare (*al-masalih al-mursalah*) 73, 75, 79
Purity Brotherhood, the (*Ikhwan al-Safá*) 214

INDEX

al-Qalquili, Sheikh Abdullah 227, 252
al-Qaradawi, Sheikh (Dr) Yusuf 77, 233-4
al-Qarafi, Imam 82
al-Qastallani, Ahmad 16, 161, 197
Qiyas see analogy
Qurʾan, the 3, 6–8, 13–14, 17–20, 26–8, 31, 33–4, 36, 41–6, 48, 51–2, 55–6, 60–4, 73–5, 77, 79–80, 83, 115, 117–18, 133–5, 146–8, 150–2, 155, 157, 174, 188–9, 202–4, 206–7, 216, 218–19, 223, 229, 232–4, 237, 249–50, 252; and family planning 85–112
al-Qurtubi, Abu Abdellah M. Ibn Ahmad 128, 156

Rabat Conference of Islam and Family Planning 1971 62, 187, 189, 208–9, 214–16, 234
radiation 185
al-Ramli, Shahabuddin 197
al-Rassi, Imam al-Qasim 151
Razik, Abdel 100
recreation 67
reliance on Allah (*tawakkul*) 1, 8, 89–92, 111, 160, 171, 212–3, 257
religion 67, 82, 141, 188, 190, 215, 218, 224, 251, 255–7; for all times 675–9, 97; of moderation 61; the Muslim 217, 219; for planning 62–5; for quality 62
religious education 39, 218
religious war (*jihad*) 57
reproduction 233, 253
repudiation of children 3, 196–7
resources 210, 218, 220; natural 223
reversibility of sterilization 188
rheumatism 178
rights and obligations of parent and child, the 27–39
rights of women in Islam, the 56–8
Rome 157
rule of concomitance (*istishab*) 73, 75, 79
Russia 113

Sabiq, Sheikh Sayyid 2, 21, 169–70, 73, 177, 183, 189, 231, 256
al-Sadiq, Imam Jaʿfar 149-51
al-Sadiq, Imam Ismaʾil Ibn Jaʿfar 149–51
Sahnoun, Sheikh Ahmad 208–9
al-Saʿib clan, the 22
al-Saʿid, Dr Al-Saʿid Mustafa 189, 196, 207, 230, 232, 254

Saleem, Sheikh Abdel Majeed 154, 225–6, 230, 234, 248–9, 257
Salih, Tunan H. Ali 226, 250
Satan 41, 94
Saudi Arabia 189, 201
scientific achievement 183
scrotum, infection of the 185
secondary inertility 184–5
secularization 203–4
semen 9, 81, 120–1, 123, 135, 138, 154, 156–7, 160, 162–3, 185–8, 193, 196–7, 211; *see also* seminal fluid; sperm
seminal fluid 250–1
sexual hormones 185
sexual intercourse 18–19, 135, 158–9, 161, 163–4, 174, 188, 197
sexual performance 187
sexual pleasure 162
sexual promiscuity 18, 39, 203–4, 206
sexually transmitted diseases 206
al-Seyuti, Jalal al-Din 114, 116, 172
al-Shafeʿi, Imam M. Ibn Idris 77, 106–8, 117, 135, 147, 150–2, 155–7, 159, 162, 172, 229
Shafeʿi jurists 78, 162
Shafeʿi school, the 6, 78–9, 117, 147, 150, 152, 159–62, 172, 191–2, 226, 251
Shah of Persia, the 152
Shaltout, Sheikh Mahmoud 56, 60–2, 97, 169–70, 173, 177, 183, 188, 226, 251, 258
Shamsuddin, Sheikh Mohammad M. 111, 166, 189, 227
al-Shaʾrawi, Mohammad 228
Shawkani, Imam 7, 118, 136–7, 139, 141, 163, 187
al-Shaybani, Imam Ahmad Ibn Hanbal 151; *see also* Ibn Hanbal
al-Shaybani, Mohammad 150, 153–4
Shaybanis, the 148, 165-7
Shiʿite school, the 74, 148, 165–7
Shiʿites, the 147–52
Shoʿib 99–100
sickle cell anaemia 23–4
sickness 103, 212
Siddiqui, Allama Alaʾuddin 208, 230
Siffin battle (Iraq), the 147
slavery 164
social conditions 10
social development 66–7, 101; Europe 67
social unrest 212

sociology 84
sodomy 123
Somalia 18, 223
Somalia Development Plan 223
sources of Islamic jurisprudence 73–84
Southern Algeria 152
Spain 113
sperm 23, 33, 120, 185–8, 190, 235; of an animal 186; banks 186; of donors 186; mixed 186
sperm banks 186
spiritual development 101
status of women in Islam, the 40–58
sterility 217, 254
sterilization 3, 8, 184–90, 204, 208–10, 213, 217, 226–8, 230, 35, 238, 256, 258; reversibility of 188; *see also* vasectomy
still-births 178
Sudan, the 18, 151, 178, 181
Sufris, the 148
Sunnah, the 3, 6, 36, 56, 59–60, 73–5, 77, 79–80, 83, 85–6, 98, 100, 106, 146–8, 150–2, 160, 188–9, 202, 207, 213, 218–19, 231, 234; and family planning 113–42
Sunni jurists 78
Sunni schools, the 74, 79, 147–8, 151, 160, 163, 212, 254
suppositories 156
surgical treatment (or surgery) 185–6, 188
surrogacy 185–6
Sweden 236
Syria 91, 113, 151, 178, 210

al-Tabarani, Imam 8, 17, 36, 49, 58, 91
al-Tahawi, Abu Ja'afar Ahmad 118, 132, 135, 137, 140–1, 154
Talib, Ali Ibn Abi 48, 119, 133–4, 136, 156
Tantawi, Sheikh Sayyid 2, 169–70, 173, 228–9, 257-8
Tanzania 152
technological advancement 183
thalassemia 23–4
Third World, the 40, 67, 212
al-Tirmidhi, Abu Iasa M. 8, 26, 55, 57, 91, 116, 131, 138
transportation 67
tubal ligation 187
tubectomy 187
Tunisia 181
Turkey 181

Umayyad dynasty, the 146, 148
unemployment 212
United Nations 111, 212, 217
United Nations Family Planning Association (UNFPA) 2
United States of America 66, 233
urbanization 220
urethral wall 18
Utba, Hind Bint 56
uterine prolapse 178
uterine wall, the 81, 185
uterus, the 7, 81, 154, 156–7, 163, 173, 185–6, 196, 217; of an animal 186–8, 248–9; *see also* the vagina

vagina, the 6, 18, 196–7, 250–1
vasectomy 187–8
vesicle, the 188
vesico-vaginal fistula 18; *see* the vesicle
virility 31

weaning 96
West Africa 150, 158
West Sudan 150
wet nursing 157, 170
withdrawal *see* coitus interruptus
womb 135, 138
women: their rights in Islam 56–8; their status in Islam 40–58
World Fertility Survey (1975–84), the 181
World Health Organization (WHO) 38, 178, 181

Yemen 18, 113

al-Zabidi, M. Ibn M. al-Murtada 65, 136–7, 141, 160, 163, 165, 196–7
Zachariah 93
Zahiri jurists 9
Zahiri school, the 74, 78, 136, 152, 167, 192, 210, 228
Zanzibar 152
al-Zawawi, al-Sayyid Ali 228, 254
Zaydi Shi'ite school, the 7, 9, 78, 148, 151, 165, 191–2, 228
Zayid, M. 216
al-Zubair, Abu 122
al-Zurqani, Imam 117–18, 157–8, 253